T0389696

Excavations at the Seila Pyramid and Fag el-Gamous Cemetery

Harvard Egyptological Studies

Editor

Peter Der Manuelian (*Harvard University*)

Editorial Board

Harvard Egyptological Studies

This monograph series ("HES") was established in 2015 to present
scholarly publications in the field of Egyptology. It highlights, but
is by no means limited to, sites and selected aspects of the Harvard
University-Boston Museum of Fine Arts Expedition (1905–1947).
Invited topics include recent PhD dissertations; reports from excavations;
specialized studies in ancient Egyptian language, history, and culture;
conference proceedings; publications of scholarly archives; and
historiographical works covering the field of Egyptology. *Harvard
Egyptological Studies* is published by the Department of Near Eastern
Languages and Civilizations, and the Department of Anthropology, both
of which are in the Faculty of Arts and Sciences at Harvard University.

VOLUME 7

The titles published in this series are listed at *brill.com/hes*

Excavations at the Seila Pyramid and Fag el-Gamous Cemetery

Editor-in-Chief

Kerry Muhlestein

Editors

Krystal V. L. Pierce and Bethany Jensen

BRILL

LEIDEN | BOSTON

Cover illustration: Tombs at the Fag el-Gamous Cemetery. Photograph by Kerry Muhlestein.

The Library of Congress Cataloging-in-Publication Data is available online at http://catalog.loc.gov
LC record available at http://lccn.loc.gov/2019037976.

Typeface for the Latin, Greek, and Cyrillic scripts: "Brill". See and download: brill.com/brill-typeface.

ISSN 2352-7501
ISBN 978-90-04-41637-6 (hardback)
ISBN 978-90-04-41638-3 (e-book)

Dedicated to C. Wilfred Griggs

*If it were not for Dr. Griggs' inexhaustible enthusiasm for the work,
the indefatigable effort he continuously poured into the project, his
wisdom and knowledge applied to the excavation for decades, his
tenacity to persevere in the work no matter the challenges, and
his absolute love of discovery that not only drove him but also
with which he infected all those with whom he worked,
nothing in this volume would be possible.*

∵

Contents

Acknowledgements

First and foremost, we are grateful for the support from and warm colla-boration with the Ministry of Antiquities in Egypt. Over many years in Egypt, both at the national level and at the local level, we have found friends, support-ers, and valuable aid unendingly streaming from these erstwhile colleagues. Nothing in this volume would have happened without their permission, en-couragement, and aid.

We are also grateful to Brigham Young University whose administrators, from presidents and their councils to deans and department chairs, have been so very supportive. We have received funding and other forms of support from the University, from the Religious Studies Center, from the College of Religious Education, from the Department of Ancient Scripture, from the Kennedy Center for International Area Studies, from the William (Bill) Gay Research Chair at Brigham Young University, from the C. Wilfred Griggs Foundation, from the individual departments of team members, and from many generous, private donors to whom we are very indebted and for whom we are exceed-ingly grateful. Brett Nielson, founder of SPARC (the Society for the Preservation of Ancient Religious Cultures) has been the most recent generous fundraiser who has made this excavation possible.

We are also grateful to so many who have worked on the excavation over the years. The reader will find their names scattered throughout the text and notes of this volume. The gift of time and skill has been generously donated by many. They are the true heart and soul of the findings presented herein.

Emily Ensign has been particularly helpful with her copy-editing abilities.

Moreover, loved ones — most especially family and close friends — have been so supportive to so many as we have traveled to Egypt and spent count-less hours in labs, reading books, and in front of computer screens. Their sacri-fice, which has made this volume possible, should not go unheralded. They have paid a price few see.

Illustrations

Figures

Tables

Introduction

This volume has been over three decades in the making. While, as the reader can see in the bibliography, over those years the excavation team has been creating a somewhat steady stream of publications about the excavation, and while early on a very small book was produced about the early finds using what was at the time a very local press, a large volume about the finds of the excavation has not yet been published until now.

One could ask why create such a volume now? We are not finished excavating, nor have we fully finished the analysis of any given aspect of the excavation, nor have we finished compiling a database of all our finds. There is not any topic we could address in a disquisition such as we are presenting here that we could not better address in five or ten years. Yet in five or ten years we would say the same thing, as we would five or ten years after that. This is clearly not a study of everything to do with the excavation all at once. We continue to expand our data sets, both by further excavation and by carefully entering data into a database and refining it. We continue to draw upon the expanding knowledge of many fields and ever-increasing technology to better understand the data and samples we have already collected. We also continue to raise funds in order to better take advantage of increasing technological abilities. Furthermore, we continue to scour archives and libraries, as well as talk with previously involved individuals, in an effort to better understand the material we already have. Consequently, one could argue that each of the following articles are currently incomplete.

In fact, that is the very nature of the academic process. Academicians are never done. Yet we are hindered in our ability to progress if we do not share with the larger academic world what we can at reasonable intervals. There is a great deal that the information in this volume has to offer the academic world, and we are anxious to share it with our colleagues—thus hopefully making progress possible in both their and our continuing research. Furthermore, the topics addressed in the chapters of this volume are sufficiently progressed to such a point where they need to be made available to the world. Archaeology bears an onerous burden, for we destroy as we excavate, and if we do not publish, and do so somewhat regularly as we go, then we have wrought destruction for naught. This volume is one step towards paying to the academic community what this excavation owes it. The desire to do everything as fully and as thoroughly as possible has already delayed this publication for decades and must be deferred no longer. Instead, we offer what we believe is a valuable

© KONINKLIJKE BRILL NV, LEIDEN, 2020 | DOI:10.1163/9789004416383_002

contribution to a number of academic disciplines along with our pledge to press forward in further research and analysis.

In creating this volume we strove to avoid redundancy, but it is not entirely possible. Early chapters include information about the geography and history of the area in general. The history of the excavation is also addressed in these chapters. As a result, this information is left out of most other chapters, not wanting to iterate and reiterate it in all succeeding chapters. Still, some topics require that parts of that history is again included to provide greater depth and specifics when necessary for the topic of the chapter but seemed to be too much detail for the introductory chapters. In these cases, a minimum amount of redundancy was unavoidable. We also had to keep in mind that in many circumstances, chapters will be read in isolation. Thus, for example, while a more detailed history of the excavation of the pyramid is provided in a chapter dedicated to that topic, at least a brief history of that same thing must be included in the chapter about the history of the whole excavation.

While the articles presented herein certainly make reference to the larger history happening around the site during various time periods, and while we certainly hope that these articles add to our understanding of this history, we are not attempting to write a history in this volume. Where appropriate, we cite articles and books that are themselves histories yet we do not necessarily do so each time a repeated historical topic is brought up. For example, the advent of Hellenism and, subsequently, a Roman presence in Egypt is an undergirding element in most chapters. In these chapters these influences are presented as a given, they are not argued for, detailed out, or thoroughly represented in the citations. Similarly, the arrival of Christianity and the eventual near complete conversion of the Fayoumic population to that religion is presented as a given. We acknowledge that this is a process that took place on both a historical and a cultural continuum. By this we mean that it took time for Christianity to go from a religion with minimal converts in the 1st century AD, to one that was widespread in the 3rd century and was then *largely* universally adopted in the fourth and fifth centuries AD.[1] While there is no doubt that there were many

---

1 David Peacock, "The Roman Period," in Ian Shaw, ed., *The Oxford History of Ancient Egypt* (Oxford: Oxford University Press, 2000), 441; Otto F.A. Meinardus, "Coptic Christianity, Past and Present," in Massimo Capuani, *Christian Egypt: Coptic Art and Monuments Through Two Millennia*, Gawdat Gabra, ed. (Cairo: The American University in Cairo Press, 2002), 8–9; Roger S. Bagnall, *Egypt in Late Antiquity* (Princeton: Princeton University Press, 1993), 279–287. See also Lincoln H. Blumell, *Lettered Christians: Christians, Letters and Late Antique*

Christians in Egypt at the time of the Roman persecutions, their visibility and numbers took large jumps forward after Constantine embraced Christianity in the 4th century.[2] In the Fayoum specifically, Christianity was present in the 1st century AD, was well established in the 3rd century (when monasticism began to flourish in the area), and was dominant by the 5th century.[3] Additionally, we also mean that the practical elements of living and dying in a Christian cultural context also took place on a continuum. There is not as fine a line between what would be thought of as pagan and what would be considered Christian practices as we often think.[4] This is especially true as we look at burial practices. The ability to identify Christianity in material burial culture is a large and complex enough topic that it must receive its own treatment separate from this volume.[5] Still, as we discuss the life of the Fag el-Gamous cemetery we must acknowledge that during its history most of its inhabitants must have converted to Christianity,[6] whatever that means and however it is manifest.[7] This is a point that does not need to be belabored or dissected in each chapter.

It is our desire to provide small snapshots of historical life and culture through detailed analysis of things such as grains, textiles, jewelry, and pottery. This, when combined with larger pictures of burial practices in general throughout the necropolis, and the historiography of work at the site, should help produce significant portions of the tapestry of the Fayoum in the Old

---

Oxyrynchus (Leiden: Brill, 2012), 8–12; and *Christian Oxyrhynchus,* Lincoln H. Blummell and Thomas A. Waymnet, eds. (Waco, Texas: Baylor University Press, 2015), 7–9.

2   David Frankfurter, *Religion in Roman Egypt, Assimilation and Resistance* (Princeton: Princeton University Press, 1998), 19–20.

3   See Siegfried G. Richter, "The Importance of the Fayoum for Coptic Studies," in *Christianity and Monasticism in the Fayoum Oasis, Essays from the 2004 International Symposium of the Saint Mark Foundation and the Saint Senouda the Archimandrite Coptic Society in Honor of Martin Krause,* Gawdat Gabra, ed. (Cairo: The American University in Cairo Press, 2005), 2–7.

4   Bagnall, *Egypt in Late Antiquity,* 265–267. See also David Frankfurter, *Christianizing Egypt. Syncretism and Local Worlds in Late Antiquity* (Princeton: Princeton University Press, 2018).

5   For recent published work on this, see Kristin H. South, "Roman and Early Byzantine Burials at Fag el-Gamus, Egypt: A Reassessment of the Case for Religious Affiliation." Master's thesis, Brigham Young University, 2012.

6   See R. Paul Evans, David Whitchurch, and Kerry Muhlestein, "Re-thinking Burial Dates at a Graeco-Roman Cemetery: Fag el Gamous, Fayoum, Egypt," *Journal of Archaeological Science: Reports* 2 (2015): 109–114.

7   Frankfurter, *Christianizing Egypt,* 3–7.

Kingdom and the Graeco-Roman era. As we weave our portions of the tapestry, we hope that as time goes on they will be fit together with those portions created by others doing similar work. As we each play our individual parts in concert with each other, our picture will become ever clearer and our tapestry ever larger.

Kerry Muhlestein, Cairo, March, 2018.

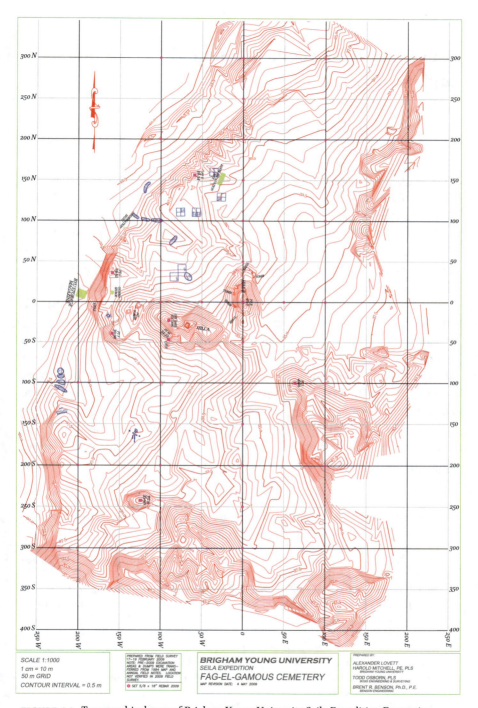

FIGURE 0.1 Topographical map of Brigham Young University Seila Expedition Excavation
Areas at Fag el-Gamous Cemetery, 4 May 2009
PREPARED BY ALEXANDER LOVETT, HAROLD MITCHELL, TODD OSBORN AND
BRENT R. BENSON

CHAPTER 1

The Fayoum, The Seila Pyramid, Fag el-Gamous and its Nearby Cities

Kerry Muhlestein, Cannon Fairbairn and Ronald A. Harris

Because the excavations discussed in this volume take place in the Fayoum and cover a time period that spans from the Old Kingdom through the Byzantine era, many readers will find it helpful to understand the history, geography, and geology of the Fayoum. Here we provide a brief outline of those subjects. This is not intended to present new information or to be a definitive discussion. Rather, it is aimed at contextualizing the rest of the material presented in this volume, and thus making all of its information more accessible. The Fag el-Gamous cemetery and the Seila Pyramid are located on the eastern edge of the Fayoum, just north of the center of the Fayoum's north/south axis.

Anciently called the "Garden of Egypt,"[1] the Fayoum sits in a large natural depression west of the Nile Valley.[2] The depression is about 65 kilometers across and covers about 12,000 square kilometers.[3] While some refer to it as the largest oasis in the Western Desert,[4] others protest that this is in fact a false classification because the Fayoum receives the majority of its water from the Nile and not an independent spring as with traditional oases.[5] No matter how one wishes to classify this region of Egypt, it is an area of unique geography, vegetation, and wildlife, with a rich history and an abundance of archaeology.

---

1 A.E. Boak, "Irrigation and Population in the Faiyum, the Garden of Egypt," *Geographical Review* 16/3 (July 1926): 355; Alberto Siliotti, *The Fayoum and Wadi El-Rayan* (Cairo: The American University in Cairo Press, 2003), 15; R. Neil Hewison, *The Fayoum: History and Guide* (Cairo: The American University in Cairo Press, 2001), 10; William J. Murnane, *The Penguin Guide to Ancient Egypt* (London: Penguin Books, 1983), 183.

2 Boak, "Irrigation and Population," 355; Mary Ellen Lane, *Guide to the Antiquities of the Fayyum* (Cairo: The American University in Cairo Press, 1985), 9; Wm. Revell Phillips, "Ancient Civilizations and Geology of the Eastern Mediterranean," in *Excavations at Seila, Egypt*, C. Wilfred Griggs, Wm. Revell Phillips, J. Keith Rigby, Vincent A. Wood, and Russell D. Hamblin, eds. (Provo, Utah: Religious Studies Center, Brigham Young University, 1988), 17; Boak, "Irrigation and Population," 354.

3 John Baines and Jaromír Málek, *Cultural Atlas of Ancient Egypt* (Oxfordshire: Andromeda Oxford Limited, 1980), 131.

4 Phillips, "Ancient Civilizations and Geology," 17; Siliotti, *The Fayoum and Wadi El-Rayan*, 4.

5 Hewison, *The Fayoum*, 2.

The landforms of the Fayoum are shaped by recent extensional tectonic activity that formed the depression,[6] and by sediment deposition associated with Lake Moeris, or Birket el-Qarun. Active faults bound the Fayoum and have caused earthquakes in the past that may have damaged some of the archeological sites in the region, such as the Seila Pyramid. Depositional features include three lake terraces: the first and highest is the el-Lahun-Hawara terrace; the second terrace exists at about modern sea level and contains cities such as Crocodilopolis (Modern Medinet el-Fayoum);[7] the third, and lowest, of the terraces lies in the northern part of the depression and contains little known ancient settlement.[8] This northern portion of the depression sits below sea level[9] and is enclosed by a rocky limestone mountain range to the north.[10] The northern Fayoum desert is also known for its Eocene and Oligocene fossil sites, which are some of the best preserved in the world.[11] These fossils are often found in the stones in which tombs were cut.

In the northwest is Birket el-Qarun, meaning "The Lake of Horns," also known as Lake Moeris. This is a large, brackish lake sitting in the lowest area of the Fayoum depression, about 44 meters below sea level.[12] Today the lake takes up only about one-fifth of the Fayoum depression.[13] The lake has diminished in

6   Timothy M. Kusky, Talaat M. Ramadan, Mahmoud M. Hassaan and Safwat Gabr, "Structural and Tectonic Evolution of El-Faiyum Depression, North Western Desert, Egypt Based on Analysis of Landsat ETM+, and SRTM Data," *Journal of Earth Science* 22/1 (2011): 75–100.

7   The modern Arabic name is Medinet el-Fayoum. The Greek name used in the Graeco-Roman era was Crocodilopolis. The Egyptian name was Shedet. In this paper we will use the name that matches the time period being spoken of.

8   Tomasz Derda, *Arsinoites Nomos: Administration of the Fayum Under Roman Rule* (Warsaw: Faculty of Law and Administration of Warsaw University, 2006), 9.

9   Phillips, "Ancient Civilizations and Geology," 17.

10   E.W. Gardner and G. Caton-Thompson, "The Recent Geology and Neolithic Industry of the Northern Fayum Desert," *The Journal of the Royal Anthropological Institute of Great Britain and Ireland* 56 (1926): 301; Noriyuki Shirai, Willeke Wendrich, and René Cappers, "An Archaeological Survey in the Northeastern Part of the Fayum," in *Proceedings of the Tenth International Congress of Egyptologists, University of the Aegean, Rhodes 22–29 May 2008*, P. Kousoulis and N. Lazaridis, eds. (Belgium: Peeters, 2015), 459; Hewison, *The Fayoum*, 2; Siliotti, *The Fayoum and Wadi el-Rayan*, 6.

11   Elizabeth Bloxam and Tom Heldal, "The Industrial Landscape of the Northern Faiyum Desert as a World Heritage Site: Modelling the 'Outstanding Universal Value' of Third Millennium BC Stone Quarrying in Egypt," *World Archaeology* 39/3 (Sep. 2007): 310.

12   H.J.L. Beadnell, *The Topography and Geology of the Fayum Province of Egypt* (Cairo: National Printing Department, 1905), 12–14; Boak, "Irrigation and Population," 356; Siliotti, *The Fayoum and Wadi El-Rayan*, 4; Baines, *Cultural Atlas of Ancient Egypt*, 131.

13   Baines, *Cultural Atlas of Ancient Egypt*, 131.

size due to drier climates, but once filled most of the Fayoum depression.[14] In
the prehistoric era, the lake was fresh water and contained many fish.[15] Until
the building of the Aswan Dam, Lake Moeris' level would fluctuate depending
on the flooding of the Nile, evaporation, and silt build-up in canals.[16] Today
and in ancient times, Lake Moeris is supplied with water by the Bahr Yusuf, or
"the Henet of Moeris," a canal branching away from the Nile just north of
Assiut,[17] cutting through the ridge Gebel el-Naqulun that separates the Fayoum from the Nile Valley.[18] Entering the ridge at Lahun, it emerges near Hawara[19] and continues to Medinet el-Fayoum.[20] Upon entering the depression,
various canals take the water from Bahr Yusuf throughout the Fayoum.[21] In
addition, there is evidence in the north of about four basins and wadis that
may have been filled with water when the lake was full and overflowing, creating smaller lakes around which many Epipalaeolithic and Neolithic artifacts
have been found,[22] and where it is clear the earliest agricultural communities
in Egypt developed.[23] The domestication of animals took place here by the

---

14   Derda, *Arsinoites Nomos*, 12; Boak, "Irrigation and Population," 356; Robert J. Wenke, Janet
      E. Long, and Paul E. Buck, "Epipaleolithic and Neolithic Subsistence and Settlement in the
      Fayyum Oasis of Egypt," *Journal of Field Archaeology* 15/1 (Spring 1988): 34.

15   Fekri Hassan, "Holocene Lakes and Prehistoric Settlements of the Western Faiyum,
      Egypt," *Journal of Archaeological Science*, 13 (1986): 493.

16   James A. Harrell and Thomas M. Bown, "An Old Kingdom Basalt Quarry at Widan el-Faras
      and the Quarry Road to Lake Moeris," *Journal of the American Research Center in Egypt* 32
      (1995): 83–84; Hassan, "Holocene Lakes and Prehistoric Settlements," 493–494.

17   Gardner, "The Recent Geology and Neolithic Industry," 301; Siliotti, *The Fayoum and Wadi
      El-Rayan*, 4; Hewison, *The Fayoum*, 3; Derda, *Arsinoites Nomos*, 62; Belinda Bolliger, Scott
      Forbes, Mary Halbmeyer, Janet Parker, and Michael Wall, eds., *Egypt: Land and Lives of the
      Pharaohs Revealed* (Australia: Global Book Publishing, 2005), 32; Murnane, *The Penguin
      Guide to Ancient Egypt*, 19; Baines, *Cultural Atlas of Ancient Egypt*, 18.

18   Beadnell, *The Topography and Geology*, 26.

19   Derda, *Arsinoites Nomos*, 10; Caton-Thompson and E.W. Gardner, "Recent Work on the
      Problem of Lake Moeris," *The Geographical Journal* 73/1 (1929): 27; Boak, "Irrigation and
      Population," 354.

20   Derda, *Arsinoites Nomos*, 10.

21   Boak, "Irrigation and Population," 354. See also Bryan Kraemer, "The Meandering Identity
      of a Fayum Canal: The Henet of Moeris/Dioryx Kleonos/Bahr Wardan/Abdul Wahbi," in
      Proceedings of the Twenty-Fifth International Congress of Papyrology, Ann-Arbor 2007,
      Traianos Gagos, ed. (Ann Arbor: Scholarly Publishing Office, The University of Michigan,
      2010), 365–376.

22   Shirai, "An Archaeological Survey," 462–463, 469.

23   Annelies Koopman, Sjoerd Kluiving, Willeke Wendrich, Simon Holdaway, "Late Quater-
      nary Climate Change and Egypt's Earliest Pre-Pharaonic Farmers, Fayum Basin, Egypt," in
      *Landscape Archaeology. Proceedings of the International Conference Held in Berlin, 6th –
      8th June 2012*, Wiebke Bebermeier, Robert Hebenstreit, Elke Kaiser, Jan Krause, eds. (Ber-
      lin: Exzellenzcluster, 2012), as in *eTopoi* 3 (2012): 63–69. Also Willeke Wendrich, R.E. Taylor,

mid-5th millennium BC.[24] While it is clear that changing lake levels affected these early civilizations, we are still in the process of refining exactly how and when.[25]

The geography changes towards the south where there are basins associated with the Fayoum, but of different origin. The Gharaq Basin in the southern area of the Fayoum is separated by a ridge, but was likely formed by a different body of water independent of Lake Moeris.[26] To the south-west of the Fayoum, also separated by a ridge from both the Fayoum depression and the Gharaq basin, is Wadi el-Rayan.[27] This area consists of two lakes – an upper lake called Qaret el-Buqairat, and a lower lake called El Midauwara – which were artificially created in the 1960s and 1970s when the Aswan Dam caused Lake Moeris to overflow.[28] In addition, there are four springs south of Wadi el-Rayan, which along with its lakes, provide water to this area.[29]

The eastern edge of the Fayoum is where the Seila Pyramid and Fag el-Gamous cemetery are located. The eastern border of this area is known as Gebel el-Rus, the ridge on which the Seila Pyramid sits. This ridge exposes Tertiary rocks and is about 8 square kilometers in size.[30] This escarpment rises

and J. Southon, "Dating stratified settlement sites at Kom K and Kom W: Fifth millennium BCE radiocarbon ages for the Fayum Neolithic," *Nuclear Instruments and Methods in Physics Research B* 268 (2010): 999–1002.

24   Veerle Linseele, Wim Van Neer, Sofie Thys, Rebecca Phillipps, René Cappers, Willeke Wendrich, Simon Holdaway, "New Archaeozoological Data from the Fayoum 'Neolithic' with a Critical Assessment of the Evidence for Early Stock Keeping in Egypt," PLoS ONE 9(10): e108517. doi:10.1371/journal.pone.0108517. Also Veerle Linseele, Simon J. Holdaway, and Willeke Wendrich, "The earliest phase of introduction of Southwest Asian domesticated animals into Africa. New Evidence from the Fayum Oasis in Egypt and its implications," *Quaternary International* 412 (2016): 11–21.

25   Rebecca Phillips, Simon Holdaway, Rebecca Ramsay, Joshua Emmitt, Willeke Wendrich, and Veerle Linseele, "Lake Level Changes, Lake Edge Basins and the Paleoenvironment of the Fayum North Shore, Egypt, during the Early to Mid-Holocene," *Open Quaternary* 2/2 (2016): 1–12.

26   Beadnell, *The Topography and Geology,* 23; Derda, *Arsinoites Nomos,* 9.

27   Beadnell, *The Topography and Geology,* 16–23.

28   Siliotti, *The Fayoum and Wadi El-Rayan,* 29–30; C. Wilfred Griggs, "Excavating a Christian Cemetery Near Seila, in the Fayum Region of Egypt," in *Excavations at Seila, Egypt,* C. Wilfred Griggs, Wm. Revell Phillips, J. Keith Rigby, Vincent A. Wood, and Russell D. Hamblin, eds. (Provo, Utah: Religious Studies Center Brigham Young University, 1988), 75; Hewison, *The Fayoum,* 3.

29   Siliotti, *The Fayoum and Wadi El-Rayan,* 41; Phillips, "Ancient Civilizations and Geology," 17.

30   Russell Dee Hamblin, "Stratigraphy and Depositional Environments of the Gebel el-Rus Area, Eastern Faiyum, Egypt" (MA diss., Brigham Young University, 1985), 61–62.

from 20 m above sea level to 125 m at its highest point.[31] It shows Eocene and Pliocene strata.[32] Gebel el-Rus exhibits "an angular unconformity between Eocene and Pliocene beds, Pliocene paleochannels filled with debris-flow deposits, a variety of sedimentary structures, trace follis, and distinctive faunas."[33] Water was carried to the area by a large canal that branched off the main water vein feeding the Fayoum. During the Ptolemaic era this canal was known as the "Canal of Kleon" in Greek. In Demotic, the Egyptian writing system most common at that time, it seems to have just been referred to as "the canal" (*tꜣ ḥnt*).[34] In the Medieval Period it would come to be known by the name it still carries: "bahr Wardan,"[35] also sometimes called the "bahr Abdallah Wahbi,"[36] though in truth the Bahr Wahbi really refers to the modern canal that parallels the ancient canal, often running in exactly the same course. Before receiving the name Bahr Wahbi, a moniker that it received from the name of the engineer who plotted out the course of the modern re-digging of the canal, the ancient canal was often called Bahr Seilah.[37] It is this ancient branch that fed the areas around the cemetery in antiquity and continues to do so today, though it was re-dug and rerouted somewhat in the early 20th century.[38] It continues to be dredged and cemented even today.[39] This canal forms the western boundary of the cemetery. The arable land was west and downhill of the canal, where irrigation happened most easily. The land uphill from the canal, where irrigation would require pumping, remained barren and was reserved for the use of the dead.

Due to the abundance of water and the milder climate (compared to the Nile Valley), the Fayoum was and is lush in vegetation, home to a variety of animals and birds, and the only substantial area of farmland outside of the Nile Valley.[40] Anciently, many plants and crops were grown in its fertile soil including grapes, olives, figs, wheat, barley, flax, onions, sesame, indigo, cabbage, sugar cane, and turnips.[41] Along with its agricultural resources, the Fayoum

---

31   Ibid., 61.

32   Ibid.

33   Ibid., 62.

34   Kraemer, "The Meandering Identity of a Fayum Canal," 367.

35   Ibid., 368. This is also sometimes called Bahr Wadan.

36   http://www.trismegistos.org/fayum/fayum2/2251.php?geo_id=2251.

37   Kraemer, "The Meandering Identity of a Fayum Canal," 367–369.

38   Ibid., 369.

39   Personal observation. 2013 is when we observed new dredging and cementing in of portions of the canal. The work has continued until the time of writing this, in 2018.

40   Phillips, "Ancient Civilizations and Geology," 17.

41   Hewison, *The Fayoum,* 18.

also contains quarries, such as those for limestone, which were used in at least the construction of the Seila Pyramid,[42] basalt, mined at Widan el-Faras during the Old Kingdom,[43] and gypsum, mined at the quarries of Umm es-Sawan.[44]

Early on, before Egypt's pharaohs began construction here, the Fayoum was a lush marshland,[45] experiencing great fluctuations in lake level.[46] Archaeology in this specific area suggests this region has been inhabited since Paleolithic and Neolithic times, though evidence is limited.[47] In fact, the Fayoum contains some of the earliest known Neolithic sites in Egypt.[48] In general, these settlements and sites have been grouped into Fayoum A and Fayoum B (also referred to as Qarunian). Fayoum B or Qarunian sites, which are often dated to around the 7th to 8th millennia BC,[49] have been unearthed north and west of the modern lake. Evidence suggests that these groups were hunter-gatherers, moving around the lake, relying on the natural resources of the oasis.[50] Caton-Thompson dated these sites to the Mesolithic; however, often they are assigned to the Epipaleolithic phase.[51]

Fayoum A, or Faiyumian, flourished around the lake during the Neolithic period, though the exact dates are debated. In general, these suggested dates

42   Keith J. Rigby, "Potential for Geologic and Interdisciplinary Research in and Around the Fayum Depression in Egypt," in *Excavations at Seila, Egypt*, C. Wilfred Griggs, Wm. Revell Phillips, J. Keith Rigby, Vincent A. Wood, and Russell D. Hamblin, eds. (Provo, Utah: Religious Studies Center, Brigham Young University, 1988), 23.

43   Elizabeth Bloxam and Per Storemyr, "Old Kingdom Basalt Quarrying Activities at Widan el-Faras, Northern Faiyum Desert," *The Journal of Egyptian Archaeology* 88, (2002): 23, 26; Harrell, "An Old Kingdom Basalt Quarry," 171–191; Bloxam, "The Industrial Landscape," 306, 311.

44   G. Caton-Thompson and E.W. Gardner, *The Desert Fayum* (London: Royal Anthropological Institute of Great Britain and Ireland, 1934), 103–123; Bloxam, "The Industrial Landscape," 306–313.

45   Siliotti, *The Fayoum and Wadi El-Rayan*, 4; Hewison, *The Fayoum*, 18.

46   Wenke, "Epipaleolithic and Neolithic Subsistence and Settlement," 34.

47   Siliotti, *The Fayoum and Wadi El-Rayan*, 16; Lane, *The Guide to the Antiquities of the Fayyum*, 10; Murnane, *The Penguin Guide to Ancient Egypt*, 19.

48   Kathryn A. Bard, ""The Emergence of the Egyptian State (c. 3200-2686 BC)," *The Oxford History of Ancient Egypt*, Ian Shaw, ed. (Oxford: Oxford University Press, 2000), 57.

49   R.J. Wenke, P. Buck, J.R. Hanley, M.E. Lane, J. Long and R.R. Redding, "The Fayyum Archaeological Project: Preliminary report of the 1981 season," *American Research Center in Egypt Newsletter* 122, (1983): 25; Wenke, "Epipaleolithic and Neolithic Subsistence and Settlement," 32.

50   Bolliger, *Egypt*, 33.

51   Stan Hendrickx and Pierre Vermeersch, "Prehistory: From the Palaeolithic to the Badarian Culture (c.700,000-4000 BC)," in *The Oxford History of Ancient Egypt*, Ian Shaw, ed. (Oxford: Oxford University Press, 2000), 35–36; Bolliger, *Egypt*, 32.

are somewhere around the 6th to 5th millennia BC.[52] Sites for this period have been discovered along the north and north-eastern ancient shorelines of Lake Moeris.[53]

It appears that the level of the lake rose during the Old Kingdom and then again during the Middle Kingdom, and finally began declining during the Ptolemaic era until it reached its modern size.[54]

Many have believed that in the Old Kingdom, the area was used mostly by royal members of society as hunting and fishing grounds and as a source of natural resources.[55] It is true that there were lush marshlands that quickly became associated with the crocodile god Sobek, remaining the center of his worship into the Roman era.[56] Undoubtedly the area around the Seila Pyramid was once more of an aquatic environment. Seashells are found in the sand deposits, and elderly farmers recount finding crocodile bones when they plowed their fields.[57] Additionally, many hold that there were not any large permanent settlements in the Fayoum until the Middle Kingdom.[58] This seems to be an increasingly inaccurate and less accepted view.[59] What we do know of the use of the Fayoum during the Old Kingdom is largely from its northern areas.[60] The Seila Pyramid and nearby cemetery (just north of the center of the Fayoum, on its eastern side), the temple at Qasr el-Sagha (though its date is

52   Wenke, "The Fayyum Archaeological Project," 25; Wenke, "Epipaleolithic and Neolithic Subsistence and Settlement," 32; Hendrickx and Vermeersch, "Prehistory," 37; Bolliger, *Egypt*, 32; Bruce Trigger, "The rise of Egyptian Civilization," in *Ancient Egypt: A Social History*, B.G. Trigger, B.J. Kemp, D. O'Connor, and A.B. Lloyd, eds. (Cambridge: Cambridge University Press, 1983), 6.

53   Trigger, "The rise of Egyptian Civilization," 21; Caton-Thompson, *The Desert Fayum*, 22–41, 54–59, 71–87; G. Caton-Thompson, "Explorations in the Northern Fayum," *Antiquity* 1/3 (1927): 331–340; Shirai, "An Archaeological Survey," 459; Gardner, "The Recent Geology and Neolithic Industry," 310–314; Wenke, "Epipaleolithic and Neolithic Subsistence and Settlement," 44.

54   Hassan, "Holocene Lakes and Prehistoric Settlements," 494, 498.

55   Hewison, *The Fayoum*, 18; Siliotti, *The Fayoum and Wadi El-Rayan*, 16–17.

56   Elaine K. Gazda, ed., *Karanis, An Egyptian Town in Roman Times: Discoveries of the University of Michigan Expedition to Egypt (1924–1935)* (Ann Arbor: Kelsey Museum of Archaeology, The University of Michigan, 1983), 32; Toby A.H. Wilkinson, *Early Dynastic Egypt* (London and New York: Routledge, 1999), 295; Lane, *The Guide to the Antiquities of the Fayyum*, 26; Hewison, *The Fayoum*, 18.

57   Personal communication with the local inhabitants in February, 2018.

58   Wenke, "Epipaleolithic and Neolithic Subsistence and Settlement," 47.

59   Miroslav Bárta, "Location of the Old Kingdom Pyramids in Egypt," *Cambridge Archaeological Journal* 15/2 (2005): 181.

60   Caton-Thompson, "Recent Work on the Problem of Lake Moeris," 42.

debated, is surely no later than the Middle Kingdom),[61] tombs at Kom Ruqqaia, mines at Widan el-Faras (along with its quarry road and quarrymen's camp),[62] and Shedet (or Crocodilopolis, later known as Arsinoe, the cult center of Sobek worship),[63] and an early Old Kingdom settlement near Kom Umm al-Atl (also known as Bacchias)[64] all date to this period. It appears that there were at least three power centers in the Fayoum during the Old Kingdom, namely Shedet, Seila, and Birket Qarun.[65] Ćwiek marshals evidence including archaeological structures, cemeteries, quarries, and titles of officials in order to demonstrate that the Fayoum was a larger and more important center during the Old Kingdom than has been previously thought.[66]

It was during this era, at the dawn of the 4th Dynasty, that the Seila Pyramid was built by Snefru. The discovery of this pyramid and the identification of its owner has been part of what has caused some to believe that the Fayoum was of greater importance during the Old Kingdom than was originally thought.[67] Additionally, Grenfell and Hunt found a small Old Kingdom cemetery near the village of Seila (not far from the pyramid),[68] and two small Old Kingdom statues were found near the pyramid, or perhaps in the cemetery.[69]

---

61   Ibid., 27; Caton-Thompson, *The Desert Fayum,* 132–138; Murnane, *The Penguin Guide to Ancient Egypt,* 184; Harrell, "An Old Kingdom Basalt Quarry," 73.

62   Bloxam, "Old Kingdom Basalt Quarrying Activities," 23–36; Harrell, "An Old Kingdom Basalt Quarry," 71–91.

63   Lane, *Guide to the Antiquities of the Fayyum,* 12–13. Also Pyr. 416 and 1564.

64   Caton-Thompson, *The Desert Fayum,* 101.

65   Andrzej Ćwiek, "Fayum in the Old Kingdom," *Göttinger Miszellen* 160 (1997): 18. Also Bárta, "Location of the Old Kingdom Pyramids," 181.

66   Ćwiek, "Fayum in the Old Kingdom," 17–22.

67   See Ćwiek, "Fayum in the Old Kingdom," 17.

68   Bernard P. Grenfell and Arthur S. Hunt, "Graeco-Roman Branch: Excavations in the Fayum and at El Hibeh," in *Archaeological Report: 1901–1902,* F. Ll. Griffith, ed. (London: Egypt Exploration Fund, 1902), 2. See also Jean Yoyotte, "Études Géographiques 11. Les Localités Méridionales de la Région Memphite et 'le Pehou d'Héracléopolis,'" *Revue d'Égyptologie* 15 (1963): 98.

69   Ludwig Borchardt, *Statuen und Statuetten von Königen und Privatleuten im Museum von Kairo, Nr. 1-1294, Teil 1. Catalogue Général des Antiquités Égyptiennes du Musée du Caire.* (Berlin: Reichsdruckerei, 1911), 6–7, plate 2, and Figures 5 and 6. Borchardt does not give anything for the provenance other than "Sile." Andrzej Ćwiek, "Date and Function of the So-Called Minor Step Pyramids," *Göttinger Miszellen* 162 (1998): 43 fn 24, stated that these statues came from a cemetery rather than the pyramid. For this he cited Grenfell and Hunt's report of work in 1900–1901. See Grenfell and Hunt, "Graeco-Roman Branch: Excavations in the Fayum," in *Archaeological Report: 1900–1901,* F.Ll. Griffith, ed. (London: Egypt Exploration Fund, 1901), 4–7. However, the cemetery he spoke of was reported in Bernard P. Grenfell and Arthur S. Hunt, "Graeco-Roman Branch: Excavations in the Fayum and at El Hibeh," in *Archaeological Report: 1901–1902,* 2–5. While Grenfell and Hunt

Yoyotte postulated that the area near Seila had become an important admin-istrative mirror to the Meidum area.[70] Dreyer and Kaiser concluded that it had become a seat of royal power and administration.[71] They were followed in this conclusion by Stadelmann[72] and then Ćwiek.[73] Ćwiek later argued that Seila may have been *the* administrative capital of the Fayoum at the time that region was growing in population and importance.[74] Zecchi points out that the statues of officials found near the Seila Pyramid indicate that there must have been a somewhat regular presence of officials in the area, meaning that the area was a large enough administrative center to host royal represen-tatives.[75] One would presume that for agriculture and population, and even the building of a pyramid, to succeed, that Bahr Seila, known from Ptolemaic times, would already have existed by the 4th Dynasty. It is not possible to tell if this is the case, but it seems an inevitable conclusion based on the needs for water.

Bárta believes that the substantial population center at Seila would have helped supply the manpower for building both the Meidum and Seila Pyramids,[76] which are 10 km apart. He also suggests that the shape and loca-tion of the Meidum cemetery indicate a close connection with the nearby Gerza cemetery (in the Fayoum), because they stretch towards each other. The

---

speak of finding a cemetery there they felt came from the Old Kingdom, they do not speak of any finds in the report, nor anywhere else we have searched in their records. They do not record anything about finding these two statues. Therefore we conclude it is best to rely on Borchardt's publication saying these were from Seila, possibly from the cemetery, though they could also have been from the pyramid, which is where Borchardt worked. It is worth noting that in another publication, See Andrzej Ćwiek, "Fayum in the Old King-dom," *Göttinger Miszellen* 160 (1997): 21, Ćwiek says that the statues "may come" from the necropolis. The exact location of the Seila necropolis cannot currently be identified.

70   Jean Yoyotte, "Études Géographiques," 98.
71   Günter Dreyer and Werner Kaiser, "Zu den kleinen Stufenpyramiden Ober-und Mittelä-gyptens," *Mitteilungen des Deutschen Archäologischen Instituts, Abteilung Kairo 36 (1980): 56–57.* See also Werner Kaiser, Günter Dreyer, Peter Grossmann, Wolfgang Meyer, and Stephan Johannes Seidlmayer. "Stadt Und Tempel Von Elephantine: Achter Grabungs-bericht." *Mitteilungen Des Deutschen Archäologischen Instituts. Abteilung Kairo,* 36 (1980/ 1981): 279.
72   Rainer Stadelmann, "Snofru – Builder and Unique Creator of Pyramids of Seila and Mei-dum," in *Echoes of Eternity. Studies Presented to Gaballa Aly Gaballa,* Ola El-Aguizy and Mohamed Sherif Ali, eds. (Wiesbaden: Harrassowitz Verlag, 2010), 35.
73   Ćwiek, "Fayum in the Old Kingdom," 21.
74   Ćwiek, "Date and Function of the So-Called Minor Step Pyramids," 42.
75   Marco Zecchi, *Geografia Religiosa del Fayyum* (Bologne: University of Bologna, 2001), 90–91.
76   Bárta, "Location of the Old Kingdom Pyramids," 182.

Gerza cemetery was in turn associated with an old and traditional trade route that connected the Nile Valley to the Fayoum.[77] This road runs right through the Fag el-Gamous cemetery and just below the Seila Pyramid, coming almost to the town of Seila (it may have come to it in earlier eras).

In some ways, the geography of the area dictates that the Seila area would have been an important part of the Fayoum. It is on the eastern-most edge of the Fayoum, meaning that it is closer to the Nile Valley than anywhere else in the Fayoum. Any road that cut across the desert from the Nile Valley in this eastern-most area would have run into the Gebel el-Rus ridge, whose extremely steep hills would have barred passage. The ridge suddenly ends just north of Seila, at the exact place the canal bends towards the east for a short distance. This is exactly where a road coming from the Nile Valley area of Meidum would enter the Fayoum, making this road the most direct route between the fertile depression and the concentration of population and culture that was next to the Nile. The Seila Pyramid sits at the southern and eastern end of the ridge, looking down on where the ancient road would have run and intersected with the canal. The need for transportation and trade, the ability to guard the way in and out of the Fayoum, and the ability to control and tax trade at such a trans-portation bottleneck, almost demanded that the Seila area become an impor-tant center. In many ways the Seila area was the gateway to the Fayoum, and the pyramid sat astride that entrance.

The Fag el-Gamous cemetery derives its name from the descendant of such a road. Literally meaning "the way of the water buffalo," the cemetery was so named because in more modern times the Fayoum was connected to the Nile Valley railroad tracks by an overland road on which water buffalo and other goods traveled. Geography dictated the road be located here, just as we have noted it would have in the past. Such a road combined with a canal (Bahr Seila) that was part of a larger canal system would create a transportation nexus that may partially explain why Seila seems to have become something of a popula-tion center in the Old Kingdom, and would be part of why the Seila Pyramid would have been built there, though surely there were other reasons as well. The inhabitants of Seila would have been able to support the cultic functions of the pyramid,[78] though the priests themselves may have lived in the foothills near the pyramid rather than in the village itself.[79] This depends somewhat on

---

77   Ibid.

78   See the two articles on the pyramid in this volume for more on these cultic activities. Also see Kerry Muhlestein, "Transitions in Pyramid Orientation: new evidence from the Seila Pyramid," *Studien zur Altägyptischen Kultur*, 44/1 (2015): 249–258, tables 37–38.

79   Ćwiek, "Fayum in the Old Kingdom," 21.

the frequency of the rituals that were performed at the pyramid.[80] If weekly rituals, something unusual, were performed, then perhaps priests could travel from the village to the pyramid to perform the rituals. If daily rituals occurred, it is unlikely that the priests would have traveled such a distance. To date, searches for domestic structures for priests near the pyramid have not been fruitful.

Dreyer and Kaiser concluded that royal residences must have been near the minor pyramids, including Seila in that conclusion.[81] Ćwiek postulates the same thing.[82] He does so based on the idea that the king would have had such a residence near all of his pyramids. This does not make it clear whether the residence demanded a pyramid be built, or vice versa. Additionally, we are not convinced that the Seila Pyramid is fully similar to the minor step pyramids, though it is often included as one of them.[83] Even if it is essentially different from minor step pyramids, that does not mean it did not hold important things in common with them, such as being in administrative centers and near royal residences. Furthermore, it makes some sense that the king would take some personal interest in a project as large as building a pyramid, even one that was only eight stories tall, such as the Seila Pyramid. It follows that his personal attention would be best accommodated if there were some kind of royal residence nearby. Still, the most we can really say is that the town of Seila seems to have been substantial during the 4th Dynasty, being large enough to support the building and maintenance of a pyramid and its cult, and that it certainly received royal attention and visits, with perhaps a royal residence being constructed there.

It is clear that there is much more to be learned about the history of the Fayoum during the Old Kingdom, particularly in the 4th Dynasty. Further studies of cemeteries, titles and histories from the Old Kingdom, archaeological work in places such as Seila, and administrative texts are necessary to better flesh out the roles and activities of the Fayoum during this era. It is also clear that the Seila Pyramid both informs and is informed by our understanding of the Fayoum and Meidum areas during this era.

In the Middle Kingdom the Fayoum witnessed more extensive growth and development. Pharaohs of the 12th Dynasty began major construction projects

---

80   See the article on ritual objects at the Seila Pyramid found in this article.

81   Dreyer and Kaiser, "Zu den kleinen Stufenpyramiden Ober-und Mittelägyptens," 56–57. See also Kaiser, Dreyer, Grossmann, Mayer, and Seidlmayer, "Stadt und Tempel von Elephantine. Achter Grabungsbericht," 279.

82   Ćwiek, "Fayum in the Old Kingdom," 21; Ćwiek, "Date and Function of the So-Called Minor Step Pyramids," 44.

83   See the article on the excavation of the Seila Pyramid in this volume.

in the area, which included land reclamation and water control.[84] Amenemhat I began efforts to cultivate and control water flow in the Fayoum, even moving the capital closer to the Fayoum at *Amenemhat-itj-tawy*, probably near Lisht.[85] He may have built flood gates near Lahun.[86] This focus on the Fayoum reached new heights during the reign of Senusret II (son of Amenemhat II). In order to control the waters of Lake Moeris, Senusret II implemented a new irrigation system, including a dam and canals, thereby lowering the water levels and creating cultivatable land in the rich soil revealed by the receding shoreline.[87] Senusret II even built his own pyramid at Lahun.[88] It may also have been during his reign that the temple at Qasr es-Sagha in the northeastern part of the Fayoum was built.[89] However some argue that this temple was built in the Old Kingdom and was maintained throughout the Middle Kingdom, a view supported by Caton-Thompson and Gardner.[90] Amenemhat III built his second pyramid at Hawara along with a mortuary temple called the "labyrinth" by Herodotus, and two 18 m tall statues.[91] Amenemhat III also appears to have lead a land reclamation and irrigation project in the area to provide large amounts of land for agricultural use.[92] He was even worshipped later as the god of the Fayoum, Poremanres.[93]

Evidence for occupation and activity during the Second Intermediate Period is limited, but there are three small cemeteries – Maiyana, Abusir el-Melek, and Gurob – near the entrance to the oasis that contain burials dated to this time.[94]

84   Caton-Thompson, "Recent Work on the Problem of Lake Moeris," 43; Bruce G. Trigger, *Early Civilizations: Ancient Egypt in Context* (Cairo, Egypt: The American University in Cairo Press, 1993), 33; Murnane, *The Penguin Guide to Ancient Egypt*, 19; Baines, *Cultural Atlas of Ancient Egypt*, 18; Wenke, "The Fayyum Archaeological Project," 25.

85   Caton-Thompson, "Recent Work on the Problem of Lake Moeris," 26; Miroslav Verner, *The Pyramids: The Mystery, Culture, and Science of Egypt's Greatest Monuments* (New York: Grove Press, 2001), 384; Gae Callender, "The Middle Kingdom Renaissance," in *The Oxford History of Ancient Egypt*, Ian Shaw, ed. (Oxford: Oxford University Press, 2000), 148, 158; Murnane, *The Penguin Guide to Ancient Egypt*, 181; Harrell, "An Old Kingdom Basalt Quarry," 89.

86   Boak, "Irrigation and Population," 358.

87   Verner, *The Pyramids*, 386; Callender, "The Middle Kingdom Renaissance,"164.

88   Caton-Thompson, "Recent Work on the Problem of Lake Moeris," 43.

89   Callender, "The Middle Kingdom Renaissance," 164.

90   Caton-Thompson, "Recent Work on the Problem of Lake Moeris," 45–46.

91   Caton-Thompson, "Recent Work on the Problem of Lake Moeris," 43–44.

92   Boak, "Irrigation and Population," 358; Lane, *Guide to the Antiquities of the Fayyum*, 14; Callender, "The Middle Kingdom Renaissance," 169; Harrell, "An Old Kingdom Basalt Quarry," 89.

93   Callender, "The Middle Kingdom Renaissance," 169.

94   Janine Bourriau, "The Second Intermediate period (c. 1650-1550 BC)," in *The Oxford History of Ancient Egypt*, Ian Shaw, ed. (Oxford: Oxford University Press, 2000), 199.

There is little Fayoumic evidence from the New Kingdom or Late Period. A site just north and east of Harageh (near el-Lahun) near the cemetery at Gurob, seems to have been founded in the 18th Dynasty and lasted until the 23rd. It was about 200 meters square.[95] Little else is known from in the Fayoum from these dynasties. Towards the end of the 23rd Dynasty and just afterwards, as early as the 7th or 8th centuries BC, land in Egypt, including in the Fayoum, was granted to Greek and Macedonian veterans as a reward for successful military service,[96] though, as will be noted below, this practice greatly increased in the Ptolemaic era. Both Herodotus (ca 484 – 425 BC) and Strabo (ca 63 BC – 24 AD) visited the Fayoum and wrote highly of its natural resources and prosperity, indicating that it was flourishing before, during, and after the Ptolemies.[97] In addition, hundreds of papyri fragments have been discovered in the Fayoum from these eras.[98] In fact, it has been suggested that nearly one third of the documentation amassed for Egypt was discovered in the Fayoum.[99]

The Ptolemaic and Roman periods saw great improvements in irrigation and agriculture in the Fayoum.[100] Land grants in the region increased at this time, especially during the rule of Ptolemy II Philadelphus (ca 284 – 246 BC) who promoted policies designed to enhance Greek colonization and reclaim more land for arable use.[101] The Fayoumic lands given to soldiers by Ptolemy II and his successors created a population boom and an area of great ethnic diversity.[102] Ptolemy II also renamed the area, calling it the Arsinoite Nome after his sister Arsinoe II. Due to a need for more cultivatable land, he reduced the size of Lake Moeris,[103] and witnessed dramatic increases in agricultural production. Such projects to reclaim and maintain land for cultivation continued throughout the reign of the Ptolemies and during this time the amount of land used for cultivation reached its peak.[104] The Fayoum became one of Egypt's

---

95   Reginald Engelbach, *Harageh* (London: British School of Archaeology in Egypt, 1923), 17–18; Lane, *Guide to the Antiquities of the Fayyum*, 15–16.

96   Marjorie Vent, "Two Early Corinthian Alabastra in Alexandria," *Journal of Egyptian Archaeology* (Egypt Exploration Society) 71 (1985): 186.

97   Caton-Thompson, "Recent Work on the Problem of Lake Moeris," 20–21; Boak, "Irrigation and Population," 353.

98   Lane, *Guide to the Antiquities of the Fayyum*, 17.

99   Derda, *Arsinoites Nomos*, 7.

100   Lane, *Guide to the Antiquities of the Fayyum*, 18.

101   Richard Alston, *The City in Roman and Byzantine Egypt* (New York, 2002), 58.

102   Boak, "Irrigation and Population," 361; Lane, *Guide to the Antiquities of the Fayyum*, 18; Baines, *Cultural Atlas of Ancient Egypt*, 131.

103   Siliotti, *The Fayoum and Wadi El-Rayan*, 26.

104   Caton-Thompson, "Recent Work on the Problem of Lake Moeris," 49–50; Murnane, *The Penguin Guide to Ancient Egypt*, 19, 47.

most prosperous and populated areas.[105] As a result, many people migrated to the lush Fayoum depression, including Syrians, Jews, Persians, Greeks, Macedonians, and Samaritans.[106]

During this time the settlement of the Fayoum reached its greatest height both in terms of population and agricultural output.[107] For example, just before the Ptolemaic expansion, Fayoum population is estimated to be 60–80 people per square kilometer.[108] By the Roman era the towns of the Fayoum had about 120 people per square km.[109] Many of the known cities in the Fayoum were founded or expanded during the Ptolemaic period,[110] including Karanis, Philadelphia, Bacchias, Philoteris, and Dionysias.[111] After a small decline near the end of the reign of the Ptolemies, the Fayoum once again became a point of interest and prosperity under the Romans,[112] as is seen in the revival of Karanis during this period.[113] During its time under Roman rule, the Fayoum became a considerable source of grain for the empire.[114] However, it appears that many (possibly all) of the towns and cities established or flourishing during this era were in serious decline or even abandoned by the 4th or 5th century AD.[115] These include Karanis,[116] Bacchias,[117] Dimayh,[118] Tebtunis,[119]

---

105   Baines, *Cultural Atlas of Ancient Egypt*, 18.
106   Kerry Muhlestein and Courtney Innes, "Synagogues and Cemeteries: Evidence for a Jewish Presence in the Fayoum," *Journal of Ancient Egyptian Interconnections* 4/2 (2012): 55–57.
107   Wenke, "The Fayyum Archaeological Project," 25.
108   D.W. Rathbone, "Villages, Land and Population in Graeco-Roman Egypt," *Proceedings of the Cambridge Philological Society* 36 (1990): 132.
109   Andrew Monson, "Communal Agriculture in the Ptolemaic and Roman Fayyum," in *Graeco-Roman Fayum – Texts and Archaeology*, Sandra Lippert and Maren Schentuleit, eds. (Wiesbaden, Harrassowitz Verlag: 2008), 178.
110   Baines, *Cultural Atlas of Ancient Egypt*, 131.
111   Phillips, "Ancient Civilizations and Geology," 18; For Philoteris, see Bernard P. Grenfell, Arthur S. Hunt, and David G. Hogarth, *Fayum Towns and their Papyri* (London: Egypt Exploration Fund, 1900), 62–63.
112   Boak, "Irrigation and Population," 362.
113   Gazda, *Karanis*, 9.
114   Derda, *Arsinoites Nomos*, 281.
115   Kraemer, "The Meandering Identity of a Fayum Canal," 367; Boak, "Irrigation and Population," 362; Lane, *Guide to the Antiquities of the Fayyum*, 25.
116   D.G. Hogarth and B.P. Grenfell, "Cities of the Faiyum: Karanis and Bacchias," *Archaeological Report (Egypt Exploration Fund)* (1895–1896): 14–19; Gazda, *Karanis*, 32; Lane, *Guide to the Antiquities of the Fayyum*, 40; Hewison, *The Fayoum*, 21, 71.
117   Lane, *Guide to the Antiquities of the Fayyum*, 50; Hewison, *The Fayoum*, 21, 96.
118   Caton-Thompson, *The Desert Fayum*, 153–158; Caton-Thompson, "Recent Work on the Problem of Lake Moeris," 27, 48–49; Boak, "Irrigation and Population," 364; Lane, *Guide to the Antiquities of the Fayyum*, 59; Murnane, *The Penguin Guide to Ancient Egypt*, 184; Harrell, "An Old Kingdom Basalt Quarry," 73.
119   Lane, *Guide to the Antiquities of the Fayyum*, 80; Hewison, *The Fayoum*, 21.

Philadelphia,[120] Theadelphia,[121] and Dionysias.[122] The ruins of Crocodilopolis, the cult center of Sobek which was often the capital of the Fayoum,[123] are spread over four square kilometers from this time period. Among the predominately Graeco-Roman ruins lie a Middle Kingdom temple.[124] Karanis (Kom Aushim),[125] which lies on the northern edge of the Fayoum, was one of the largest cities in the Fayoum during the Graeco-Roman period[126] and contains two temples dedicated to various forms of the crocodile god.[127] Bacchias (Kom Umm al-Atl) is the site of a Graeco-Roman village, including a temple to Sobek, that flourished during the 3rd century AD.[128] Tebtunis (Umm al-Burigat) is another of the Fayoum's largest sites.[129] Dionysias (Qasr Qarun) contains two temples from the Late Period and was the starting point of an ancient caravan route.[130]

The Fayoum continued to be inhabited into the Byzantine period, when there were about 198 towns and 300,000 people living in the region.[131] It was an important populated area in early Islamic Egypt as well.[132] It is during the pre-Islamic eras that the cities and villages whose citizens were buried in the Fag el-Gamous cemetery flourished.

There were a few villages near Fag el-Gamous. Their inhabitants must have been the primary users of the huge necropolis. Tanis, also known as Manashinshana (also referred to as Kom 2 by Petrie), was the closest settlement.[133] Seila lies due east of the southern edge of the cemetery, and further south lies Bandiq. Somewhere close to these sites, but with a location not fully identified,

---

120   Hewison, *The Fayoum*, 21.

121   Grenfell, *Fayum Towns and their Papyri*, 51–53; Boak, "Irrigation and Population," 364.

122   Hewison, *The Fayoum*, 21.

123   Siliotti, *The Fayoum and Wadi El-Rayan*, 21; Lane, *Guide to the Antiquities of the Fayyum*, 12–13, 61–62; Hewison, *The Fayoum*, 38–41; Wilkinson, *Early Dynastic Egypt*, 295.

124   Murnane, *The Penguin Guide to Ancient Egypt*, 185.

125   Grenfell, *Fayum Towns and their Papyri*, 27–34, 40–42; Hogarth, "Cities of the Faiyum," 14–19.

126   Boak, "Irrigation and Population," 354; Siliotti, *The Fayoum and Wadi El-Rayan*, 23; Hewison, *The Fayoum*, 69–71

127   Gazda, *Karanis*, 32; Murnane, *The Penguin Guide to Ancient Egypt*, 183.

128   Hewison, *The Fayoum*, 69, 95–96; Lane, *Guide to the Antiquities of the Fayyum*, 50.

129   Lane, *Guide to the Antiquities of the Fayyum*, 80; Hewison, *The Fayoum*, 69, 83–86.

130   Murnane, *The Penguin Guide to Ancient Egypt*, 185.

131   Ibid., 19.

132   Wenke, "The Fayyum Archaeological Project," 25.

133   On the identification of these locales, see the article on Mummy Portraits in this volume. It is not universally agreed that these are the same sites. For example, Kraemer, "The Meandering Identity of a Fayum Canal," figure 1, lists Manashinshana and Tel Shinshana as different sites.

was Alabanthis.[134] Even further south is Hawara. Not far to the north is Phila-delphia with Roda and Farqus further to the west. As was noted above, this area was partially settled by mercenaries. The presence of axe wounds on sev-eral Fag el-Gamous skeletal remains accords with the idea of a mercenary pop-ulation within the cemetery. Such a population would have inhabited the region with diverse ethnic backgrounds. In some measure this accounts for the full range of hair color encountered in the cemetery and indicates that the cemetery probably has a multi-racial population. Philadelphia and Tanis are the two closest settlements to the cemetery, with Seila being nearly as close. Unfortunately, we know little about the Graeco-Roman settlement there, though it seems to have borne the same name.[135] Thus Seila may have been an ancient contributor to the cemetery as well, but if so we are hampered in our ability to use textual evidence about that site.

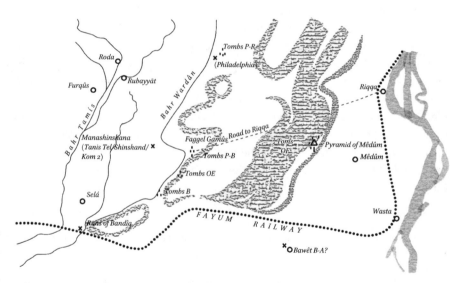

FIGURE 1.1   Map of Fag el-Gamous and surrounding areas, based on a map by Grenfell and
Hunt. Map made by Aimee Maddox

134   http://www.trismegistos.org/fayum/fayum2/97.php?geo_id=97. In using papyrological
information we will often refer to the sources made available by www.Trismegistos.org.
See M. Depauw and T. Gheldof, "Trismegistos. An Interdisciplinary Platform for Ancient
World Texts and Related Information," in *Theory and Practice of Digital Libraries – TPDL
2013 Selected Workshops*, Ł. Bolikowski, V. Casarosa, P. Goodale, N. Houssos, P. Manghi, and
J. Schirrwagen, eds. (Cham: Springer, 2014), 40–52; and *Papyrus Collections World Wide*, W.
Clarysse and H. Verreth, eds. (Brussels: KVAB, 2000).
135   www.trismegistos.org/place/2108.

We assume this area was similar to the rest of the Fayoum in that the majority of land was owned privately rather than by temples or the state.[136] At the same time, there was probably a higher proportion of public land in the Fayoum than elsewhere in Egypt, and this public land was likely more communal than in the rest of Egypt on the whole.[137] All the towns and villages near the Fag el-Gamous cemetery were serviced by and made fertile because of the nearby canal, Canal Kleon (Bahr Wardan/Bahr Seila). Tanis was close to the incoming water source, and Philadelphia received its water from Tanis.[138] Besides the importance of the canal, Philadelphia and the nearby villages Tanis and Seila were important locations because of their position by the main road that led from the Nile Valley to the Fayoum. This is the same route that made Seila an important center in the Old Kingdom. This vital artery of travel gave life to the towns and villages on the eastern edge of the Fayoum, and the death of their inhabitants created the Fag el-Gamous cemetery.

As was noted above, the inhabitants of Seila were probably buried at the Fag el-Gamous cemetery. Yet we know so little of Seila from this time period. Its name is attested in Greek and Demotic in papyri from the 1st century BC through the 8th century AD. Still all these references tell us is that it was a village (*epoikion*; *chorion*), in the *meris* of Herakleides, and that it was considered to be under the jurisdiction of the undertaker's guild that was centered in that *meris*.[139] Thus our discussion will focus on what we learn about the inhabitants of the cemetery from the population centers of Tanis and Philadelphia.

As we try to paint a picture of the settlements whose inhabitants were interred at Fag el-Gamous, some attention can be paid to changes over time, but for the most part our evidence for each era is so fragmentary that we may gain

---

136   Monson, "Communal Agriculture in the Ptolemaic and Roman Fayyum," 180–182.

137   Ibid., 180–183 and 186.

138   Ibid.

139   It is attested in regard to the necropolis, written in Demotic in the 1st century BC, in four papyri, P. Hawara 16a/TM 41469 (www.trismegistos.org/text/41469), P. Hawara 16b/TM 41470 (www.trismegistos.org/text/41470), P. Hawara 17a/TM 41471 (www.trismegistos.org/text/41471), and P. Hawara 17b/TM 41472 (www.trismegistos.org/text/41472) where it is written with an "r" instead of an "l" in Demotic. All of these attestations list it as part of the necropoleis guild of Ptolemais Hormou, Syron, Hormou, Syron Kome, Kerkesoucha, Orous, Psinharyo, Seila, and Alabanthis. See https://www.trismegistos.org/fayum/fayum2/747.php?geo_id=747. It is also mentioned in several other texts in Greek from the 6th through the 8th centuries AD. See for example P. Baden 4 90/TM 31143 (www.trismegistos.org/text/31143); or P. Lond. 2/TM 37002 (www.trismegistos.org/text/37002). See also Herbert Verreth, *Toponyms in Demotic and Abnormal Hieratic Texts from the 8th Century BC till the 5th Century AD, Trismegistos Online Publications vol. 5,* Willy Clarysse, Mark Depauw, and Heinz-Jozef Thissen, eds. (Köln/Leuven: Trismegistos, 2011), 577–578.

a better overall picture by assuming that if some industries or establishments were present at one time, they were likely present for much of the life of the town or village. While this creates a picture with only broad brush strokes, such a picture can give an impressionistic view of life that is useful.

Tanis is attested in papyri from the mid-3rd century BC to the 7th or 8th century AD.[140] The inhabitants of Tanis were known as Tanitai.[141] We know that at least some of them were given land in Tanis as a reward for their military service in Memphis.[142] Residents of a village like Tanis would likely have been preponderantly farmers, with many of them farming communal public lands (such as lands owned by the state or temples) as divided out by village elders.[143] Often this took the shape of lands farmed by groups of families working together.[144] Such farmers were thought of as rent paying tenants.[145] Some leased lands in both Tanis and Philadelphia.[146] Payments were sometimes, perhaps often, made in harvest of grain rather than monetary reimbursement.[147]

We know from the Zenon papyri cache, found in nearby Philadelphia, that a number of inhabitants of Tanis leased land for agricultural use that was administered by inhabitants of Philadelphia.[148] This is not surprising since Tanis fell under Philadelphia's administrative jurisdiction, and many administrators and wealthy landholders resided there. During the Roman era the area was known for its vineyards,[149] suggesting that many of the villagers would have been involved in viticulture. Fruit and olive trees were also cultivated there in at least some periods.[150] The presence of an oil seller[151] suggests that at least some of the olives were used to create oil locally. Today the area produces wheat abundantly.[152] That, combined with a papyrus that mentions a tax on

---

140   http://www.trismegistos.org/fayum/fayum2/2251.php?geo_id=2251.

141   P. Mich. X 593 and http://www.trismegistos.org/fayum/fayum2/2251.php?geo_id=2251.

142   P. Cairo Zen. II 59297 and http://www.trismegistos.org/fayum/fayum2/2251.php?geo_id=2251.

143   Monson, "Communal Agriculture in the Ptolemaic and Roman Fayyum," 183.

144   J. Rowlandson, "The Organisation of Public Land in Roman Egypt," in L' agriculture institutionnelle en Égypte ancienne: état de la question et perspectives interdisciplinaires, CRIPEL 25, (2005): 173–196.

145   Monson, "Communal Agriculture in the Ptolemaic and Roman Fayyum," 183.

146   See in Katelijn Vandorpe, Willy Clarysse, and Herbert Verreth, Graeco-Roman Archives from the Fayum, Collectanea Hellenistica – KVAB, VI (Peeters: Leuven, 2015), 162–163.

147   Ibid.

148   http://www.trismegistos.org/fayum/fayum2/2251.php?geo_id=2251.

149   Caton-Thompson, "Recent Work on the Problem of Lake Moeris," 49.

150   http://www.trismegistos.org/fayum/fayum2/2251.php?geo_id=2251.

151   http://www.trismegistos.org/fayum/fayum2/2251.php?geo_id=2251.

152   Personal observation, 2008–2018.

grain,[153] along with the presence of barley in some of the ancient tombs,[154] suggests that village inhabitants would have also been involved in harvesting barley. At least some of this came from royal lands.[155] The high quality and quantity of textiles found in the cemetery[156] also suggests that the weaving industry may have been an important part of the local economy. Spinning seems to have been solely performed by women,[157] and weaving was almost the same way.[158] Splicing and spinning flax roughens the skin, and thus a number of women in the area probably had very rough hands.[159] Papyrological evidence also indicates that there were shops and shopkeepers in Tanis,[160] such as some who sold soup.[161] There was also a bathhouse.[162] There were professional dancers and those who employed them.[163]

By the Roman period there was a high number of soldiers, including some from the cavalry, many of them having Roman names. Yet there were also a number of inhabitants with Egyptian names.[164] At least one priest lived in the village,[165] and possibly more when considering the fact that the neighboring town of Philadelphia had at least eleven operating temples within its borders.

Villages typically consisted mostly of houses made of sun-dried mudbrick.[166] In Tanis there were probably also granaries and wine presses, and perhaps even buildings committed to weaving, though this may have taken place largely in houses and their courtyards instead. Homes typically had their own grinding stones. Most rural villages of the day also had dovecotes.[167] It is very likely

---

153   http://www.trismegistos.org/fayum/fayum2/2251.php?geo_id=2251 and P. Hamb. III 212.
154   See the botanical report in this volume.
155   SB IV 7474 and http://www.trismegistos.org/fayum/fayum2/2251.php?geo_id=2251.
156   See the article on textiles and jewelry as well as the article on the death of common people in this volume.
157   See Christina Riggs, *Unwrapping Ancient Egypt* (New York: Bloomsbury Academic: 2014), 115.
158   Ibid., 116.
159   Ibid., 115.
160   P. Cairo Zen. III 59450. See also http://www.trismegistos.org/fayum/fayum2/2251. php?geo_id=2251.
161   http://www.trismegistos.org/fayum/fayum2/2251.php?geo_id=2251.
162   Ibid.
163   Ibid.
164   Ibid.
165   P. Bodl. I 150.
166   Roger S. Bagnall, *Egypt in Late Antiquity* (Princeton: Princeton University Press, 1993), 111–112.
167   Ibid., 113.

that the villagers engaged in other kinds of animal husbandry. Pigs, cows, and sheep are specifically mentioned in papyri.[168] Based on pottery found at the cemetery it is likely that besides having access to professionally made ceramic vessels made in a pottery factory we know existed in the village,[169] some villagers were seemingly very adept at making their own local variations as well.[170] They clearly also accessed jewelry made of metal, ceramics, glass and shells. Some of these items seem to have been locally made.[171] Villagers were also engaged in quarrying and brickmaking,[172] with at least some of the bricks making their way into the cemetery. Furniture in the village was probably made of wood.[173] Based on finds from the cemetery we assume tunics were commonly worn and at least a number of women used wooden or ivory/bone hairpins in their hair.

Life in Tanis would have centered on families. Based on the demographics of the cemetery, Tanis and its surrounding villages probably experienced a juvenile mortality rate of about 33%, which means that their children had about twice as much chance of surviving to adulthood as did most children in Egypt.[174] While we do not know why this is the case, it is probably at least partially due to the quality and quantity of food available in the highly arable land in which they lived and grew crops.

Philadelphia (Kom el-Hammam) was the largest nearby town to the Fag el-Gamous cemetery.[175] At its height it was just under 120 people per square kilometer, making it about as densely populated as Theadelphia and Karanis, two of the larger towns of the Fayoum,[176] though considerably smaller than

---

168   http://www.trismegistos.org/fayum/fayum2/2251.php?geo_id=2251.

169   Ibid.

170   See the article on pottery with kill holes in this volume.

171   See the article on textiles and jewelry in this volume.

172   http://www.trismegistos.org/fayum/fayum2/2251.php?geo_id=2251.

173   Suzana Hodak, "Archaeological Remains of Everyday Life in the Fayoum," in *Christianity and Monasticism in the Fayoum Oasis*, Gawdat Gabra, ed. (Cairo: The American University in Cairo Press, 2005), 217.

174   R. Paul and Kerry Muhlestein, "Death of a Child: The Demographic and Preparation Trends of Child Burials in the Greco-Roman Fayoum of Egypt," in Lesly Beaumont, Matthew Dillon, and Nicola Harrington, eds. *Handbook of Children of Antiquity* (Routledge, forthcoming). While paleodemographic studies have limitations that mean the demographic results are always tentative, this is equally, perhaps more, true for papyrological demographic studies. Thus it is worth comparing and contrasting the results of such studies.

175   For more on Philadelphia, see John Gee in this volume.

176   Monson, "Communal Agriculture in the Ptolemaic and Roman Fayyum," 178.

Arsinoe.[177] Estimations place the size of the city at 60 hectares at its height.[178] It was at various times described as a *kome* (town) or *polis* (city), even with neighborhoods (*vici*) within its precincts.[179]

It has its own sizable necropolis nearby, and is often thought to have also used Rubayyat as a necropolis, where many mummy portraits were discovered.[180] Thus, Fag el-Gamous may not have received many burials from this population center, though the fact that Fag el-Gamous is larger than the necropolis of this, the largest town in the area, suggests that perhaps some residents of Philadelphia may have used Fag el-Gamous for their interment. In fact, the northern end of Fag el-Gamous is just as close to Philadelphia as is Rubayyat, possibly signifying that the residents of this city may very well have used both cemeteries, perhaps being a major contributor to the large cemetery population. This idea is somewhat strengthened by the fact that for a substantial period of time the rights for embalming and burying the people of Tanis were owned by people who lived in Philadelphia.[181] Furthermore, while both Tanis and Philadelphia were inhabited throughout the Ptolemaic period, very few burials in Fag el-Gamous come from that era. One thing that may account for this is the theory that the cemeteries often associated with Philadelphia were filling up by the Roman era and they had to expand into Fag el-Gamous. All things considered, the likelihood that many Philadelphia inhabitants were buried at Fag el-Gamous makes it worth trying to extrapolate information from Philadelphia as we try to understand the growth of Fag el-Gamous and the lives of those who rest in death within it.[182]

As with Seila, there are geographical reasons for the settlement of Philadelphia. It too sat at the place where the local hills first allowed access from the Nile Valley to the depression of the Fayoum and a canal system. Thus, Philadelphia sat ideally positioned to aid in trade, to protect the Fayoum, and to collect taxes and distribute goods.[183] Being near an existing canal allowed inhabitants

---

177   Bagnal, *Egypt in Late Antiquity*, 111.

178   Gregory Marouard, "'Completamente distrutte': Réévaluation archéologique de Philadelphie du Fayoum, Égypte," in *Essays for the Library of Seshat: Studies Presented to Janet H. Johnson on the Occasion of Her 70th Birthday*, SAOC vol. 70, Robert K. Ritner, ed. (Chicago: The Oriental Institute, 2017), 132.

179   http://www.trismegistos.org/fayum/detail.php?tm=1760.

180   Lane, *Guide to the Antiquities of the Fayyum*, 52; Murnane, *The Penguin Guide to Ancient Egypt*, 185.

181   Vandorpe, Clarysse, and Verreth, *Graeco-Roman Archives from the Fayum*, 432.

182   On the excavation of Philadelphia, see Paul Viereck, *Philadelpheia: Die Gründung einer hellenistischen Militärkolonie in Ägypten* (Leipzig: J.C. Hinrichs, 1928).

183   This conclusion was independently reached by Marouard, "Completamente distrutte," 122, 146.

to take advantage of both a venue for transportation and to properly exploit the fertile possibilities of the area.

Large amounts of papyri have been unearthed from the town, as have wax tablets and ostraca.[184] Combining that with papyri found elsewhere that mention the city allows us to say that the town seems to have been founded and settled early in the Ptolemaic era,[185] and flourished at least from the middle of the 3rd century BC until end of the 4th century AD.[186] The establishment of a military fortress at the beginning of the 4th century indicates it was still flourishing then, but the end of the use of that fortress about 100 years later suggests that the heyday of Philadelphia was ending.[187] Other records mention the town until the 8th century AD, though the last few centuries were probably a slow decline after the area had steeply descended from its apex, reached just before the time of Hadrian.[188] This larger span roughly matches the dates of the burials at Fag el-Gamous.

The city began as a place for settling mercenaries,[189] a pattern which continued to fuel its growth for some time.[190] Throughout its history many of its inhabitants had some kind of military connection.[191] It was one of three Fayoum towns that had a large military fortress built in it at the beginning of the 4th century AD,[192] ensuring a renewed military growth during that time period. The military background and ensuing sudden, imposed settlement could account for the town's orderly grid layout.[193] It is worth noting that though the first inhabitants were foreign mercenaries, the houses seem to be a syncretic combination of Greek and Egyptian styles.[194]

In the middle of the 1st century AD the town had about 1000 tax paying inhabitants.[195] There were very low Nile floods in AD 45 and 47, which was

184   P. Viereck and F. Zucker, *Papyri, Ostraka und Wachstafeln aus Philadelphia im Fayûm*, Aegyptische Urkunden aus den Königlichen Museen zu Berlin, Griechische Urkunden, VII (Berlin, 1926).

185   Probably during the reign of Ptolemy II. See Marouard, 121–122.

186   See the article on Philadelphia in this volume.

187   Marouard, "Completamente distrutte," 147.

188   See the article on Philadelphia in this volume; also Marouard, "Completamente distrutte," 122–123.

189   Marouard, "Completamente distrutte," 146.

190   Bagnall, *Egypt in Late Antiquity*, 111, and footnote 8.

191   Vandorpe, Clarysse, and Verreth, *Graeco-Roman Archives from the Fayum*, 239–240; Marouard, 146–147.

192   Marouard, "Completamente distrutte," 146.

193   See the article on Philadelphia in this volume. Also, P. Viereck, *Philadelphia: die Gründung einer hellenistischen Militärkolonie in Ägypten*.

194   Marouard, "Completamente distrutte," 123.

195   Vandorpe, Clarysse, and Verreth, *Graeco-Roman Archives from the Fayum*, 257.

probably a major contributor to about a ten year economic decline during which time its tax collectors were consistently unable to bring in the taxes they were supposed to.[196] Eventually the town started to flourish again. It became a large and densely populated center.[197] Besides numerous temples, it contained buildings such as a theater, a *stoa*, a gymnasium and a palace.[198] The use of the surrounding lands includes fields of sesame and *kiki* (castor),[199] orchards, vineyards, fields of grain, fields of legumes, and houses for raising pigeons,[200] as well as raising other kinds of animals, including at least donkeys, sheep and pigs.[201] Of course these activities would give rise to merchants who sold this kind of produce.[202] Moreover we know that a group of at least 80 weavers found the city of Philadelphia an attractive place to live,[203] which is interesting given the number of high quality textiles found in the cemetery.

It is clear that there was a multi-national presence in Philadelphia.[204] This is also true of the villages nearby, such as Tanis and Alabanthis.[205] Some of the diversity in the area was due to the number of veterans who had settled in the area. For example, we know that for at least a time a group of Arab bowmen lived in Philadelphia, as well as Syrian cavalrymen.[206] Intermarriages, both between racial backgrounds and between varying social classes, occurred.[207] Many inhabitants were Roman citizens.[208] At least some of the inhabitants that were not native to Egypt took up Egyptian religious practices to some degree.[209] The multitude of temples in the city suggests that in the pre-Christian era there would have been many priests, and we know the names of some who held hereditary priestly offices.[210] At least one temple was dedicated

---

196   Ibid.

197   See the article on Philadelphia in this volume.

198   Willy Clarysse and Katelijn Vandorpe, *Zenon, un homme d'affaires grec à l'ombre des pyramides* (Leuven: Presses Universitaires de Louvain, 1995), 51.

199   Michael Rostovtzeff, *A Large Estate in Egypt in the Third Century b.c.* (Madison: University of Wisconsin Press, 1922), 56.

200   Vandorpe, Clarysse, and Verreth, *Graeco-Roman Archives from the Fayum*, 238, 240.

201   Ibid., 240–245, 257.

202   For example, we know of wine merchants in Philadelphia. See Vandorpe, Clarysse, and Verreth, *Graeco-Roman Archives from the Fayum*, 408.

203   Rostovtzeff, *A Large Estate in Egypt in the Third Century b.c.*, 69; and Marouard, "Completamente distrutte," 132.

204   See Muhlestein and Innes, "Synagogues and Cemeteries," 55.

205   Ibid., 56.

206   Vandorpe, Clarysse, and Verreth, *Graeco-Roman Archives from the Fayum*, 241, 244.

207   Ibid., 244.

208   Ibid.; and Marouard, "Completamente distrutte," 147.

209   Vandorpe, Clarysse, and Verreth, *Graeco-Roman Archives from the Fayum*, 364.

210   See Ibid., 181–182.

to Hathor,[211] and another to Anubis, whose temple collected payments from citizens who wished to receive services from that god.[212] There was also an Isieion and a Sarapieion that were connected by a processional route,[213] along with temples to other deities in the Egyptian pantheon and to Ptolemy II and Arsinoe.[214] Presumably as Christianity became more and more accepted by the inhabitants of the area there would have been Christian ecclesiastical leaders as well. There was at least one sizable police station that kept good records.[215]

Philadelphia was the administrative center for the area. Many of its residents owned considerable land holdings which they rented to farmers in the surrounding villages.[216] Some leased public land in order to sub-lease it to others.[217] They also rented land for grazing to those who owned the flocks and herds of Tanis, as was mentioned above.[218] There was also royal land attached to the town, with men from as far away as the Memphite nome overseeing groups who farmed that land.[219] Additionally, land owners from places like Antinoopolis and Ptolemais Euergetis appointed residents of Philadelphia to be agents for them in renting out their land for grain, palm or olive harvests.[220]

Some who lived in Philadelphia owned shops in the nearby villages.[221] Within the town we know of people who owned what seem to be commercial mills.[222] There were people of considerable means within the city. One example would be Aurelius Ol, who leased several sizable fields from the village leaders who made the land available to him because those who had been using it could no longer pay their taxes. Ol also loaned people money and had more than 50 sheep and goats.[223] Another example is found in Flavius Abinnaeus, a

211   Ibid.
212   Ibid., 364.
213   Marouard, "Completamente distrutte," 131.
214   For more on the temples, see the article on Philadelphia in this volume.
215   Vandorpe, Clarysse, and Verreth, *Graeco-Roman Archives from the Fayum*, 322.
216   http://www.trismegistos.org/fayum/fayum2/2251.php?geo_id=2251.
217   Vandorpe, Clarysse, and Verreth, *Graeco-Roman Archives from the Fayum*, 408.
218   Ibid.
219   Ibid., 184–185.
220   Ibid., 204–205.
221   http://www.trismegistos.org/fayum/fayum2/2251.php?geo_id=2251.
222   See P. Graux II; P. Michigan XII; P. Wisc. II; all as summarized in Vandorpe, Clarysse, and Verreth, *Graeco-Roman Archives from the Fayum*, 80.
223   See P. Gen I 12, 66–70, as summarized in Vandorpe, Clarysse, and Verreth, *Graeco-Roman Archives from the Fayum*, 97–98.

Syrian who was probably a Christian and who became the commander of the fortress of Dionysias and who married Nonna, a citizen of Alexandria. They owned property in Alexandria that they leased to others. They also owned property and resided in Philadelphia, where they managed land on which they grew wheat. They owned slaves and had relations with people in Philadelphia, Alexandria, and Hermopolis.[224] The Zenon papyri reveal the workings of a different very large estate that oversaw considerable lands and the construction of many buildings.[225] As part of this it was also involved in creating canal and irrigation systems and dykes.[226] The estate included a palatial house, a court, gardens, stables for cattle, store-houses, space for servants and employees, wine cellars, baths, and more.[227] It probably also included elements other estates in the city had, such as olive and wine presses, stables for horses, a bakery, and a large kitchen.[228] Its holdings included goats, horses, cattle, and the growing of olives, grain, sesame, nut trees, and vineyards.[229]

The surface ruins of Philadelphia contain a number of visible granite and basalt features, indicating a degree of prosperity in the city. Based on a surface survey of pottery, and a brief initial comparison of pottery from the various parts of the city, the area near the canal seems to have been a wealthier area than other parts of the city.[230] The city also seems to have contained industrial elements, as indicated by what seem to be the remains of a lime smelting kiln.[231] In other words, Philadelphia was a city of inhabitants from a variety of cultures, classes, and vocations. This diverse group of people potentially represent a range of possible inhabitants of the Fag el-Gamous cemetery.

Philadelphia, Tanis, and all the surrounding area went into decline in the 4th and 5th centuries AD, and largely disappear in the 7th and 8th centuries. At least some of the reason for this decline was likely the silting up and other damage to the Bahr Seila, which was the agricultural lifeblood for the communities of the northeast Fayoum.[232] Still, no one fully understands the reasons

---

224 Vandorpe, Clarysse, and Verreth, *Graeco-Roman Archives from the Fayum*, 138–142.

225 Rostovtzeff, *A Large Estate in Egypt.*

226 Ibid., 57–59.

227 Ibid., 69–70.

228 Ibid., 70.

229 Ibid., 57–70.

230 Kerry Muhlestein, Giovanni Tata, Ron Harris, Deb Harris, R. Paul Evans, Lincoln Blumell, Catherine Taylor, Brian Christensen, John Gee, Kristin South, Joyce Smith, Casey Kirkpatrick, Manal Saied Ahmed, "The Fag el-Gamous 2014 Excavation Season," a report submitted to the Ministry of Antiquities in 2014.

231 Ibid.

232 Kraemer, "The Meandering Identity of a Fayum Canal," 372.

for the steady shrinking of the Fayoum economy and population. Unsurprisingly, the Fag el-Gamous cemetery discontinues at about the same time as the nearby villages and towns also fell out of use. As the villages passed from use they also passed from history. Their stories lie largely untold, buried beneath the sand of the cities and cemeteries.

CHAPTER 2

History of the Excavations at Fag el-Gamous and the Seila Pyramid

Kerry Muhlestein and Bethany Jensen

The Brigham Young University (BYU) Egypt Excavation Project covers an area on the eastern edge of the Fayoum. It includes the Seila Pyramid and the Fag el-Gamous cemetery and has historically included the Graeco-Roman township of Philadelphia as well. The Seila Pyramid was built by Snefru, father of Khufu (builder of the Great Pyramid) and founder of the Fourth Dynasty. It sits atop a high escarpment overlooking the edge of the Fayoum toward the Nile valley. It is exactly ten kilometers due west of the Meidum Pyramid, also built, at least in large degree, by Snefru.[1]

1 The Seila Pyramid

The excavation of the Seila Pyramid has taken place in non-continuous stages and is discussed more fully in another chapter of this volume. Still, as we here discuss the history of excavation in this area, it is worthwhile to present a very brief recap of the work done at the Seila Pyramid.

It took some time to realize what the Seila Pyramid was. Before excavations it was not apparent that architecture visible at the top of a remote escarpment in Gebel el-Rus was actually a pyramid.[2] Petrie did brief work in the area but did not survey enough to determine that it was more than a mastaba, which was his belief.[3] Later, Borchardt performed more serious, though still cursory,

---

1   See, for example, Mark Lehner, *The Complete Pyramids* (London: Thames & Hudson Ltd., 1997), 97.

2   On the geologic makeup of the area, see Russel D. Hamblin, "The Geology of the Gebel El-Rus Area and Archaeology Sites in the Eastern Fayum, Egypt," in *Excavations at Seila, Egypt* C. Wilfred Griggs, ed. (Provo, UT: Religious Studies Center, Brigham Young University, 1988), 45–73.

3   William M.F. Petrie, *Illahun, Kahun and Gurob 1889–90* (London: David Nutt,1891), 31 and plate xxx.

work. He determined that it was a pyramid.[4] Because only some of its layers were visible and because not enough was known about its characteristics, it was thought of as one of the largest of the minor step pyramids, an idea which still represents the *communis opinio* today.[5] Various other surveys took place over time, as is noted in the chapter on the excavation of the pyramid in this volume.

In 1981 the first sustained and systematic excavation was undertaken by a joint UC Berkeley – BYU team. In that year, an initial survey was performed by Leonard Lesko, assisted by C. Wilfred Griggs, in which a layer of sand was removed and the four corners then visible were cleared.[6] During the next year, Lesko moved to Brown University and the concession fell solely to BYU. During the first year excavation efforts had been split between the pyramid and the Fag el-Gamous cemetery, which lies 1.5 km northwest of the pyramid. However, because the cemetery lay in greater danger of encroachment by modern agricultural activity and illicit digging than did the pyramid, it was decided to focus efforts on the cemetery. Thus, excavation of the pyramid waited for some time.

Excavation of the pyramid was finally conducted in earnest during the 1987 and 1988 seasons. While Griggs oversaw the efforts, he was assisted by Nabil Swelim.[7] It was during the 1987 season that two stelae were found, one of which was inscribed with the *nsw-bity* and Horus names of Snefru, at last identifying the builder of the monument. Areas around the pyramid, in particular the eastern side, were further investigated in 1995, at which time a causeway was found.

In 2009 an extensive examination of the pyramid measurements was undertaken by a team of engineers, and their analysis has done a great deal to help reconstruct the original size of the pyramid as well as the method used to build it. It was determined that the pyramid was originally about eight stories high (23.4 m).

Although Griggs was continually working on publishing the results of the excavation, he did not do so before his retirement in 2011. At that time, Kerry Muhlestein became the director of the excavation. He has continued working

---

4   Ludwig Borchardt, "Die Pyramide von Silah: Auszug aus einem Berichte," in *Annales du Service des Antiquités de l'Égypte* 1 (Cairo: 1900): 211–214.
5   See, for example, Rainer Stadelmann, "Snofru – Builder and Unique Creator of the Pyramids of Seila and Meidum," in *Echoes of Eternity: Studies presented to Gaballa Aly Gaballa*, Ola El-Aguizy and Mohamed Sherif Ali, eds. (Wiesbaden: Harrassowitz Verlag, 2010), 35. Here Stadelmann speaks of Seila as one of the most curious of the small step pyramids.
6   Leonard H. Lesko, "Seila 1981," *JARCE* XXV (1988): 223–235.
7   Nabil Swelim, "Reconstructions of the Layer Monument of *Snfrw* at Seila," in *Echoes of Eternity: Studies Presented to Gaballa Aly Gaballa*, Ola El-Aguizy and Mohamed Sherif Ali, eds. (Wiesbaden: Harrassowitz Verlag, 2010), 40–56.

with the team of engineers in addition to poring over the available excavation notes and analyzing the excavation reports of Snefru's other pyramids in an effort to better understand this pyramid. In 2014 a geological structural survey was conducted. In the 2018 season some areas of the pyramid, including its causeway, were re-excavated in order to obtain measurements that had not been recorded the first time. Work on publishing the pyramid is now earnestly under way.

2 The Cemetery

The Fag el-Gamous cemetery lies about 1.5 km north and slightly west of the Seila Pyramid. It lies on the edge of arable land in the eastern desert edge of the Fayoum, just under 100 km south and a little west of Cairo. The Bahr Seila canal runs directly adjacent to it and seems to have created its western edge. It appears to have been demarcated by a large limestone stela, which is now so weathered that it is impossible to tell if it ever carried an inscription (Figure 2.1). The necropolis is very large, encompassing about 300 acres (or 125 hectares). It includes several mudstone shelves that have natural caves and also have a number of tombs carved into them, most of which date to the Graeco-Roman era. These tombs have yielded ceramic coffins, mummy portraits, and even a mummy with a golden mask. A few tombs date to the Middle Kingdom (see below), and some of the cemetery is from the Old Kingdom.[8]

Below these shelves lies the sand floor that makes up the majority of the cemetery. Here, largely Roman-era burials are densely interred, being buried just under the surface of the sand and continuing until about three meters deep. The upper meter or so contains burials spread throughout the loose sand. At around a meter deep, the sand becomes very compact (but not yet sandstone), requiring one to chip away at this substratum rather than just sift through and dig in the loose sand. In this material, shafts were dug for burials, always on an east-west axis with slight variation seemingly due to changing solar alignment during the course of a year (Figure 2.2). A shaft was typically reused, with several burials occupying the same vertical shaft. A dramatic change in burial patterns became evident during the first few seasons of excavation and has been observed consistently ever since. The lowest burials, which generally occur between one and four meters deep (typically dating to

8 Bernard P. Grenfell and Arthur S. Hunt, "Graeco-Roman Branch: Excavations in the Fayum and at El Hibeh," in *Archaeological Report* (*Egypt Exploration Fund*): *1901–1902*, F.Ll. Griffith, ed. (London: Egypt Exploration Fund, 1902), 2–3.

FIGURE 2.1   The limestone stela amid the mudstone shelving of the
Fag el-Gamous cemetery

around the 1st century AD, though some date to early in the Ptolemaic era), are
almost universally oriented toward the west, with their head lying to the east.
Within one or two layers of burials, they almost universally shift to an eastern
orientation, with their head lying towards the west.[9] This pattern has remained

9   C. Wilfred Griggs, "General Archaeological and Historical Report of 1987 and 1988 Seasons at
Fag El Gamous," in *Actes du IVe Congrès copte, Louvain-la-Neuve, 5–10 Septembre 1988. Tome I:
Art et archéologie*, Marguerite Rassart-Debergh and Julien Ries, eds. (Leuven: Peeters Publish-
ers, 1992), 196.

FIGURE 2.2   Burial shafts in the sand cemetery of Fag el-Gamous
PHOTO BY KERRY MUHLESTEIN

consistent throughout the many seasons of excavation.[10] Other changes in burial trends have been noted in other articles and are further explored in this volume.

The burials are quite dense. Throughout this area the burial density varies from 1.3 to 3.0 burials per square meter. While some areas of the cemetery are undoubtedly less densely used, such as the few areas where the rare rains have created washes, this density still suggests a staggering number of burials in the 125 hectares of the cemetery. We are still unable to determine which and how many population centers would have contributed to this heavily used necropolis, though it seems that Tanis and Philadelphia would have been the main sources.

The sand cemetery's use reached its high point during the Roman and late Roman periods, and stretched throughout the Byzantine era. Because of this

10   C. Wilfred Griggs, "Excavating a Christian Cemetery Near Seila, in the Fayoum Region of Egypt," in *Excavations at Seila, Egypt*, C. Wildfred Griggs, ed. (Provo, UT: Religious Studies Center, Brigham Young University, 1988), 82–84; C. Wilfred Griggs, Marvin Kuchar, Scott Woodward, M. Rowe, R. Paul Evans, Naguib Kanawati, and N. Iskander, "Evidences of a Christian Population in the Egyptian Fayum and Genetic and Textile Studies of the Akhmim Noble Mummies," in *BYU Studies* 33 (1993): 218–219; C. Wilfred Griggs, "Early Christian Burials in the Fayoum," in *Christianity and Monasticism in the Fayoum Oasis*, Gawdat Gabra, ed. (New York: The American University in Cairo Press, 2005), 189.

time span, it is certain that most, if not all, of the local inhabitants converted to Christianity during the lifetime of the cemetery. The various elements present at this site create a unique opportunity for researchers from many disciplines to better understand ancient Egyptians over a time period stretching from 2600 BC until about AD 600.

3   History of Excavations at the Cemetery

The earliest known excavations at the Fag el-Gamous cemetery began in the early 1900s and were conducted by Oxford's Bernard Grenfell and Arthur Hunt.[11] Grenfell and Hunt began working together in the 1895–96 season investigating Graeco-Roman sites in the Fayoum and continued to do so for many years.[12] In 1901 they began work at Fag el-Gamous,[13] and in 1902 they found mummy portraits there.[14] Among the Roman burials at Fag el-Gamous, Grenfell and Hunt also found an impressive array of at least 26 intact glass vessels from the Roman Period.[15] In addition to the glass and well-preserved mummies, they found metal jewelry composed of "a varied assortment of beads, which were often buried in small wooden boxes."[16] They first called the cemetery the Tanis necropolis and described it as being the place where the road known as Fag el-Gamous began. Soon they referred to the cemetery as Fag el-Gamous, though not consistently.[17]

Many of Grenfell and Hunt's field notebooks have vanished over the years (or they were not consistent in making such notebooks), and the scanty publication of their finds at Fag el-Gamous leaves much to be desired. Thorough

---

11   Bernard P. Grenfell and Arthur S. Hunt, "Graeco-Roman Branch: Excavations in the Fayum," in *Archaeological Report: 1900–1901*, F. Ll. Griffith, ed. (London: Egypt Exploration Fund, 1901), 4–7; Grenfell and Hunt, "Graeco-Roman Branch: Excavations in the Fayum and at El Hibeh," 2–5.

12   J.G. Milne, "Bernard Pyne Grenfell: b. 16 Dec. 1869. d. 18 May 1926," *Journal of Egyptian Archaeology* 12 (1926): 285; M.L. Bierbrier, "Fayum Cemeteries and Their Portraits," in *Portraits and Masks: Burial Customs in Roman Egypt*, M.L. Bierbrier, ed. (London: British Museum Press, 1997), 16.

13   Grenfell and Hunt, "Graeco-Roman Branch: Excavations in the Fayum," 6.

14   Grenfell and Hunt, "Graeco-Roman Branch: Excavations in the Fayum and at El Hibeh," 2–3. See also Susan Walker, "Mummy Portraits and Roman Portraiture," in *Ancient Faces: Mummy Portraits from Roman Egypt*, Susan Walker, ed. (New York: Metropolitan Museum of Art, New York, 2000), 24.

15   These are pictured in the Egypt Exploration Society archives photograph GR 133.

16   Grenfell and Hunt, "Graeco-Roman Branch: Excavations in the Fayum and at El Hibeh," 3.

17   See the article on mummy portraits in this volume.

searches among the pertinent archives at Oxford, the Egypt Exploration Society, and the British Museum have turned up no further record of their excavations at the cemetery, though some of the photographs found in these archives have been helpful. The article in this volume on the mummy portraits from Fag el-Gamous gives a more complete account of Grenfell and Hunt's activities at Fag el-Gamous. Besides the predominantly Graeco-Roman discoveries, they also found burials they believed to be pre-dynastic and Old Kingdom.[18] Yoyotte believed that this small Old Kingdom cemetery was a mirror to that of Meidum.[19] He, and later Ćwiek, postulated that some kind of important administrative center was rising there.[20]

Grenfell and Hunt's spectacular finds at Oxyrhynchus are likely partially responsible for their not having published more about their work at Fag el-Gamous. These same finds are almost certainly the reason they did not return to the site. After their brief work at Fag el-Gamous, it lay largely untouched for the better part of a century.

As was mentioned above, in 1981 BYU and UC Berkeley jointly excavated in the area. While Lesko concentrated his work at the Seila Pyramid during this first season, Griggs worked at the Fag el-Gamous cemetery. The concession also included the Graeco-Roman town of Philadelphia founded by Ptolemy II, though excavation has not been done there by the BYU team. During that first season, surveys and seismometer work was performed at the cemetery by which Griggs discovered rock cut tombs containing skeletal remains.[21]

During that first year of excavation they also searched in the sand cemetery surrounding the rock cut tombs and found a number of Coptic era burials that had both textile remains and jewelry.[22] They believed future seasons could provide textiles and demographic information. At this point, excavators believed there were originally two cemeteries roughly five miles apart.[23] It now appears to be one large continuous cemetery, though it may have originally begun as two separate cemeteries.

Excavations were slowed the year the project unexpectedly fell solely to BYU. The next year, 1983, a detailed mapping survey was conducted, and

---

18   Grenfell and Hunt, "Graeco-Roman Branch: Excavations in the Fayum and at El Hibeh," 2.

19   Jean Yoyotte, "Études géographiques. II: Les localités méridionales de la région memphite et 'le Pehou d'Héracléopolis," *Revue d'Égyptologie* 14 (1962): 98.

20   Ibid., and Andrzej Ćwiek, "Fayum in the Old Kingdom," *Göttinger Miszellen* 160 (1997): 17.

21   Leonard Lesko, "Excavation Report: Seila in the Fayoum, 1981," in "The Eighty-Third General Meeting of the Archaeological Institute of America," *American Journal of Archaeology* 86/2 (1982): 275.

22   Ibid.

23   Ibid.

excavations and geological surveys began in 1984.[24] From that year onward excavations continued regularly, predominantly at the cemetery. Griggs was persistent and indefatigable in this work. The life of the excavation and the artifacts and results it has yielded are due to him and the staff he assembled and directed.

As work progressed there was a continual process of refining their work of archaeological analysis. In the storage magazine we have uncovered copies of *Human Osteology: A Laboratory and Field Manual;*[25] *The Essentials of Forensic Anthropology;*[26] and copies of four different articles of the *American Journal of Physical Anthropology,*[27] that spanned several years of the first decade of the excavation. This lead to at least seven iterations of the chart they used to record osteological information about burials. The storage magazine also contains a photocopy of a book about "modern" archaeological techniques, covering topics from excavation to cataloguing to field conservation. Unfortunately, the pages that contained the author, title, and publication information are missing. Yet enough remains to make it clear that this was a primary source for the creation of a field manual by Griggs which was designed to make the excavation consistent in its methods and ability to record information. In this manual he says, "I have attempted to break down all the individual components into their simplest form. . . . I have included detailed background information, where appropriate, on various procedures using the currently most acceptable and most accurate anthropologic and forensic methodology. Supplemental information is also included to assist in verifying the accuracy of our observations and conclusions."[28] The general field methodology was outlined in a flow

---

24   C. Wilfred Griggs, "Introduction," in *Excavations at Seila, Egypt,* C. Wilfred Griggs, ed. (Provo, UT: Religious Studies Center, Brigham Young University, 1988), xii.

25   William M. Bass, *Human Osteology: A Laboratory and Field Manual of the Human Skeleton,* 2nd ed, (Columbia, MO: University of Missouri, 1971).

26   T.D. Stewart, *Essentials of Forensic Anthropology, Especially as Developed in the United States* (Springfield, IL: Charles C Thomas, 1979).

27   Judy Myers Suchey, Dean V. Wisely, Richard F. Green and Thomas T. Noguchi, "Analysis of Dorsal Pitting in the *Os Pubis* in an Extensive Sample of Modern American Females," *American Journal of Physical Anthropology* 51/4 (1979): 517–539; Patricia A. Owings Webb and Judy Myers Suchey, "Epiphyseal Union of the Anterior Iliac Crest and Medical Clavicle in a Modern Multiracial Sample of American Males and Females," *American Journal of Physical Anthropology,* 68/4 (1985): 457–466; Darryl Katz and Judy Myers Suchey, "Age Determination in the Male Os Pubis," *American Journal of Physical Anthropology,* 69/4 (1986): 427–435; and Jean Dittrick and Judy Myers Suchey, "Sex Determination of Prehistoric Central California Skeletal Remains Using Discriminant Analysis of the Femur and Humerus," *American Journal of Physical Anthropology,* 70 (1986): 3–9.

28   Typewritten copy of "Field Manual" as preserved in the Fag el-Gamous storage magazine.

chart that went from "Body Identification" to "Body Removal" to "Covering Description" to "Unwrapping" to "Gross Body Examination" to "Sample Collection" to "Bone Preparation" to "Clavicle Examination" (with many subsets of
this, broken down into Adult and Subadult categories) to "Storage" to "Write-
up." Each of these sections had a detailed methodology. For example, "Body
Identification" consisted of "Square ID," "Body ID#," "Location," "Orientation,"
"Depth," and "Artifacts." Copies of osteological drawings were also included in
the manual. Additionally, various forms for recording textiles were created and
employed over time, as well as forms for recording information about locations. Eventually, stamps were created to be put on each page of the field book
to insure that all the necessary information was recorded for each burial. The
amount and type of information recorded continually evolved as the excavation progressed.

Field books for seasons prior to 1987 cannot currently be located. All available field books have now been digitized, and the process of entering the information into a database is ongoing. Some analyses of those field books and
some reports of various excavation seasons are contained in this volume.

Work was focused on the sand cemetery from 1984 through 1987; the latter
year marking the renewal of work at the pyramid, though it was also perhaps
the busiest year of excavating in the cemetery.

The two hills near the storage magazine contained rock cut tombs, some of
which were examined in the first season. In the 1988 season, several depres-
sions or small holes that had been observed in these hills, Hill A and Hill B,
were investigated. The first one explored, now numbered Hill B Tomb 1,[29]
opened into a tomb containing 12 small chambers, with mudbrick helping
complete each chamber, and evidence of plaster on the walls. This tomb contained artifacts such as a wooden mallet, a metal chisel, a trowel, reed baskets
containing a grain offering,[30] cartonnage burial masks, oil lamps, mummified
cats, a wooden shuttle-cock, and pottery.[31] Plundering was evident, as was a
roof collapse. Both of these may have caused the damage that each of the six
ceramic sarcophagi inside had experienced.

Two semi-intact burials were found in this tomb. One was a female distinguished by the elaborate rhomboid patterned wrappings on her body

---

29   If they numbered these tombs at the time, beyond recording their North/South, East/
      West coordinates, we can find no record of it. Thus we (re)numbered the tombs in the
      2018 season.
30   For more about this grain offering see the botanical report in this volume.
31   See Griggs, "General Archaeological and Historical Report of 1987 and 1988 Seasons at Fag
      el Gamous," 197–198.

FIGURE 2.3   The burial from Hill B Tomb 1 with rhomboid wrappings
PHOTOGRAPH BY R. PAUL EVANS

(Figure 2.3).[32] Another was well preserved and was the only burial from the site that exhibited gold leafing glued to the linen over his fingers (which were

---

32   C. Wilfred Griggs, "Burial Techniques and Body Preservation in the Fag el Gamous Cem-
      etery," *Actas del I Congreso Internacional de Estudios sobre Momias, 1992* (Santa Cruz de
      Tenerife, Spain: Museo Arqueologico de Tenerife, 1995), 661.

individually wrapped), a practice known in many other instances in Egypt at the time period.[33] These were the only largely-complete burials found in Hill B Tomb 1.[34] A more full publication of this tomb and its findings is planned for the future.

Three other tombs were excavated in 1987. We are still in the process of piecing together old reports, field books, photographs, modern observations, and modern photographs in order to determine which photographs and reports belong to which tomb. When this complicated process is over, and the analyses that will ensue completed, they will also be included in a publication about the tombs of Fag el-Gamous. At the present time, we can merely report that in Hill B three more tombs were found, one with four chambers extending from an unfinished room/pit; another with a deep shaft leading to three horizontal shafts, which in turn lead to a total of six chambers; and the last being another room with ten chambers branching off of it, some of which were unfinished. It is also worth noting that a tomb with 158 cat burials was discovered that same year in that same area.[35]

In Hill A some of the tombs were Ptolemaic, but a few were Middle Kingdom.[36] These Middle Kingdom tombs were excavated in the 1984 season, and perhaps also in adjacent seasons. There are three of these tombs, with vertical shafts that are reported to be 15–23 m deep, with horizontal shafts extending from their sides.[37] One of these horizontal shafts led to a 3×3 m room hewn into the mudstone ridge, which leads to a 4–5 m horizontal shaft which then turns east into an unfinished chamber.[38] We are still searching for more detailed reports of these shaft tombs, but if we fail to find them re-excavation will be considered.

33   Mark Smith, *Traversing Eternity: Texts for the Afterlife from Ptolemaic and Roman Egypt* (Oxford: Oxford University Press, 2009), 33–34; See, for example, EA6704 at the British Museum; or A.1911.210.3 at the National Museum of Scotland.

34   Griggs, "General Archaeological and Historical Report of 1987 and 1988 Seasons at Fag el Gamous," 197.

35   C. Wilfred Griggs, Marvin C.J. Kuchar, Mark J. Rowe, and Scott R. Woodward, "Identities Revealed: Archaeological and Biological Evidences for a Christian Population in the Egyptian Fayum," in *The Ancient Near East, Greece, and Rome*, T.W. Hillard, R.A. Kearsley, C.E.V. Nixon, and A.M. Nobbs, eds. (Grand Rapids: Eerdmans, 1998), 1:83.

36   C. Wilfred Griggs, "Burial Techniques and Body Preservation in the Fag el Gamous Cemetery," 659–660.

37   C. Wilfred Griggs, "Excavating a Christian Cemetery Near Seila, in the Fayum Region of Egypt," 76.

38   Ibid., 76–77.

FIGURE 2.4   Golden mummy from Fag el-Gamous
PHOTOGRAPH COURTESY OF REVEL PHILLIPS

Regarding the other tombs carved into Hill A and Hill B, carbon dating places burials in these tombs as early as 200 BC.[39] Eventually 22 tombs were excavated. One of the more significant of these was found in the 1989 season (Figure 2.4). Discovered in February, a mummy with a golden mask extending to her shoulders was found in a heavy wooden coffin in a chamber cut below the floor level of a tomb (Hill B, Tomb 4).[40] This female in her thirties had scenes depicted on her torso from the Book of the Dead stretching from her shoulders to her knees. The gold head-covering depicts several symbols: a scarab pushing a sun disk over the forehead, a vulture with outstretched wings wearing the crown of Osiris, and the four sons of Horus. The Golden Mummy, as she has been affectionately called by the excavators, had four flower garlands wrapped around her body: near the neck, at the middle of the abdomen, on the lower abdomen,

---

39   Kristin H. South, Marvin C. Kuchar, and C. Wilfred Griggs, "Preliminary Report of the Textile Finds, 1998 Season, at Fag el-Gamus," *Archaeological Textiles Newsletter* 27 (Fall 1998): 9.

40   C. Wilfred Griggs et al., "Evidence of a Christian Population in the Egyptian Fayum and Genetic and Textile Studies of the Akhmim Noble Mummies," 219.

and on the legs.[41] She was also laid on a bed of flowers and had a spray of flowers placed within the linen wraps over her heart. Pottery found in the tomb and 14C analyses date the burial to about 220 BC.[42] There were some initial attempts to translate the inscription on the foot of the coffin,[43] but our ability to translate writing from the time period has progressed a great deal since the 1980's and we are currently in the midst of retranslating the inscription. We can now discern recognized names. A future publication will contain the results of this translation effort.

Between the door of the burial chamber and the coffin of the Golden Mummy was a small burial. The burial, which had a wooden nose, is thought to be that of a juvenile. The body was compressed so that it would fit within the width of the burial chamber; the femurs had been pushed up into the thoracic cavity, and the upper vertebrae had been pushed down into the upper chest cavity.[44] It was originally thought that the juvenile was much younger and that the femurs of the burial may have been swapped for the femurs of someone older. A closer analysis has shown that the femurs belong to the burial, and because of the epiphyseal union that had occurred, the juvenile is older than the original estimate of six to eight years.[45] This burial, along with the Golden Mummy, has been moved to the Museum of Egyptian Antiquities in Cairo.

Besides the seasons spent on these hills, each excavation season has focused on one or more 5×5 meter squares in the sand cemetery. These squares were designated by their coordinates as given in 10-meter grids, with the square being designated as being in the northeast, northwest, southeast or southwest corner of a 10-meter grid. The cemetery survey is gridded in meters from a reference point north or south and east or west of a central datum point. Thus, every burial is identified by the 25-meter square, the quadrant within that area, and the number order in which the burials were found. The region of the cemetery that was most heavily used by Graeco-Roman Egyptians, as identified thus far, spans from 50 North to 220 North and from 50 West to 70 East, a surface area of 20,400 square meters.

Analysis was performed by a number of individuals. Geological surveys were conducted by William Revell Phillips and J. Keith Rigby, professors of geology at BYU, as well as their student, Russel D. Hamblin, who studied the area

---

41   C. Wilfred Griggs, "Early Christian Burials in the Fayoum," 186–187.

42   Griggs, "Evidence of a Christian Population," 219.

43   Ibid.

44   Mark J. Rowe et al., "Ancient History and Modern Biological Tools: Endoscopic Sampling and Mitochondrial DNA Analysis of Ancient Tissue," 78.

45   Griggs, et al., "Evidence of a Christian Population," 219; Rowe, et al., "Ancient History and Modern Biological Tools," 78; personal communication with R. Paul Evans.

as part of the work for his master's thesis. References to their work can be found in the bibliography in this volume. Vincent A. Wood, D.D.S., brought x-ray equipment and performed paleopathological work for several seasons. Sadly, his untimely death prevented him from finishing his work or his publications.[46] Marvin Kuchar, professor of textiles at BYU, analyzed, cleaned, and did some conservation work on the burial textiles for many years, which became one of the main focuses of the research done by the team (see the bibliography in this volume to see the various publications on this topic). Later as Kuchar, who specialized in textiles in general, retired, Giovanni Tata brought an even greater specialization in Egyptian textiles to the team. He was joined by Joyce Smith and Kristin South, forming a team that moved textile analysis into a serious component of the excavation's work. Recently Anne Kwaspen has also joined the textile analysis and conservation team.

Since Kerry Muhlestein of BYU became the director of the excavation project in 2011, the emphasis has been on more fully analyzing (using technology now available) and publishing the excavations already conducted, as well as on conserving the artifacts already found. Under his directorship, excavations have been slowed and aimed at doing that which allows for better understanding of the material reported or partially reported in earlier excavations. For example, 14C dating has been done, which has helped to determine that although the tombs carved into the mudstone escarpments contain both Ptolemaic- and Roman-era burials, the burials of the sand cemetery seem to come from largely the Roman era; though the lowest burials often date to the Ptolemaic period. C14 dating has also helped identify that important shifts in burial practice, which might indicate conversion to Christianity, such as the change in body orientation, seem to have occurred around the turn of the 3rd century.[47] More 14C analyses are currently under way, as is further study regarding which markers in material burial culture may indicate Christianity.

Assembling and carefully analyzing quantifiable data from the excavations has allowed studies to be done that have determined that children were buried in largely the same manner as adults. We have also found that between the

46   See Vincent A. Wood, "Paleopathological Observations and Applications at Seila," in *Excavations at Seila, Egypt*, C. Wilfred Griggs, ed. (Provo, UT: Religious Studies Center, Brigham Young University Press, 1988), 31–44, for work he did and an explanation of plans to do more.

47   R. Paul Evans, David M. Whitchurch, and Kerry Muhlestein, "Rethinking Burial Dates at a Graeco-Roman Cemetery: Fag el-Gamous, Fayoum, Egypt," *Journal of Archaeological Science: Reports* 2 (2015): 209–214. These dates are contra what was thought earlier by the excavation team. See, for example, C. Wilfred Griggs, "Burial Techniques and Body Preservation in the Fag el Gamous Cemetery," 660–661.

ages of 15–35, the female mortality rate was double that of males, presumably due to childbirth.[48] One interesting study revealed that in a sample of 752 burials, there was approximately a 32 percent juvenile and child (all burials 15 and younger) mortality rate at the cemetery, much lower than rates at many other locations elsewhere in Egypt,[49] and even from some sections of the cemetery when examined in isolation.[50] Isolated sections largely match this overall figure. For example, in one section of the cemetery, 26% of the burials were between the ages of 0–6 and 10% between the ages of 7–15. Similarly, the burials from the 1984 season consisting of 115 identifiable burials from four 5×5 meter squares excavated from between 100 and 150 meters north and 30 to 70 meters east of the datum point, exhibited a 36.5% juvenile mortality rate.[51] Both of these are a fairly close match to the sample of 752 burials from various places throughout the cemetery. Other information gained from recent quantification analyses is presented in this volume.

The excavation has also concentrated on conserving the artifacts already excavated. This is an ongoing effort that has begun with cleaning some artifacts (others are best left uncleaned), placing artifacts in acid-free environments, and creating more viable, museum-quality storage containers. While this work continues, a second phase has begun – that of photographing and analyzing the artifacts in greater detail than was done in the past. From this a catalogue will be produced as will several other publications. At this point, every object in the Kom Aushim magazine, the official government storage site, has been provided an acid-free environment and has had its presence and condition verified and recorded. The same has happened for the majority of artifacts still at Fag el-Gamous.

---

48   Griggs, "Excavating a Christian Cemetery," 150.

49   R. Paul Evans and Kerry Muhlestein, "Death of a Child: The Demographic and Preparation Trends of Child Burials in the Greco-Roman Fayoum of Egypt," in *Handbook of Children of Antiquity*, Lesly Beaumont, Matthew Dillon, and Nicola Harrington, eds. (Routledge, forthcoming).

50   C. Wilfred Griggs, "Excavating a Christian Cemetery Near Seila, in the Fayum Region of Egypt," in *Coptic Studies, Acts of the Third International Congress of Coptic Studies*, Wlodzimierza Godlewskiego, ed. (Warsaw: Panstwowe Wydawnictwo Naukowe, 1990), 150; and Griggs, et al., "Evidences of a Christian Population," 232. Here Griggs and his co-authors point out that in one season the juvenile mortality rate was about 66%, which matches better that reported in other studies of Egypt. See Roger S. Bagnall and Bruce W. Frier, *The Demography of Roman Egypt* (Cambridge: Cambridge University Press, 1994), 75–90; and Tim G. Parkin, *Demography and Roman society* (Maryland: John Hopkins University Press, 1992), 94.

51   C. Wilfred Griggs, "Excavating a Christian Cemetery Near Seila," 82–83.

Many papers in this volume highlight the scholarship that has been done in the last few years, including the small amount of work that was done in Philadelphia. Since 2011 a modern cemetery has begun encroaching on the land designated as an archaeological site there, creating a situation where excavation needed to be done quickly. Fortunately, the French Institute has recently done two seasons of work at Philadelphia, which helped preserve some of its archaeological record. As the modern cemetery rapidly expands, the need for work, perhaps even salvage archaeology, becomes crucial. BYU's excavation team's brief survey work is included in order that it may be of help to any who work on this important project.

A bibliography that lists the publications that have dealt with the various components that are part of the BYU Egypt Excavation Project is also part of this book. The history of the excavation team since 2011 is best understood by reading the articles of this volume.

CHAPTER 3

Excavations at the Seila Pyramid and Ritual Ramifications

Kerry Muhlestein

1   History of Excavation of the Pyramid

In modern times it was not apparent that the structure many travelers had seen atop the remote escarpment in Gebel El-Rus was actually a pyramid.[1] Before its excavation it was locally known as *el-Qalah*, meaning "the fortress,"[2] though it has since come to be called *Harem Seila*, or the Seila Pyramid. Even before excavation it could be easily seen as far away as Hawara when the air was clear.[3] Though it stood six miles straight west of the Meidum Pyramid, there was nothing about the visible square covered in aeolian sand that would make explorers or archaeologists think it was another Snefru pyramid. Even the first real archaeologists to survey the area did not realize what it was. Petrie briefly explored there, but his cursory examination did not uncover enough to dissuade him from what met his initial glance: that he was looking at a mastaba.[4] Petrie estimated the height to be about 25 feet, which is less than a third of what it originally was. He also thought it was most likely a 12th Dynasty tomb. A layer on the west side had been removed at some point, though Petrie could not tell this at the time. Its removal made the pyramid seem more rectangular than it really was, causing it to look more like a mastaba. He wisely wrote that it would take more exploration to tell what was really going on with the monument.[5]

---

1   On the geologic makeup of the area, see Russel D. Hamblin, "The Geology of the Gebel El-Rus Area and Archaeology Sites in the Eastern Fayum, Egypt," in *Excavations at Seila, Egypt*, C. Wilfred Griggs, ed. (Provo, UT: Religious Studies Center, Brigham Young University, 1988), 45–73.
2   Nabil Swelim, "The BYU Expedition to Seila, in the Fayum, Egypt: The Pyramid of Seila Locally Called 'el Qalah': The Season of 1987" accessed May 2019, http://nabilswelim.com/downloads/Seila_n_let.pdf.pdf.
3   See W.M.F. Petrie, *Illahun, Kahun and Gurob 1889–90*, (London: D. Nutt, 1891), 31.
4   Ibid., and plate XXX.
5   Ibid.

There must have been some reports that the structure was a pyramid, for when Grenfell and Hunt excavated in the nearby cemeteries, they wrote that they were "south of the 'pyramid' of Sêla, an Old Empire mastaba."[6] While they averred that the structure was a mastaba, their quotations around the word makes it clear that some regarded it as a "pyramid."

Later, Borchardt performed more serious, though still brief, work. It was he who published that the structure was indeed a pyramid, calling it a step pyramid.[7] He mentioned that the antiquities service guards called it a pyramid.[8] That, combined with Grenfell's and Hunt's use of the term, suggests that the locals had known all along that it was a pyramid, and that it took some time for foreigners to accept the idea.

While working there, Borchardt reports having recovered a double statue of a man and a woman and a painted statue of a man, both recovered from what he called unauthorized excavations.[9] The painted statue of a man who is wearing a kilt and is striding with his hands clenched and hanging to his side, is about 55.5 cm tall. The statue of an official who is striding with his arms at his side next to a woman (presumably his wife), who is standing and has one arm around him while the other is at her side, is about 70.5 cm tall. Because they seem to have been produced from local illicit digging, it is difficult to tell where exactly they were found. To be clear, Borchardt does not state that the statues were from the pyramid, but rather just lists "Sile," as the provenance. Thus it is possible that the statues were uncovered at the village of Seila. Still, since Borchardt did not concentrate his work there but rather at the pyramid, the village seems an unlikely provenance. While Borchardt reports that he did not find any kind of cemetery in that area,[10] Grenfell and Hunt did, indicating that there surely was one in the area.[11] An Old Kingdom necropolis seems a likely site for such statues. Thus it appears that either the pyramid, but perhaps even

---

6   Bernard P. Grenfell and Arthur S. Hunt, "Graeco-Roman Branch: Excavations in the Fayum and at El Hibeh," in *Archaeological Report: 1901–1902*, F.Ll. Griffith, ed. (London: Egypt Exploration Fund, 1902), 2.

7   Ludwig Borchardt, "Die Pyramide von Silah: Auszug aus einem Berichte," *Annales du Service des Antiquités de l'Egypte* 1 (1900): 211–214.

8   Borchardt, "Die Pyramide von Silah," 211.

9   Ludwig Borchardt, *Statuen und Statuetten von Königen und Privatleuten im Museum von Kairo, Nr. 1–1294, Teil 1* (Berlin: Reichsdruckerei, 1911), 6–7 and plate 2. Figures 5 and 6 are the single and double statues respectively.

10   Borchardt, "Die Pyramide von Silah," 214.

11   See the article on the background of the Fayoum in this volume.

more likely, the necropolis of Seila are the possible potential origins of these statues.[12]

Borchardt performed limited exploration at the pyramid, only measuring some of its most exposed layers. He estimated that the base was 30 long strides,[13] an observation that would prove to be close to accurate (assuming that a stride was about a meter). Borchardt noted that he thought it was an Old Kingdom structure.[14] He also noted its orientation, building material, and some construction elements, all of which lead him to believe it to be one of the largest of the minor step pyramids,[15] an idea which many still hold today.[16] The ritual elements present at the pyramid are an important part as to why the current

---

12   Andrzej Ćwiek, "Date and Function of the So-Called Minor Step Pyramids," *Göttinger Miszellen* 162 (1998): 43 fn 24, stated that these statues came from a cemetery rather than the pyramid. For this he cited Grenfell and Hunt's report of work in 1900–1901. See Bernard P. Grenfell and Arthur S. Hunt, "Graeco-Roman Branch: Excavations in the Fayum," in *Archaeological Report: 1900–1901*, ed. F.Ll. Griffith (London: Egypt Exploration Fund, 1901), 4–7. However, the cemetery he spoke of was reported in Bernard P. Grenfell and Arthur S. Hunt, "Graeco-Roman Branch: Excavations in the Fayum and at El Hibeh," in *Archaeological Report: 1901–1902*, F.Ll. Griffith, ed. (London: Egypt Exploration Fund, 1902), 2–5. While Grenfell and Hunt speak of finding a cemetery there which they felt came from the Old Kingdom, they do not speak of any finds in the report, nor anywhere else we have searched in their records. They do not record anything about finding these two statues. In another publication, see Andrzej Ćwiek, "Fayum in the Old Kingdom," *Göttinger Miszellen* 160 (1997): 21. Ćwiek says that the statues "may come" from the necropolis. Therefore we conclude it is best to rely on Borchardt's publication saying these were from Seila, possibly, though not certainly, from the pyramid.

13   Borchardt, "Die Pyramide von Silah," 212.

14   Ibid., 213.

15   Ibid., 212–213.

16   See, for example, Rainer Stadelmann, "Snofro – Builder and Unique Creator of Pyramids of Seila and Meidum," in *Echoes of Eternity: Studies Presented to Gaballa Aly Gaballa*, Ola El-Aguizy and Mohamed Sherif Ali, eds. (Wiesbaden: Harrassowitz Verlag, 2010), 35. Here Stadelmann speaks of Seila as one of the most curious of the small step pyramids. He also felt it was built even before the Meidum pyramid. See also Alexander Badawy, *A History of Egyptian Architecture, Vol. 1, From the Earliest Times to the End of the Old Kingdom* (Cairo: Studio Misr, 1954), 125; and Jan Bock, "Die kleinen Stufenpyramiden des frühen Alten Reiches. Ein Überblick," *Sokar* 7, no. 12 (2006): 21–22. The most recent publication, Franck Monnier, "The satellite pyramid of Meidum and the problem of the pyramids attributed to Snefru," *The Journal of Ancient Egyptian Architecture* 3 (2018): 14, refers to it as a "provincial" pyramid, but compares its structure to the Meidum pyramid. It should also be noted that the pyramid was at times proposed to be the burial place of Huni or Hetepheres. Ćwiek, "Date and Function of the So-Called Minor Step Pyramids," 47–48 (though he does not hold to this theory); and Jean-Philippe Lauer, *Histoire monumentale des pyramides d'Égypte, tome 1* (Cairo: Institut Français d'Archéologie Orientale, 1962), 230. This theory has been disregarded both because there is no apparent burial chamber and because of the Snefru stela found on site.

excavator does not support this opinion.[17] This conclusion is further augment-
ed by the presence of angled casing stones and a knowledge of its original size,
which was extensively larger than has been commonly reported.[18] Apparent
connections with the Meidum Pyramid are further reason.[19] These last two
ideas will be explored more fully in future publications.

Borchardt published a few photographs of the pyramid that help document
its state over the years.[20] He also reports having found a worked ("bearbeitet")
basalt block.[21] Swelim, who excavated later, also reports finding three fragments of basalt, but does not record where.[22] Two small basalt fragments were
discovered in the 2018 season on the eastern side near the causeway. The northern desert of the Fayoum contains a basalt quarrying site, at Widan el-Faras.
This is the likely source for whatever basalt was used at the pyramid. Because
limestone casing for the pyramid has been found, it seems most likely that the
"worked" basalt belonged to the cultic structures on either the north or east
side. Since Borchardt says he saw the stone while ascending to the pyramid,
and because one ascends to the pyramid on the north side, this seems the most
likely place Borchardt would have seen the basalt. Thus it seems likely that the
northern cultic porch had some basalt in it, a feature that would be employed
by Snefru's son in the cultic structures around his pyramid. At the same time
the presence of a few basalt fragments on the eastern side suggests that the
cultic area there may also have been paved in basalt.

The next time the pyramid was investigated was in 1938 when Pochan curso-
rily explored the monument. He did not add very much new information, but

---

17   This opinion was reached independently by the author, but was also held by Nabil Swelim
      and Gunther Dreyer. See Ćwiek, "Date and Function of the So-Called Minor Step Pyra-
      mids," 42. Ćwiek was of the opinion that the Seila Pyramid held more in common with the
      minor step pyramids than it had as a difference, but also felt that the Seila Pyramid was
      the key to understanding the others.

18   As was presented by Kerry Muhlestein and Brent Benson in a lecture titled "(Re)Con-
      structing Snefru's Pyramids: Insights Gained from Precise GPS Measurements," (presenta-
      tion, ARCE Annual Meeting, Cincinnati, OH, April 2013).

19   Ibid., and a lecture by Kerry Muhlestein titled "Discovering and Understanding Parallel
      Programs at Snefru's Pyramids," (presentation, Society for the Study of Egyptian Antiqui-
      ties Annual Scholars Colloquium, Toronto, ON, November 2009); and a lecture by C. Wil-
      fred Griggs and Kerry Muhlestein, titled "The Seila Pyramid, Ritual Considerations
      and Parallels," (presentation, ARCE Annual Meeting, Berkeley, CA, April 2010). Some of
      these connections were already anticipated by Jean Yoyotte, "Études géographiques II:
      Les localités méridionales de la région memphite et 'le Pehou d'Héracléopolis,'" Revue
      d'Égyptologie 14 (1962): 98.

20   Borchardt, "Die Pyramide von Silah," figures 1, 3, and 4.

21   Ibid., 213–214.

22   Nabil Swelim, "The BYU Expedition to Seila," 6.

he did take five timely and important photographs that help preserve a knowledge of its state at the time.[23] Lauer drew a reconstruction in the early 1960's
after a short survey.[24] Again, because it had not yet been more fully excavated,
the reconstruction was somewhat faulty, but his measurements were much
more accurate and it was he who first recognized that there may have been an
outer facing. Lauer also postulated that the pyramid was a 3rd or 4th Dynasty
tomb for a king or queen.[25]

Kaiser and Dreyer briefly surveyed the pyramid as part of their exploration
of minor step pyramids.[26] In this exploration they theorized that, while it was
in many ways similar to the minor step pyramids, it was also unique because of
its larger size and distance from the Nile.[27] They also posited that it was a 3rd
or 4th Dynasty structure. Gunter and Dreyer provided accurate measurements
of what had been excavated at that point, noted the use of headers and stretch-
ers, and determined that the mortar was a mixture of sand and clay.[28] Still, the
full extent of the pyramid had not yet been uncovered.

2   The Lesko Excavation

In January 1981, the first sustained and systematic excavation was undertaken
by a joint University of California, Berkeley – Brigham Young University (BYU)
team.[29] In that year, headed by Leonard Lesko who was assisted by C. Wilfred
Griggs, an initial clearing of sand and two sondages were accomplished. The
work of beginning to clear the sand was substantial. Wind is almost always
present at the crest of the escarpment. The loose sand from the desert is carried up, and as the wind encounters the end of the hill it drops the sand it had
carried with it. This happens continually, but each spring a *khamseen* brings
strong enough winds to move large amounts of sand up to the summit where
it is left on top of the pyramid. Thus the large structure had become almost

---

23   André Pochan, *Pyramide de Seila (au Fayoum)*, BIFAO 37 (1938): 161, plates 1–2.
24   Laure, *Histoire monumentale des pyramides d'Égypte*, Fig. 61 and plate LXIX; also Lauer,
      "*Les petites pyramides à degrés de la IIIe dynastie*," RA 2 (1961): 5–15.
25   Lauer, "*Les petites pyramides*," 10, 15; Lauer, *Historie monumentale*, 224.
26   Gunter Dreyer and Werner Kaiser, "Zu den kleinen Stufen pyramiden Ober-und Mittelä-
      gyptens," *MDAIK* 36 (1980): 42.
27   Ibid., 50, 55.
28   Ibid.
29   Leonard Lesko, "Excavation Report: Seila in the Fayoum, 1981," in "The Eighty-Third Gen-
      eral Meeting of the Archaeological Institute of America," *American Journal of Archaeology*
      86/2 (1982): 275; and Leonard Lesko, "Seila 1981," *JARCE* 25 (1988): 223–235.

completely buried over time. Clearing the loose sand from about half of the pyramid and excavating to uncover the corners revealed that the pyramid was larger than had been thought. The visible bottom of the pyramid in the center of the western wall, the part that had been cleared before, was not really the bottom of the pyramid. The hill had not been completely leveled, but rather part of it had been incorporated into the pyramid structure. The corners of the pyramid were significantly lower than the bottom of the middle of the western wall.[30] Thus the pyramid was substantially taller than had been once thought. Additionally, considerable amounts of the outer wall on the south and east sides had been plundered, making it appear smaller than it originally had been, though enough stonework remained, especially of the headers, that the size of the walls could be determined.[31] The blocks of the pyramid measured, on average, 1 x 0.5 x 0.5 meters.[32]

Lesko found a small ancient coin inside the debris of the east wall. While it was illegible, Lesko felt it recognizable enough to theorize that the wall had been at least partially cleared in late antiquity, and that perhaps some of the stone blocks present in the nearby late antique cemetery had come from the pyramid.[33] Looking for subsidiary structures, Lesko cleared small spaces around the east, south and west sides, finding nothing. He also conducted a seismometer test in these areas around the pyramid during this season. He found no anomalies, suggesting that there are no underground cavities, though the geological material there is not ideal for conducting seismic waves.[34]

No consequential objects were found that year. Further, nothing that helped determine who the builder was had been uncovered. Thus the excavators speculated that the structure was either 3rd or 5th Dynasty.[35] While this theory was incorrect, a few very important things were accomplished that season. Enough of the surface was cleared to find what was assumed to be the corners of the building, allowing for a better estimation of its size to be made, though that would be modified over time. Removing sand from the top layer made

---

30   Leonard Lesko, "Seila 1981," 226.

31   Ibid.

32   C. Wilfred Griggs, "Excavating a Christian Cemetery Near Seila, in the Fayum Region of Egypt," in *Coptic Studies, Acts of the Third International Congress of Coptic Studies*, ed. Wlodzimierza Godlewskiego (Warsaw: Panstwowe Wydawnictwo Naukowe, 1990), 145.

33   Lesko, "Seila 1981," 226.

34   See Nabil Swelim, "An Aerial View of the Layer Monument of Snfrw at Seila," in *Zeichen aus dem Sand. Streiflichter aus Ägyptens Geschichte zu Ehren von Günter Dreyer*, Menes – Studien zur Kultur und Sprache der ägyptischen Frühzeit und des Alten Reiches, Eva-Maria Engel, Vera Müller, and Ulrich Hartung, eds. (Wiesbaden, Germany: Harrassowitz, 2008), 5:652.

35   Lesko, "Excavation Report: Seila in the Fayoum, 1981," 275.

FIGURE 3.1   Northern side of the pyramid with the "looting trench" visible
PHOTO BY KERRY MUHLESTEIN

something Petrie had found even more apparent. The pyramid had been plundered from the north side, right into its core. Presumably someone had
assumed the existence of a northern entrance to what could have been a
chamber, and the plundering was in search of such a feature.

We cannot tell when, during the 4600 year life of the pyramid, this plundering occurred. In later excavation of some of the rubble left by these plunderers,
a tobacco label was uncovered[36] which suggests that the plundering might
have taken place when one of its early 19th or 20th century excavators had
been at work. Yet Petrie noted the trench cutting into its north side when he
did the first modern published exploration.[37] He did not investigate enough to
see that the plundering was as extensive as it was, so it is possible that a trench
had begun before his day, while the disassembly of so much of the pyramid
was done by later excavators. There has even been speculation that Mariette or
Maspero could have dug such a trench before Petrie got there,[38] though we
have no record of their having worked at Seila. Petrie thought that the trench
looked recent (like at Dashur and Kula) and was cleared down to three feet

36   Ibid.; and Swelim, "An Aerial View," 652.
37   Petrie, *Illahun, Kahun and Gurob 1889–90*, 31.
38   Nabil Swelim, "The BYU Expedition to Seila."

below the pavement level.[39] Borchardt thought that the trench was probably dug in antiquity, but might also be more modern.[40] It is also possible that later archaeologists examined the pile of debris as well, and that this was when the cigar wrapper became part of those remains. Most likely the full plundering of the pyramid happened before Petrie's day, probably long before, though we will never be sure.

The plundering makes it impossible to tell if there was a chamber in the pyramid. Yet it is most plausible that there was not, since it seems likely a plunderer or excavator would stop when they encountered a chamber, leaving at least its floor intact. At present there is no trace of anything suggesting the remains of a chamber has been uncovered.

3   The 1987 Season

After the first season in 1981 Lesko moved from UC Berkeley to Brown University, and the Egypt Antiquities Organization asked BYU to continue the project, headed by Griggs. Part of the concession included a large necropolis known as Fag el-Gamous, which had also received survey attention in the inaugural season. Because modern agriculture was threatening to encroach upon the cemetery site, Griggs determined that the cemetery would take priority and that work on the Seila Pyramid would have to wait several years.

Work on the pyramid began again in February 1987.[41] At this point, Griggs assumed that the pyramid was a 3rd Dynasty step pyramid.[42] As a result of this assumption, Nabil Swelim, who had been working on minor step pyramids for some time, was invited to direct the work at the pyramid. He was assisted by two foremen who regularly worked for the German Archaeological Institute, Aly Awaad and his assistant, El Tayeb Hassan. This work was at the behest of, and was overseen by, Griggs, who personally headed the work that continued at the cemetery below. Revell Phillips, a professor of geology from BYU, and George Homsey, a professional architect and a founding partner of the architectural firm, *Esherik, Homsey, Dodge, and Davis,* based in San Francisco, also

---

39   Petrie, *Illahun, Kahun and Gurob 1889–90,* 31.

40   Borchardt, "Die Pyramide von Silah," 212–213.

41   Swelim, "The BYU Expedition to Seila," 1–6; Swelim, "An Aerial View," 647–653; Swelim, "Reconstructions of the Layer Monument of *Snfrw* at Seila," 39–56.

42   C. Wilfred Griggs, "Excavating a Christian Cemetery Near Seila, in the Fayoum Region of Egypt," in *Excavations at Seila, Egypt,* C. Wilfred Griggs, ed. (Provo, UT: Religious Studies Center, Brigham Young University, 1988), 76.

assisted with the work. While many of the details of the excavation work were either not recorded or have been lost, we are fortunate that Swelim published a few articles in *Festschriften*[43] as well as self-publishing a number of descriptions, pictures, and drawings of the excavation of the Seila Pyramid. Without his careful work during and after excavation, we would know far less about this monument.

During this season, a few angled, smooth facing stone fragments were found. At some point, more were found but it is not clear when. At least one was found near the northern porch on the north side of the pyramid, and two were found on the eastern side, one just north of the eastern porch and one just south.[44] These angled facing stones are in addition to fragments of facing stones which we cannot tell whether or not were angled. Fragments of facing stones were discovered in the northwest corner of the pyramid. Four facing fragments were found near the outside edge of the northern porch/chapel, labeled Stone Objects B, C, D, and H. These could have been for the facing of the pyramid or instead could have faced a chapel if something covered the porch pavement on the northern side. Four examples of outer casing stones were found near the eastern chapel. Stone Object A was found south of the chapel/porch, a fragment labeled as being part of object H was found south of the chapel/porch, and two pieces of H were uncovered north of the chapel/porch.[45] Of the pyramid facing stones, Swelim wrote "the dressed limestone of the outer facing was bound by a hard white gypsum mortar. Its foundation was built over steps dug in the gravel to reach an all-round level for the pyramid base."[46] The 2018 season rediscovered some limestone blocks that had natural gypsum infusions on the surface, causing them to look almost as if they were burnished grey granite. We cannot tell if this is the kind of gypsum mortar to which Swelim referred.

---

43   Swelim, "An Aerial View," 647–653; Nabil Swelim, "Reconstructions of the Layer Monument of *Snfrw* at Seila," in *Echoes of Eternity: Studies Presented to Gaballa Aly Gaballa*, Ola El-Aguizy and Mohamed Sherif Ali, eds. (Wiesbaden: Harrassowitz Verlag, 2010), 39–56.

44   These positions are based on personal communications with Wilfred Griggs, studying drawings made at the time of excavation, and at least one angled stone still visible on the southern side of the eastern porch.

45   Nabil Swelim, "The Architecture: minor step pyramids or archaic benbens," accessed May 2019, http://nabilswelim.com/downloads/3.pdf.pdf, 12–13.

46   Nabil Swelim, "The Layer Monuments," 1, accessed May 2019, http://nabilswelim.com/downloads/LM%20for%20enc%20cancelled.pdf.

All of these facing stones, especially the angled ones, indicate that the pyramid was likely originally fully faced with angled stones and was thus probably a true pyramid. It is possible that the facing was never finished, though it had been for all the rest of the pyramids built at the time (for dating the pyramid see below) and plundering of facing stones is common.[47] Thus, while we cannot be sure, it is likely that this was a true pyramid akin to its early 4th Dynasty contemporaries. We are currently undertaking a number of analyses that will further address this question and will be part of a future full publication of the pyramid.

It seems likely that the upper facing stones were removed fairly early on, exposing the mudstone blocks of the upper layers of the pyramid to erosion. Flakes, or spalls, from these blocks fell around the pyramid over time, creating a pile over a meter thick in many areas, even up to 2 meters in places. The lower facing stones were removed much later since the falling flakes of the mudstone fell around where these stones once lay, leaving a negative impression of their presence.[48]

Among the most important finds were objects at the center of the northern wall and others at the center of the eastern wall. A small porch, or "naos" as Swelim first called it,[49] was found on the northern side of the pyramid. Mudbricks were laid squarely on a level gravel base to create the porch. On the outermost (northern) edge the remains of a brick wall were found, 4.4 meters from the pyramid.[50] This raises the possibility that the porch had been enclosed, forming a ritual chapel. The aforementioned basalt block found by Borchardt was likely part of this structure, possibly from the floor if it is somewhat similar to Khufu's pyramid temple. Early on, Griggs referred to this structure and/or the pavement on the eastern side as "the remains of a temple pavement," and called the artifacts found there "temple artifacts," though he did not use this terminology for long.[51] Further dimensions of the porch were not

47   Swelim, "The BYU Expedition to Seila," 1 and fn 2, felt that the defacement of the facing stones happened in the 5th Dynasty. His only evidence for this was that other 4th Dynasty pyramids had been plundered during the 5th Dynasty.

48   Swelim, "An Aerial View," 6.

49   Ibid.

50   Nabil Swelim, "Reconstructions of the Layer Monument of *Snfrw* at Seila," 41.

51   C. Wilfred Griggs, Marvin C.J. Kuchar, Mark J. Rowe, and Scott R. Woodward, "Identities Revealed: Archaeological and Biological Evidences for a Christian Population in the Egyptian Fayum," in *The Ancient Near East, Greece, and Rome*, T.W. Hillard, R.A. Kearsley, C.E.V. Nixon, and A.M. Nobbs, eds. (Grand Rapids: Eerdmans, 1998), 1:82.

recorded, and the bricks were removed during the archaeological process of determining whether there was something beneath them, thus making it impossible to recover the dimensions via re-excavation. It is hoped that as we continue the search for excavation notes that perhaps we may one day find these dimensions. Based on the architectural drawings, the porch/chapel was likely about a meter going from east to west and half a meter going from south to north.

A floor surface was made atop the bricks by laying down powdered limestone mixed with sand.[52] On or near this floor, the remains of a stone table and thirty fragments of a small stone statue were found.[53] In 1987 a somewhat unique libation altar was also found.[54] A more detailed description of the altar and statue are in another chapter in this volume. At this time it was determined that the statue was made of a very white travertine, and it was suspected that the altar was as well. Travertine is often referred to as "Egyptian Alabaster," and is a calcium-carbonate stone.

Some plant material was also found in this area. Recent analysis (see the chapter in this volume) has determined that it was from the *Cyperus* family, likely one of two forms of sedge tubers.[55] Though we cannot be sure, it is hard to picture why such vegetation would be present if it were not part of a ritual offering, possibly with symbolic significance because it is a sedge. Because members of the *Cyperus* family were used as food in Egypt,[56] it seems probable that the vegetable remains were part of a food offering that accompanied the liquid offerings we know took place in that area. The remains of at least three 4th Dynasty ceramic vessels were also found, though not enough information was recorded about these vessels to determine more about their nature or use. They certainly could have been part of food offerings if such a thing took place at this ritual structure.

---

52   Swelim, "An Aerial View," 648.

53   Ibid.

54   C. Wilfred Griggs, "General Archaeological and Historical Report of 1987 and 1988 Seasons at Fag el Gamous," in *Actes du IVe Congres copte, 1988. Tome I: Art et archéologie*, eds. Marguerite Rassart-Debergh and Julien Ries (Louvain: Peeters, 1992), 195; Swelim, "The BYU Expedition to Seila," 6; and I.E.S. Edwards, "The Pyramid of Seila and its Place in the Succession of Snofru's Pyramids," in *Chief of Seers: Egyptian Studies in Memory of Cyril Aldred*, E. Goring, N. Reeves, and J. Ruffle, eds. (London: Routledge, 1997), 89.

55   See the botanical report in this volume.

56   Mary Anne Murray, "Fruits, Vegetables, Pulses and Condiments," in *Ancient Egyptian Materials and Technology*, Paul T. Nicholson and Ian Shaw, eds. (Cambridge: Cambridge University Press, 2000), 636–637.

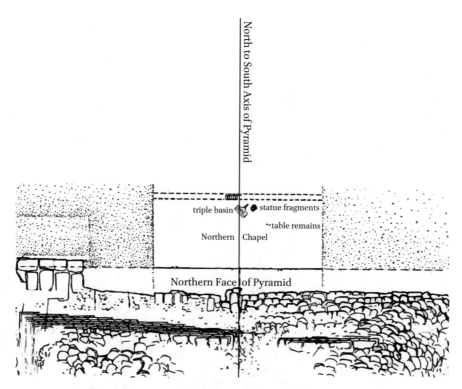

North to South Axis of Pyramid

triple basin   statue fragments

table remains

Northern | Chapel

Northern Face of Pyramid

FIGURE 3.2 Diagram of the central part of the northern face of the pyramid
DIAGRAM BY KATHRYN STUBBS

Two round topped stelae were found on the eastern side. The extant remains of one is just over a meter tall (1.3 m),[57] and the other is almost two meters, though they have both clearly been broken. The shorter stela is 0.6 m wide and 0.37 m thick.[58] The taller stela was uninscribed, though it is broken enough that we cannot be certain that it did not once carry an inscription. The shorter stela contained the inscribed Horus name *neb-ma'at*, and the *Nsw-bity* (King of Upper and Lower Egypt) name "Snefru." The identity of the pyramid's builder had finally been revealed.[59] The discovery that the Seila Pyramid had been built by

---

57   In a letter to I.E.S. Edwards written by C. Wilfred Griggs, April 5, 1990, in the British Museum archives, Griggs lists the stela as being 1.4 meters tall. It is possible that some of it was broken during transport, or that this measurement was just a little off.

58   Ibid.

59   Swelim, "Seila," 1, felt that this was the first of Snefru's pyramids. If it was begun while the Meidum Pyramid was being finished, its size dictates that it would probably have been finished first.

FIGURE 3.3 The inscribed stela
            PHOTO BY SAYED SAʿAD

Snefru caused some to begin to rethink the history of the Fayoum during the
Old Kingdom.[60]

Near these stelae, several fragments of travertine were discovered. They
were of a similar composition to the libation altar found on the northern side.
This suggests that some kind of altar was present on the eastern side as well,
though we cannot be sure.

Even with the extensive excavation conducted that season, the north and
west outer walls were not fully cleared, so Swelim felt they still could not determine the size of the pyramid.[61]

---

60   See Andrzej Ćwiek, "Fayum in the Old Kingdom," *Göttinger Miszellen* 160 (1997): 17; and
     the chapter on the history of the Fayoum in this volume.
61   Swelim, "The BYU Expedition," 5.

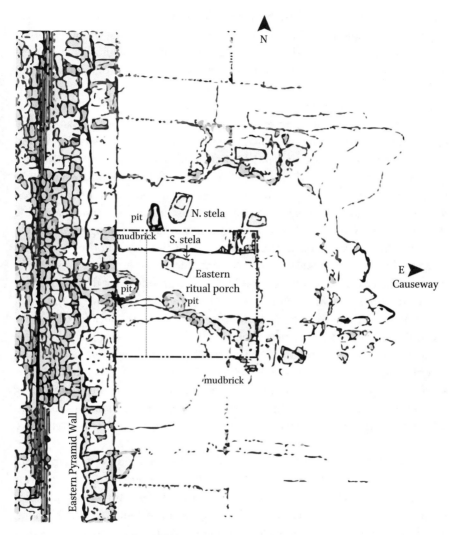

FIGURE 3.4 Diagram of the eastern face of the pyramid
           DIAGRAM BY KATHRYN STUBBS

4   The 1988 Season

During the next season, further excavation continued at the pyramid from February 7 – March 3, 1988. Besides those who had participated before, the team was joined by more architects from Homsey's firm, namely Melissa Harris, James McLane and Charles Davis, another founding partner of the firm. I.E.S. Edwards also visited the site and worked with the excavation team that season,

and continued to consult with the team for many years following.[62] John Rutherford, an engineer from San Francisco, also came. While he did not publish
the results of his study, Rutherford determined that the pyramid lay due west
of the Meidum Pyramid and was at a similar elevation to the top of that seemingly sister structure.[63]

During this excavation season, which focused solely on the eastern side, a
mud-brick porch or pavement extending along the length of the eastern side
of the pyramid was found. It appears that a layer of bricks was laid down on
top of a layer of compacted sand fill and mud packing and seems to have
abutted directly against where the facing stones of the pyramid would have
lain. Some sort of structure seems to have formed a wall that joined the porch
floor to the pyramid, though only four stretcher and three headers abutting
the pyramid now remain of this structure, consequently making it impossible
to determine more about it. The bricks in both the north and east porches
measured 22×11×7.5–8 cm.[64] On the eastern side, these mud-bricks were laid
on an artificially built up terrace that leveled the ground extending to the east
side of the hill somewhat before the landscape fell steeply down to the wadi.
Much of this terrace was covered with gravel which served as a level base for
most of the bricks.[65] The terrace itself was built largely of chippings from the
same kind of stone the pyramid was made of (labeled limestone initially, but
recent geological analysis reveal it to be mudstone, though some of the chips
seen in old photographs do appear to be limestone, probably from facing
stones). Presumably, these chips were created from the quarrying process.
The pavement extended east from the pyramid wall for about three more
meters.

The porch was not perfectly rectangular, but seems to have conformed to
the contours of the hill. It was about 3 m wide on its northern side and grew
wider as it moved south. Because the hillside is not level in this area, with a rise
occurring in the center of eastern side, the gravel base could not provide a full
ability to level the terrain. In order to remedy this, the pavement was further
leveled by inserting two courses of masonry on the northern side and one
course on the southern.[66] As a result, this pavement, which was called a "court"

---

62   Correspondence between Edwards and Griggs about the pyramid as late as 1990 are held
      in the British Museum archives.
63   Personal communication with Wilfred Griggs, to whom Rutherford reported the results of
      his work.
64   Homsey's drawings preserve these measurements.
65   Swelim, "Reconstructions of the Layer Monument," 42–44.
66   Swelim, "An Aerial View," 650.

in the earliest reports, was "almost perfectly horizontal," or level.[67] Seismic settlement over time could easily account for any aberrations in this assertation.

In the center of this paved porch, a kind of chapel with the remains of a mudbrick wall around it extended out another 1.57 meters.[68] The remains do not allow us to determine the original height of this wall, and neither Swelim's nor Griggs' publications inform us of how many courses still stood when they excavated. None of it remains now; it must have been disassembled during excavation. There is some confusion about the width of this chapel since the preliminary report filed at the end of the 1988 season describes it as consisting of two rows of bricks running parallel eastward,[69] but Swelim's scaled drawings show the chapel to be about five meters wide.[70] While the bricks have all been removed now, the 2018 re-excavation revealed a backfilled space that matches most closely Swelim's measurements.

During these excavations, they uncovered five holes that had been carved into the bedrock along the eastern porch.[71] Griggs noted that the diameters of the holes were enlarged below the surface of the ground,[72] which would make them similar to holes that held pots at the Bent Pyramid's "Valley Temple," and Red Pyramid's Valley Temple,[73] suggesting that the Seila holes may have been created for the same reason. Presumably, offerings were made in these bowls.

Further refinement of this picture was made possible by re-excavation in the 2018 season. A sixth hole was uncovered. Two of the six holes lie in a straight axis south of the central chapel. Only one of the two holes on the southern side was excavated in 2018 because the hole visible in pictures that lay even further south was outside of the area that we were able to excavate during this season. These are the only two holes for which we have good photographs from the earlier excavation seasons. These photos show that both were bell shaped and

---

67   "Preliminary Report for the Brigham Young University Fag El Gamous, Seila Excavation, Jan. – March, 1988," as filed with the Egyptian Antiquities Organization, 2. We are grateful to Yasmin Omar and Rasha Elhadad, Ministry of Antiquities inspectors who searched through Ministry of Antiquities archives to find this and other reports.

68   Swelim, "Reconstructions of the Layer Monument," 44, and information from the 2018 excavation season.

69   "Preliminary Report for the Brigham Young University Fag El Gamous, Seila Excavation, Jan. – March, 1988," as filed with the Egyptian Antiquities Organization, 2.

70   Swelim, "Reconstructions of the Layer Monument," 44.

71   Personal correspondence with Wilfred Griggs.

72   Ibid.

73   Ahmed Fakhry, "The Excavation of Snefru's Monuments at Dashur: Second Preliminary Report," ASAE 52 (1952): 574.

fairly uniform in size. Measurements for the hole that was unearthed in 2018 show that "the top of the pit is ovoid in shape, measuring 25x35 cm in size. At its widest point inside the pit, it is 35x42 cm in size. Its slightly rounded base narrows to 21x26 cm, and it is 42 cm deep. The sides of not only this pit, but all the subsurface pits, consist of the hard bedrock material."[74] No artifacts were recovered from the pit, but two thin slabs of limestone were wedged into the northern part of this cavity at its widest point. One of these exhibited a surface of glossy gypsum infusion. As noted above, these two holes likely held pots or bowls. Because the libation altar was on the north side it is reasonable to postulate that food offerings may have been made in these bowls, which would work in tandem with the liquid offerings as has been noted in other settings.[75]

In contrast to how earlier excavators had remembered the other holes, they were not bell shaped, nor were they in a straight line with each other. The 2018 re-excavation not only found an additional hole, but revealed that these remaining four holes, just north of the central chapel, formed an almost perfect square. These four holes had generally straight walls. They were of varying width and depth, though the erosion of the surface in that area makes it difficult to determine how much they now vary from their original depth. Moreover, they are placed in an area where the ground slopes, which may account for their varying sizes. In any case, the shape and position of the four holes makes it appear that they were intended to hold four posts which could have supported some kind of roof.

Many small stone fragments were found in the area of the eastern central chapel, though it is no longer possible to determine what they are fragments of. Additionally, Swelim reports finding a large slab of stone, Stone Object F, he felt may have been the roof of a chapel for a model boat. The slab was very large, measuring 75 cm long, 67.5 cm wide, and 45 cm thick.[76] Swelim also found a small wooden oar, such as are included in model boats. It is 14 cm long, 2 cm wide at the blade, and was painted white with traces of red pigment.[77] It was the presence of this oar that gave rise to the theory of a model boat, and thus a model boat chapel.[78] Yet it is quite possible that this large carved stone could have been used for something else.

---

74   This description was provided by Deborah Harris in our preliminary excavation report.
75   Regina Hölzl, "Libation Basins from the Old to the New Kingdom: Practical Use and Religious Significance," in *L'Acqua nell'antico Egitto: Vita, Rigenerazione, Incantesimo, Medicamento*, Alessia Amenta, Michela Luiselli, and Maria Novella Sordi, eds. (Rome: L'Erma di Bretschneider, 2005), 313.
76   Swelim, "Reconstructions of the Layer Monument," 41–47.
77   Personal observation.
78   Swelim, "Reconstructions of the Layer Monument," 41.

Additionally, three pits were found around or under the porch. Their purpose is unknown. Swelim felt that two of them may have been where the stelae stood.[79] A steep embankment of stonework was encountered at this point. Based on this and a sondage made by Lesko in the 1981 season,[80] the team supposed that a causeway had been found, though it would be several more years before they excavated the causeway. Several sondages were also made in the eastern wadi, but, besides the evidence of the causeway and a few loose pottery sherds, no evidence was found for anything else in the area.[81]

During this (the 1988) season, in the space next to the pyramid, covered by falling spalls from the exposed rock that eroded due to the harsh climate, the remains of a cord basket and a small wooden box with a sliding lid were found. Swelim dated the box to the Middle Kingdom, which suggests that there was some kind of activity there in the Middle Kingdom (as there was at the Bent Pyramid). It would follow that the structure lay undisturbed for long enough afterwards that the Middle Kingdom layer was slowly covered by natural erosion.[82] While Swelim published pictures of these objects,[83] their whereabouts are currently unknown and we cannot verify the dating of the box. On top of the rubble that covered these objects were the remains of what was judged to be a 3rd or 4th century amphora, as well as a Philomator coin. Though we can only now examine a grainy black and white photograph of the amphora, its appearance is more like a Ptolemaic vessel, based on the placement of the handle and shape of the rim. This would make it match more closely the date of the coin. Interestingly, in the 2018 season in the loose sand on the descent from the pyramid another ancient coin was found, containing the double eagle of Ptolemy VI. The three coins found in the pyramid area suggests that there was activity around the pyramid in the Ptolemaic era, supporting Lesko's conclusion that plundering of the blocks of the pyramid had taken place during the Ptolemaic era.[84]

Having uncovered a previously unknown step of the pyramid made it clear that it was larger than had originally been thought. At this time, Swelim estimated that the length of the base of the pyramid was about 30 m.[85] Griggs,

79   Swelim, "An Aerial View," 650.
80   "Preliminary Report for the Brigham Young University," 2.
81   Ibid.
82   Swelim, "The BYU Expedition to Seila," 1.
83   Nabil Swelim, "Seven Layer Monuments of the Early Old Kingdom, Forthcoming," 34, accessed May 2019, http://nabilswelim.com/downloads/MSP_Pre.pdf.pdf. Confirmation of the dating is not possible at this time.
84   Lesko, "Seila 1981," 226.
85   Swelim, "Reconstructions of the Layer Monument," 56.

FIGURE 3.5   The outermost steps of the pyramid visible at the northwest corner
PHOTO BY KERRY MUHLESTEIN

however, estimated it was about 25 m,[86] though he would elsewhere say that it
was 25 m from the center of the pyramid to its furthest corner and the sides
were about 35.5 m long, presumably meaning that this would be the length
with the casing stones intact.[87] Both were short of what later engineers would
find, though Swelim was close and Griggs' later estimate was very close. Clearly
more work needed to be done.

5   Later Work

In 1992, at the behest of the Egyptian Antiquities Organization, the two stelae
were moved to the excavation's storage magazine. The preliminary report filed
for this year states that in the process of moving the stelae they discovered yet

86   Personal communication.
87   Griggs to Edwards, 5 April 1990, in British Museum Archives. These measurements as re-
       corded in this letter are referred to by Edwards in I.E.S. Edwards, "The Pyramid of Seila
       and its Place in the Succession of Snofru's Pyramids," 92.

another step, lower than those exposed thus far and still buried. They also report having discovered mudbrick paving for a temple courtyard on the east side of the pyramid.[88] This is somewhat confusing because the 1988 report also spoke of the pavement for a temple courtyard and described it in some detail. In any case, these discoveries convinced the team that they needed to do more work on the eastern side of the pyramid.

The work was undertaken during the 1995 season. Because Nabil Swelim, who was a detailed note taker, was not present for this season, we have less information available for it than for the earlier seasons. It was in this year that another key element of the pyramid was fully uncovered. Extending straight east from the center of the pavement, connecting to the small chapel, is a causeway made of large limestone blocks. The causeway is not evenly preserved, but its original measurements can still be determined. Because either precise measurements were not recorded or have been lost, we focused on obtaining this information during re-excavation in the 2018 season. The dimensions of the causeway are 7 m long by 8.4 m wide. Downslope angles range from 35 degrees along the steepest part of the structure. Near the top, the angle shallows to 22 degrees as it nears the platform/porch area. The overall angle was originally estimated to be 29 degrees.[89] The causeway has a clear ending, with the bottommost blocks, which run perpendicular to the rest of the stones of the causeway, anchored into a lip carved into the bedrock. This allows those lowest stones to serve as an anchor for the rest of the causeway, preventing any of its stones from slowly working their way downhill as gravity inexorably pulls on them.

On the south-eastern corner a small foundation deposit jar was found, butted up against the large anchor stone. Inside the jar black and red dirt had been placed in 2 distinct layers. The intention of drawing on the symbolism of Black Land and Red Land is clear. No traces of a structure at the bottom of the causeway have been found; there does not appear to be any kind of Valley Temple.

In the 2009 season, a team of three engineers and a student from BYU conducted GPS mapping of both the Seila and Meidum Pyramids, in addition to producing a topographical map of the necropolis. Harold Mitchell, Brent Benson, Todd Osborn, and Alexander Lovett, began to produce a detailed structural analysis of the Seila Pyramid. Since that time Benson has continued the

---

88   C. Wilfred Griggs, "Preliminary Report of the Brigham Young University 1992 Excavation Season," as filed with the Egyptian Antiquities Organization, 1. We are grateful for Rasha Elhadad and Yasmin Omar, inspectors for the Ministry of Antiquities, for helping us obtain this report.

89   Swelim, "Reconstructions of the Layer Monument," 44.

FIGURE 3.6 An anchoring stone in the causeway
PHOTO COURTESY OF REVELL PHILLIPS

FIGURE 3.7 The eastern side of the pyramid with the causeway exposed
PHOTO BY KERRY MUHLESTEIN

work, and, with the use of sophisticated software, has been able to determine with impressive accuracy the original size and structure of the pyramid, finding it to be larger and much higher than was originally thought. By looking at the third step of the pyramid, which is the step with the most complete and visible remains, he identified all four corners of the pyramid. Performing a best fit analysis of these corners, he was able to determine that the pyramid was oriented 0.45 degrees west of true north, or at 359.55 degrees, meaning that it was less than half a degree off of perfect cardinal orientation. Preliminary estimates indicate that the fully cased pyramid was over 36 meters at the base and nearly 8 stories tall (23.4 m). Full details of architectural features will be published in a more comprehensive volume in the future. Benson has also done a great deal of work on the structural relationship between the Seila and Meidum Pyramids, which will also be published in due time.

In 2014, further geological analysis of the stones of the pyramid was performed by Ronald Harris of the BYU Department of Geological Sciences. While all earlier reports described the pyramid as having been built of limestone, this was largely, though not completely, inaccurate. Most of the pyramid is constructed of blocks less than one meter in any dimension that consist mostly of mudstone with some interlayers of siltstone and limestone. The blocks are cemented together using a mud mortar with sand and rock fragments less than 4 cm in diameter. Of course the different types of stones in the pyramid erode at varying rates. This differential erosion is in the process of making the pyramid unstable. Mortar mud preferentially erodes out from under the mudstone blocks, which are much more indurated than the mortar, and thus form overhangs. Many of the overhanging mudstone blocks are collapsing from the structure.

Limestone, confirmed by XRF analysis, is found in blocks lying near the pyramid and included as blocks within it or interlayers within mudstone blocks. The limestone is the material most resistant to erosion of those materials used to construct the pyramid. Perhaps this is why the builders of the pyramid used it as a facing stone, which would prevent the rapid erosion of the clay-rich materials, such as the mudstone blocks, which lay under the limestone facing.

Mutually perpendicular natural fractures encrusted with hematite that are found throughout the mudstone blocks indicate that many of the blocks used to construct the pyramid were likely already broken into rectangular pieces before quarrying. Many such blocks are visible in outcrops surrounding the pyramid.[90]

---

90   For this analysis and description we are indebted to Ronald Harris, and is largely derived
       from Kerry Muhlestein, Giovanni Tata, Ronald Harris, Deborah Harris, R. Paul Evans,

FIGURE 3.8 The southeast corner of the pyramid, where erosion and resulting overhangs are
visible
PHOTO BY KERRY MUHLESTEIN

The 2018 season, completed just days before this was written, was conducted
by Kerry Muhlestein, Deborah Harris, and Bethany Jensen, with some assis-
tance from Kristin South. Additionally, our skilled foreman, Gabr Abd il-Ati,
was key in accomplishing the work. As was noted above, the causeway was re-
excavated, as was some of the paved porch and the holes on the eastern side.

Lincoln Blumell, Catherine Taylor, Brian Christensen, John Gee, Kristin South, Joyce
Smith, Casey Kirkpatrick, and Manal Saied Ahmed, "The Fag el-Gamous 2014 Excavation
Season," *Annales du Service des Antiquités de l'Egypte,* 2014.

Some details of this work have been included in this article, but more will be presented in the future.

6   Ritual Ramifications

Some key similarities between the Seila and Meidum Pyramids have already been noted, explored and preliminarily published.[91] In particular, the presence of cultic elements on both the northern and eastern side is important in pyramid history. Before Snefru, pyramids largely had a north-south axis as their primary orientation.[92] Snefru's Dashur pyramids had a greater east-west axis as their primary orientation,[93] the details of which will be discussed more fully below. Snefru's son, Khufu, built the Great Pyramid and set a pyramid complex standard that would be closely followed thereafter, though most of what he did was based on his father's work at Dashur. The Meidum Pyramid is typically viewed as a transitional pyramid, standing programmatically between pyramids that pre-dated Snefru and the architectural program of the Dashur pyramids and those that followed.[94] Hence pyramids with an east-west orientation are often referred to as "post-Meidum" pyramids, though it should be noted that the Dashur Pyramids are also somewhat transitional.

The Meidum Pyramid had a north-south oriented burial chamber and a northern entrance, like the pyramids before it.[95] Yet the Meidum Pyramid had something else: a temple structure erected on the eastern side of the pyramid.[96]

---

91   Most of what is presented below was also discussed in another article. See Kerry Muhlestein, "Transitions in Pyramid Orientation: new evidence from the Seila Pyramid," *Studien zur Altägyptischen Kultur* 44/1 (2015): 249–258, tables 37–38.

92   Ann Macy Roth, "Social Change in the Fourth Dynasty: The Spatial Organization of Pyramids, Tombs, and Cemeteries," *JARCE* 30 (1993): 33.

93   This is often thought to be due to a rise in the emphasis of the sun cult. For example, see Dieter Arnold, *The Monuments of Egypt. An A–Z Companion to Ancient Egyptian Architecture*, (London: I.B. Tauris & Co Ltd., 2009), 183. But see James P. Allen, *The Ancient Egyptian Pyramid Texts*, (Atlanta: SBL Press, 2005), 12, about a shift to south-north motion rather than eastwards in the pyramids, related to the Northern Stars.

94   Roth, "Social Change in the Fourth Dynasty," 33. Arnold, *The Monuments of Egypt*, 145, writes that Meidum consisted originally of a north-south axis, but was converted to an east-west axis.

95   G.B. Johnson, "The Pyramid of Meidum Part One," *KMT* 4/2 (1993): 66; Miroslav Verner, *The Pyramids: Their Archaeology and History*, Steven Randall, trans. (London: Atlantic Books, 2001), 162.

96   George B. Johnson, "The Pyramid of Meidum Part Two," *KMT* 5/1 (1994): 74.

This pyramid temple[97] also contained two un-inscribed stelae[98] and a crude offering table.[99]

From the temple a causeway extended, running eastward.[100] While large mud bricks have been found at the end of this causeway, nothing that suggests a valley temple has been unearthed.[101] The new structure suggests that while the elements usually associated with burial – entrance to the pyramid and the chamber – were still oriented north-south, ritual activity was centering on the east.

The Dashur Pyramids, also built by Snefru, continued the practice of creating an entrance on the northern side.[102] Yet the Bent Pyramid, compounding its dual orientation, actually has an entrance on both the north and west sides.[103] Both entrances lead to chambers with a north-south orientation. A pyramid temple is also present on the east side of this pyramid.[104] It was small in comparison to later 4th Dynasty pyramid temples, yet larger than the one built at Meidum.[105] Two inscribed stelae were erected here, as well as an altar.[106] A causeway leads out from the complex,[107] but instead of running straight east

97   Often referred to as a mortuary temple.

98   W.M. Flinders Petrie, *Medum* (London: David Nutt, 1892), 8; Alan Rowe, "The Eckley B. Coxe, Jr., expedition excavations at Meydum, 1929–30," *Penn. Univ. Mus. Journal* 22/1 (1931): 32; and Martin Isler, *Stick, Stones, and Shadows: Building the Egyptian Pyramids* (University of Oklahoma Press, 2001), 125.

99   Ali el-Khouli, *Meidum,* The Australian Centre for Egyptology: Reports 3, Geoffrey T. Martin, ed. (Sydney, Australia: Australian Centre for Egyptology, 1991), 13; Rowe, "The Eckley B. Coxe, Jr., expedition," 32; Petrie, *Medum*, 8.

100   W.M. Flinders Petrie, Ernest Mackay, and Gerald Wainwright, *Meydum and Memphis (III)* (London: School of Archaeology in Egypt, 1910), 6; Stadelmann, "Snofro – Builder and Unique Creator of Pyramids of Seila and Meidum," 37.

101   Nabil Swelin, *Some Problems on the History of the Third Dynasty,* (Alexandria: The Archaeological Society of Alexandria, 1983), 84.

102   See Ahmed Fakhry, *The Pyramids,* (Chicago: University of Chicago Press, 1969), 93; and I.E.S. Edwards, *The Pyramids of Egypt, 5th ed.* (Baltimore: Penguin Books, 1993), 80–81.

103   Ibid. Also Alexander Badawy, *A History of Egyptian Architecture Vol. 1: From the Earliest Times to the end of the Old Kingdom,* (Giza: Sh. Studio Misr, 1954), 134; and Hadyn R. Butler, *Egyptian Pyramid Geometry,* (Mississauga, ON: Benben Publications, 1998), 151.

104   Philip J. Watson, *Egyptian Pyramids and Mastaba Tombs of the Old Kingdom,* (Essex: Princes Risborough, 1987), 26; and Ahmed Fakhry, *The Monuments of Sneferu at Dashur,* (Cairo: General Organization for Government Printing Offices, 1959), 1:39.

105   Herbert Ricke, "Baugeschichtlicher vorbericht über die kultanlagen der südlichen pyramide des Snofru in Dahschur," *Annales du Service des Antiquités de l'Égypte* 52 (1954): 609, argues that the mortuary temple at the Bent Pyramid predates that at Meidum.

106   Ahmed Fakhry, *The Monuments of Sneferu at Dashur* (Cairo: General Organization for Government Printing Offices, 1959–1961), 26; and Ahmed Fakhry, "The excavation of Snefru's Monuments at Dashur," 563–594; Ricke, "Baugeschichtlicher vorbericht über die kultanlagen der südlichen pyramide des Snofru in Dahschur," 606–607.

107   Colin Reader, "On Pyramid Causeways," *JEA* 90 (2004): 63–71.

from the pyramid temple, it begins on the eastern corner of the north side, and then bends to head largely east, but slightly north.[108] Its course was likely influenced by the topography of the area.[109] This causeway leads to a "Valley Temple," though this Valley Temple is different from it successors, for after the Valley Temple the causeway continued for 148 meters more, ending in an apparent "harbor basin."[110] The Bent Pyramid also had a small chapel on its northern side that contained an altar.[111]

The Red Pyramid is more like its successors than Snefru's other pyramids. It too has a northern entrance.[112] The passage from this entrance leads to two chambers that run north-south, but these lead to the burial chamber, which is on an east-west axis for the first time.[113] Snefru constructed a temple on the eastern side which is larger than those at his other pyramids, though still small compared with its successors at Giza or Abu Rowash.[114] There are early excavation reports of the remains of a causeway (which may have only been used for transporting materials)[115] and a valley temple to the east of the pyramid.[116] There are also the remains of holes for holding pots, though the reports do not provide sufficient detail to compare to similar finds elsewhere.

---

108   Fakhry, *The Monuments of Sneferu at Dashur*, 36.

109   Nicole Alexanian, Wiebke Bebermeier, Dirk Blaschta, Arne Ramisch, Brigitta Schutt, and Stephan Johannes Seidlmayer, "The Necropolis of Dahshur. Seventh Excavation Report Autumn 2009 and Spring 2010," *German Archaeological Institute*: 11–15.

110   Nicole Alexanian, Felix Arnold, Dirk Blaschta, Josuah Pinke, and Stephan Johannes Seidlmayer, "The Necropolis of Dahshur. Ninth Excavation Report Autumn 2011 and Spring 2012," *German Archaeological Institute/Free University of Berlin*, 5–6.

111   Miroslav Verner, *The Pyramids: The Mystery, Culture, and Science of Egypt's Great Monuments*, Steven Rendall, trans. (New York: Grove Press, 2001), 178. Edwards, "The Pyramid of Seila and its Place in the Succession of Snofru's Pyramids," 90. Fakhry, *The Monuments of Sneferu at Dashur*, 70.

112   Fakhry, *The Pyramids*, 97.

113   Nils Billing, "Monumentalizing the Beyond: Reading the Pyramid before and after the Pyramid Texts," *SAK* 40 (2011): 56. On the change, see Roth, "Social Change in the Fourth Dynasty," 45.

114   Rainer Stadelmann, Nicole Alexanian, Herbert Ernst, Günter Heindl, and Dietrich Raue, "Pyramiden und Nekropole des Snofru in Dahschur. Dritter Vorbericht über die Grabungen des Deutschen Archäologischen Instituts in Dahschur," *MDAIK* 49 (1993): 263–265; Rainer Stadelmann, "Die Pyramiden des Snofru in Dahschur. Zweiter Bericht über die Ausgragungen an der nördlichen Stein pyramide," *MDAIK* 39 (1983): 228–229; Rainer Stadelmann and Hourig Sourouzian, "Die Pyramiden des Snofru in Dahschur," *MDAIK* 38 (1982): 379–393; Edwards, "The Pyramid of Seila and its Place in the Succession of Snofu's Pyramids," 90.

115   On issues regarding the causeway, see Butler, *Egyptian Pyramid Geometry*, 163; Isler, *Stick, Stones, and Shadows*, 214–215; and Verner, *The Pyramids: The Mystery, Culture, and Science of Egypt's Great Monuments*, 187.

116   Lehner, *Complete Pyramids*, 105; Arnold, "Red Pyramid," in *The Monuments of Egypt: An A-Z Companion to Ancient Egyptian Architecture*, 199.

Of Snefru's four pyramids, Seila and the Bent Pyramid are the only ones to exhibit evidence for ritual activity on the north side, though both have larger structures on the east and contain evidence for ritual activity there as well (at Seila in the form of the holes for pots, the presence of stelae where offerings could have been centered is indicated,[117] and in the fragments of what seems to be an altar). The Seila Pyramid had stelae on the eastern side, as did the Bent and Meidum Pyramids. The Meidum stelae were both uninscribed, the Bent stelae were all inscribed, and the Seila Pyramid had one inscribed stela and one that was perhaps uninscribed. It seems to be identical to the Meidum Pyramid in having a causeway on the east with no structure attached to the lower part of that causeway. At the same time, as will be seen in the chart below, it has many shared affinities with the Bent Pyramid. These cultic elements are summarized in the following table:

TABLE 1   A comparison of ritual structures at Snefru's pyramids.

Pyramid	Burial chamber orientation	Side of entrance	Adjacent structure	Causeway	Valley temple	Altars
Seila	None (uncertain)	None (uncertain)	Porch on East and North	East	No	Two on north, perhaps one on east
Meidum	North-South	North	East temple	East	No	One on east
Bent	North-South	North and West	East and North temple	North-East, largely East	Yes	One on east, one on north
Red	East-West	North	East temple	East	Yes	One on east

The Seila Pyramid sits at the junction of pyramid cultic activity that focused on the north of the pyramid and an emerging cultic focus on the east. Future publications will explore: the purpose of the Seila Pyramid, which was clearly not intended to house the king's dead body; the timing of when the Seila Pyramid was built as compared to Snefru's other pyramids; questions about what

---

117   Stadelmann, "Snofro – Builder and Unique Creator of Pyramids of Seila and Meidum," 38; Andrzej Ćwiek, "Date and Function of the So-Called Minor Step Pyramids," 52.

kinds of activities would have happened in Seila's cultic structures; the relationship between the Seila Pyramid and Snefru's other pyramids, asking what can looking at all of them together tell us about the development of the pyramid complex; and analyzing what the Seila Pyramid's relationship is to the minor step pyramids and what that relationship can tell us about the development of the concept of pyramids. Clearly there is more work to be done in exploring and analyzing the Seila Pyramid. Yet it is already apparent that the Seila Pyramid was a site of innovation in architecture, in orientation, in titular inscription, in ritual activity, and in use of spatial geography. We look forward to creating future publications that will further all of these topics and thus will allow us to better understand the beginning of the pyramid age.

CHAPTER 4

Ritual Objects from the Northern Side of the Seila Pyramid

Kerry Muhlestein, Brian D. Christensen and Ronald A. Harris

Of Snefru's four pyramids, the Seila Pyramid and the Bent Pyramid are the only two which both have ritual structures and objects on their northern sides.[1] As we investigate the Seila Pyramid, the objects associated with this northern chapel are worth analyzing and reporting because of their intrinsic significance, because not everything published about them in the past has been fully accurate,[2] and also so that other scholars who research similar structures and rituals from the same era can compare them with the objects at Seila.

In the 1987 excavation season, a small porch was found abutted to the north face of the pyramid.[3] Mudbricks topped by a mixture of powdered limestone and sand covered an area of roughly 4.5 square meters. These bricks were laid on a gravel base that leveled the area out. The remains of a wall on the northern side of the porch suggest that the porch was at least partially, if not completely, enclosed.[4] The walls were probably made of smooth stone, and the

---

1 On the northern side of the Bent Pyramid, the remains of a cultic chapel and *ḥtp* altar were found. See Ahmed Fakhry, *The Monuments of Sneferu at Dashur, vol. 1, The Bent Pyramid* (Cairo: General Organization for Government Printing Offices, 1959), 41–46; I.E.S. Edwards, "The Pyramid of Seila and its Place in the Succession of Snofru's Pyramids," in *Chief of Seers: Egyptian studies in memory of Cyril Aldred*, E. Goring, N. Reeves, and J. Ruffle, eds. (London: Routledge, 1997), 90. Additionally, a pit was found on the northern side of the Bent Pyramid that serves an unknown function. See Mark Lehner, *The Complete Pyramids of Egypt* (New York: Thames and Hudson, 1997), 104.

2 For example, see Marco Zecchi, *Geografia religiosa del Fayyum* (Bologna: University of Bologna, 2001), 89–91, who reports all the objects being found on the east side, when in fact many were found on the north. Also see Rainer Stadelmann, *Die großen Pyramiden von Giza* (Graz, Austria: Akademische Druck- und Verlagsanstalt, 1990), 90, who has a wonderful report about the statue, but seems to misunderstand where it was found. None of these scholars can be faulted, proper publication of this information will make it much easier for people to accurately discuss these finds.

3 Nabil Swelim, "The Layer Monuments," accessed May 2019, http://nabilswelim.com/downloads/LM%20for%20enc%20cancelled.pdf.

4 Nabil Swelim, "Reconstructions of the Layer Monument of *Snfrw* at Seila," in *Echoes of Eternity: Studies Presented to Gaballa Aly Gaballa*, Ola El-Aguizy and Mohamed Sherif Ali, eds., (Wiesbaden: Harrassowitz Verlag, 2010), 39–56.

© KONINKLIJKE BRILL NV, LEIDEN, 2020 | DOI:10.1163/9789004416383_006

porch perhaps even had a roof, though we cannot tell. Thus the structure must have been a cultic porch (without a roof), or perhaps even a cultic chapel (with a roof). Some faced stone fragments were found adjacent to the chapel/porch. They could have been part of the architecture of the chapel/porch, though they could have come from the pyramid instead. When Borchardt performed the first real examination of the Seila Pyramid he reported seeing a dressed basalt stone in this area.[5] While it is not clear exactly where the stone was seen, the later presence of basalt floors in pyramid temples suggests that it may have been part of the chapel/porch on the northern side. For more on the excavation of this chapel/porch, see the article about the pyramid excavations within this volume.

The fragments of what appears to be a large limestone table were found on the chapel/porch, as well as the remains of at least three 4th Dynasty ceramic

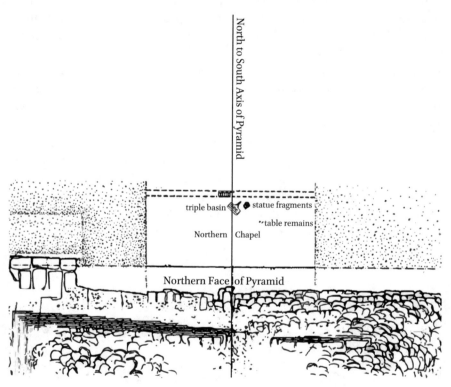

FIGURE 4.1   Diagram of the northern cultic structure and associated artifacts
            DRAWING BY KATHRYN STUBBS

5   Ludwig Borchardt, "Die Pyramide von Silah: Auszug aus einem Berichte," *Annales du Service des Antiquités de l'Egypte* 1 (1900): 213–214.

vessels.[6] Because good photos and detailed descriptions of these objects were not made, little can be said about them other than that it seems likely they were used in cultic activity at the pyramid.[7]

Two other very interesting objects were also discovered at the northern cultic structure about which more can be said: the remains of a small statue and a libation altar.

1   Seated-Figure Statue

In order to better understand the altar and statue at the Seila Pyramid, we examined their geologic composition. Ronald Harris, professor of geological sciences at Brigham Young University, conducted x-ray fluorescence (XRF) tests using a Brucker portable XRF analyzer. This definitively demonstrated that the altar and statue found at the pyramid are composed of travertine[8] with abundances of various trace elements; these elements help to compare the altar's and statue's compositions with other travertine artifacts and deposits found throughout Egypt and the surrounding region. The Seila objects are largely similar in composition to travertine commonly found in Egypt, though travertine objects always contain their own variety of trace elements based on where the travertine originated.

Many objects in Egypt have been identified as "alabaster." Alabaster refers to either calcite ($CaCO_3$), or gypsum ($CaSO_42H_2O$). The calcite form of alabaster is really travertine, which is sometimes referred to as "Egyptian alabaster." It is formed by the rapid precipitation of calcium carbonate, or, in other words, travertine is calcite deposited by groundwater. Travertine is similar to limestone but is more translucent, which makes it desirable for fine objects and beautiful vessels.

---

6   Nabil Swelim dated the pottery to the 4th Dynasty, but does not state on what grounds, and left no detailed drawings or other evidence.

7   On the significance of cultic structures existing on both the northern and eastern side of the pyramid, see Kerry Muhlestein, "Transitions in Pyramid Orientation: New Evidence from the Seila Pyramid," *Studien zur Altägyptischen Kultur*, 44/1 (2015): 249–258, tables 37–38.

8   Pictures and a description of the statue were first made in Rainer Stadelmann, "Snofru—Builder and Unique Creator of the Pyramids of Seila and Meidum," in *Echoes of Eternity: Studies Presented to Gaballa Aly Gaballa*, Ola El-Aguizy and Mohamed Sherif Ali, eds., (Wiesbaden: Harrassowitz Verlag, 2010), 34. Here Stadelmann states that the statue was made of a white stone resembling alabaster.

It is presumed that this is a travertine statue of Snefru,[9] though it does not contain any fragments of the face. The details of the statue's carving reveal the sculpture to be a refined masterwork reflecting a sophisticated understanding of human anatomy. It is clearly of a higher quality than the other two small Old Kingdom statues found nearby.[10] No process marks, except for the bottom filing to level the base, are visible, in contrast to the libation altar of the same material, which has a less refined finish and less consistency of form. The fragments reveal a three-quarter view of the seated figure with the base and back wall forming an L-shaped profile. Even with only a few fragments available it is clear that the statue is in the "frontal," or "fixed axis" style that was the rule of the era.[11] The figurative elements include feet and ankles up to mid-calf positioned on a flat, rectangular base; a left hand on a draped left knee; and a left arm, including the deltoid and upper arm as well as partial forearm. One fragment has a trace of black on it, which could be the remains of paint, though this is not certain. A small fragment appears to be the right arm at the bend of the elbow. As Stadelmann observed, "several longitudinal fragments with three smoothed faces and two sharp edges attest the existence of a back slab."[12] Almost certainly this was originally a refined depiction of King Snefru, and its presence in the chapel, along with the libation altar and table (which could have been a non-libation altar), suggests that the royal cult was practiced on this northern side.[13]

The anatomy of the upper left arm and deltoid suggest a muscularity that is likely specific to a male figure and is similar to statuary art of the period.[14] The musculature is executed with the elegant realism that is a hallmark of high sculpture of the era.[15] The fragment of exposed pectoral muscle and arm

9   C. Wilfred Griggs, "General Archaeological and Historical Report of 1987 and 1988 Seasons at Fag el Gamous," in *Actes du IVe Congrès Copte, 1988. Tome 1: Art et Archéologie*, Marguerite Rassart-Debergh and Julien Ries, eds. (Leuven: Peeters Publishers, 1992), 195–196.

10   Ludwig Borchardt, *Statuen und Statuetten von Königen und Privatleuten im Museum von Kairo, Nr. 1–1294, Teil 1* (Berlin: Reichsdruckerei, 1911), 6–7 and plate 2.

11   While this style has long been referred to as frontal, Heinrich Schäfer, *Principles of Egyptian Art*, Emma Brunner-Traut, ed., and John Baines, ed. and trans. (Oxford: Griffith Institute, 2002), 311–312, argues that it is more precise to use the term "fixed-axes."

12   Stadelmann, "Snofru," 34.

13   See the article on the excavation of the Seila Pyramid and ritual ramifications in this volume.

14   This style is common in the 4th and early 5th Dynasties, and changes somewhat thereafter. See Edna R. Russmann, "A Second Style in Egyptian Art of the Old Kingdom," *Mitteilungen des Deutschen Archäologischen Instituts, Abteilung Kairo* 51 (1995): 269.

15   Dorothea Arnold, *When the Pyramids Were Built: Egyptian Art of the Old Kingdom* (New York: The Metropolitan Museum of Art, 1999), i. Also David P. Silverman, *Ancient Egypt* (New York: Oxford University Press, 1997), 216.

combined with the hand on an ornately draped horizontal knee leads the viewer to imagine a seated, high-status male. The wavy pattern on whatever material was depicted as draping the leg on which the left hand rests is undoubtedly a representation of a kilt that ends mid-thigh. This statue seems to be similar to Djoser statues in which the king is also depicted as seated with the left hand resting on his knee, but wearing a jubilee cloak.[16] It is also similar to the depiction of a seated Snefru on a stela from the Bent Pyramid, now housed in the open air court of the Cairo Museum.[17] In this depiction the left hand lies on the knee and the right hand is raised holding the flail. Yet the Seila statue differs from these depictions and represents a small transition, since before its discovery seated figures of the king in a short *shendyt* kilt were first attested in depictions of Snefru's son, Khufu.[18] The kilt appears to be similar to

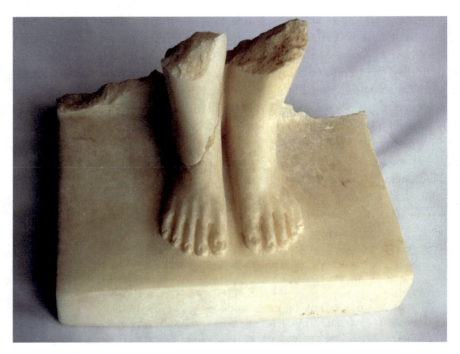

FIGURE 4.2   Base of statue
PHOTO BY BRIAN D. CHRISTENSEN

16   Hourig Sourouzian, "L'iconographie du roi dans la statuaire des trois premières dynasties,"
      in *Kunst des Alten Reiches. Symposium im Deutschen Archäologischen Institut Kairo am 29.
      und 30. Oktober 1991* (Mainz: Verlag Philipp von Zabern, 1995), 143–144; also Stadelmann,
      "Snofru," 34–35.
17   JE 89289.
18   Stadelmann, "Snofru," 35.

FIGURE 4.3   Left arm and knee of statue
PHOTO BY BRIAN D. CHRISTENSEN

those worn by Snefru in his statues found in the so-called "valley temple" of the
Bent Pyramid, though these statues are of Snefru striding rather than seated.[19]
The wavy lines of the kilt appear to be exactly the same on both the Dashur
statues and the one from Seila.[20] Thus it is clear that in some ways the Dashur
statues are quite innovative, just as the Seila statue appears to be. We are in the

---

19   See Ahmed Fakhry, *The Monuments of Sneferu at Dahshur, vol. 2, The Valley Temple, Part
      1.—The Temple Reliefs* (Cairo: General Organization for Government Printing Offices,
      1951), 3–4, and plates XXXIII–XXXVII.
20   Ibid., plate XXXV.

FIGURE 4.4   Close up of statue left hand, knee
PHOTO BY BRIAN D. CHRISTIAN

process of researching and writing about the high number of innovations attested in Snefru's day, including his statuary and titulary.

We measured the fragments of the travertine seated figure; however, not enough of the statue survives for us to create an accurate estimate of its height. This is especially the case because we do not know if the head would have sported a wig, a crown (some of which could be quite high), or no head covering at all. If it was similar to the depiction of the seated Snefru of the Dashur Stela, he would be wearing the crown of Lower Egypt. If it was similar to the striding statues in a short kilt from Dashur it would be wearing the crown of Upper Egypt. In trying to proportionally place how the fragments would probably have been assembled, and following that proportion, we estimate that the statue would have been between 25 and 30 cm tall without any kind of adornment on the head. The measurements of these extant fragments are presented in table 4.1.

It has been suggested that the statue may have been placed on top of the pyramid.[21] Other suggestions (see below) seem more likely, though this one cannot be ignored.

---

21   Rainer Stadelmann, *Die Großen Pyramiden von Giza*, 78.

TABLE 4.1   Dimensions of Statue Fragments

Dimension	Height, width, depth (in centimeters)
Foot pedestal	17x15x3
Feet	7x7x9
Left hand on knee	10x4x4
Left arm	13x7x3
Largest backing slab fragment	12x6x2
Foot fragment	7x4x3
Grooved pedestal fragment	13x4x3

2   Libation Altar

2.1   *Royal Libations*

The mere presence of a libation altar at the pyramid is interesting since no others are attested at Snefru's other pyramids. Known altars at these pyramids are large, are in the shape of the *ḥtp* glyph, and are clearly not for libations. Further, it is difficult to assess the ritual meaning of the Seila libation altar since the pyramid is somewhat unique, apparently never having been intended for a burial. Because of this, the presence of a small royal statue, and because libation altars in a funerary context were not common until the 5th Dynasty,[22] it is more likely that the libations were associated with the living royal cult than that they were funerary in nature.[23] It is also possible that, as in other places, the basins could be a symbolic representation of lakes and thus a connection with creative waters.[24] This would especially make sense because the Seila Pyramid could not be connected to a quay and canal as many other pyramids were, though that was not necessarily a standardized idea at this time, and one would then expect such a symbol to be on the east side associated with the causeway rather than the northern side.

---

22   Regina Hölzl, "Libation Basins from the Old to the New Kingdom: Practical Use and Religious Significance," in in *L'Acqua nell'antico Egitto: Vita, rigenerazione, incantesimo, medicamento*, Alessia Amenta, Michela Luiselli, and Maria Novella Sordi, eds. (Rome: L'Erma di Bretschneider, 2005), 310.

23   This is more in keeping with the assumption many have made of the minor step pyramids. Namely, that they were a manifestation of royal power. For example, see Andrzej Ćwiek, "Date and Function of the So-Called Minor Step Pyramids," *Göttinger Miszellen* 162 (1998): 42–43.

24   Hölzl, "Libation Basins," 314.

Most of what we know about royal cult libations comes from later time periods, when libations were often part of New Kingdom funerary temples[25] and, at least in the Late Period, regular parts of the daily rituals for gods.[26] In these periods it seems there were times when at least priests came to the temple specifically and solely for libations.[27] Yet most of these rituals seem to have earlier Middle[28] or Old Kingdom predecessors.[29] Additionally, there are clear references to libations in the texts of the Old Kingdom. In the Pyramid Texts libations were often associated with liquid that came from Osiris being returned to him in order to make him whole or rejuvenate him.[30] The liquid emanating from Osiris could simultaneously be associated with the rejuvenating flood.[31] While we do not know what liquid(s) was offered at the Seila Pyramid (see below), every known libation liquid was in some way associated with rejuvenation,[32] suggesting that this was likely part of the meaning of whatever ritual took place at the pyramid. Still, there are many forms of and purposes for rejuvenation, making further investigation worthwhile.

Towards that end, a Late Period ritual text has been tied to a Pyramid Text precursor that mentions libations, and thus that text may have some relevance.[33] Therein, libation is associated with fresh water issuing from the Nile and/or Osiris. Such water then played a role in transformation and glorification,

25   Gerhard Haeny, "New Kingdom 'Mortuary Temples' and 'Mansions of Millions of Years,'" in *Temples of Ancient Egypt*, Byron E. Shafer, ed. (Ithaca: Cornell University Press, 1997), 97–98, 113.

26   See the 22nd Dynasty Papyrus Berlin 3055. See also Ragnhild Bjerre Finnestad, "Temples of the Ptolemaic and Roman Periods: Ancient Traditions in New Contexts," in *Temples of Ancient Egypt*, Byron E. Shafer, ed. (Ithaca: Cornell University Press, 1997), 205.

27   Stephen E. Thompson, "The Anointing of Officials in Ancient Egypt," *Journal of Near Eastern Studies* 53/1 (1994): 20.

28   Françoise Dunand and Christiane Zivie-Coche, *Gods and Men in Egypt, 3000 BCE to 395 CE*, David Lorton, trans. (Ithaca: Cornell University Press, 2002), 90–91.

29   Emily Teeter, *Religion and Ritual in Ancient Egypt* (New York: Cambridge University Press, 2011), 47.

30   Pyr. 22–23; Pyr. 166–167; Pyr. 868; Pyr. 2031. See also Jan Assmann, *Death and Salvation in Ancient Egypt*, David Lorton, trans. (Ithaca: Cornell University Press, 2001), 355–363.

31   Pyr. 788; Pyr. 1360; Pyr. 2007.

32   See Mu-Chou Poo, "Liquids in Temple Ritual," in UCLA *Encyclopedia of Egyptology*, Willeke Wendrich ed., (Los Angeles: http://digital2.library.ucla.edu/viewItem.do?ark=21198/zz-0025dxbr), 5.

33   Rita Lucarelli, "A Libation Text in the Book of the Dead of Gatseshen," in *L'Acqua nell'antico Egitto: Vita, rigenerazione, incantesimo, medicamento*, Alessia Amenta, Michela Luiselli, and Maria Novella Sordi, eds. (Rome: L'Erma di Bretschneider, 2005), 325, 328.

or *sȝḥw*,[34] of individuals.[35] This idea would be particularly appropriate for a pyramid connected with the royal cult. In fact, water was very important in a variety of royal rituals because the king had to be purified and glorified by water.[36] The king also had to master and use water, especially to bring about rebirth or fertility, which provided a circular association with the king's own rebirth and fertility.[37] Thus royal libation offerings were necessary for the king to fulfill his transcendent role in life and in death.[38] The purposes of the cult of the living king and of the dead king were not necessarily separate. Indeed, they were somewhat intertwined, and while we are not yet sure of the purpose of the Seila Pyramid and even less sure of the purpose of its libation rituals, they were almost surely somehow connected with the transformation of Snefru.

2.2   *The Physical Altar*

The altar is a flat rectangular slab of travertine with three conical basins and converging channels leading to a triangular spout with a separate cover over the spout. We are unaware of any similar altars from this area or era. The closest parallels we have found are 8th Dynasty funerary altars from Saqqara, as shown to us by Dr. Vasil Dobrev at his excavations.[39] These 8th Dynasty altars are not true parallels, but they are closer than other altars.

The carving marks on the altar are consistent with traditional stone carving using metal tools. A point chisel seems to have been employed for roughing and left point marks in the low spots and bruises in the translucent stone. No tooth chisel or flat chisel marks are evident, but it is likely that after the slab was split, its form was roughed into shape, first by pitching with a flat chisel and then by modeling with a point chisel. On the whole this piece is not as refined as the statue, largely because it shows the process of creation transparently by not having all of the process marks smoothed away.

---

34   See Jan Assmann, "Egyptian Mortuary Liturgies," in *Studies in Egyptology Presented to Miriam Lichtheim*, Sarah I. Grollj, ed. (Jerusalem: Magnes Press of Hebrew University, 1990), 3–9.

35   Lucarelli, "Libation Text," 327–328.

36   Pyr. 529f, 1454b.

37   Pyr. 132c. See also Aaron Smith, "Kingship, Water and Ritual: The Ablution Rite in the Coronation Ritual of Pharaoh," in *L'Acqua nell'antico Egitto: Vita, rigenerazione, incantesimo, medicamento*, Alessia Amenta, Michela Luiselli, and Maria Novella Sordi, eds. (Rome: L'Erma di Bretschneider, 2005), 330.

38   Smith, "Kingship, Water and Ritual," 330–332.

39   We are grateful to Dr. Dobrev for showing us these altars and await his publication of them.

The parallel flatness of the top and bottom slab surfaces was achieved by filing through the rough stone from edge to edge. This technique is best viewed in the marks left by flattening the side edges of the stone, but it can be assumed that this technique was employed in achieving basic dimensionality and symmetry in the stone. It is also noteworthy that the base of the figure of Snefru, from the same type of stone at the same site, was leveled and flattened in the same way, even though the figure bears no other tool marks. On the altar, after filing to level, the flanges above the file marks were pitched off with a flat chisel and the surface sanded flat to the level of the file marks. Visible evidence indicates that the edge of a file was used for square-edged cuts, and a flat file was used to further smooth the top surface after pulverizing the high points with a bush hammer or some similar tool (see the marks on and around the triangular spout).

The three bowls were likely hollowed out by point chisels and sanded smooth. There are very few tool marks or bruises in the bowls, except for a few peck marks. They are perfectly symmetrical and smooth, indicating that they were compassed and carefully ground into shape. The converging channels running into the bowls are ruler straight and seem to be filed for accuracy in channeling liquids. The dimensions of the altar are presented in Figure 4.9.

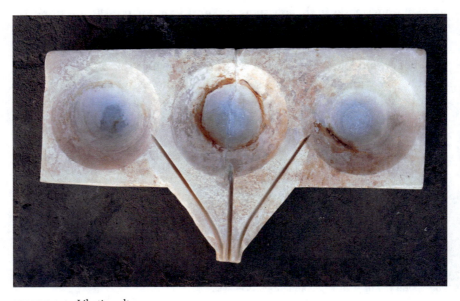

FIGURE 4.5   Libation altar
PHOTO BY BRIAN D. CHRISTENSEN

FIGURE 4.6   Libation altar with light revealing rings in basins
PHOTO BY BRIAN D. CHRISTENSEN

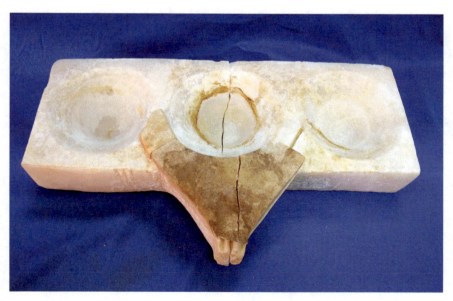

FIGURE 4.7   Libation altar (before repairing its crack) with the cover on its channels
PHOTO BY KERRY MUHLESTEIN

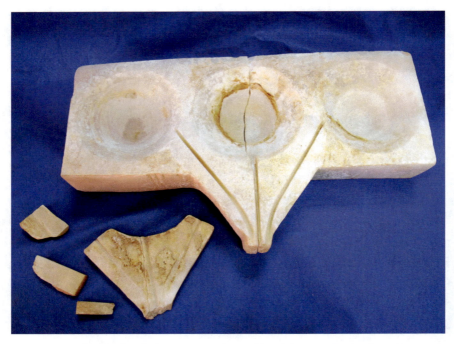

FIGURE 4.8   Libation altar (before repairing the crack) and the cover for the channels
PHOTO BY KERRY MUHLESTEIN

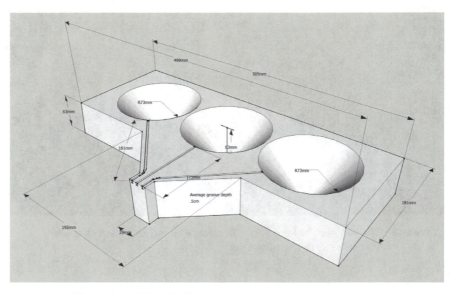

FIGURE 4.9   Illustration by Brian D. Christiansen

2.3   The Offering Material and Method

The central basin possesses a colored ring that is the result of residue from some kind of liquid. Harris conducted an XRF analysis of this ring in an attempt to determine what kind or kinds of liquids were offered in the altar. The ring is very similar in composition to bronze, which is typically 90 percent copper, with tin and zinc being common alloys; the ring consists of copper with small amounts of zinc, iron, tin, arsenic, and palladium also present. This information was quite interesting, but it did not seem to help identify the offering liquid.

As we continued with XRF analyses of objects from the larger excavation site, including the cemetery that lies 1.5 km away, we discovered that the metal jewelry from the cemetery exhibited the same elemental properties as the ring in the libation basin. In other words, the residue ring in the altar's basin was made of the same material as that of the (seemingly locally made) jewelry worn by the local inhabitants thousands of years later. This suggested a few possibilities for the creation of the residue ring. The ring may have been made by the constant presence of water that had been poured from a metal container (such as the copper bowls and ewers that are commonly found in Old Kingdom tombs), which process thus transferred the metal's elements into the water and then onto the stone of the altar. Even more likely is the possibility that a cast bronze object was submerged in liquid in the center bowl, leaving a ring of dissolved oxides from the metal. A likely candidate for this could be a wet bronze or copper bowl (copper bowls of similar shape were common in the Old Kingdom) being placed inside the libation altar's bowls for long periods of time. Acidic liquids like wine, beer, or milk would accelerate oxidation on bronze or copper, but water would have an effect as well, as is demonstrated by the colorful stains on marble and bronze fountains in other contexts. While there is a long history for offering wine[40] and beer,[41] and somewhat later milk,[42]

---

40   Wine was associated with pyramid offerings. See PT 442 and 581. Also, Poo, "Liquids," 1–2. The earliest known depiction of offering what may be wine is from two generations later and is not certain. See Mu-Chou Poo, *Wine and Wine Offering in the Religion of Ancient Egypt* (London: Kegan Paul International, 1995), 40. On Pyramid Text wine liturgies see Poo, *Wine and Wine Offering,* 71–78.

41   Beer was a common offering, probably even in the 4th Dynasty, though our evidence for it all dates to a later period. See Poo, "Liquids," 3.

42   Milk was a common, though much less common, substance for offering as well. It is best known in later rituals at Philae. The evidence for milk offerings is all late, and it is possible that it was not a regular offering during the 4th Dynasty. See Poo, "Liquids," 3. See also Janice W. Yellin, "Abaton-style Milk Libation at Meroe," *Meroitic Studies, Meroitica,* 6/8 (1982), 151–155.

the strongest history is for libating water.[43] Alternatively, if the altar lay in the sand for some time and collected what little rainwater percolated through the sand, and if that sand also contained the trace elements of the local metals, then the elements could have been carried by rainwater through the sand into the altar. None of these theories can account for why one basin has a heavy residue, one has a trace on one side, and the third has no residue at all in normal viewing, though photo enhancement of colors reveals a light orange trace ring in the third bowl as well. One potential theory is that during the years the altar lay unattended in the sand, a bronze object was in the basin lying at an angle (see below). During these many years rainwater penetrated the sand to also fill the basin with enough liquid to oxidize the bronze object. This theory is complicated because there was no bronze object found near the altar and because there was a crack in the middle basin, discussed below. In any case, it seems most likely that water was the liquid offered in the altar because no traces of other liquids have been detected. Still, the oxidizing qualities of beer, wine and milk mean that they cannot be ruled out.

Interestingly, the ring seems to have been made by liquid that was at about a twenty degree angle, meaning that the ring was left while the altar was at an angle, not level. This would make sense if the altar had fallen and landed on something and then lain in the sand for millennia filling with rainwater, as has been postulated above. Yet the altar is broken cleanly along the line of the incoming center channel, right in the middle of the basin that contains the residue. One would assume that it broke as it fell, and thus it would no longer have held water. Alternatively, if the cult at the pyramid had at some time been ended, the altar could have been broken as a form of "decommissioning" it.[44] Neither of these scenarios lends itself to the theory that the residue ring was created as it lay for millennia collecting rainwater. The residue ring and the break in the altar leave open at least as many questions as they answer.

The Ministry of State for Antiquities in Egypt requested that we repair the break. Thus, at their request, in 2014 Brian Chistiansen, professor of art at Brigham Young University, applied an epoxy polymer resin mixed with dolomite marble dust to rejoin the halves of the altar into its original form. This allowed us to test, for the first time, how the libations may have been performed.

---

43   Water was a very common offering and is attested in all time periods. For some examples of Old Kingdom evidence, see PT 230, 436, 460, 553, 676, 679 and Poo, "Liquids," 5. See also Aylward Blackman, "The Significance of Incense and Libations in Funerary and Temple Ritual," *Zeitschrift für Ägyptische Sprache und Altertumskunde* 50 (1912): 69–71.

44   For more on the idea of decommissioning objects, see the article on kill holes in Fag el-Gamous pottery in this volume.

From the time of the discovery of the altar, it was supposed that the long neck with channels was designed to carry liquid into the conical bowls of the altar.[45] The cover for the channeled neck would have concealed the movement of the liquid and could have made it seem that the liquid just suddenly appeared in the bowls. Yet the base of the altar is not completely level; it actually leans toward the neck. This causes liquid in the channels to flow away from the basins rather than channel into them. We had to tilt the altar at about twenty degrees in order to make the liquid funnel into the basins well. While it is extremely interesting that this is about the same angle as the residue ring in the middle basin mentioned above, it still does not seem like the altar was intended to have some object placed under it in order to put it at a twenty degree incline. Furthermore, the chisel marks are still visible on the bottom of the altar, indicating that this was its original base, not a broken form that would have changed the incline. Thus, we conclude that it does not seem as if the altar was intended to have liquid flow into the basins via the channels.

This means we must consider the possibility that the channels were created for liquid to flow the other way: out of the basins. The channels are not deep and only appear at the very top of the basins. When we placed the altar on a level surface and filled the basins all the way to the top, liquid indeed flowed from them into the channels. Yet it would only do so for seconds before the level of the liquid fell below the level of the channels. This is in keeping with funerary tables from the late Old Kingdom, which, whether they had basins for offerings or not, had channels and spouts that were designed to collect the overflow of liquids and carefully channel them to a chosen spot or vessel.[46] Thus it seems quite possible that the channels with their lid were designed to ensure that the libation could be filled to the top but that any overflow could be properly disposed of, as should happen to a substance which had just become sacred. This may be the exact purpose of the pottery vessels found nearby. Perhaps whatever small amount of liquid flowed from the basins into the channels was then used to libate the nearby statue or was used in other ritual purposes. This would be in keeping with the Pyramid Text imagery mentioned above of returning the efflux that flowed from Osiris to Osiris for purposes of revivification and transformation. Perhaps it was intended that a small amount of water would overflow, be collected, and then be poured on an object associated with the royal cult, perhaps even the statue of the king found nearby.

---

45   Griggs, "Report of 1987 and 1988 Seasons," 195.
46   Hölzl, "Libation Basins," 315–316.

3   Conclusion

Ritual architectural elements—such as the structure of the pyramid itself, the structure of the chapels, the foundation deposit found on the southeast corner of the causeway, and the stelae—will be discussed in forthcoming publications. Fragments of other ritual objects were found elsewhere around the pyramid. For example, broken pieces of travertine were found on the eastern porch. A small wooden oar such as would be on a model boat was found nearby. Holes were carved into the ground around the eastern porch that suggest ceramic vessels were enclosed there, presumably for some kind of offering. Yet of the small objects found in the northern cultic structure, only these two—the statue and the libation altar—survived well enough for us to analyze and publish here. Their existence makes it sure that cultic activity was a part of the Seila Pyramid's presence on the northern side in at least the early 4th Dynasty.

CHAPTER 5

Death of a Common Man

Kerry Muhlestein and Cannon Fairbairn

The burials of ancient Egypt have long been a fascinating topic for many. The care put into preparing burials and the intricate rituals and efforts put into the spectacular burials of the elite have made their way in to museums, novels, movies and imaginations throughout the world. Yet, as with so many other cultural aspects, we know much less about the burials of non-elites.[1] Although in some ways[2] they are well represented in the archaeological record, they have traditionally been proportionally under-published in comparison with their elite contemporaries,[3] though that trend has been in the process of being reversed in recent research. Fag el-Gamous represents an opportunity to continue to bring to light the lives of a large number of the non-elite of Egypt in the Graeco-Roman era.

As noted in the chapter on the history of the excavation, the Fag el-Gamous cemetery is very large and has a variety of burial styles associated with it. In Hill A there are some Middle Kingdom shaft tombs, stretching about 15 meters vertically into the hill before branching out horizontally into chambers on either side.[4] Tombs carved into the mudstone escarpment (Hill A and Hill B) around the sandy portion of the cemetery have yielded wealthier burials. Some

---

1   See John Baines and Peter Lacovara, "Burial and the dead in ancient Egyptian society: Respect, formalism and neglect," in *Journal of Social Archaeology* 2/1 (2002): 6, 12–14.

2   Baines and Lacovara, Ibid., 6–7, note that there are areas for which we know surprisingly little about this subject.

3   Edward Bleiberg, *To Live Forever: Egyptian Treasures from the Brooklyn Museum* (London: Giles, 2008), 106. For example, in Christina Riggs, *The Beautiful Burial in Roman Egypt* (Oxford: Oxford University Press, 2006), one finds an impressive discussion of many funerary aspects of the Roman Era. Yet one will search the pages in vain for information about the common burial, it is not represented in this, or most, publications about burial in Roman Egypt. Of course, this is both due to the focus of that publication and also because of the lack of archaeological publications about common burials on which authors can draw. As Baines and Lacovara, "Burial and the dead," 6, note, "Some gaps in the published record are due to inadequate recording and publications; traditional excavations were seldom designed to address these questions."

4   C. Wilfred Griggs, "Burial Techniques and Body Preservation in the Fag el Gamous Cemetery," in *Actas del I Congreso Internacional de Estudios sobre Momias, 1992,* (Santa Cruz de Tenerife, Spain: Museo Arqueologico de Tenerife, 1995), 659–660; and C. Wilfred Griggs, "Excavating a Christian Cemetery Near Seila, in the Fayoum Region of Egypt," in *Excavations at Seila, Egypt,*

FIGURE 5.1   Burial shafts in the compacted sand of Fag el-Gamous
                PHOTOGRAPH COURTESY OF REVEL PHILLIPS

of these, such as a mummy with a gold head covering (described in this volume in the chapter on the history of the excavations), have been fantastic. Yet the majority of the cemetery consists of burials laid in the sand (referred to here-after as the "sand cemetery"), with some in shafts carved vertically into the compacted sand (not to be confused with what we Egyptologists typically call "shaft tombs," which were far more elaborate), and some are "surface burials," interred in the loose upper layer of sand that creates the visible landscape of the cemetery. It is the burials of the sand cemetery, the vast majority of those who were interred at Fag el-Gamous, that will be the focus of this chapter as we examine the most common burial practices exhibited in the cemetery.

In the upper most levels of the sand we find burials densely placed in a somewhat random pattern throughout the cemetery. Though the placement appears random, in all cases they maintain their east-west axis. At greater

C. Wilfred Griggs, ed. (Provo, UT: Religious Studies Center, Brigham Young University), 76–77.

depths, around one meter deep, we consistently find vertical shafts cut into the compacted sand. These shafts can be up to two meters deep and usually have multiple burials placed inside, with sand between each burial. The shafts are placed near one another so that any given area is taken up largely by shafts that almost always contain multiple burials. This, in part, accounts for the density of burials found in the cemetery.

We will never know exactly which combination of factors came to determine the manner of burial in the cemetery. Family, religious ideas, age at death, cause of death, social position, and economic ability must have all played a role (though we have found that age did not play a significant difference in most practices).[5] Even though we cannot tease out the way all these factors and others played out in creating the types of burials found at Fag el-Gamous, of one thing we can be sure. The sheer number of burials in the sand cemetery (as opposed to in tombs carved into the escarpment), averaging about 20,000 burials per hectare,[6] with an estimated 125 hectares as part of the cemetery, mandates that they are the burials of the ordinary, for it would be a contradiction to call that many people the elite, or anything but common. While as researchers we can quibble about the socio-economic status of those buried at Fag el-Gamous, or what kinds of labels best apply, the quantity of burials dictates that these are the common, or ordinary, burials and burial customs of their time and place. Thus, whatever the cause of the burial practices found there, as a result of having excavated so many of these burials, we are afforded an excellent opportunity to learn how the common person prepared their loved ones for burial in this area of the Fayoum during the Roman era.

The burials from the cemetery of Fag el-Gamous begin in the Ptolemaic era, but date primarily to the Roman and Byzantine eras.[7] The burials stop at about the time Islam became the dominant religion of the people. In analyzing these burials, we must not assume that our findings are representative of all burials from this time period. Burial practices can vary throughout the country, or even throughout the Fayoum. Variations can even be found within the same cemetery. In our cemetery, the sand burials are largely homogenous, though there are important distinctions, as will be noted below. Still, they cannot be

---

5   See Kerry Muhlestein and R. Paul Evans, "Death of a Child: The Demographic and Preparation Trends of Child Burials in the Greco-Roman Fayoum of Egypt," in *Handbook of Children of Antiquity*, Lesly Beaumont, Matthew Dillon, and Nicola Harrington, eds. (Routledge, forthcoming).

6   See the article on the history of the excavations presented in this volume.

7   R. Paul Evans, David Whitchurch, and Kerry Muhlestein, "Re-thinking Burial Dates at a Graeco-Roman Cemetery: Fag el Gamous, Fayoum, Egypt," *Journal of Archaeological Science: Reports* 2 (2015): 109–114.

taken as being representative of all burials in Egypt during the Roman Era. Further comparative studies are necessary before that issue can be addressed. Yet we can safely say that, on the whole, Fag el-Gamous seems to mirror the larger trend towards less grandiose and conspicuous burials throughout Egypt.[8]

In discussing the burial practices at Fag el-Gamous, we will use varying sample sizes in our analysis. This was determined by the available data. While a very large number of burials have been uncovered, not all of the information we wished to analyze was available or recorded for every burial. As the excavation progressed, so did an awareness of what details would be useful to record, and even then a poor state of preservation can prevent a burial from yielding the desired information. Burials included in statistical analyses presented herein are from those seasons which recorded information about burial place, depth, age, sex, grave goods, textiles, cordage, and color of textiles. Thus, unless otherwise noted, the data set presented is from 336 burials that record this information. This data set consists of the burials from the 1987–1989, 1992, 1994, 1998, 2000, 2002, 2003, and 2009–2014 seasons (with no excavation happening in the 2011 season) that recorded all of this information. This thorough recording happened most consistently in the 2009–2014 seasons, with much smaller representation from the earlier seasons listed.

At the same time, when speaking of whether an element was present in the cemetery or not, we considered all available information. For example, if a particular burial contained a figurine, but did not have some other key specific information recorded which caused it to be excluded from our set of 336 burials, it would not be used when analyzing such things as arm position, presence of textiles, etc. Yet it would still be considered when we ask whether figurines were present in the cemetery.

Similarly, the burials interred in the tombs of the escarpment designated at Hill B are considered when we ask whether a practice was present at all in the cemetery. They are not, however, part of the data set of 336 used in statistical analyses. This is because they were part of the earliest excavations of the cemetery and thus from before better record keeping practices were employed, and because, while they are certainly part of the cemetery, they do not represent the kind of burial that constitutes the vast majority of the cemetery. Thus, they lie outside of the statistical considerations, but within the larger questions of whether a certain practice occurred at all in the cemetery.

Almost all burials that were interred outside of Hills A and B were buried without a tomb. Several mudbrick structures have been discovered in the

---

8 Mark Smith, *Traversing Eternity: Texts for the Afterlife from Ptolemaic and Roman Egypt* (Oxford: Oxford University Press, 2009), 48.

cemetery. Some were clearly small tombs, but with many others it is difficult to determine whether they were tombs or either public or private chapels, which were a regular feature in cemeteries by the mid-4th century AD.[9] Analyzing these structures and comparing them to other tombs and chapels from the same time period will be the focus of a large study that is already underway, but is too large a topic to be included in this disquisition. As interesting as these structures are, a very small percentage of the burials of Fag el-Gamous were associated with any kind of edifice at all.

In contrast, many were buried in small vertical shafts, as was noted above. Unfortunately, until the 2013 excavation season, shafts were not given numbers and were not kept track of in the field books. Between this and the fact that many of the burials were surface burials placed in loose sand, there is no way to designate the location of any of these burials except by the excavation square and the burial number within that square. The database which we plan to publish will also include all burial information. The analysis presented in this article is not meant to include specific burial numbers for every burial presented, which would become overly pedantic and burdensome for the reader. Rather, here we focus on the larger picture painted by the conglomeration of the details that make up our data set of 336 burials. Details about these burials will be part of the publication of a larger database.

As we continue excavations, which also allows us to refine our ability to properly use data from earlier field books, we will have even better data sets in the future. This article presents a status update of what has been unearthed and analyzed until this point, for with a project of this size it is unreasonable to withhold publication of findings until all excavation is done and all possible data and analysis is accounted for.

In order to understand the burials of this cemetery, we will compare them to the most commonly known features of burials in the Roman era. This will allow us to see what is common, unique, or a local variation at Fag el-Gamous. Of course, there is a great deal of variation in burial techniques in every era, including the Roman era.[10] Still, comparison to frequently known practices is useful. It should be noted that the data available and the questions addressed here are inevitably influenced by the questions and practices of interest to academic archaeology and Egyptology.[11]

9 Peter Grossmann, "Churches and Meeting Halls in Necropoleis and Crypts in Intramural Churches," in *Egypt in the First Millennium AD: Perspectives from New Fieldwork,* Elisabeth R. O'Connell ed. (Leuven: Peeters, 2014), 93.

10 See Christina Riggs, *Unwrapping Ancient Egypt* (New York: Bloomsbury Academic: 2014), 99–108.

11 Ibid., 32–33.

1   Coffins

Although the use of anthropoid sarcophagi decreased during the Roman period, other types of funerary encasings grew in usage, such as wooden coffins
and cartonnage.[12] While in many places in Egypt one can reasonably expect to
find a coffin or a cartonnage body casing,[13] this is not the case at Fag el-Gamous.
It is true that several of the wealthy burials interred in tombs carved into the
mudstone escarpment were found in ceramic or wooden coffins (such as were
found in Hill B). In fact, it is not uncommon for contemporary cemeteries to
have a few burials that exhibit such characteristics. For example, ceramic coffins were also found at the Graeco-Roman cemetery of Quesna, though there
they also make up a small percentage of the total burials.[14] This is mirrored in
the non-elite Roman era cemetery of Thebes.[15] So far, no coffins have been
found among the sand cemetery burials at Fag el-Gamous.[16] The vast majority

FIGURE 5.2   Ceramic coffins at Hill B at Fag el-Gamous
PHOTOGRAPH COURTESY OF REVEL PHILLIPS

12   Salima Ikram, *Death and Burial in Ancient Egypt* (London: Longman, 2003), 125.
13   Ibid.
14   Joanne Rowland, "The Ptolemaic-Roman Cemetery at the Quesna Archaeological Area,"
       The Journal of Egyptian Archaeology 94 (2008): 70, 73.
15   Nigel Strudwick, "Some aspects of the archaeology of the Theban necropolis in the Ptol-
       emaic and Roman periods," in *The Theban Necropolis: Past, Present, and Future*, Nigel
       Strudwick and John H. Taylor, eds. (London: British Museum Press, 2003), 182.
16   In an article, earlier excavators said that the burials in the sand were interred "usually
       without coffins." This implies that sometimes they were. Yet the prior director has never
       spoken to us personally about having found a coffin in the sand cemetery, and there is no

of burials were surrounded by nothing but sand. This same lack of coffins is evident in other Roman era burials that appear to be of the same socio-economic status, such as those at Thebes[17] and Ismant el-Kharab.[18]

Exhibiting a practice that is absent at Fag el-Gamous, several Graeco-Roman cemeteries, such as Ismant el-Kharab, Quesna, and Deir el-Bahri, are dense with pit graves,[19] a practice that continues in the later phases of the Roman era with Christian burials.[20] At the same time, during the Greek and Roman eras some burials were covered in bricks or stones,[21] such as those found at Ismant el-Kharab.[22]

These coffin-like graves have also been found among the sand cemetery burials of Fag el-Gamous, mostly made of limestone. 45 of the 336 burials considered here (13.39%) were found accompanied by stone markers of some kind. Most often the limestone or mudstone placed on or around the body were simply fieldstones that were not cut or dressed in any manner. On occasion, cut blocks from buildings, sometimes even decorated, were repurposed for burial use. In at least several cases the excavators were convinced stone markers were limestone casing stones from the nearby Seila Pyramid.[23] The

record in the field books or articles about such an occurrence. See C. Wilfred Griggs, Marvin C.J. Kuchar, Mark J. Rowe, and Scott R. Woodward, "Identities Revealed: Archaeological and Biological Evidences for a Christian Population in the Egyptian Fayum," in *The Ancient Near East, Greece, and Rome*, T.W. Hillard, R.A. Kearsley, C.E.V. Nixon, and A.M. Nobbs, eds. (Grand Rapids: Eerdmans, 1998), 1:83.

17 Christina Riggs, "The Egyptian funerary tradition at Thebes in the Roman Period," in *The Theban Necropolis: Past, Present, and Future*, Nigel Strudwick and John H. Taylor, eds. (London: British Museum Press, 2003), 190.

18 Michael Birrell, "Excavations in the Cemeteries of Ismant el-Kharab," in *Dakhleh Oasis Project: Preliminary Reports on the 1992–1993 and 1993–1994 Field Seasons*, C.A. Hope and A.J. Mills, eds. (Oxford: Oxbow Books, 1999), 33, 41; Arthur C. Aufderheide, Michael Zlonis, Larry L. Cartmell, Michael R. Zimmerman, Peter Sheldrick, Megan Cook, and Joseph E. Molto, "Human Mummification Practices at Ismant el-Kharab," *The Journal of Egyptian Archaeology* 85 (1999): 198.

19 Birrell, "Excavations in the Cemeteries of Ismant el-Kharab," 38; Rowland, "The Ptolemaic-Roman Cemetery at the Quesna Archaeological Area," 73; Christina Riggs, "Beautiful Burials, Beautiful Skulls: The Aesthetics of the Egyptian Mummy," *British Journal of Aesthetics* 56/3 (July 2016): 252; Adam Łajtar, "The Theban Region under the Roman Empire," in *The Oxford Handbook of Roman Egypt*, Christina Riggs, ed. (Oxford: Oxford University Press, 2012), 182.

20 John H. Taylor, *Death and the Afterlife in Ancient Egypt* (Chicago: University of Chicago Press, 2001), 155; Sue D'Auria, Peter Lacovara, and Catharine H. Roehrig, *Mummies and Magic: The Funerary Arts of Ancient Egypt* (Boston: Museum of Fine Arts, 1988), 25; Riggs, *The Beautiful Burial in Roman Egypt*, 2.

21 Wolfram Grajetzki, *Burial Customs in Ancient Egypt* (London: Duckworth, 2003), 126.

22 Birrell, "Excavations in the Cemeteries of Ismant el-Kharab," 38.

23 For example, see Fieldbook 1987A, 18. This fieldbook contains numerous such examples.

FIGURE 5.3   Fag el-Gamous burial covered by limestone
PHOTOGRAPH COURTESY OF R. PAUL EVANS

lowest burials in a shaft are almost always placed in a niche at the bottom/side of the shaft and are almost always covered by stone.[24]

In some places, such as Quesna or Kellis, they have found several burials where mudbrick was stacked around the body to form a type of coffin.[25] This is common enough at Kellis that Peter Sheldrick has created a typology for this kind of burial, classifying various types of mudbrick "coffins" around burials.[26] At Fag el-Gamous we have only found this kind of construction on one occasion, covering three different burials that were next to each other. Uncovered during the 2013 season, the bricks of all three burials were nearly uniform, suggesting they had been made using the same mold. The bricks consistently measured 31 cm long and 17 cm wide, with an average height of 11 cm. While the length and width dimensions were completely constant, the height of the bricks varied slightly, suggesting that the mold was open at the top and when the mud

24   Griggs, et al., "Identities Revealed," 83.

25   Rowland, "The Ptolemaic-Roman Cemetery at the Quesna Archaeological Area," 73; Olaf E. Kaper, "The Western Oases," in *The Oxford Handbook of Roman Egypt*, Christina Riggs, ed. (Oxford: Oxford University Press, 2012), 727–728.

26   Personal communication, November 2014.

was leveled it was done inconsistently. The most expansive use of mudbrick was for the adult male. Bricks were not laid under the body, but were laid along the side, forming a kind of wall. Other bricks were placed on either side of the burial at an angle, so that they leaned against each other, forming a peaked arch that covered the body. Adjacent to this we found an adult female burial that was also buried with mudbricks. In this instance, mudbrick was laid along the side, but on the lower half of the body a single brick was laid across the body, forming a flat cover. On the upper torso and head two bricks lean against each other, forming a small arch similar to that made for the entire body of the male.

FIGURE 5.4 Makeshift mudbrick coffin found in 2013
PHOTOGRAPH BY KERRY MUHLESTEIN

Near this adult female was a small child burial. This burial also had bricks laid along the side and was completely covered by mudbricks laid flat across the body with an extra brick placed over the child's head.

As noted above, the uniformity of the bricks in these burials suggests that they were made at roughly the same time, using the same brick molds. That, combined with their proximity, suggests that this may have been a family burial, though this must remain speculation until DNA analysis is performed. In the 2000 season a burial was found that used rough limestone to make a peak over the burial's head in roughly similar fashion.

As was noted above, on the whole, the Roman era sand cemetery contains very few tombs. Yet one area serves as a striking contrast to this norm. In the 1987 season, 9 mud brick structures and one low stone structure were found in a 15x20 meter area. Some of these had extremely well dressed and preserved burials within them, and some had no evidence of burials. We presume that some of these served as tombs, and others may have served as either a kind of chapel or an embalming structure, ideas that will be further explored in the future (as was noted above).

The unusually concentrated number of structures found in this season serve as an important reminder. Similarly, coffin-like structures were only found in a single season, 26 years later and 60 meters apart. If either one of these seasons had not taken place, we would say that there are almost no examples of tombs and no examples of coffins at Fag el-Gamous. Clearly the general practice at the cemetery was to inter burials without tombs or coffins. Yet we cannot ever safely assume that a practice never took place. These two seasons also highlight that the cemetery varies in practice from one location in the cemetery to another. In our general sample of 336 burials spread over several years and various areas of the cemetery, only 14 burials (4%) are associated with mudbrick of any kind (4 head-east and 10 head-west burials). As noted above, 45 of these burials had stone associated with them. Thus, a total of 69 (17.5%) burials had some kind of stone or brick associated with them. Yet in one 5x5 meter square of the 1987 season, 7 of 18 burials (39%), more than twice as many, had such features. This area is clearly dissimilar from most of the cemetery in this practice. This is part of why having a large sample size spread from throughout the excavated cemetery is important as we try to develop a representative picture of burial practices. Yet it is also important to note the exceptions as we try to understand the necropolis.

2   Texts

During this time period many burials were interred with sacred texts intended to aid the deceased in their journeys into the afterlife. These manuscripts were often recorded on papyri and contained texts such as the Book of the Dead, as well as a host of new texts, such as The Book of Traversing Eternity, Thé Book of Thoth, The Book of the Fayoum, and the Book of Breathings. At Fag el-Gamous, we have found no papyri texts at all, except for a fragment of a receipt of some kind that was repurposed as part of a sandal.[27] While we cannot conclude that no texts were interred with any burials at Fag el-Gamous, the fact that none have been found among the hundreds of excavated burials strongly suggests that it was extremely uncommon. It is safe to conclude that the general burial practice here does not include texts. There are probably several reasons behind the lack of texts among the burials. Undoubtedly one important factor behind this is that those who were interred in this cemetery could not afford such works. It is worth noting that the Book of Thoth records that in the afterlife kindly beings could revivify a corpse that had no papyrus texts accompanying it.[28] Thus hope for a desired kind of afterlife was not lost for these poorer burials that had no texts accompanying them in death. Furthermore, the Demotic tale of Setne Khamwas, the creation and copying of which stems from the same time period as the Fag el-Gamous cemetery, teaches that the state of a person in the afterlife has more to do with the person's character and ensuing success or lack thereof in judgment than it does with burial preparations and accoutrements.

3   Body Positioning

The burials in the Fag el-Gamous cemetery demonstrate a consistent trend in regards to body position at burial. Over time the direction of the head switched. In the earliest group of burials, those at a depth of over 251 cm, 4 of the 7 burials (57%) were head-east and 3 (43%) were head-west. In the 201–250 cm group, 15 of 36 (42%) were head-east and 21 (58%) were head-west. In the 151–200 cm group, 23 of 64 (36%) were head-east and 41 (67%) were head-west. In the 101–150 cm group, 17 of 76 (22%) were head-east and 59 (78%) were head-west. In the 51–100 cm group, 2 of 80 (3%) were head-east and 78 (98%) were head-west. Finally, in the 0–50 cm group, 1 of 34 (3%) was head-east and 33 (97%) were head-west. The pattern of moving towards a nearly universal head-west orientation seen here seems to reflect the Christian practice of orienting

---

27   See the article in this volume for a translation of the text.

28   Richard L. Jasnow and Karl-Theodor Zauzich, *The Ancient Egyptian Book of Thoth: A Demotic Discourse on Knowledge and Pendant to the Classical Hermetica* (Wiesbaden: Harrassowitz: 2005), 318–324.

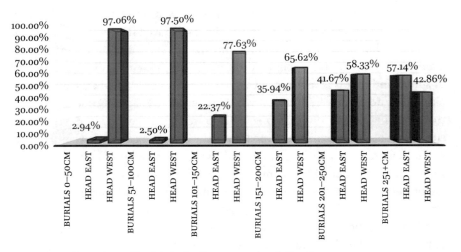

FIGURE 5.5 Percentage of burials in depth group per head direction

the body head-west,[29] though we cannot be certain this is the reason for the shift in direction. This phenomenon continues to be thoroughly researched by the team.[30]

Another choice those arranging a burial had to make was how to position the arms. Throughout the cemetery, the placement of the arms is inconsistent across burials. Information regarding arm position was not recorded for much of the history of the excavation and the state of any particular burial does not always make it possible to determine arm position. For the burials with arm position recorded, the most common position was with arms at the sides. This is also the most common arrangement for later Christian burials.[31] This same pattern can be found in the cemeteries of the Roman period at Dush, Ismant

29   Salima Ikram and Aidan Dodson, *The Mummy in Ancient Egypt: Equipping the Dead for Eternity* (London: Thames and Hudson, 1998), 131.

30   We are currently continuing to work on this topic. For work done in the recent past see Kristin H. South, "Roman and Early Byzantine Burials at Fag el-Gamus, Egypt: A Reassessment of the Case for Religious Affiliation," (master's thesis, Brigham Young University, 2012); and Kerry Muhlestein and Bethany Jensen, "You Can't Take it With You: Material Markers of the Conversion to Christianity in the Fayoum of Egypt," (presentation, Religious Landscapes of Egypt, Late to Greco-Roman Period, Zürich, February 2017).

31   Ikram, *Death and Burial in Ancient Egypt,* 73; Ikram and Dodson, *The Mummy in Ancient Egypt,* 131.

el-Kharab, and Quesna.[32] In the sample of 336 burials, 39 had their arm position recorded. Of these 39, 23 (59%) had their arms to their sides. Some of those had their arms at their sides with their wrists angling in towards the body. One (3%) had both arms crossed over their body in a fashion similar to the traditional royal pose with arms crossed across the chest. Eight (21%) had their left arm bent over their body. One (3%) had the right arm bent over their body. Five (13%) had both arms bent over their body to meet at the pelvis. Only one (3%) had their hands inside the thigh. These arm positions seem to reflect the trends of Egypt as a whole.[33]

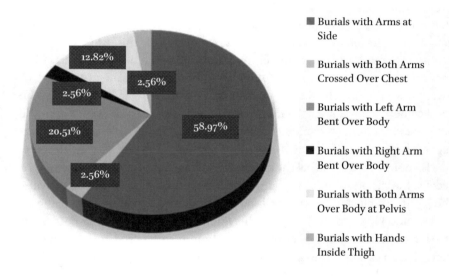

FIGURE 5.6   Arm positions of sample of 39 burials

32   Aufderheide, "Human Mummification Practices at Ismant el-Kharab," 207; Birrell, "Excavations in the Cemeteries of Ismant el-Kharab," 41; Rowland, "The Ptolemaic-Roman Cemetery at the Quesna Archaeological Area," 75–93.

33   Janet Davey, John T. Taylor, and Olaf H. Drummer, "The Utilisation of Forensic Imaging in the Investigation of Graeco-Roman Child Mummies," *Journal of Egyptian Archaeology* 100 (2014): 204–205; Smith, *Traversing Eternity*, 34.

4   Mummification

Mummification is a visible hallmark of Egyptian burials, though it was far from universally practiced.[34] During the Roman period this was no different, although there was an increase in mummification during the Graeco-Roman era in general.[35] While mummification was still practiced, this didn't always include embalming.[36] It should be remembered that the physical transformation of the dead body was an important part of mummification, but the most important aspect was the rituals performed on behalf of the deceased.[37] While having such rituals performed by a priest could have been prohibitively costly in the pre-Christian era, one would assume that all Christians were able to avail themselves of such religious services at the death of a loved one, though by then the thought and purpose behind the rituals had significantly changed, even if the practices remained largely the same. The performance of rituals that don't involve physically transforming the body leaves no trace, and thus cannot be detected by us, and therefore remains outside this discussion.

Thus, we must ask, are there fully embalmed and mummified burials at Fag el-Gamous? In the truest sense of mummification, no, there are not, except for a very few elite burials in the tombs of the escarpment (Hills A and B). The sand cemetery burials, for the most part, do not provide evidence for even the simplest embalming techniques described by Herodotus as he outlined varying levels of mummification,[38] except for the wrapping of the body. To some, this is enough to call a burial a mummy, using language such as "the poor might receive the simplest burial as plainly bandaged mummies."[39] Still, we typically think of the inclusion of other techniques when speaking of mummification.

It should be noted that in one publication the previous director noted that there were "some attempts at mummification in some pre-Christian burials, including an abdominal incision for removal of internal organs, removal of the brain through the nose, and application of preserving agents to retard

---

34   Baines and Lacovara, "Burial and the dead in ancient Egyptian society," 15.

35   Davey et al., "The Utilisation of Forensic Imaging," 196.

36   Łajtar, "The Theban Region Under the Roman Empire," 182.

37   Jan Assmann, *Death and Salvation in Ancient Egypt*, David Lorton, trans. (Ithaca: Cornell University Press, 2001), 33; Baines and Lacovara, "Burial and the dead in ancient Egyptian society," 15–16, and J.C. Goyon and P. Josset, *Un corps pour l'éternité: Autopsie d'une momie* (Paris: Léopard d'Or, 1988); and Riggs, *Unwrapping Ancient Egypt*, 78–79, 90–94.

38   Herodotus, *The Histories* (Baltimore: Penguin Books, 1954).

39   David Peacock, "The Roman Period," in *The Oxford History of Ancient Egypt*, Ian Shaw, ed. (Oxford: Oxford University Press, 2000), 441.

decomposition."[40] No information about location of these burials is given. There is no evidence of any of this in the burials of the sand cemetery to my knowledge, and the previous director typically thought of the sand cemetery as largely Christian while the tombs of Hills A and B were considered pre-Christian. Thus, it seems almost certain that the description of mummification attempts was about the burials in Hills A and B, where we know such attempts were made.

Assuming this is the case, the sand cemetery burials exhibit no evidence for removal of viscera, or excerebration (brain removal) which was a common practice even during the Ptolemaic and Roman periods,[41] though perhaps a bit less common than earlier.[42] It is worth keeping in mind that many of the burials were so decayed that if the practice had been done no evidence would now be visible. In the rock cut tombs of the escarpment, a few burials have been found whose brains were removed and also exhibit an incision on the left side.[43] We have never found canopic jars or the box placed between legs that tended to replace the canopic jars in the Ptolemaic and Roman eras.[44] This alone indicates that the full mummification process as typically outlined was not taking place.[45]

There was also no evidence for body repairs, another part of the mummification process.[46] To the contrary, we have found evidence that seems to be the exact opposite of the careful mummification process. In one of the burial shafts, we found the remains of a man who was over seven feet tall. He was placed in a shaft that had been dug and used prior to his death. His body was bent almost in half when it was buried, presumably so that he would fit inside a shaft that had been made for much shorter people.[47]

The full mummification process immerses the body in natron for a period of time. This is what causes much of the desiccation process.[48] The burials we

---

40   Griggs, "Burial Techniques and Body Preservation," 559.

41   Ikram, *Death and Burial in Ancient Egypt*, 71.

42   Davey, et al., "The Utilisation of Forensic Imagine," 196, 204.

43   Griggs, "Report of 1987 and 1988 Season," 201.

44   Smith, *Traversing Eternity*, 31; David Aston, "Canopic Chests from the 21st Dynasty to the Ptolemaic Period," *Ägypten und Levante* 10 (2000): 159–178.

45   Placing certain bodily organs in a container was part of ancient mummification instructions, such as those on P. Boulaq 3, 2/16–17, as translated in Smith, *Traversing Eternity*, 220, 227.

46   Ibid.

47   Personal communication with C. Wilfred Griggs, 2009. Unfortunately, we have not yet identified this exact burial in the field books to provide more specific details.

48   Joyce Filer, *The Mystery of the Egyptian Mummy* (New York: Oxford University Press, 2003), 9; Smith, *Traversing Eternity*, 32.

encounter in the Fag el-Gamous sand cemetery have not been saturated in natron, as is the case with many other non-eviscerated burials from the Roman
and Coptic periods.[49] While we do not have precise enough recording to do a
statistical analysis, one excavation report states that a majority of burials from
the cemetery are "coated with salt crystals."[50] This phenomenon must be inconsistent, for it has not been observed frequently by the current excavation
team. A small number of our burials were found with large bunches of salt
placed next to the body (one of the burials in the sample had crystal salts
around and perhaps in the body). Presumably this was the commoner's attempt at desiccation. Although there is a great lack of information in regard to
early Christian burials in Egypt, later Christian mummies (4th – 6th centuries
AD) were often dried using salt.[51] Mummiform bundles (such as are found at
Fag el-Gamous) were sometimes accompanied by handfuls of salt throughout
Egypt up until about 800 AD.[52]

   A common practice among those who were mummified was that of pouring
a hot resin[53] (typically from the sap of coniferous trees, but could also contain
bitumen or beeswax) over the body, and stuffing wadded up linen into body
cavities, presumably to help the burial better hold its shape.[54] Besides several
examples in Hills A and B, no evidence of the former practice has been recorded at the Fag el-Gamous cemetery, and only a few examples of the latter
have been manifest. Since the current director began excavations and recording

---

49   Ikram, *The Mummy in Ancient Egypt*, 109; Herodotus, *The Histories*, 133–134; Christina
      Riggs, "Tradition and Innovation in the Burial Practices of Roman Egypt," in *Tradition and
      Transformation: Egypt under Roman Rule* (Leiden: Brill, 2010), 345; Sofia Torallas Tovar,
      "Egyptian burial practices in Late Antiquity: the case of Christian mummy labels," in *Cul-
      tures in Contact: Transfer of Knowledge in the Mediterranean Context: Selected Papers,* Sofia
      Torallas Tovar and Juan Pedro Monferrer-Sala, eds. (Cordoba: CNERU–CEDRAC 2013), 17;
      Aufderheide, "Human Mummification Practices at Ismant el-Kharab," 202; Arthur C. Auf-
      derheide, Larry Cartmell, Michael Zlonis, and Peter Sheldrick, "Mummification Practices
      at Kellis Site in Egypt's Dakhleh Oasis," *JSSEA* 31 (2004): 68.
50   C. Wilfred Griggs, R. Paul Evans, Kristin H. South, George Homsey, Anne Ellington and
      Nasry Iskander, "Seila Pyramid/Fag el Gamous Cemetery Project Report of the 2000 Sea-
      son," in *Bulletin for the Australian Center for Egyptology* 12 (2001): 14.
51   Ikram, *Death and Burial in Ancient Egypt*, 73; Ikram and Dodson, *The Mummy in Ancient
      Egypt*, 131; Taylor, *Death and the Afterlife in Ancient Egypt*, 91.
52   Elisabeth R. O'Connell, "Settlements and Cemeteries in Late Antique Egypt: An Introduc-
      tion," in *Egypt in the First Millennium AD, Perspectives from New Fieldwork*, Elisabeth R.
      O'Connell, ed. (Leuven: Peeters, 2014), 7.
53   S.A. Buckley and R.P. Evershed, "Organic Chemistry of Embalming Agents in Pharaonic
      and Graeco-Roman Mummies," *Nature* 413 (2001): 837–841; Aufderheide, "Human Mum-
      mification Practices at Ismant El-Kharab," 201.
54   Smith, *Traversing Eternity*, 32.

evidence for the site, he noted what seemed to be the remains of bitumen in one burial which was unusually well preserved in its skin, brain, tongue, and fingernails, suggesting that bitumen and other elements may have been applied and produced a bit of a preserving affect.[55] This leads us to wonder if such practices had been observed earlier but were not recorded in the excavation notes.

Other substances that were frequently applied elsewhere, such as anointing the head with incense, oil, or unguent,[56] do not leave enough trace for us to know whether or not they were present in the burials of Fag el-Gamous. They have not been observed, but this is really no indication as to whether or not they were used.

Frequently, though still in a minority of cases, the ribs of palm fronds were attached to the Fag el-Gamous burials, presumably to provide a rigidity that would support the body.[57] In Egyptian mummification practices, bodies were often repaired with palm ribs to reattach body parts or as substitutes for missing limbs.[58] In other instances, palm fronds would be used as a type of substitute coffin placed over the body, similar to the mudbrick method previously discussed. There may be further significance to the presence of palm fronds. At the Roman era catacombs of Kom el-Shakafa in Alexandria, where both the elite and those of lower socio-economic status were buried,[59] there are many depictions of gods and goddesses presenting palm fronds to the deceased, suggesting there was a religious meaning behind their presence,[60] perhaps associated with the presentation of *renpet*, or the counting of years. Regardless of what may have been the purpose, 35 of the 336 burials (10%) in this sample were associated with palm sticks or spines. There have been cases of up to 9 reed sticks running the length of the body.[61]

---

55   This was for burial 91 of the 2013 season (130/140 N 20/30 W NW #91).

56   See, for example, P. Boulaq 3, 2/1–5, 7/1–7, as translated in Smith, *Traversing Eternity*, 225, 236.

57   Riggs, "The Egyptian funerary tradition at Thebes in the Roman Period," 190.

58   Ikram, *Death and Burial in Ancient Egypt*, 71; Filer, *The Mystery of the Egyptian Mummy*, 11; Birrell, "Excavations in the Cemeteries of Ismant el-Kharab," 35; Aufderheide, "Human Mummification Practices at Ismant el-Kharab," 204–208.

59   David Peacock, "The Roman Period," 442.

60   Personal observation of these catacombs, March 2018. See also Anne-Marie Guimier-Sorbets, Andre Pelle, Mervat Seif el-Din, *Resurrection in Alexandria: The Painted Greco-Roman Tombs of Kom al-Shuqafa* (Cairo: American University in Cairo Press, 2017), 30, 33, 44, 62, 109, 112, 113, and 151 for examples.

61   Griggs, et al., "Report of the 2000 Season," 13.

What those who prepared burials for Fag el-Gamous did well in their attempts to mummify was provide textile wrappings,[62] which may have been considered the most important part of the physical elements of the ritualized process of transforming the deceased.[63] Clothing said something about a person, and was culturally significant, in both life and death.[64] While many cultures dressed their dead, at Fag el-Gamous the number of wrappings, combined with many attempts to use ribbon or torn strips to create a diamond or rhomboid shaped pattern similar to that which occurred on many fully embalmed mummies,[65] suggests that this was an intentional attempt to imitate at least some aspects of the full mummification process.

Coptic period burials are well known for the textiles associated with them,[66] and the burials of Fag el-Gamous are no exception. By now, many burials are skeletalized and very little of their original wrappings survive. However, even in these skeletal burials we often find small remains of textiles, suggesting that they had been wrapped originally, and many burials are still in their elaborate wrappings. 196 (58%) of the burials in a sample of 336 still contained textiles.

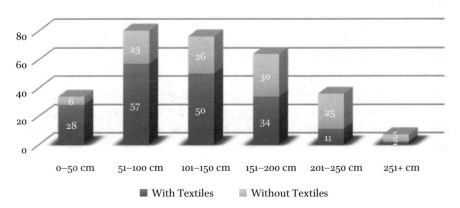

FIGURE 5.7   Presence of textiles by burial depth

62   Griggs, "Excavating a Christian Cemetery Near Seila, in the Fayoum Region of Egypt," 80.
63   Riggs, *Unwrapping Ancient Egypt*, 79–81.
64   Ibid., 120; and Jochen Sokoly, "Textiles and Identity," in *A Companion to Islamic Art and Architecture*, Finbarr Barry Flood and Gülru Necipoğlu, eds. (New York: John Wiley & Sons, 2017), 275.
65   See, for example, A.1911.210.3 in the National Museum of Scotland. For an example of strips of linen used in a manner very similar to many burials at Fag el-Gamous, see EA24800 in the British Museum.
66   Jung-Im Han, "A Study on the Characteristics of the Designs on Coptic Textiles of Ancient Egypt," *Fashion Business* 15/3 (2011): 112–124.

FIGURE 5.8   An intricate pattern from the burial wrappings at Fag el-Gamous
PHOTOGRAPH BY THE FAG EL-GAMOUS EXCAVATION CONSERVATION TEAM

The wrappings are usually made of linen, though often small amounts of wool were employed,[67] a characteristic that was new in this era.[68] Egypt was known for its production of linen, and the fabric formed the bulk of textiles used by both the living and the dead.[69] The wrappings are usually found in multiple layers, as was common throughout Egyptian history including the time period to which the cemetery belongs.[70] Earlier burials were typically interred with fewer and lesser-quality textiles. Among what seem to be the earliest burials, those in the sample that were more than 250 cm deep, only 2 of the 7 (29%) had textiles. The burials in the range of 201–250 cm, 11 of the 36 (31%) were found with textiles. As the cemetery aged, burial trends changed and the quantity of textiles increased. This is illustrated by the fact that 64 of the burials (53%) between 151 and 200 cm and 76 of the burials (66%) between 101–150 cm

---

67   For more on the kind of weave employed in Fag el-Gamous burials, see the article on textiles and jewelry and the article on basket weave in this volume.
68   Riggs, *Unwrapping Egypt*, 117.
69   Ibid., 109–111.
70   O'Connell, "Settlements and Cemeteries in Late Antique Egypt: An Introduction," 7.

FIGURE 5.9   Burials wrapped in a colored textile at Fag el-Gamous
            PHOTOGRAPH COURTESY OF REVEL PHILLIPS

also contained textiles, or evidence of textiles, although some of this is also
due to rate of preservation at those depths. 80 of the burials (71%) discovered
between 51–100 cm contained textile remains and 34 of the burials (82%)
found between 0 and 50 cm had textiles. We can see about the same time the
quality and quantity of textiles increased, the head direction also shifted to a
greater number of head-west orientation, causing the majority of burials to
share this correlation.

Earlier burials typically employed a few layers of textiles that had been used
in life and had been repurposed for burial,[71] though it has been argued that
repurposing textiles could instead be viewed as imbuing identities carried in
life onto the afterlife existence.[72] This reuse of clothing for burial is similar to
the trend seen in Coptic period burials in which individuals were buried in
their own clothing.[73] At Fag el-Gamous, the later burials are typically buried in
clothing that does not appear to have been used in life, meaning that they were
created specifically for burial.[74] They were also, on the whole, higher quality
textiles,[75] though a lower quality kind of weave was often used. For example,

71   C. Wilfred Griggs, Marvin Kuchar, Scott Woodward, M. Rowe, R. Paul Evans, Naguib
     Kanawati, and N. Iskander, "Evidences of a Christian Population in the Egyptian Fayum
     and Genetic and Textile Studies of the Akhmim Noble Mummies," in BYU Studies 33
     (1993): 223, discuss how microscopic analysis reveals which burials had fabrics that ex-
     hibit the wear that comes from use, and which exhibit no signs of wear.

72   Riggs, Unwrapping Ancient Egypt, 120–121.

73   Ikram, Death and Burial in Ancient Egypt, 73; Tovar, "Egyptian burial practices in Late An-
     tiquity: the case of the Christian mummy labels," 17.

74   Griggs, et al., "Evidences of a Christian Population," 223.

75   Ibid.

FIGURE 5.10 A child's tunic used in burial
PHOTOGRAPH BY KERRY MUHLESTEIN

the most common weave at Fag el-Gamous is 1 warp 2 weft and 2 warp 2 weft basket weave.[76]

Burials with textiles that are well preserved are usually wrapped in a high number of layers (approximately 10–25). Contemporary burials from other sites, such as Ismant el-Kharab, also note a high quantity of textiles used to wrap burials.[77]

In the better-preserved burials, intricate, colorful designs were frequently woven into the wrappings. These colorful threads are made of wool, since wool

---

76   South, et al., "Face Bundles," 3. See also the article on basket weave in this volume.
77   Riggs, "Tradition and Innovation in the Burial Practices of Roman Egypt," 346; Birrell, "Excavations in the Cemeteries of Ismant el-Kharab," 35.

holds dye better than linen.[78] Sometimes tunics or aprons were also included. For example, in the 1998 season of 111 burials, 99 still contained textile remains. Of these 99, ten tunics were found, with an additional five that were woven in a manner most consistent with tunics, though the remains were too fragmentary to be sure that they were tunics.[79] Ten other pieces were sewn/woven in a manner that was consistent with either tunics or blankets but the remains were so small that it could not be determined which, if either, of these they were.[80] The ten that were certainly tunics were made of wool and were dyed in various colors.[81]

For the cemetery as a whole, even when colorful patterns were not used, typically decoration was part of any piece of linen. This usually took the form

FIGURE 5.11 Pile weave as decoration in a textile from Fag el-Gamous
PHOTOGRAPH COURTESY OF REVEL PHILLIPS

---

78   Han, "A Study on the Characteristics of the Designs on Coptic Textiles of Ancient Egypt,"
      112–124. Riggs, *Unwrapping Ancient Egypt,* 117, notes that while the cellulose in linen made
      it so most dyes won't work, safflower dyes could yield a kind of yellow and iron oxide
      could yield shades of orange and red.
79   Kristin H. South, Marvin C. Kuchar, and C. Wilfred Griggs, "Preliminary Report of Textile
      Finds, 1998 Season, at Fag el-Gamus," *Archaeological Textiles Newsletter* 27 (1998): 10.
80   Ibid.
81   Ibid.

of combining various forms of weaving, such as creating weft ribs, open warp, pile weave, pile loops, or fringes.[82]

The heads of burials were frequently wrapped, often with layers of hair nets.[83] From our sample of 336 burials, 69 of the 196 burials (35%) that were found with textiles had textiles that had retained color and pattern, though on others color could have faded or the remains were too fragmentary to tell. Colored and patterned textiles became a primary characteristic of Coptic textiles.[84] The motifs woven into the burial shrouds of Fag el-Gamous include colorful and skillfully crafted patterns. Yet with the thousands of shrouds analyzed at Fag el-Gamous, no shroud has exhibited what would often be thought of as a typical design in funerary shrouds in early Roman Egypt, such as images of Osiris, Isis, Nephthys, Anubis, or the sons of Horus.[85] We cannot say why this is the case. It is tempting to ascribe it to the lower economic class of the cemetery's denizens, yet as this type of design became less popular in Egypt and gave way to the colorful and intricate designs of the Coptic era, the shrouds of Fag el-Gamous exhibit detailed and intricate designs, such as pomegranates,[86] geometric designs, vegetative designs, all kinds of animals, rosettes, crosses and other images.[87] Thus it seems as if during the era of traditional Egyptian religion the people around Fag el-Gamous did not find ways to marshal enough resources to create images in their shrouds, but they were motivated enough to do so during the Christian era.

Another textile related feature found in the burials from Fag el-Gamous is the use of cordage to bind the wrappings around the body. The use of ribbons/ropes/torn strips as a kind of bandage overwrapping layers of beautiful shrouds and tunics, is to be expected.[88] As Assmann has noted, there is a long tension

---

82   Kristin H. South, Joyce Y. Smith, Giovanni Tata, and C. Wilfred Griggs, "Textile Finds from a Typical Early Christian Burial at Fag el-Gamus (Fayum), Egypt," in *Purpureae Vestes III: Textiles y Tintes en la ciudad antigua* C. Alfaro, J.-P. Brun, Ph. Borgard, R. Pierobon Benoit, eds. (Valencia, Spain: University of Valencia Press, 2011), 131.

83   Griggs, "Excavating a Christian Cemetery," 78.

84   Maribeth C. Clarke, Rachel P. Haitt, Marvin C. Kuchar, and Mary H. Farahnakian, "Indexing and Cataloging Textiles From the Fag el Gamous Cemetery in Fayum, Egypt to Determine Their Relationship With Known Coptic Textiles," *Clothing and Textiles Research Journal* 21/3 (2003): 123.

85   Riggs, *The Beautiful Burial in Roman Egypt*, 251–256.

86   David M. Whitchurch and C. Wilfred Griggs, "Artifacts, Icons, and Pomegranates: Brigham Young University Egypt Excavation Project," *Journal of the American Research Center in Egypt* 46 (2010): 215–231.

87   Griggs, "Report of 1987 and 1988 Seasons," 197; and Griggs, "Burial Techniques and Body Preservation," 660.

88   See, for example, EA6723 and EA6714 at the British Museum, or 97-121-114A and E16234 at the University of Pennsylvania Museum of Archaeology and Anthropology.

FIGURE 5.12 Hair net on a burial at Fag el-Gamous
PHOTOGRAPH COURTESY OF REVEL PHILLIPS

in Egyptian thought between the need to bind the body for practical mummification purposes, and simultaneously allow for the resurrected, transfigured
body to be unbound and beautifully robed.[89]

The effect of conversion to Christianity on burial practices is an ongoing
study at many sites,[90] including ours. At Fag el-Gamous it is clear that the move
towards Christianity, a slow process that existed on a continuum for both individuals and communities,[91] correlates with a trend towards use of ribbons in
burials,[92] though the nature of that correlation is unclear. For example, in one

---

89   Jan Assmann, *Death and Salvation in Ancient Egypt*, David Lorton, trans. (Ithaca: Cornell
       University Press, 2001), 344–346.

90   O'Connel, "Settlements and Cemeteries in Late Antique Egypt: An Introduction," 8.

91   See David Frankfurter, *Christianizing Egypt: Syncretism and Local Worlds in Late Antiquity*
       (Princeton: Princeton University Press, 2018).

92   Kristin H. South, "Minor Textile Burials and Religious Affiliation: An Archaeological Case
       Study from Roman Egypt," in *Dressing the Dead in Classical Antiquity*, Maureen Carroll
       and John Peter Wild, eds. (Stroud, Gloucestershire: Amberly Publishing, 2012), 65–68.

season none of the lower burials used ribbons while the majority of east facing (head-west) burials with textiles did.[93] While we cannot say whether this correlation means that the ribbons are associated with Christianity, it is clear that the introduction and use of ribbons woven for funerary purposes begins at about the same time we would expect Christianity to arrive in Egypt, and continues on a corresponding curve thenceforth.[94] There are parallels to these ribbons in places such as Saqqara, Lisht, Dashur, Hibeh, Qarara, Kom el-Ahmar, Antinoe, and Thebes.[95]

In our sample, 28 (8%) of the burials used torn strips of linen. Over time the linen strips were largely replaced by a standardized white (or undyed) and red (or less commonly white and brown) woven ribbon.[96] On occasion the ribbons were wrapped horizontally and/or vertically around the body.[97] More often,

FIGURE 5.13 Ribbons wrapped in a diagonal or rhomboid pattern, close up
PHOTOGRAPH BY KRISTIN H. SOUTH

93   South, et al., "Preliminary Report of Textile Finds," 10.
94   Ibid.
95   Ibid., 68–71.
96   Undyed linen was initially a pale yellow or cream, but natron, sun, and time whitened it.
      See Riggs, *Unwrapping Ancient Egypt*, 117.
97   South, et al., "Textile Finds from a Typical Early Christian Burial," 128.

FIGURE 5.14
Ribbons wrapped in a diagonal or rhomboid pattern on
entire burial
PHOTOGRAPH BY R. PAUL EVANS

these ribbons were wrapped around the body in a diagonal pattern seemingly
mimicking the rhomboid shapes present in the diagonal wrapping of many
mummies in this time period. 81 (24%) of the Fag el-Gamous burials had
ribbons.[98]

Throughout Egypt as a whole, among wealthier burials it was common to
gild portions of the mummy with gold, such as on the face, the fingernails, or
at the center of the rhomboid wrappings.[99] Examples of individually wrapping
digits and genitalia are also somewhat frequently found. At Fag el-Gamous,
while one burial with golden fingernails was found in the tombs carved in the
upper escarpment (Hill B), no traces of this guilding practice have been found
in the large sand cemetery. Some of the burials in the rock-cut tombs, including the one that had gold fingernails, had individually wrapped toes, fingers

---

98   Ikram, *Death and Burial in Ancient Egypt*, 71; Edward Bleiberg, *To Live Forever: Egyptian
      Treasures from the Brooklyn Museum* (London: Giles, 2008), 104; Riggs, "Tradition and In-
      novation in the Burial Practices of Roman Egypt," 349.
99   Smith, *Traversing Eternity*, 33–34. See, for example, EA6704 at the British Museum; or
      A.1911.210.3 at the National Museum of Scotland.

and ears, and individually wrapped genitals for males, as well as outer rhomboid wrappings.[100]

Many of the burials of Fag el-Gamous do possess a rather striking feature.
Most of those that still have textiles contain what we have designated as a "face
bundle." From our sample of 336, 50 burials were found with a face bundle (or
evidence of a face bundle). This accounts for 26% of the burials containing
textiles,[101] or 15% of all the burials in the sample.[102] This percentage is skewed
since many of the burials exhibiting textiles had such small textile remains
that it is impossible to tell whether or not a face bundle had been present. In
later years better recording allows us to account for this problem. For example,
in the 2009 season, every burial that had enough textile remains to be sure
whether or not it would have had a face bundle did indeed have one.[103] A close

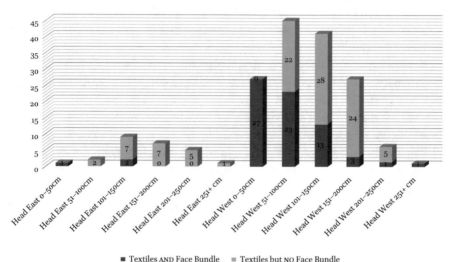

■ Textiles AND Face Bundle   ■ Textiles but NO Face Bundle

FIGURE 5.15 Presence of textiles *and* face bundles by head direction and depth

---

100   Griggs, "Report of 1987 and 1988 Seasons," 201. Unfortunately, we cannot provide individ-
      ual burial numbers for these features.

101   This statistic is smaller than our general impression. See Kristin H. South, "Minor Textile
      Burials and Religious Affiliation: An Archaeological Case Study from Roman Egypt," 63–
      64. The observations may actually be more correct since it is hard to statistically state
      when there is enough of a textile presence left for a face bundle to truly be declared "not
      present."

102   The presence of 3 head-east burials with face bundles in our sample is very small, but is
      still contra South, "Minor Textile Burials," 64, who states that there are no head-east buri-
      als with face bundles.

103   Kristin H. South, Joyce Y. Smith, Giovanni Tata, and Charles Wilfred Griggs, "'Face Bun-
      dles' in Early Christian Burials from the Fayum, Egypt," *Archaeological Textiles Newsletter*
      48 (2009): 2–3.

examination of the field books, excavation photos and textile analysis notes for every season between 2009 and 2018,[104] reveals that of the 38 burials that had enough remains at the head to know definitively whether it had a face bundle or not, 37 had face bundles. Thus it is clear that face bundles were much more common than the statistics above indicate.

The face bundles found at the cemetery generally consist of strips of linen folded over, one on top of the other, with the uppermost layer twisted together. Sometimes the twisted strip contains a few stitches to hold the twist shape together.[105] This twisted strip looks identical to the hieroglyph for twisted flax;[106] it is, in fact, actually twisted flax (since linen is made from flax). The strips are typically 3–6 cm wide and 13–20 cm long, though they are folded in half so that the practical length is half that.[107] There are some interesting exceptions. The area excavated in 1984 (4 squares in the large area of 100 to 150 N and 30 E to 70 E) yielded no face bundles made from linen strips, but many made of linen and palm fiber ropes.[108]

Face bundles are different from the phenomenon of stuffing linen inside a body cavity to hold its shape, for face bundles are carefully arranged textiles placed external to the body. Yet they may serve the same function, that of trying to maintain basic body shape after decomposition. Structures over the faces of contemporary burials have been found elsewhere.[109] Those from Deir el-Bahri were made of plaster and linen,[110] and burials at Qau el-Kebit and Ismant el-Kharab were found with cartonnage mummy masks.[111] At Kom el-Ahmar/Sharuna they used wads of linen and palm sticks to create a triangular shape.[112] Burials at Qarara from this era use ribbons that are similar to those at

104   The 2011 season was ended by the revolution before excavation began, and several seasons were either study seasons, conservation seasons, or the excavation took place at the pyramid instead of the cemetery.
105   South, et al., "Face Bundles," 3.
106   Sign v28.
107   South, et al., "Face Bundles," 3.
108   Griggs, "Excavating a Christian Cemetery near Seila," 78.
109   Bernard P. Grenfell and Arthur S. Hunt, "Graeco-Roman Branch. Excavations at Hibeh, Cynopolis and Oxyrhynchus," *Archaeological Report: 1902–1903*, F.Ll. Griffith, ed. (London: Egypt Exploration Fund, 1903), 3; Christina Riggs, "Funerary rituals (Ptolemaic and Roman Periods)," in UCLA *Encyclopedia of Egyptology*, Jacco Dieleman, Willeke Wendrich, eds. (2010), 2.
110   Łajtar, "The Theban Region Under the Roman Empire," 182.
111   Grajetzki, *Burial Customs in Ancient Egypt*, 126; Birrell, "Excavations in the Cemeteries of Ismant el-Kharab," 33.
112   Beatrice Huber, "Al-Kom al-Ahmar/Sharuna: Different Archaeological Contexts – Different Textiles?" in *Textiles in Situ: Their Find Spots in Egypt and Neighbouring Countries in the*

Fag el-Gamous (though black is frequently employed with the red at Qarara), and face bundles that are somewhat similar, though the internal contents are not made of the neatly folded linen as they are at Fag el-Gamous.[113] Something that was at least somewhat similar to a face bundle is described for some of the 6th to 7th century burials at the Monastery of Epiphanes.[114] In these other locales, face bundles are often made of non-woven vegetable material, which, as was noted above, occurs at Fag el-Gamous on rare occasion, though the majority are made of woven linen.

FIGURE 5.16
A burial with bundles at the face and feet, and rhomboid pattern wrappings
PHOTOGRAPH BY JOYCE Y. SMITH

First Millennium CE, Sabine Schrenk, ed. (Riggisberg: Abegg-Stiftung, 2006), 65–67; South, et al., "Face Bundles," 4.

113   South, et al., "Face Bundles," 4.
114   Ibid.

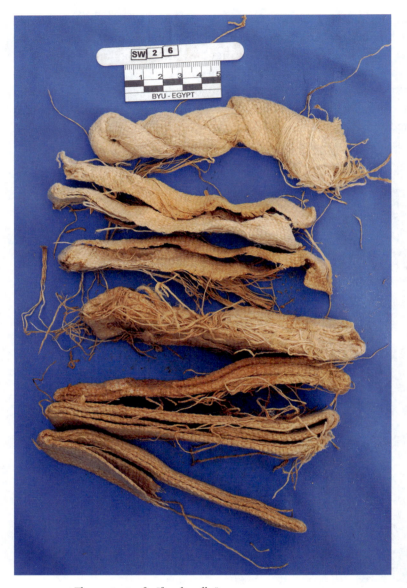

FIGURE 5.17 The contents of a "face bundle."
     PHOTOGRAPH BY DAVID M. WHITCHURCH

FIGURE 5.18 The rhomboid pattern of one of the wealthy burials from the hillside tombs
PHOTOGRAPH BY R. PAUL EVANS

We theorize that these bundles ensured that the wrapped bodies continued to look like they had a head and face, even after the desiccation process would normally have caused the head area to cave in somewhat. It seems to be a variation on the long-standing trend of giving special attention to preserving, or even enhancing, the head and face of a burial.[115] For those who could afford it, "an image of the deceased was integral to the design of the mummy mask, shroud, coffin, or tomb."[116] Yet for the poor burials of the Fag el-Gamous sand cemetery, not one instance has been found of masks or shrouds that try to preserve the likeness of the deceased. These face bundles were as close as the sand cemetery burials seemed to be able to come to preserving their faces in any way at all. In contrast, in the tombs carved into the escarpment (Hills

---

115   Smith, *Traversing Eternity*, 35. Examples somewhat similar to those at Fag el-Gamous can be found as EA6723 and EA6714 in the British Museum. Besides masks, attempts to artificially recreate faces/heads in other ways can be seen as AMM 25-b and AMM 10-b in the Rijksmuseum; M14048 at the World Museum of Liverpool; and EA6704 at the British Museum.

116   Riggs, *The Beautiful Burial in Roman Egypt*, 245.

A and B) a gilded mask was present, as was a cartonnage mask, and in unknown portions of the cemetery several mummy portraits were found.[117]

In addition to the face bundles, we have also found bundles created at the feet. Like the face bundles, we think that the foot bundles were used to maintain a look of having feet after the body had begun to decompose. Such foot casing was a common feature of Roman era burials in Egypt,[118] and are sometimes called "foot projections."[119] However, in contrast to the face bundles, the foot bundles were not made in a consistent manner nor with the same kinds of materials as the face bundles. The focus on recreating a lifelike aesthetic for the wrapped body is consistent with many other Graeco-Roman period burials that all seem to give priority to recreating a lifelike body in burial.[120]

5   Grave Goods

Following the trend seen elsewhere in Roman Egypt,[121] no shabtis have been found at Fag el-Gamous, though 8 figurines have been found (most of those are not in the data set being numerically analyzed here). Most of the bodies in the cemetery were interred without any grave goods. Of our sample of 336, only 75 burials (22%) were associated with any kind of burial goods. Those burials that did include objects show a wide diversity. Examples include: 33 burials with pottery, 12 with jewelry, eight with reed mats, seven with glass, six with baskets, four with plant wreaths, three with terracotta figures, three with pieces of wood, three with faience, three with date seeds and pits, three with shells, two with ropes, one with charcoal, one with a metal object, one with an olive branch, one with an oyster, one with a wooden peg, one with a box lid, one with a stone pillar drum, one with remains of a fire, and one with a jewelry box. Burials of the Roman era were characterized by the inclusion of everyday

---

117 See the article about mummy portraits in this volume for more information about these burials and their location.
118 Grajetzki, *Burial Customs in Ancient Egypt*, 126; Smith, *Traversing Eternity*, 35–36; Marjorie Susan Venit, *Visualizing the Afterlife in the Tombs of Graeco-Roman Egypt* (New York: Cambridge University Press, 2016), 173, 177. For examples, see the exaggerated feet on the Mummy of Artimedora at the Metropolitan Museum of New York; EA6723 at the British Museum, or 97-121-114A and E16234 at the University of Pennsylvania Museum of Archaeology and Anthropology.
119 Riggs, *The Beautiful Burial in Roman Egypt*, 247.
120 Venit, *Visualizing the Afterlife in the Tombs of Graeco-Roman Egypt*, 170.
121 Smith, *Traversing Eternity*, 44–45.

objects as opposed to the more traditional objects associated with burials from earlier periods.[122] Items that are often seen in contemporary burials are similar to those that have been found at Fag el-Gamous, such as jewelry, glass vessels, wreaths, baskets, lamps, figurines, foodstuffs, weavers' shuttles, needles, baskets and brooms,[123] all of which have been found somewhere in the Fag el-Gamous cemetery, if not in the particular data set being considered here.

As noted above, 33 (10%) of the burials had pottery interred with them. When the pottery is intact or the remains have enough diagnostic shapes to determine what the pots were, the vast majority of pottery interred with the burials are wine amphorae or cups.[124] It has been theorized that this is evidence of a funerary eucharist,[125] though we really cannot be sure of this.

FIGURE 5.19 Cups found in one season at the cemetery
PHOTOGRAPH COURTESY OF REVEL PHILLIPS

---

122   Venit, *Visualizing the Afterlife in the Tombs of Graeco-Roman Egypt,* 170; Riggs, *The Beautiful Burial in Roman Egypt,* 75.

123   Venit, *Visualizing the Afterlife in the Tombs of Graeco-Roman Egypt,* 170; Łajtar, "The Theban Region Under the Roman Empire," 183. Also, Smith, *Traversing Eternity,* 44; and Riggs, *The Beautiful Burial in Roman Egypt,* 95.

124   Griggs, et al., "Identities Revealed," 84.

125   Ibid.

All of these various uses of textiles and other kinds of grave goods bring up an important issue. While the burials from the Fag el-Gamous sand cemetery were poor in comparison to burials that had gone through the full mummification process, they should not be dismissed as truly poor. The textiles used in each burial represent an astounding amount of resources for these common people. Written sources tell us that the provincial well-to-do would spend around 600 drachmas on the linen for their burials, which was the equivalent of a year's worth of wages for a worker.[126] While most of the poorer burials of Fag el-Gamous are not quite as fine or numerous as the linen of the wealthier burials, they are not entirely dissimilar. The quality and quantity often rival that of the wealthy. For example, besides some impressive use of color and pattern, among their burials we have seen a style of weaving that has not been previously attested in any other burials in Egypt, suggesting a high degree of craftsmanship.[127]

6   Conclusion

The burials of the Fag el-Gamous sand cemetery may represent those of lower socio-economic status, but they are not all "poor" to the same degree, and from a funerary perspective, their burials suggest that they were not really poor at all. For in some way (perhaps in an investment of time and talent) they were able to marshal considerable resources for their burials and seem to have invested those resources in the types of funerary preparations that they either deemed most important or were most able to provide. This is especially true when it is recognized that a careful comparison of the textiles at Fag el-Gamous with several sample sets of Coptic textiles from elsewhere in Egypt revealed that, on the whole, the Fag el-Gamous textiles were more detailed in their design, had a tighter weave, and generally were of a higher workmanship than the comparative samples.[128] The people around the Fag el-Gamous cemetery may not have been able to provide the full mummification process, but they poured an astounding amount of their resources into their funerary practices. Textual evidence reveals cases of people elsewhere in Egypt selling their jewelry, slaves,

---

126   Dominic Montserrat, "Death and Funerals in the Roman Fayum," in *Portraits and Masks: Burial Customs in Roman Egypt*, M.L. Bierbrier, ed. (London: British Museum Press, 1997), 37.

127   Giovanni Tata, "Original Weave at Fag el-Gamous," (presentation, Annual Meeting of ARCE, Seattle, WA, April 2008).

128   Clarke, "Indexing and Cataloging Textiles from the Fag el Gamous Cemetery," 126–127.

or livestock in order to afford the costs of burial.[129] Often, the loved ones of those interred at Fag el-Gamous succeeded in producing a burial that reflected an understanding of the importance of a proper burial, even if their version was more of an adaptation rather than an adoption of the practices used by those with greater means.

All of this demonstrates that while the average person could not afford the same kind of interment as the wealthy burials for which Egypt is so famous, still the common did their best to provide a proper burial for their dead. The common burial typically had no coffin, though occasionally makeshift coffins were used. Sometimes their burials were accompanied by deposits of salt, but this was not typical. The burial could be very well preserved at times, but this was largely because of the sand and not due to any formal preservation process. Yet the quantity, quality, and creative use of textiles was impressive, as was the use of other resources, such as mudbricks, palm fronds, and ceramics. Despite a lack of wealth and resources, the common resident of this part of the Fayoum used what they had to honor their dead with respectable burials.

---

129   Montserrat, "Death and Funerals in the Roman Fayum," 36.

CHAPTER 6

The Mummy Portraits of Fag el-Gamous

Bethany Jensen and Kerry Muhlestein

The necropolis of Fag el-Gamous has been under excavation by Brigham Young University for more than thirty years.[1] During this time more than 1000 burials have been discovered; however, not a single mummy portrait has been found despite the fact that many of the burials fit the appropriate time period. While no mummy portraits have been found in the last thirty years, recent research has shown that Fag el-Gamous is the source of at least seven mummy portraits unearthed at the turn of the 20th century. Although only two of these portraits are explicitly said to have come from Fag el-Gamous, evidence from previous excavators and logical reasoning assign five others to this site. This paper will outline the research that occurred in the process of determining that each of these seven portraits should be attributed to Fag el-Gamous, while also providing some historical background for the excavators who discovered the portraits and brief descriptions of the physical appearance of each portrait.

One of the difficulties in establishing the provenance of artifacts from this area derives from the failure of previous archaeologists to provide precise descriptions of the find-spot of the artifacts.[2] It is believed that the Fag el-Gamous cemetery was likely the burial ground for multiple villages, including the settlements of Seila (sometimes spelled "Sela" or "Sila" by earlier archeologists) and Tanis, the latter sometimes referred to as Tel Shinshana or Manashinshana or Kom 2 (see figure 6.2).

The Fag el-Gamous cemetery is very large, encompassing about 300 acres (or 125 hectares). Its northern edge lies east and about a kilometer north of Manashinshana/Tanis/Kom 2, approaching the southern edge of Philadelphia. It extends southward until the southern edge lies directly east of Seila. Thus, it was likely the cemetery for both Tanis and Seila, with Philadelphia also being a

---

1   An earlier and less developed version of this paper was previously published in a student journal. See Bethany Jensen and Kerry Muhlestein, "The Mummy Portraits of Fag el-Gamous," in *Studia Antiqua* 12/1 (2013): 51–64.

2   This is not uncommon regarding mummy portraits. See Barbara E. Borg, "The Face of the Elite," Glenn W. Most, trans., *Arion* 8/1 (2000), 65–66. Borg rightly complains about how the lack of details in regards to the early finds of mummy portraits hampers our understanding of them. The current article can help slightly alleviate that by at least restoring the proper find spot to several mummy portraits.

likely contributor (possibly beginning as two cemeteries that eventually con-joined[3]). The cemetery's size and its service for two or three villages is part of what leads to confusion regarding the provenance of some artifacts. When re-cording their findings, the early excavators had the tendency to generalize or even mislabel the true provenance of an artifact. This occasionally occurred as an object found in the cemetery was recorded as being found in one of the three villages located nearby. Groups of objects, some funerary and some household, were also often clumped together as all being from the cemetery when in reality, a portion of those artifacts came from a village and a portion from the cemetery. Additional sources of confusion include archaeologists originally crediting an object as having come from one location, such as Manashinshana, but then later referring to that same object as having come from the cemetery, or using a different name for the same village. Even if the reports claim an artifact came from a village, we assume that all mummies and the items found with them came from the cemetery and not a settlement. In the midst of the confusion that arises from some of this imprecise reporting, much of our attempt to find which mummies came from the Fag el-Gamous cemetery centers around making sense of the provenance labeling system used in early excavation reports and museum registries.

1   Mummy Portraits

Mummy portraits were first made around 30–40 AD and continued to be cre-ated until about the mid-3rd century,[4] with a few outliers in the 4th century.[5] The portraits are a blend of two traditions: Graeco-Roman portrait painting and Egyptian mummification processes.[6] The portraits served as a way to re-cord how the deceased appeared in life or how they would like to look in

---

3 See the article on the background of the Fayoum in this volume.
4 Susan Walker, "A Note on the Dating of the Mummy Portraits," in *Ancient Faces: Mummy Portraits from Roman Egypt*, ed. Susan Walker (New York: Metropolitan Museum of Art, New York, 2000), 36. See also Barbara Borg, *Mumienporträts. Chronologie und kultureller Kontext* (Mainz: Philipp von Zabern, 1996), and Barbara E. Borg, "Portraits," in Christina Riggs, ed., *The Oxford Handbook of Roman Egypt* (Oxford: Oxford Handbooks Online, 2012), 13–14.
5 Barbara E. Borg, "Painted Funerary Portraits," in Willeke Wendrich (ed.), UCLA *Encyclopedia of Egyptology*, (Los Angeles, 2010), 4, found at http://digital2.library.ucla.edu/viewItem .do?ark=21198/zz0021bx22; and Elisabeth R. O'Connell, "Settlements and Cemeteries in Late Antique Egypt: an Introduction," in Elisabeth R. O'Connell, ed., *Egypt in the First Millennium AD, Perspectives from new fieldwork* (Leuven: Peeters, 2014), 7.
6 Kurt Gschwantler, "Graeco-Roman Portraiture," in *Ancient Faces: Mummy Portraits from Ro-man Egypt*, ed. Susan Walker (New York: Metropolitan Museum of Art, New York, 2000), 21.

death,[7] though there is not full agreement on this.[8] The influence of Roman artistic culture is evident in these portraits. The clothing, hairstyles, and jewelry reflect styles that were in vogue in the imperial court.[9]

The first mummy portraits discovered were found in 1615 in Saqqara by Pietro della Valle, an Italian traveler.[10] In the early 19th century several mummy portraits were discovered by British and French excavations, but toward the end of the century the number of portraits that were uncovered expanded greatly. In 1887, a major cemetery near er-Rubayat, just north of Manashinshana/Tanis/Kom 2, was discovered and dozens of mummy portraits were uncovered. W.M. Flinders Petrie found a major Roman cemetery at Hawara, several miles south of Seila, around this same time. Here Petrie uncovered many portraits in 1887–9 and again when he returned in 1911.[11] Although the portraits are sometimes called the "Fayoum portraits," portraits have been found all over Egypt from Upper Egypt to the Mediterranean coast west of Alexandria.[12]

2   Work around Fag el-Gamous

Bernard Grenfell and Arthur Hunt excavated in Egypt for many years in the late 1800s and early 1900s. They first began working together in the 1895–1896 season investigating Graeco-Roman sites in the Fayoum.[13] Between the years 1895

---

7   Susan Walker, "Mummy Portraits and Roman Portraiture," in *Ancient Faces: Mummy Portraits from Roman Egypt*, ed. Susan Walker (New York: Metropolitan Museum of Art, New York, 2000), 23.

8   Borg, "Painted Funerary Portraits," 7–8. See also Barbara E. Borg, *Mumienporträts: Chronologie und kultureller Kontext*, 111–149.

9   Susan E.C. Walker, "Mummy Portraits in their Roman Context," in *Portraits and Masks: Burial Customs in Roman Egypt*, M.L. Bierbrier, ed. (London: British Museum Press, 1997), 4.

10   See Borg, "Painted Funerary Portraits," 1; and Borg, "The Face of the Elite," 63–34.

11   William M. Flinders Petrie, *Hawara, Biahmu, and Arsinoe* (London: Leadenhall Press, 1889); W.M. Flinders Petrie, *The Hawara Portfolio: paintings of the Roman age, found by W.M. Flinders Petrie, 1888 and 1911* (London: School of Archaeology in Egypt, 1913). See also Morris Bierbrier, "The Discovery of the Mummy Portraits," in *Ancient Faces: Mummy Portraits from Roman Egypt*, Susan Walker, ed. (New York: Metropolitan Museum of Art, New York, 2000), 32.

12   R.S. Bagnall, "The Fayum and its People," in *Ancient Faces: Mummy Portraits from Roman Egypt*, Susan Walker, ed. (New York: Metropolitan Museum of Art, New York, 2000), 26.

13   J.G. Milne, "Bernard Pyne Grenfell: b. 16 Dec. 1869. d. 18 May 1926," *Journal of Egyptian Archaeology* 12 (1926): 285.

FIGURE 6.1   Bernard Grenfell and Arthur Hunt in Egypt
PHOTOGRAPH COURTESY OF THE EGYPT EXPLORATION SOCIETY

and 1903, Grenfell and Hunt found mummy portraits in the Fayoum.[14] In 1902, they found some of these portraits at Fag el-Gamous. Unfortunately, many of their field notebooks have vanished over the years[15] and their publication of the finds is somewhat limited. Thankfully, the Egypt Exploration Society (EES) has preserved some glass-plate negatives from their excavations. Morris Bierbrier, formerly the Assistant Keeper of the Department of Antiquities, British Museum, used these plates along with the Archaeological Reports of the Graeco-Roman Branch of the Egyptian Exploration Fund (EEF) to determine that some of the mummy portraits featured in the photographs came from Fag el-Gamous. Three of the negatives depict mummy portraits from the 1901–1902 excavation season.[16] In the 1900–1901 Archaeological Report, Grenfell and

14   Morris L. Bierbrier, "Fayum Cemeteries and their Portraits," in *Portraits and Masks: Burial Customs in Roman Egypt*, M.L. Bierbrier, ed. (London: British Museum Press, 1997), 16.
15   Susan Walker, "Mummy Portraits and Roman Portraiture," in *Ancient Faces: Mummy Portraits from Roman Egypt*, Susan Walker, ed. (New York: Metropolitan Museum of Art, New York, 2000), 24.
16   Bierbrier, "Fayum Cemeteries and their Portraits," 16.

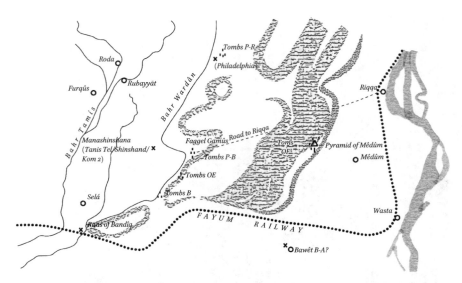

FIGURE 6.2 Map of the Fag el-Gamous area based on the map made by Grenfell and Hunt
MAP CREATED BY AIMEE MADDOX

Hunt reported finding a Ptolemaic cemetery at Manashinshana,[17] which they identified with Tanis based on a mummy label.[18] The following season they reported that they excavated near Seila but didn't find anything, so they returned to Manashinshana. This time Manashinshana was much more productive for them and they discovered several portraits, as will be further outlined below.[19]

3   About the Site

Fag el-Gamous is a very large necropolis located on the edge of the eastern Fayoum. When Grenfell and Hunt excavated here the site was initially sometimes referred to as Manashinshana, the necropolis of Tanis.[20] Afterwards, the

---

17   Bernard P. Grenfell and Arthur S. Hunt, "Graeco-Roman Branch: Excavations in the Fayum," in *Archaeological Report: 1900–1901*, F.Ll. Griffith, ed. (London: Egypt Exploration Fund, 1901), 6.

18   SB XII 10833. See also http://www.trismegistos.org/fayum/fayum2/2251.php?geo_id=2251.

19   Bernard P. Grenfell and Arthur S. Hunt, "Graeco-Roman Branch: Excavations in the Fayum and at El Hibeh," in *Archaeological Report: 1901–1902*, F.Ll. Griffith, ed. (London: Egypt Exploration Fund, 1902), 3.

20   The Tanis they are referring to is located in the eastern Fayoum. This is not the same Tanis that is located in the Nile Delta where Petrie worked.

term Manashinshana was used as a term for the village (Tanis) and Fag el-Gamous was the term used for the cemetery, though this terminology is not used consistently. The exact location of Manashinshana as found by Grenfell and Hunt is no longer known, making it difficult to determine the modern parallel of the exact location of the mummy portraits. The village today known as Shanashinshana is likely the site known to Grenfell and Hunt as Manashinshana. It lies several hundred meters straight west of the necropolis.[21] A note from Grenfell and Hunt substantiates this theory, reading, "the site of the necropolis is by Fagg el Gamus,[22] the name of the road leading from the Fayum across the desert to Riqqa in the Nile Valley."[23] The road began at the edge of the necropolis, right at the border of the cultivated land that spans the western side of the Bahr Seila canal and leads across the desert to the train station in the Nile Valley.[24] In the same source, Grenfell and Hunt referred to Tanis as "probably identical with the ruins of an ancient village called Manashinshana about five miles south of Rubayyat, the cemetery of it being at Fagg el Gamus, where a desert road crosses over into the Nile valley."[25] Thus, over time, the cemetery took on the name of the road and came to be referred to as the Fag el-Gamous cemetery or necropolis. On a map created by Grenfell and Hunt[26] the road from Riqqa runs through and ends at the current excavation site. They also placed a few tomb locations on the map which are within the concession area.

Grenfell and Hunt provided further landmarks to describe the location of this cemetery. They state that they excavated "at a cemetery in the Fayum on the edge of the desert about halfway between Manashinshana and the Sela railway station; and somewhat south of the 'pyramid' of Sela (an Old Empire mastaba)."[27] The Seila Pyramid is north of the Fag el-Gamous necropolis and is close enough to the cemetery to be included in the same archaeological

---

21   Personal communication with the locals who live in that area today, multiple times ranging from May 2012—February 2018.

22   The transliteration of the name of the cemetery has not been consistent over time. Both the word "Fag" and the word "Gamous" can receive a variety of spellings. While this volume uses the spelling Fag el-Gamous, when we quote original sources we use their spelling.

23   Bernard P. Grenfell, Arthur S. Hunt, and Edgar J. Goodspeed, *The Tebtunis Papyri: Part 2*, vol. 52 of *Graeco-Roman Memoirs* (1907; repr., London: Egypt Exploration Society, 1970), 345.

24   More about the road and canal is discussed in the chapter on the history and geology of the Fayoum in the volume.

25   Grenfell, et al., *The Tebtunis Papyri: Part 2*, 403.

26   Grenfell and Hunt, *Tebtunis Papyri, Part 2*, Plate III.

27   Grenfell and Hunt, "Graeco-Roman Branch: Excavations in the Fayum and at El Hibeh," 2.

concession. As was noted above, the Fag el-Gamous cemetery is on the border of the desert and cultivated land, separated by the Bahr Seila canal.[28] It parallels the distance from Manashinshana/Tanis to Seila with the center of the necropolis being about halfway between them, thus matching Grenfell's and Hunt's description of the cemetery being halfway between the two villages. All of the descriptions combined make it clear that the cemetery they began calling Fag el-Gamous is the same Fag el-Gamous cemetery being excavated today, though only a small portion of it has been excavated.

The site of Manashinshana has also been identified as Petrie's Kom 2,[29] which was a Roman village north of the Seila railway. Petrie writes of a mastaba being a major landmark near the cemetery,[30] which we now know to be the Seila Pyramid.[31] On Petrie's map, he marks the location of Kom 2 in relation to the pyramid as the same location that Manashinshana is in relation to the pyramid, thus we can be sure that Petrie's Kom 2 is the same site as ancient Manashinshana.

To sum up, evidence points towards the modern village of Seila being in the same location as the ancient village. Manashinshana/Tel Shinshana /Tanis/ Kom 2 is almost certainly the modern village of Shanashinshana, a site located several hundred meters from the edge of the Fayoum that is at least roughly in the same area and carries a name that seems to preserve the memory of some of the names of the earlier village.[32]

Because it is somewhat difficult to keep track of all the geographic points we have just gone through while assigning them to all of the various names given them at different points in time, a summary may be helpful.

1)   The ancient cemetery currently known as Fag el-Gamous is on the eastern edge of the Fayoum, just beyond the cultivated land across the canal Bahr Seila.

---

28   See Bryan Kraemer, "The Meandering Identity of a Fayum Canal: The *Henet* of Moeris/ Dioryx Kleonos/Bahr Wardan/Abdul Wahbi," in *Proceedings of the Twenty-Fifth International Congress of Papyrology, Ann-Arbor 2007*, Traianos Gagos, ed. (Ann Arbor: Scholarly Publishing Office, The University of Michigan, 2010), 365–376, on the identity of this canal. Bahr Wardan is the ancient canal, which is largely followed by (though sometimes separate from) the modern canal Bahr Wahbi.

29   Paola Davoli, *L'archeologia urbana nel Fayyum di età ellenistica e romana* (Napoli: G. Procaccini, 1998), 165.

30   W.M. Flinders Petrie, *Illahun, Kahun, and Gurob* (1891; repr., Encino, California: Joel L. Malter & CO, 1974), 31.

31   See the article on the history of the excavations at Seila and Fag el-Gamous in this volume.

32   Besides the work presented above, Davoli, *L'archeologia urbana nel Fayyum di età ellenistica e romana*, 165.

2) This cemetery is very large and stretches from just east of Manashinsha-
    na to just east of Seila.

3) Manashinshana is also referred to as Tanis, Kom 2, and Tel Shinshana.

4) We assume that any burials reported to have come from the village of
    Manashinshana/Tanis/Kom 2 or Seila really came from what is known
    today as the Fag el-Gamous necropolis.

With these geographic points in mind, we can examine the provenance of
burials that possessed mummy portraits, looking for those that came from any
of the above listed sites, and then assign those mummies to Fag el-Gamous.

4   The Finding of Mummy Portraits in Fag el-Gamous

As previously mentioned, in the 1900–1901 excavation season Grenfell and
Hunt found a large Ptolemaic cemetery near Manashinshana. There, they
found many mummies with cartonnage in good or fair condition. They also
obtained a large quantity of Greek and Demotic papyri, the majority of which
date to the 3rd century BC.[33] Unfortunately, the report doesn't detail how many
mummies with cartonnage were found or whether those mummies had portraits or not.

During the following season (1901–1902) when Grenfell and Hunt returned
to Manashinshana from what they felt were unproductive excavations in the
area around the Seila railway station, they found several "papyrus mummies."[34]
The Roman and Byzantine tombs they found contained well-preserved portraits on wood, glass vases, and many other small objects. Unfortunately, the
report does not note how many portraits were found. A "handsomely decorated stucco mummy" was also found at Manashinshana and was retained by the
Cairo Museum.[35] Interestingly, this mummy is referred to in a catalogue from
the EEF's annual exhibition in 1902 as having come from Seila.[36] If this is the
same mummy, it is an excellent example of the previously discussed discrep-
ancies in provenance assignment—being labeled as having come from either
of two villages when in reality it was found in the shared cemetery. Similarly,

---

33   Grenfell and Hunt, "Graeco-Roman Branch: Excavations in the Fayum," 7.
34   Grenfell and Hunt, "Graeco-Roman Branch: Excavations in the Fayum and at El Hibeh,"3.
35   Grenfell and Hunt, "Graeco-Roman Branch: Excavations in the Fayum and at El Hibeh," 3.
36   B. Grenfell and A. Hunt, "Graeco-Roman Branch," in *Catalogue of Egyptian antiquities,
     found by Prof. Flinders Petrie at Abydos and Drs. Grenfell and Hunt in the Fayum (Egypt Ex-
     ploration Fund) and drawings from the temple of the kings (Sety I), (Egyptian Research Ac-
     count) 1902: exhibited at University College, Gower Street, London July 1st to 26th*, by W.M.
     Flinders Petrie and Egypt Exploration Fund (London: Egypt Exploration Fund, 1902), 8.

other funerary objects listed in the catalogue as having come from Seila should also be attributed to the Fag el-Gamous necropolis. These other items include: cartonnage of early Ptolemaic mummies (3rd-2nd centuries BC) and "objects of the Roman and Byzantine periods, including three well preserved mummy portraits."[37]

The objects mentioned as having been found along with the portraits are not explicitly detailed but it can be inferred that included with the portraits were glass vases, jewelry, beads, and other objects similar to those found at Manashinshana.[38] These glass vases may help us to further solidify the location of the site. In the report of the 1901–1902 season, the only location that Grenfell and Hunt reported where glass vases were found is Manashinshana. In a catalogue for the Cairo Museum about Graeco-Egyptian glass, there are several vases that come from Fag el-Gamous and one from Seila. In the introduction to the catalogue, some vases said to come from Seila are later listed as coming from Fag el-Gamous. The vases that are listed in the contents of the catalogue from Fag el-Gamous were found by Grenfell and Hunt in 1902. This indicates that the vases found at Manashinshana in 1902 were actually from the Fag el-Gamous cemetery. This helps confirm our assumption that the portraits found with the glass vases would be attributed to the same location—Fag el-Gamous.[39]

Distribution lists from the EEF record that portraits were sent to Boston, Chicago, Brussels, and Oxford in 1902 from Grenfell's and Hunt's 1901–1902 excavation.[40] Below we will address the portraits sent to each of these locations, as well as the stucco mummy mentioned above. The three portraits mentioned in the EEF 1902 catalogue may be the portraits that are currently in Chicago, Boston, and Oxford.[41] As no provenance is given in the catalogue for these portraits, we assume the portraits at these locations can be attributed to Fag el-Gamous.

Another catalogue of the Cairo Museum (*Graeco-Egyptian Coffins*) gives us the record of two mummy portraits in the museum. Portrait no. 33283 and

---

37   Ibid., 8.
38   Ibid., 8–9.
39   M.C.C. Edgar, *Catalogue général des antiquités égyptiennes du Musée du Caire 32401–32800, Graeco-Egyptian Glass* (1905; repr., Osnabrück, Germany: Otto Zeller Verlag, 1974), III.
40   EES Distribution Lists, transcription in EES archives. Can also be accessed at http://egyptartefacts.griffith.ox.ac.uk/sites/default/files/pdfs/Transcription%20EES%20distribution%20reg%201900-1913.pdf.
41   Bierbrier, "Fayum Cemeteries and their Portraits," 17.

33284 are listed as coming from Fag el-Gamous after being found by Grenfell and Hunt.[42] Both of these portraits are said to be in very poor condition.

5   Cairo Portraits

Following are some details about the condition and appearance of the two Cairo Museum mummy portraits. Grenfell and Hunt describe portrait no. 33283 as a portrait of a young man, the angle of the painting showing more of the right side of his face. The man has a short beard and moustache, similar in style to many other portraits, and a gilded wreath in his hair. The background of the painting was white when first painted, but was gilded after the portrait was fixed in place. Wax colors (encaustic)[43] were used to paint the portrait, which is among the most common methods of creating the portraits.[44] At the time the catalogue was put together the portrait was said to be in "very bad condition," and the coloring and detail were unrecognizable. The wood is broken and eaten "all round," the preserved portion is full of holes, the surface is badly damaged and discolored, and the back is coated with cloth and pitch.[45]

Portrait no. 33284 is also described as being in "very bad condition." It is broken "all round," and most of the left side of the face is broken off.[46] There is an impression of cloth on the surface, the back is coated with cloth and pitch, and the item is very fragile." The portrait features the head of a bearded man straight on, but shows slightly more of the right side. "There is a strip of white with a lilac border across the front of the neck" which may be the top of a chiton. The man has thick, wavy hair that covers much of his forehead. His beard is also thick and wavy. According to Edgar, he has "rather Jewish features,"[47] a "fair, ruddy complexion, dark hair, and brown eyes." The forehead is wrinkled

---

42   M.C.C. Edgar, *Catalogue général des antiquités égyptiennes du Musée du Caire 33101–33285, Graeco-Egyptian Coffins* (1905; repr., Osnabrück, Germany: Otto Zeller Verlag, 1977), 131.

43   See Borg, "Portraits," 12.

44   Borg, *Mumienporträts*, 1–11.

45   Edgar, *Catalogue général des antiquités égyptiennes du Musée du Caire 33101–33285*, 131.

46   Ibid., 131–132.

47   It is true that such identification was done with horrible intent during the Third Reich (see Borg, "The Face of the Elite," 67), Edgar's description predates this usage. While we would eschew such a phrase today, and while it is not realistically possible to make such an identification from such a portrait, we have included this description in order to not rob the historical characters of the past of their voice, and thus our understanding of their voice, because it offends our modern sensibilities and carries with it another historical story of persecution. See Borg, "Painted Funerary Portraits," 5; and Barbara E. Borg, *"Der*

with "vertical lines above the nose and a strongly marked line below the inner corner of the eye." His eyebrows are thick and arched. He has a hooked nose and his lips curve downward in the middle. The portrait is painted on a white background. It was painted with wax colors (encaustic) and there are marks of a hard point (especially on the forehead). There is "strong light on the nose, forehead, and cheek, shading on the left side of the nose" (the deeper shading is a yellowish brown color), his "hair was rendered by curving black strokes on a brown ground; brown strokes round the outside."[48] The pictures that we have been able to locate of these portraits show that the portraits are indeed in poor condition, but the surviving portions depict very detailed paintings.

6   Brussels

One portrait from Fag el-Gamous is in the Royal Museums of Art and History in Brussels, Belgium. Portrait E 4859 was sent to Brussels by the Egypt Exploration Fund (EEF) in 1902 but was not registered until 1913.[49] In 1914, Adolphe Reinach reported that at least one portrait that went to Brussels was from Manashinshana.[50] The records in Brussels and those of the EEF give no indication of the provenance for E 4859. There seems to be a great deal of disagreement about the origin of the portrait; one source says the portrait is from Tanis, another from Manashinshana, and another from Fag el-Gamous.[51] We can now make sense of this confusion since all of these terms point to the same necropolis. Distribution lists show that this portrait was found at the same time as a few other portraits attributed to Fag el-Gamous.[52] This fragmentary portrait depicts a middle aged man that is slightly turned to the right. The right half of his head is broken off. He wears a short beard on his chin and cheeks and has a short moustache. He has dark curly hair and dark eyes. He is wearing

---

      zierlichste Anblick der Welt": Ägyptische Porträtmumien (Mainz am Rhein: Philipp von Zabern), 37.

48   Edgar, *Catalogue général des antiquités égyptiennes du Musée du Caire 33101–33285,* 131–132.

49   Bierbrier, "Fayum Cemeteries and their Portraits," 17.

50   Adolphe Reinach, "Les portraits gréco-égyptiens," *Revue archéologique,* 4th ser., XXIV (1914): 32.

51   Harco Willems and Willy Clarysse, *Keizers aan de Nijl* (Leuven, Belgium: Peeters, 1999), 209; Musée d'archéologie méditerranéenne (Marseille, France), *Egypte romaine: l'autre Egypte* (Marseille, France: Musées de Marseille, 1997), 156; *The Global Egyptian Museum* (International Committee for Egyptology), s.v. "Mummy portrait," accessed March 12, 2012, http://www.globalegyptianmuseum.org/detail.aspx?id=711.

52   EES distribution list.

a white tunic with a dark trim around his wide neck. The portrait is painted on a white background.[53]

7   Oxford

Located in the Ashmolean Museum, E 3755 has been attributed to Fag el-Gamous by Morris Bierbrier.[54] The portrait was registered in 1908 with no surviving contemporary note of its provenance. When it was registered later, it was said to come from Tanis.[55] This portrait was photographed by Hunt during the 1901–1902 excavations. EEF Photograph Hunt no. 126 is a picture of this portrait of a young man. The young man has dark, seemingly straight hair, dark, thick eyebrows, dark eyes, and a long thin nose. He has a short, thin beard on his cheeks and chin, and a thin moustache. He appears to be wearing a red and yellow garment. The background of the portrait is white. This portrait went on display in the Ashmolean Museum in October 2011.

8   Stucco Mummy

The Stucco Mummy was found at Manashinshana in the 1901–1902 excavation season, as previously mentioned.[56] In a later exhibition catalogue, a stucco mummy is included in the exhibition but was said to come from Seila.[57] The descriptions of the two items are so similar that they are almost surely the same mummy whose location had been confused, rather than two different mummies. Two photographs from the EES archives are from Grenfell and Hunt's expedition in 1901–1902. Hunt no. 128 and 129 are photographs of a stucco mummy from Seila. The coffin is currently being housed in the Egyptian Museum (Cairo Inv. 17|10/16|1). The provenance of the mummy was unknown until Bierbrier brought to light the photographs that showed that this was, in fact, the same piece found in 1902 from Fag el-Gamous.[58] These photographs have been instrumental in verifying the provenance of some of these mummy portraits from Fag el-Gamous.

---

53   Harco Willems and Willy Clarysse, *Keizers aan de Nijl*, 156.
54   Bierbrier, "Fayum Cemeteries and their Portraits," 17.
55   Ibid.
56   Grenfell and Hunt, "Graeco-Roman Branch: Excavations in the Fayum and at El Hibeh," 3.
57   B. Grenfell and A. Hunt, "Graeco-Roman Branch," in *Catalogue of Egyptian antiquities*, 8.
58   Bierbrier, "Fayum Cemeteries and their Portraits," 17.

FIGURE 6.3   E3755 or GR.NEG.126
          PHOTOGRAPH COURTESY OF THE EGYPT EXPLORATION SOCIETY

Lorelei Corcoran discussed this mummy in her catalogue of portrait mummies in Egyptian museums.[59] The portrait probably dates to 330–350 AD. The

---

59   Lorelei H. Corcoran, *Portrait Mummies from Roman Egypt (I–IV Centuries A.D.): with a Catalog of Portrait Mummies in Egyptian Museums*, Studies in Ancient Oriental Civilization 56 (Chicago: Oriental Institute of the University of Chicago, 1995).

FIGURE 6.4 GR.NEG. 128 / GR.NEG.129
        PHOTOGRAPH COURTESY OF THE EGYPT EXPLORATION SOCIETY

mummy is covered in a layer of stucco around the head, along the front, and around the footcase. Where actual feet would be on the mummy, there are feet modeled at the bottom of the wrappings. Above the feet are three sections on the front of the body that depict mythological scenes. The first scene is a depiction of the purification of the deceased by Thoth and another deity. The second scene depicts the ram of Mendes above the body of a female mummy, a scene of procreative power and revivification. The top scene is a depiction of the conception of Horus, child of Osiris. The upper torso of the mummy is a portrait of the deceased, an adult woman. Parts of the portrait are modeled in stucco, giving it a three-dimensional appearance. These elements include: a crown of leaves inlaid with "gems" and a star medallion, a medallion necklace, the breasts, and a small vessel in the right hand. She appears to be wearing a red chiton with black clavi. She is also wearing many bracelets and rings. The portrait is painted directly onto the linen and is surrounded by a stucco frame inlaid with stucco "gems."[60]

9   Boston/Chicago

Two other portraits have been attributed to Fag el-Gamous through a series of deductions. These portraits are shown in EEF Photograph Hunt no. 127, which is from Seila. As noted above, we assume that items related to burial must come from the necropolis, not the village. Furthermore, since early excavation photographs of the portraits in EEF Photographs Hunt no. 126 and 128–129 are mummy portraits that came from Fag el-Gamous, it is highly likely that no. 127 is also from Fag el-Gamous. The portraits in EEF Photograph Hunt no. 127 are currently in the collections of two American institutions. One of these portraits is in the Museum of Fine Arts Boston (02.825). This portrait was acquired from the EEF in 1902 and is said to come from er-Rubayat, a site just north of Manashinshana.[61] The museum currently lists the portrait's provenance as "el-Rubayat," found in 1902, and says that it was excavated by W.M.F. Petrie for the Egypt Exploration Fund.[62] This cannot be correct. Petrie never excavated in er-Rubayat and in 1902 he was in Abydos, where he worked from 1899 to 1904.[63] The incorrect labeling on this artifact, combined with the Hunt picture that indicates a provenance of Seila, which is consistently associated with Fag el-Gamous, strongly suggest that this was a Fag el-Gamous portrait. The portrait

---

60   Lorelei H. Corcoran, "Stucco Mummy No. 22," in *Portrait Mummies from Roman Egypt* (*I–IV Centuries A.D.*): *with a Catalog of Portrait Mummies in Egyptian Museums*, Studies in Ancient Oriental Civilization 56 (Chicago, Illinois: Oriental Institute of the University of Chicago, 1995), 194–202.

61   Bierbrier, "Fayum Cemeteries and their Portraits," 17.

62   "Funerary portrait of a man," Museum of Fine Arts Boston, accessed March 20, 2012, http://www.mfa.org/collections/object/funerary-portrait-of-a-man-131643.

63   "The Archaeological Record: Flinders Petrie in Egypt," Digital Egypt for Universities, accessed March 12, 2012, last modified 2002, http://www.digitalegypt.ucl.ac.uk/archaeology/petriedigsindex.html.

FIGURE 6.5   GR.NEG. 127. The Boston portrait is on the left, the Chicago portrait is on the
right
PHOTO COURTESY OF THE EGYPT EXPLORATION SOCIETY

depicts a middle-aged man with a short beard and moustache. He has dark
hair that hangs long over his ears and forehead. The eyebrows are thick and
dark and come together above the bridge of the nose. The man is wearing a
white chiton and a gray mantle over his left shoulder. The background of the
portrait is gray.[64]

The other portrait in this photograph is in the Oriental Institute, Chicago
(2053). This portrait is said to have been acquired in 1897 from Hawara, several
miles south of Seila. Given the fact that this portrait is in the same picture as
the previous portrait, it is very unlikely that they were found at two different
times, in two different locations—especially since the picture (Hunt no. 127) is
labeled Seila.[65] Another problem is that there were no excavations in Hawara

64   "Funerary portrait of a man," Museum of Fine Arts Boston, accessed March 20, 2012,
      http://www.mfa.org/collections/object/funerary-portrait-of-a-man-131643.
65   Bierbrier, "Fayum Cemeteries and their Portraits," 17.

in 1897. The closest time period was in 1892 when three portraits were found, none of which match in description to this portrait.[66] For these reasons, we deduce that both of the mummy portraits depicted in the photograph Hunt no. 127 were discovered at the Fag el-Gamous necropolis.

This portrait depicts a young man. He has dark, curly hair, a short, curly beard, and a moustache. He has dark, thick eyebrows. He is wearing a red garment with what appears to be white trim or a white undergarment around the neck. The background is beige.

10   Additional Portraits

In Parlasca's *Ritratti di Mummie*, he incorrectly attributes nine other portraits to Fag el-Gamous that currently reside in the Phoebe A. Hearst Museum of Anthropology in Berkeley, California.[67] These portraits are actually from Tebtunis. The provenance from Berkeley is very clear on this point.[68] The Egypt Exploration Fund reports that in the 1899–1900 season Grenfell and Hunt were working for the University of California excavating at Umm el-Baragat, the site of ancient Tebtunis. There they worked with several groups of tombs, including a Ptolemaic cemetery. While the report from the EEF does not say whether any portraits were found here, it does say that they found "mummy-cases constructed of papyrus in the same manner as those discovered by Petrie in Gurob."[69] The fact that these portraits are in Berkeley and that Parlasca says they were discovered in 1899–1900[70] indicate that these portraits must have come from the excavations at Tebtunis. Grenfell and Hunt did not find portraits in Fag el-Gamous until 1902—as previously stated.

11   In Summary

Tracking down these portraits has been an important part of our excavation research. One of our aims as a research team is to try to understand more about

---

66   A.L. Frothingham Jr., "Archaeological News: Summary of Recent Discoveries and Investigations," *The American Journal of Archaeology and the History of the Fine Arts* 8/1 (January–February 1893): 103.

67   Klaus Parlasca, *Ritratti di Mummie*, A. Adriani, ed., Repertorio d'Arte dell'Egitto Greco-Romano, Serie B (Roma: L'Erma di Bretschneider, 1977), II:76.

68   Bierbrier, "Fayum Cemeteries and their Portraits," 16.

69   F.G. Kenyon, "Graeco-Roman Egypt," in *Archaeological Report: 1899–1900*, F.Ll. Griffith, ed. (London: Egypt Exploration Fund, 1900), 44.

70   Parlasca, *Ritratti di Mummie*, 76.

the culture and society of the people who are represented in the cemetery. There are some obstacles to this goal. In an ironic twist to what commonly happens at excavations, one of the largest obstacles we face is that we are finding little in the way of elite burials. Many of the elites who we do know of were excavated nearly a century ago. Consequently, we have a large data set for the average citizens in the cemetery, yet we know little of the more wealthy and prestigious. Many factors must have been part of determining whether a burial had such a portrait attached to it, including cultural background, the expectations of various social circles, economic ability, and cultural aspirations of the family. Undoubtedly, the combined desire and ability to include such a portrait indicated a higher social and economic niche than was average. Thus, the mummy portraits represent a higher status demographic, and so studying them affords us the opportunity to learn about a part of the population about which we have little information from elsewhere in our excavation. This allows us to develop a more well-rounded picture of this specific regional society.

Knowing which portraits come from our cemetery helps us understand the larger cultural phenomenon of Roman portraiture in Egyptian embalming practice in general. This cross-cultural interaction is a fascinating area of study, and we can be more accurate in our analysis of this practice since we now know more of which mummies come from what area of the country. As we make these findings public, we will enable others to make more accurate assessments as well. Furthermore, we will be more informed contributors to conversations we are engaging in with other excavations dealing with the same time period. A fuller picture allows the entire academic community to be more well-rounded in its research.

Clearly the villages around Fag el-Gamous were inhabited by a culture that was experiencing a number of influences from Mediterranean culture. Roman influence is evident in the portraits and Christianity was spreading throughout its population at the time. Even though these were small villages that were very much out of the way, they were becoming part of a global culture. After millennia of being more of a cultural donor than borrower, Fayoum residents were finding their roles reversed. The presence of so many Roman mummy portraits attests to the Roman cultural influence in the area. In the light of these discoveries, we will be better guided in our interpretation of existing artifacts, and in our discovery of more. Further research in all of these areas is more possible because we now have a better provenance for the mummy portraits discussed in this article.

CHAPTER 7

An Introduction to the Textiles of Fag el-Gamous: The Use of Basket Weave Linen in Burials of the Necropolis of Fag el-Gamous

Kristin H. South

1 Introduction

Textiles are among the most ubiquitous finds in the excavations at Fag el-Gamous due to their importance in funerary custom.[1] While other funerary goods were optional, all burials included wrappings, many of which have been preserved to a significant degree. As the common thread that literally binds the rest of the funerary finds together, textiles deserve a closer look and not only because understanding the basic elements of textiles is crucial to understanding many other analyses reported in this volume.

Multiple types of textile finds have emerged in the course of work at Fag el-Gamous, sortable by fiber, weave, and shape. To date, every textile from this necropolis has been made of either linen or wool or a combination of the two, with the large preponderance made of plain linen. Wool, the rarer fiber at this site, is used predominantly for clothing and for colored decoration in linen textiles.[2] Narrow, purpose-woven bands of about 1 cm in width were frequently used to hold burials together, and sprang hairnets also occur with regularity but not high frequency on female burials. We have also found one instance of nålebinding in a pair of child's socks. The most common weaves, as described below, are 1×1, 1×2, or 2×2 variations on plain weave, with tapestry weaves less frequently used for decoration. The large majority of textiles were woven as rectangular sheets, with a smaller number of woven-to-shape and sewn tunics

---

1 A version of this article was published as Kristin South, "The Use of Basket-Weave Linen in Burials of the Necropolis of Fag el-Gamus, Egypt," in *Excavating, Analysing, Reconstructing. Textiles of the 1st Millennium AD from Egypt and Neighbouring Countries* (*Proceedings of the 9th conference of the research group "Textiles from the Nile Valley,"* 27–29 November 2015), Antoine De Moor, Cäcilia Fluck, and Petra Linscheid, eds. (Tielt, Belgium: Lannoo International, 2017), 88–107.

2 Some have argued that before this era wool does not seem to have been used in Egyptian burials. See Christina Riggs, *Unwrapping Ancient Egypt* (New York: Bloomsbury Academic: 2014), 117.

that were placed as clothing on the bodies or used as wrapping and padding pieces to supplement the rectangular sheets.

A more detailed report on the variety of finds at Fag el-Gamous is in preparation,[3] while this report focuses on one particular aspect of the textile finds from the 2010 and 2013 seasons.

In the 5×5 meter square excavated in 2010 and 2013, a total of 67 burials were numbered and recovered.[4] This section, located in the northwest quadrant of the square defined by the measurement of 130–140 meters to the north of datum point and 20–30 meters west of it, had no unusual distinguishing features to mark it out as extraordinary in any way. It is part of an extensive necropolis that has been calculated as covering 300 hectares and each square thus far excavated has yielded a similar density of burials. This means that there is an extremely high number of burials in the cemetery, although calling them "mummies" oversteps the traditional concept of a mummy. The vast majority of the burials were deposited directly in the hot, dry sand of Egypt's desert, causing natural desiccation to take place and preserving them, in some instances, quite thoroughly. In only a small minority of the burials is there evidence of the traditional pharaonic process of mummification and, even then, most do not include the signature elements of cartonnage, papyri, coffins, and amulets.

Twenty of the 67 burials were completely or almost completely skeletalized.[5] An additional four have not yet been studied.[6] For the other 43, however, at least some textiles were found associated with the human remains although none of them were perfectly preserved. In most cases, for instance, the textiles in the region of the torso were greatly blackened and deteriorated. The best preserved samples usually came from the lower body only.

Regarding dates: Burial NW 3, one of the shallowest and thus likely one of the latest burials, was associated with a piece of 4th century AD pottery. It is the only datable object found in this quadrant. Unfortunately, while the

---

3 Kristin H. South and Anne Kwaspen, report to be presented at VII Purpureae Vestes International Symposium, Granada, Spain, 2019; with intent to publish the report in the proceedings.

4 2010 season finds were numbered 1–23, and 2013 started at 50 and ended at 95. NW 6 was a numbering error that did not correspond to an actual burial, and NW 12, although identified, was not removed from the ground in 2010. It was renumbered in 2013 as NW 51 and was the second burial removed in that year.

5 Defined here as including no more than two numbered textiles in a sufficiently stable condition to acquire a thread count.

6 NW 57, 63, 84, and 85. NW 57 was numbered but fell almost entirely outside of the square and so was not excavated.

original field notes describe the pottery as 4th century, no other information was given whereby we can verify the dating of this pottery, making our dating tentative. The few radiocarbon dates we have obtained at this site generally place the burials in the 1st through 6th centuries AD.[7] However, for this particular quadrant and section of the necropolis that one piece of pottery provides the only specific date. Thus we can be fairly certain that the burials in this study fall within that five century date range but further studies will be needed to pinpoint dates more accurately.

The finds from the quadrant excavated in 2010 and 2013, when compared to burials excavated in previous seasons, can be considered typical of this portion of the necropolis and as such may have relevance for more general burial patterns throughout the cemetery. A close study of several burials in comparison to one another has revealed a pattern in the order in which different types of textiles were placed on the bodies. This paper will begin by describing this pattern then follow with a description of three specific burials to show how this pattern played out in actual instances. It ends with some general observations, ideas, and further questions.

2   Observed Patterns

As noted above,[8] the burials at Fag el-Gamous usually include many layers of linen and minimal amounts of wool. Wool is used in three ways: to decorate linen sheets with colored patterns and images, as ground cloth for sheets made entirely of wool, and as tunics. Linen, on the other hand, occurs overwhelmingly as simple rectangular sheets.[9]

These rectangular sheets are generally of two types: plain weave or basket weave (fig. 7.1). Plain weave (also known as "tabby" weave) is the most basic and simple weave. It is created by alternating one weft thread (the threads that

---

7   [5] R. Paul Evans, David M. Whitchurch, and Kerry Muhlestein, "Rethinking Burial Dates at a Graeco-Roman Cemetery: Fag el-Gamous, Fayoum, Egypt," *Journal of Archaeological Science: Reports* 2 (2015): 209–214.

8   See for instance Kristin H. South, Joyce Y. Smith, Giovanni A. Tata, and C. Wilfred Griggs, "Textile Finds from a Typical Early Christian Burial at Fag el-Gamous (Fayoum), Egypt," *Purpureae Vestes III: Textiles y Tintes en la Ciudad Antigua,* C. Alfaro, J.-P. Brun, Ph. Borgard, R. Pierobon Benoit, eds. (Valencia: University of Valencia Press, 2011); and Kristin H. South, "Minor Burial Textiles and Religious Affiliation: An Archaeological Case Study from Roman Egypt," in *Dressing the Dead in Classical Antiquity*, Maureen Carroll and John P. Wild, eds. (Stroud, Gloucestershire: Amberley Publishing, 2012).

9   Other seasons have revealed tunics made of linen; in this quadrant, however, tunics are all made of wool.

pass back and forth between the warps) over and one weft thread under a set of warp threads (the threads that are affixed to the loom). Basket weave is a kind of shortcut: it is a variation of plain weave in which two or more weft threads at a time are sent over and under two or more warp threads. Basket weave has a coarser appearance, more like a basket, and is easier and faster to make than a plain weave. Although basket weaves do exist at other sites in Egypt, they rarely receive much notice in publications. At Fag el-Gamous the basket weaves have two warp threads and two wefts; those that are called "half-basket" have one weft passing over two warps at a time. Most (98 of 110, or 89%) of the linen sheets designated as basket weave are in the classic two-over-two style, but 12 (11%) were constructed in one-over-two half-basket.[10] For the sake of convenience, both are referred to as basket weaves as they are used in a similar fashion that is notably distinct from the use of the plain weaves.

Of the 43 burials studied, all included plain-weave linen while only six did not include any basket weave linen. Of the six burials without basket weave, it is possible to say with certainty that three of them[11] (9%, n=43) never included any basket weave, as all of the layers of wrappings were preserved at least in part. The other three are burials of young children or infants.[12] This means that 91% of preserved adult burials include basket weave and 73% of child and infant burials (8 of 11) do as well. All three of the child burials without basket weave, though, are part of the same cluster burial, meaning that they were buried at the same time (and were thus at least from the same time period, if not also related to one another and prepared for burial by the same individuals with the same expectations and perhaps the same economic resources). Additionally, one of the three adult burials without basket weave (NW 88) was part of that same cluster. This coincidence of usage implies a deliberate choice of when to include or omit basket weave layers, and suggests that, apart from these four linked burials, it was rare for an individual to be buried without at least some basket weave linen. The basket weave sheets share several distinguishing features including self-bands, extensive fringes, and similar thread counts.

Although not the main focus of this paper, a note must be inserted regarding self-bands. 75% of the basket weaves were constructed with the inclusion of extra weft threads or one much coarser thread in one shot (a single pass of weft

---

10   The half-basket samples are spread over seven different burials (NW 1, 4, 5, 17, 19, 65, and 78). Based on the counts and location found on the body, it is likely that 65.3 and 65.4 are actually two fragments of the same original sheet, and are counted only once.

11   NW 11, NW 23, and NW 88.

12   NW 89, NW 91, and NW 92.

threads through the warp), to create a ribbed look. These "self-bands," by comparison occur on only 24% of the plain weaves. The usual pattern at Fag el-Gamous, where self-bands occur in multitudes, is for one shot of extra wefts to be followed by two shots (one of each shed) of plain weave, followed by another set of extra threads, then two more plain shots, then a third set of extra threads.[13] Like four tunics from Egypt now in the Louvre and dated to the 5th to 7th centuries,[14] many of our basket weave linen sheets have self-bands that continue throughout the entire length of the cloth and are separated at regular intervals (fig. 7.2). Already in use by the 4th Dynasty as recorded in the finds of the Rowad Trench at Giza,[15] this decorative technique appears to have changed little in the intervening 3000 years. At Fag el-Gamous, self-bands appear both as irregular or infrequent markings at seemingly random intervals or as more regular elements. In those pieces of cloth large enough to detect an overall pattern, the self-bands repeated sometimes at very regular distances (17 samples) but twice as often at approximate distances (38 samples) within a range that varied by up to 2 cm—indicating, perhaps, that the weaver was eyeing the distances rather than counting wefts. The most common distances between self-bands were 4–5 cm, but these samples came from two burials in total (NW 68 and NW 78), suggesting that the increased incidence is due to preservation. 27% (n=30) of the basket weave sheets included preserved fringes. The fringes ranged from 1–19 cm in length, and the majority were 18 cm or longer. The fringes in each case were simple, with no special treatment to fix the final weft threads in place or create any kind of decoration. In three cases, all from the same burial,[16] they were uncut. The longer fringes were often treated as part of the cloth and tucked around the feet.[17]

---

13   Lise Bender Jorgensen, "Self-bands and Other Subtle Patterns in Roman Textiles," *Purpureae Vestes II. Vestidos, Textiles y Tintes. Estudios Sobre la Producción de Bienes de Consumo en la Antigüedad*, C. Alfaro and L. Karali, ed. (Valencia, Spain: University of Valencia Press, 2008): 135–141 remarks that these and other "subtle patterns" have been noted most often as a design feature in linen textiles, but are more common at Mons Claudianus among the wool textiles. At Fag el-Gamous, they occur predominantly among the linen samples. Where they are less than 10% of the total sample at Mons Claudianus (Jorgensen, "Self-bands," 135), they occur on the majority of pieces at Fag el-Gamous.

14   Roberta Cortopassi, "Late Roman and Byzantine Linen Tunics in the Louvre Museum," in *Ancient Textiles: Production, Crafts, and Society*, Carole Gillis and Marie-Louise Nosch, eds. (Oxford: Oxbow Books, 2007), 139–142. Here they are separated by 1.5 to 3 cm, but on our pieces the distances are more varied.

15   Edward D. Johnson, "GPMP 2004 Field Season Report on Textiles from the Road Trench," *Bulletin of the Egyptian Museum* 5 (2008): 46.

16   NW 78.

17   Examples include NW 60.4, 68.14, 68.16, 73.20, and 78.5.

The basket weaves tend to have very similar thread counts. They are over-whelmingly warp-faced (92 of 96 with useable thread count data) with only four listed as balanced weaves[18] and 0 confirmed cases of weft-faced weaves.[19] A large number of sheets have similar or identical counts: 16 sheets were 18/10 (with an additional three at 18/8) and 21 were 14/8 (plus 1 at 14/10). Those at 16/8 and 16/10 made up another 21 total. The uniform look and thread counts of the basket weave show that they are the products of a thriving and regulated state industry rather than homemade products. Documents from ancient Tebtunis, a nearby city, confirm this impression, with a charge to an official whose func-tion was to inspect the weaving factories to make certain "that the linen is of good quality and has the number of threads prescribed in the ordinance."[20] The basket weave linen of Fag el-Gamous was indeed of good, uniform quality.

With these details about basket weave sheets in mind, consider next their pattern of use: basket weaves are by far the most numerous sheets in the buri-als that preserved each layer of wrappings. In these "complete" burials, basket weaves always occur as the middle layers of wrapping, i.e. the second from the body up to the second from the outside. There are no instances of plain weave and basket weave layers intermixed: the pattern of plain weave outer layer, bas-ket weave middle layers, and plain weave innermost, is ubiquitous. The only exceptions, which seem to prove the rule, use basket weave as the outermost layer as well as the middle layers (NW 73 and NW 74) but still had plain weave as the layer closest to the body. Generally, though, the pattern was plain weave, followed by basket weave, followed by plain weave again. The following exam-ples will illustrate this pattern.

3   Burials NW 68, 73, and 78 (and other associated, similar burials)

Because of the better state of their preservation, three burials yielded some of the most complete data for the quadrant. Each was an adult, buried directly in

---

18   NW 52.1, 78.24 (a half-basket), NW 73.5A, and NW 82.5.

19   One piece (NW 14.3), recorded by an inexperienced student, was listed at 14/20, but no photographic evidence exists to confirm her analysis, which was also not double-checked by a regular member of the team.

20   Papyrus Tebtunis 703 from Michel M. Austin, *The Hellenistic World from Alexander to the Roman Conquest: A Selection of Ancient Sources in Translation* (Cambridge: Cambridge University Press, 1981), 255–256, as quoted in Gillian E. Bowen, "Texts and Textiles: A Study of the Textile Industry in Ancient Kellis," *The Artefact* 24 (2001): 24. In a discussion of the weaving industry in Kellis, Bowen notes that although this is a description that dates from the Ptolemaic era, the regulations continued into Roman times as well.

the sand alongside and similar to all of the others in this section of the necropolis. We were able to determine without question the number and order of the textile remains on the lower half of each body, although in each case the upper halves, including the torso, were not well preserved (fig. 7.3). These three burials (NW 68, NW 73, and NW 78) included great similarities that seem to indicate a set of burial practices that were common to all three and likely common to many of the others. A brief description of the "normal" course of these burials follows.

NW 68 (length 165 cm, burial depth 113 cm, a female between 21–25 years old) had as its outer layer a comparatively fine weave with a 21/18 count, self-bands, open warp, and fringe (fig. 7.4). It was tucked under the feet and sewn in place. The typical red-and-white "ribbons"[21] covered and secured the outer layer and were also used between the outermost and second layers.

Ten separate basket weave sheets followed,[22] consistently with thread counts of 16–18/10. For the inner (hidden) layers, torn strips of linen held the wrappings together (rather than purpose-made ribbons).

Closest to the body (68.19, 68.21, and 68.22) were small fragments of plain weave with wide oxidized[23] false purple stripes (now dark green) (fig. 7.5), pile with 2 cm loops, and open warp sections (fig. 7.6).[24] The feel and look of this layer closest to the body (68.19) was similar to the outermost layer (68.2).

In sum, Burial NW 68 included at least 12 layers of linen (Table 7.1). The innermost and outermost layers were constructed in plain weave, and the middle layers were all basket weave. The outermost layer of ribbons holding the burial together were constructed in a decorative red and white pattern, while the hidden inner bandages were held together with strips of linen torn from the selvedge edges of the basket weave shrouds.

NW 73 (length 171 cm, burial depth 138 cm, a female between 21–25 years old) followed the same general pattern (Table 7.2), with one difference: the burial made use of 11 layers of basket weave wrapping (14–16/8) *including* the

---

21   Kristin H. South and Kerry Muhlestein, "Regarding Ribbons: The Spread and Use of Narrow Purpose-Woven Bands in Late-Roman Egyptian Burials," in *Drawing the Threads Together: Textiles and Footwear of the First Millennium AD from Egypt,* Antoine De Moor, Cäcilia Fluck, Petra Linscheid, eds. (Tielt, Belgium: Lannoo Publishers, 2013).

22   A discrepancy of a missing number for the fifth shroud in the field analysis, however, makes it possible that only nine basket weave layers were present.

23   I am indebted to Emilia Cortez for this suggestion of how to understand our frequent finding of wool that started as false purple but has now turned green.

24   NW 68.19, 68.21, 68.23, 68.24, and 68.27. Please note that the dyes have not been analyzed, but it is safe to assume that all mention of "purple" in this chapter refers not to true purple but to a mixture of less expensive dyes. See the article on purple dyes in the volume.

outermost layer. An additional six sheets were cut and folded and placed over different parts of the body (torso to knees, ankles), perhaps as padding. Torn strips of basket weave linen were used to hold each sheet in place, and the outermost layer appeared to have been sewn in place around the feet (fig. 7.7). Each sheet had a repeating pattern of self-bands. The layer next to the body, in plain weave, (NW 73.21 and 73.22) incorporated all of the usual decorative elements: open warp, fringe, colored wool, and self-bands (fig. 7.8). A second piece of plain weave, found around the torso, probably came from the same sheet originally, but now has only had a wide band of z-twist false purple wool preserved.

NW 78 (length 180 cm, burial depth 104 cm, a male between 35–40 years) displayed the same pattern (Table 7.3). In this case, a half-basket outer layer was followed by nine basket weave sheets, (most with thread counts of 14/8), completely wrapped around the body and an additional seven cut and folded pieces covering smaller portions of the body. Although the innermost layers are not well preserved, they seem to consist of two separate plain weave layers, one with open warp and a long fringe (thread count 14/8) and the innermost with self-bands, open warp, and thin lines of green/purple wool near the ends. A face bundle made predominantly of basket weave layers made way for a layer of plain weave linen right next to the face.[25]

Although these are the three best preserved and recorded burials, at least 10 others[26] reinforce the observed pattern: plain weave is the outermost layer when two or more layers of plain weave are present, the middle layers are basket weave, and the layer closest to the body is constructed of plain weave. Where only one layer of plain weave exists, it is next to the body rather than outermost.

4   General Observations and Further Questions

Several other aspects of these burials were uniform enough to make generalizations, which follow below:

In all three of the above-mentioned burials, and as found in most of the other burials, the basket weave pieces had both selvedges cut off anciently before they were employed for burial. The torn strips of linen used to wrap the

---

25   For more on face bundles typical of this site, see Kristin H. South, "'Face Bundles' in Early Christian Burials from the Fayoum," *Archaeological Textiles Newsletter* 48 (2009): 2–5.

26   NW 4, 17, 21, 23, 54, 64, 74, 79, 82, and 95.

bodies almost certainly came from these same linen sheets: the thread counts, self-band, and distances between self-bands, were often identical.

Colored wool decoration occurs on all three burials on a layer closest to the body. The small sample makes it difficult to generalize, but this placement of wool decoration next to the body seems to be the prevailing pattern whenever weft shots of wool are present: in five of seven burials, a linen sheet that includes weft wool bands is placed directly next to the body, and the placement on the other two is inconclusive.[27] This pattern of usage suggests that the people preparing the bodies for burial knew of certain expectations that they followed regularly, even on layers that would never be seen, and that those expectations included decorative elements next to the body.

More generally, wool figured as a decorative element in 17 of the burials, with 28 textile pieces, total, including wool. Two were sprang caps on the heads of the deceased (NW 1 and NW 51.1), seven or eight were all-wool pieces, at least five of which were tunics.[28] Notably, of all five burials that included wool-ground tunics, each was a burial of a child or infant.[29] A closer examination of child burials is a large and important topic currently being researched.[30]

The addition of wool to an otherwise all-linen piece requires an extra level of effort, so it would be logical to expect wool to occur only in those pieces that were constructed in plain weave, if it is accurate to suppose that the presence of basket weave is due to a desire for cheap filling layers. Observation bears this out: none of the pieces employing wool were constructed in basket weave. Rather, some of them included even more decorative elements, indicating additional higher value: self-bands occurred on three pieces into which weft bands of wool had been inserted,[31] and two of the three pieces also incorporated

27   NW 68, 73, 74, 78, and probably 79. NW 82 uses linen with colored wool bands as the outermost and second layers; while NW 88 has a linen sheet as the second of four layers (counting from the outermost). Textiles of NW 82 and NW 88 were very incomplete or deteriorated, though, so the pattern may have held here as well.

28   NW 5.5 (yellow wool tunic); NW 8.1 (undyed wool tunic); NW 8.2 (probable tunic, undyed wool); NW 89.3 (probable tunic with plant motifs on wool ground, but not enough remains for certain identification); NW 91.4 (wool ground tunic); NW 92.5 (wool ground tunic); NW 92.6 (probable tunic, used as shroud); NW 92.8 (tunic wadded into a face bundle, not yet analyzed).

29   NW 5, 8, 89, 91, and 92.

30   R. Paul Evans and Kerry Muhlestein, "Death of a Child: The Demographic and Preparation Trends of Child Burials in the Greco-Roman Fayoum of Egypt," in *Handbook of Children of Antiquity*, Lesly Beaumont, Matthew Dillon, and Nicola Harrington, eds. (Routledge, forthcoming).

31   NW 68.19 and 68.24 are counted as one piece; NW 82.8, NW 73.21 and 73.22 are also counted as one piece. Additionally, a warp-faced plain weave piece, NW 88.4, may have had

open warp sections near a fringe. This shows that the most technically compli-cated textiles in the necropolis—apart from reused tunics—used plain weave and a mix of self-bands, colored wool, open warp, and a well-defined fringe for their decoration. Such a combination never occurs in basket weave, where the decoration is limited to repeating self-bands.

Apart from the reused tunics, the textiles used for the burials were all rect-angular in shape. The basket weave sheets, in particular, appeared to have been purpose-woven for burial use. As such, it seems reasonable to use the term "shroud" in discussing them: three pieces appear quite new in every well-preserved case, giving the impression that they were created specifically for burial. They show no sign of wear, are bright in color, and are flexible, crisp, and clean to the touch and appearance (fig. 7.9). Unpublished SEM analysis com-pleted in 2012 on similar pieces from this site shows smooth fibers that even under great magnification display little breakage or abrasion (fig. 7.10). The plain weaves, on the other hand, appear to vary in their pre-burial use. Many more show visible signs of wear, although this is hard to determine accurately because they were placed either next to the body, where they are the first to deteriorate, or on the outside of the burial, where they are more likely to be in contact with abrasive sand.

The most striking and consistent finding in this study of one discrete set of burials pertains to the use of basket weaves. They were cheap, easy to produce, and plentiful, and yet in this set of burials they were never placed as the layer closest to the body. That position seems to have been reserved for plain weave sheets that often included several decorative elements: weft bands of colored wool, open warp sections, long fringes, and self-bands. Among these burials, at least, none of the adults appear to have been clothed before being wrapped in rectangular sheets, although children and babies were often dressed or wrapped in wool tunics. No tunics constructed in basket weave have been found at Fag el-Gamous.

The observed textile placement pattern in these burials appears to demon-strate that plain weave was the ideal, and hence it was used whenever possible for the layer that was seen (outermost) and the layer that actually touched the body (innermost). Plain weave, especially when finished with one or more decorative elements, is of a higher quality than basket weave linen, and thus more respectful to the deceased. The unseen middle layers, when necessary, could be filled out with the more inexpensive basket weave. If this conjecture accurately describes an economic motivation behind the observed patterns,

two ribs present, but they may instead have only been two extra thick linen wefts used, so this piece was omitted. Another eight pieces with colored wool wefts had no self-bands.

then the three adult burials[32] that employed only plain weave sheets (with no basket weaves present) would be expected to demonstrate other indications of wealth. This is, indeed, the case:

- NW 11, a well-preserved adult burial, included carefully-made red and white ribbons, a face bundle, and symmetric wrapping (fig. 7.11). It was also partially enclosed in a limestone covering, which is unusual for this site (fig. 7.12).
- NW 23 included purpose-woven red and white ribbon and had eight long supporting palm sticks wrapped parallel to the body in the innermost layer of cloth. The skull was exposed, so it is not possible to say if a face bundle was originally present. This burial, like NW 11, was separated from the mass of burials. In this case, the separation was enacted by the use of a line of mud bricks along one side. Again, this is an unusual inclusion for burials at this site.
- NW 88 also had palm sticks placed parallel to the body underneath the burial in the sand as supports, and others wrapped inside the linen along the sides of the body (fig. 7.13). This burial included the most colorful type of ribbon found on site (fig. 7.14), woven of three colors of dyed linen (red, white, and brown). The head was missing as a result of exposure during the 2010 season, so the presence or absence of a face bundle is unknown. This burial was part of a cluster that included three children,[33] all of which were buried with wool tunics (comprising five of the total of eight tunics found). It makes sense to suppose that these child burials with wool tunics are indicative of greater-than-average wealth. Supporting this idea, these three child burials are the only other well-preserved burials without any basket weave present.

Half-basket weaves present a complication to the picture that is emerging. Half-basket weaves would take longer to make than a traditional two-over-two basket weave and hence would probably sell at a higher price, although still less than plain weaves. If economic conditions informed the use of half-basket weaves, we would expect to find other indications of potential above-average wealth in the seven burials that make use of them instead of traditional basket weave. This does turn out to be accurate in at least four of the seven cases: NW 1, with 10 layers of half-basket weaves, also included a face bundle and a red

---

32   NW 11, NW 23, and NW 88. Four additional intact child burials did not include any basket weave. These burials are discussed below.

33   NW 89, NW 91, and NW 92.

and green sprang cap.[34] NW 5, although very poorly preserved, included a beautifully dyed red outer ribbon, wooden sticks to support the body, more than one layer of plain weave, and a tunic. NW 17, also very poorly preserved, included both four layers of half-basket weave and a fine plain-weave sheet next to the body, as well as bits of limestone, wood, and palm ribs around the body—indicating a richer burial with a possible wooden coffin or at least a delineated lining. NW 65 included two types of purpose-woven ribbon, one in white and one in red, as well as glass, faience, and potsherds (fig. 7.15). Rope associated with a set of reeds makes it likely that the entire burial was placed atop a now-deteriorated mat.

NW 78, the final instance of a use of half-basket weave, presents a picture of possible poverty rather than abundance. For NW 78, it seems that the people who prepared the body for burial understood a clear hierarchy of quality: the hidden middle nine layers are all two-over-two basket weaves, and the innermost layer is a plain weave, but for the outermost layer, they used half-basket. Torn strips are used to hold it together. A moderately lower economic status seems thus to be indicated both by the use of torn strips instead of ribbons and by the inability to procure plain weave for the outermost layer. This choice of inclusion order for the three types of weaves would also seem to show that the layer closest to the body matters even more than the one visible on the outside.

In sum, the primary motivation for using basket weave shrouds (either of a regular two-over-two pattern or of a one-over-two half-basket pattern) appears to be economic necessity,[35] but they were used in such a way that their presence was not obvious and they did not come into contact with the body itself. The differences follow a wholly consistent pattern: the unobserved middle layers are the place where cheap basket weave can be inserted, but the body itself should be shrouded in finer material. The visible outer shroud, where possible, should be made of the highest quality, sheer linen (fig. 7.16). Economic

---

34   NW 4, the burial of a baby, was too poorly preserved to determine much from its remains, except that it included both the innermost and outermost layers of plain-weave linen, and the middle layers were all half-basket weave. NW 19 also did not include other indications of wealth, but the burial itself followed the usual pattern of a plain-weave outermost layer and another plain-weave innermost layer, with six layers of half-basket weave in between, held together with torn strips of linen.

35   Undoubtedly, many factors beyond economy contributed to the way a body was prepared for burial (see Christina Riggs, *Unwrapping Ancient Egypt*, 79–94). Yet, despite this truism, in the case of the use of basket weave, it truly does seem to be economic, for it was clearly a style that those who prepared the burial wished to remain unseen.

constraints make the use of basket weave possible, but when it could be avoided, it was.

The present conclusions regarding economic motivations vary from past speculations about possible religious motives for observed differences in burials at this site.[36] In this section of the necropolis, the burials are more similar to one another than in some other areas—for instance, other sections do include adults clothed in wool tunics—and so these slight differences stand out against a backdrop of uniformity. This could arise from their possibly deriving from a shorter historical span or from a time period after the major changes in religion and burial practices had occurred. Further research comparing similar but disparate burials is needed for a greater understanding of the range of acceptable burial practices in the eastern Fayoum in the Late Roman and Early Byzantine eras.

TABLE 7.1   Layers of linen wrappings extant on Burial NW 68

Textile #	make	warp / cm	weft / cm	longest remaining edge (cm)	of note	Basket weave present?	Excavation notes and observations
68.1	undyed ribbon						*Outermost decorative binding ribbon.* Two sheds of 6 warps each, of which 2 on each side have 2 threads/shed. The middle threads may have been dyed slightly darker. A knot of this ribbon is centered over the top of the foot bundle.
68.2	plain weave	21	18		selvedge self bands		*Fine linen outer layer.* 8 cm between self-band patterns. 3.5 cm wide open warp then 2.5 cm woven, then fringe. Around the foot area, 68.2 is gathered and stitched into place

36   See, for instance, South and Muhlestein, "Regarding Ribbons;" and South, "Minor Burial Textiles and Religious Affiliation."

Textile #	make	warp / cm	weft / cm	longest remaining edge (cm)	of note	Basket weave present?	Excavation notes and observations
68.3	torn strips (basket weave)	18	10	1 m+	torn strips self bands	x	*Torn strips used as binding* over 2nd shroud, with overall self-band pattern 4–5 cm apart. Strips are 1–5 cm wide. One piece of the wide torn strip is actually 10 cm wide and splits to be tied and twisted around the feet.
68.4	basket weave	18	10		self bands	x	*First basket weave shroud.* 4–5 cm between sets of self bands. Same measurements as 68.3 (likely the shroud from which the strips were torn).
68.5	basket weave	18	10	120	self bands	x	*Second basket weave shroud.* Fully wrapped around body. Large, well-preserved. 4–5 cm between weft self bands. Neither selvedge is present, although the textile is well preserved. Both appear cut. Probably used as torn strips.
68.6	basket weave	18	10	122	self bands	x	Only *over feet* (so not numbered as an overall shroud)—folded and placed on feet. self bands 4–5 cm apart overall on piece. When unfolded, a wool thread of dark green (oxidized?) was present but not woven or sewn in.

TABLE 7.1   Layers of linen wrappings extant on Burial NW 68 (*cont.*)

Textile #	make	warp / cm	weft / cm	longest remaining edge (cm)	of note	Basket weave present?	Excavation notes and observations
68.7	basket weave	18	10	116	self bands	x	*3rd overall shroud.* Basket weave. Self bands similar to others of this burial, with same distances. No selvedges: torn on each side. Not preserved enough in warp direction to get definitive length. Placed on left side of front of body, then folded all the way under the body, then ends along right leg.
68.8	basket weave	18	10	113	self bands	x	*4th overall shroud.* Same self-band pattern as above. One edge along left side of body, wraps around, ends over other edge on right side of body (same pattern as with 3rd). Fringe 13.5 cm long.
68.9	torn strips (basket weave)	18	10	1 m+	fringe	x	*Torn strips used as binding.* Tied in knot over top of foot—*over basket weave shroud #5.* Includes selvedge. Includes a piece 6 cm wide that forks to go around feet.
68.10	basket weave	16	10	111	self bands	x	*6th overall shroud.* twisted at feet and piled at bottom of feet. Wrapped from right leg (at top) around body. Same self-band pattern as others.

Textile #	make	warp / cm	weft / cm	longest remaining edge (cm)	of note	Basket weave present?	Excavation notes and observations
68.11	basket weave	16	10	111	self bands fringe	x	*7th overall shroud.* Starts under the left leg, wraps toward the right, goes under, ends over left leg. Same self-band pattern as others. 19 cm fringe.
68.12	basket weave	18	10	63	self bands	x	Laid over *the top of the feet.* Cut to a rectangle (63 × 46) and folded three times to 10.5 cm width and 29 cm length. Same self-band pattern as above except in one spot where a second band runs along directly next to the expected one for 14 cm.
68.13	basket weave	16	10	62	self bands fringe "smocked"	x	A single piece of linen folded and placed *between the legs*, ending before the feet. Folded to 18 am width. Same self-band pattern. Along three of the ribbed sections one part (ca 3–4 cm current width) appears smocked—the rib wefts are pulled tight and cannot be opened completely. This appears to be coincidental and not deliberately decorative or functional.

TABLE 7.1   Layers of linen wrappings extant on Burial NW 68 (*cont.*)

Textile #	make	warp / cm	weft / cm	longest remaining edge (cm)	of note	Basket weave present?	Excavation notes and observations
68.14	basket weave	16	10	118	self bands fringe	x	Weft count is 8–10. Piece starts on *left leg*, wrapped under (to the left) and returning to the left—not wrapped all the way around. Fringe 16 cm long, tucked up over the feet. Warp length of 58 excludes the fringe. Weft length of 118 is without selvedges, both of which are cut. Self-band pattern as before, overall. Distance between sets is 5–7 cm.
68.15	basket weave	18	10	101	self bands fringe	x	This is laid symmetric to 68.14—over the *right leg*, folded behind, and back to the front. Same self-band pattern. Long fringe (19 cm).
68.16	basket weave	18	10	113	self bands fringe	x	*8th overall shroud*—outermost edge is along the bottom of the body with fringe (16 cm) tucked up over the top of the feet and wrapped at least twice around. Wrapping starts on left leg, wraps to the right, goes all around the body twice, then ends underneath the body.
68.17	basket weave	18	10	112	self bands	x	*9th overall shroud.* self bands as above. End folded over feet from below. Outermost edge of shroud underneath the body.

Textile #	make	warp / cm	weft / cm	longest remaining edge (cm)	of note	Basket weave present?	Excavation notes and observations
68.18	basket weave	16	10	104	self bands fringe	x	*10th and final basket weave shroud.* Fringe end (14 cm) is folded up from under the body and comes nearly to the knees. Weft count is 8–10.
68.19	plain weave	13	8		self bands wool		Multiple small fragments. *Layer closest to the body at the lower legs,* similar in appearance to 68.2 (outermost layer). Two individual lines of wool. Wool is green (oxidized?).
68.20	un-dyed and red ribbon						*Binding* under one layer of plain weave. Ribbon poorly preserved but has at least 2 red warps. Found at the outer edge of the burial, so: ribbon/plain weave / ribbon (68.20) then basket weave. (Numbered in turn of observation, not of order found. It appears to have been at the same level as the torn strips 68.3, but from another part of the body.)
68.21	plain weave with added col-ored wool	23	16, 28		wool		*Down center of body* is a well-preserved purple band with alternating purple and undyed threads. Only runs for 8 cm of the 40 cm preserved band. Weft counts are 16 for linen, 28 for wool. Location on the body relative to other shrouds not recorded.

TABLE 7.1   Layers of linen wrappings extant on Burial NW 68 (*cont.*)

Textile #	make	warp / cm	weft / cm	longest remaining edge (cm)	of note	Basket weave present?	Excavation notes and observations
68.22	plain weave	26	17		face bundle self bands		Fine woven shroud on the *face bundle*—18 layers of fine weave with weft ribs. Probably same fabric folded over multiple times.
68.23	plain weave	19	12		pile weave		Pile weave fragment with fine plain weave. Context on the body uncertain, *possibly shoulder or upper chest.* No body fluid stains. Pile loops are 2 cm long, repeat 1.5 cm apart.
68.24	plain weave	12	9		self bands "purple" wool open warp fringe		From *shoulder?* Context uncertain. Fine weave. Random self bands with no repeating pattern. Purple wool threads in weft direction. Open warp, fringe or frayed.
68.25	basket weave					x	Multiple small pieces of basket weave numbered together for convenience. Location not recorded.
68.26	basket weave	18	10		face bundle	x	*Face bundle.* Multiple layers folded back on itself. Standard basket weave with self bands. Typical of shrouds on lower body and may be the upper extension of one of the inner basket weave shrouds.

Textile #	make	warp / cm	weft / cm	longest remaining edge (cm)	of note	Basket weave present?	Excavation notes and observations
68.27	weft face plain	26	16, 28		"purple" wool		Found as *closest layer over the head.* Weft-faced plain weave with additional purple weft sections. Wool weft is 28/cm. Very fine. Purple bands on a linen field. Some discoloration to green. Linen bands are very fine and tightly woven. Note that the counts are nearly identical to 68.21 and may indicate the same piece.
68.28	basket weave					x	Multiple layers of basket weave folded randomly about *head.*
68.29	plain weave	18	12	33	pile weave "purple" wool		*Head covering.* Probably the same piece of pile weave as 68.23, but this piece also displays a weft wool purple band.

TABLE 7.2   Layers of linen wrappings extant on Burial NW 73

Textile #	make	warp / cm	weft / cm	longest remaining edge (cm)	of note	Basket weave present?	Excavation notes and observations
73.1	basket weave	20	8		torn strips self bands	x	*Outermost binding.* Folded once to width of nearly 2 cm. Distance between self bands: 7 cm, 11 cm.

TABLE 7.2   Layers of linen wrappings extant on Burial NW 73. (*cont.*)

Textile #	make	warp / cm	weft / cm	longest remaining edge (cm)	of note	Basket weave present?	Excavation notes and observations
73.2	basket weave	16	10		self bands	x	*Outermost shroud.* Weft self bands. Distances vary 11–14 cm. Possibly sewn over the ends to keep the shroud in place. One sewn thread appears to hold it. Tucked under the feet and extends 40 cm up the underside of the body on both sides.
73.3	basket weave	18	10	54	self bands fringe	x	Folded and placed on top from the *knees to the feet.* No selvedges (cut). Self bands 3–4.5 cm apart. Fringe 3 cm.
73.4	basket weave	16	10		torn strips self bands	x	*Torn binding strips* over full length of remaining body. 2 cm folded. Includes a 14 cm wide strip torn in middle then wrapped around feet and knotted over the tops of the feet.
73.5	basket weave	20	10	101	self bands fringe	x	*2nd overall shroud.* Covers feet and extends under body with upper edge along right leg. Both weft edges cut. Fringe present (5 cm). Self bands.
73.6	basket weave	12	8	108	self bands fringe	x	*3rd overall shroud.* Wrapped all the way under. Both selvedges cut. Self band pattern, repeats every 6–7 cm.

Textile #	make	warp / cm	weft / cm	longest remaining edge (cm)	of note	Basket weave present?	Excavation notes and observations
73.7	basket weave	16	8	108	self bands fringe	x	*4th overall shroud.* Does not wrap over feet. Extends under body. Self bands 5–6 cm apart. Fringe 2–3 cm.
73.8	basket weave	16	8	110	self bands fringe	x	*5th overall.* Cut on both sides and possibly on fringe end as well. One fringe remains, 2 cm long. Self bands repeat 5–9 cm. The shroud was centered under the body then wrapped up over the top.
73.9	basket weave	14	8		self bands fringe	x	*Over torso, ends below knees* with fringe (2–3 cm) at bottom. Too deterio-rated on bottom for overall measurements. Was wrapped under body and two ends met over the top.
73.10	basket weave	18	8		self bands	x	Smaller piece, ends *near/below the knee,* like 73.9. Self bands with 6.5 - 7.5 cm repeat. General note: Most of these shroud pieces are oriented with the weft running across the body. This piece, however, is perpendicular, with the weft in line with the head-to-foot line of the body. Cut edges.
73.11	basket weave	14	8	108	self bands	x	Folded over the *ankles, ends around top of thigh.* Vertical to the body like 73.10. Self bands repeat 9–10.5 cm.

TABLE 7.2   Layers of linen wrappings extant on Burial NW 73. (*cont.*)

Textile #	make	warp / cm	weft / cm	longest remaining edge (cm)	of note	Basket weave present?	Excavation notes and observations
73.12	basket weave	14	8	99	self bands	x	*6th overall shroud* (?) but ends at toes (does not go under the feet) and does not continue under the body—placed over the top. For dimensions: 99×58, cut in three directions and deteriorated in 4th. Self bands repeat every 8–10.5 cm.
73.13	basket weave	16	8	56	self bands	x	Small piece (padding?) ends at *knees*—goes to just under left leg. Weft vertical to body. Self bands with 10 cm repeat. Edges cut.
73.14	basket weave	16	8		self bands	x	A 22 cm wide strip that continues down the body then splits to *tie around the feet*. Goes all the way up the body as far as preserved. Self bands repeat 5–7 cm.
73.15	basket weave	14	8	144	self bands	x	*7th overall shroud*. Wraps all the way around the bottom of the body with ends tucked under the feet. Two torn edges, one cut end. Self bands repeat 7–9 cm.
73.16	basket weave	16	8	108	self bands	x	*8th overall shroud*. Wrapped fully around body. Two cut edges. Self bands repeat every 4–6.5 cm.

Textile #	make	warp / cm	weft / cm	longest remaining edge (cm)	of note	Basket weave present?	Excavation notes and observations
73.17	basket weave	18	8	142	self bands	x	*9th overall shroud.* Ends wrapped over feet instead of under as in past recent layers. Two edges cut. End cut. Self bands repeat mostly 5 cm apart but some 10–10.5 cm apart.
73.18	basket weave	16	8	94	self bands	x	*10th overall shroud.* Fringe 6 cm at ankles. Whole piece wrapped under body. Self bands repeat 5–6.5 cm. 2 cut edges.
73.19	basket weave	14	8	76	self bands	x	Single piece laid *over the top of the body* from ankles upward. Self bands repeat 5.5–6.5 cm. Two cut edges, cut end. 76 × 62 cm total size.
73.20	basket weave	16	8	106	self bands	x	*11th and final basket weave shroud.* Wrapped twice around the feet with 7 cm fringe at end tucked under the feet. Self bands repeat 6–6.5 cm. Both sides cut.
73.21	plain weave	14	10		self bands open warp fringe "purple" wool		*Closest layer to body* at feet and legs. Two sets of self bands near the open warp. Z-twist purple/green wool weft bands. Open warp and fringe also present.
73.22	plain weave	7	32		wool		Found near the *torso*. May be another piece of 73.21. Fine z-twist wool now green, possibly originally false purple. Two layers found together. Too ill-preserved to say

TABLE 7.2   Layers of linen wrappings extant on Burial NW 73. (*cont.*)

Textile #	make	warp / cm	weft / cm	longest remaining edge (cm)	of note	Basket weave present?	Excavation notes and observations
							anything about decoration—appears to be a wide single colored band. Note: An additional five textile fragments were recorded as coming from this burial, but their original location on the body could not be determined. For the purposes of this study, they have been omitted from this list.

TABLE 7.3   Layers of linen wrappings extant on Burial NW 78

Textile #	make	warp / cm	weft / cm	longest remaining edge (cm)	of note	Basket weave present?	Excavation notes and observations
78.1	basket weave	20	8		torn strips	x	*Outermost binding.* Torn strips on outermost layer of mummy. Some selvedges. Folded to 2 cm, unfold to 4–6 cm. Self bands repeat every 8–10 cm.
78.2	half basket	13	16	77		x	*Outermost shroud.* This number 78.2 also includes a 9 cm wide torn strip that is knotted over the feet— has nearly the same count as the main piece (13×14). The knotted piece includes a selvedge.

Textile #	make	warp / cm	weft / cm	longest remaining edge (cm)	of note	Basket weave present?	Excavation notes and observations
78.3	basket weave	18	8		torn strips self bands	x	*Torn binding strips around feet* (and up body, presumably but badly preserved there), on same layer as the knot noted with 78.2 Folded to 2 cm. Self bands repeat every 7.5–8 cm, one at 4 cm.
78.4	basket weave	16	8	124	self bands fringe	x	*2nd shroud.* Under the feet and wrapped over the right leg, then bunched between the legs, not in layers but as a longitudinal wad. Edges are cut. One fringe end, 5 cm.
78.5	basket weave	16	10	112	self bands fringe	x	*3rd shroud.* No torn strips between this and 78.4. Bottommost side is on right leg, then wrapped around bottom outer side of body, then over left leg and tucked under right leg at topmost edge. Nice 11.5 cm fringe over the tops of the feet.
78.6	basket weave	14	8	100	self bands	x	*4th shroud.* Cut edges. No fringe.
78.7	basket weave	14	8	128	self bands fringe	x	*5th shroud.* Cut sides. One end preserved with fringe. Bottommost edge on right leg wrapped under body, over left leg, and ends over right leg again. Fringe 6 cm.

TABLE 7.3   Layers of linen wrappings extant on Burial NW 78. (*cont.*)

Textile #	make	warp / cm	weft / cm	longest remaining edge (cm)	of note	Basket weave present?	Excavation notes and observations
78.8	basket weave	12	8	148	self bands	x	Cut edge placed along right leg, continues under soles of feet, goes up left leg (*in a u-shape*). Does not continue under body.
78.9	basket weave	14	8	100	self bands fringe	x	*Folded over top of body* with fringe (3 cm) folded to the top. Deteriorated at top. Cut edges.
78.10	basket weave	14	8	100	self bands	x	*Folded and laid over legs* similar to 78.9. Folded dimensions 50 cm x 25 xm. Cut edges.
78.11	basket weave	12	8	112	self bands loom string end	x	Folded and laid over legs *down middle of body.* Folded width 28 cm. Length 53 cm + 3 cm loom ends.
78.12	basket weave	18	4	112	self bands	x	Another piece *folded over legs and placed along central axis of body.* Folded vertically then folded again same way. Warp length 54 cm. End seems cut, no fringe.
78.13	basket weave	14	8	107	self bands fringe	x	Wrapped along *the length of the left leg.* More bunched than folded. Looped fringe (uncut). Edges are cut.
78.14	basket weave	14	8		self bands fringe	x	Same position as 78.13, only *along the right leg.* Looped fringe, very deteriorated. Cut edges. Too deteriorated for overall dimensions.

Textile #	make	warp / cm	weft / cm	longest remaining edge (cm)	of note	Basket weave present?	Excavation notes and observations
78.15	basket weave	14–18	8		self bands fringe	x	*Torn binding strips* over the next burial shroud, under 78.13 and 78.14. Also goes around the feet. Folded to 2.5 cm, but some sloppy, on the bias. Unfolded width = 5 cm. Included a looped fringe, a knot over the ankles, a large tied knot under the soles of the feet, and some strips also tied in front over feet. May come from more than one original piece—one has count of 14/8, other is 18/10. Based on self band placement, part may be same piece as 78.13.
78.16	basket weave	14	8	110	fringe	x	*6th overall shroud.* Wrapped over the top of the body and underneath.
78.17	basket weave	14	8	129	self bands fringe or loom string end	x	*7th overall shroud.* Cut edge. Very wide self bands. Fringe or loom string end, 2 cm.
78.18	basket weave	16	8	105	self bands loom string end	x	*8th overall shroud* wrapped over body and under, from right over to left leg then under body. Loom string ends.
78.19	basket weave	14	8	104	self bands	x	*9th overall shroud.* Mostly deteriorated except around feet. Cut edges and end. Irregular self bands.

TABLE 7.3   Layers of linen wrappings extant on Burial NW 78. (*cont.*)

Textile #	make	warp / cm	weft / cm	longest remaining edge (cm)	of note	Basket weave present?	Excavation notes and observations
78.20	basket weave	14	8	104	self bands	x	*10th overall shroud.* Ends and sides cut. Self bands repeat consistently. Wrapped under feet and over top.
78.21	plain weave	22	10	112	ribs open warp		[*Location not noted but found between 78.20 and 78.23.*] Consistent self band pattern. Open warp is 5.5 cm wide on one end and 4 cm on the other. Cut edges. Comparable to 78.25.
78.22	plain weave	14	8	110	open warp		[*Location not noted but found between 78.20 and 78.23.*] Long fringe (18 cm). 1.5 cm woven between fringe and open warp section. open warp 7 cm wide. two cut edges.
78.23	plain weave	22	14		open warp wool		*Innermost layer at the lower legs and feet*—plain weave with two shots of purple/ green. Very badly preserved. S-twist of wool is barely visible. Open warp 3 cm.
78.24	half basket	13	12			x	This and the next piece are from the less-preserved torso area. Seems to have been folded and *placed over the top of the body*— under first layer—count is balanced and it

Textile #	make	warp / cm	weft / cm	longest remaining edge (cm)	of note	Basket weave present?	Excavation notes and observations
							appears fairly balanced because the weft threads are fine. [Possibly same piece as the smaller one described in 78.2.]
78.25	plain weave	20	9		open warp		Piece *folded over the top of the body*. Similar to 78.21. Includes two open warp sections at one end. 3 cm fringe. Self bands are uneven.
78.26	basket weave				face bundle	x	*Face bundle twist.* Attached to textiles closer to body but none above. Twist is made of basket weave, twisted in z direction, 15 cm long (end is missing) and 3 cm wide. Underneath *next to the face was a plain weave* (not numbered or analyzed) with variegated self band pattern.

FIGURE 7.1
Example of typical basket weave linen
from Fag el-Gamous (200-210N 20-30E-
SE#45a). Note that the selvedges have
been cut off. They are frequently found in
use as binding tapes in these burials

FIGURE 7.2   NW 73.5, showing a repeating pattern of decorative self-bands

FIGURE 7.3   NW 68 in situ. For most of the burials, the area around the legs was the best
preserved

FIGURE 7.4   The cluster of textiles on the face area of NW 68. Note the outer plain weave
layer followed by layers of basket weave linen

FIGURE 7.5
This piece of cloth was found at
the layer closest to the body and
running along the torso (NW
68.21). Large sections of wool are
found only on plain weave sheets,
never basket weaves

FIGURE 7.6   This small fragment of the layer of linen closest to the body at the legs includes sections of open warp near the fringe ends and three shots of false purple wool (NW 68.19)

FIGURE 7.7   The better-preserved lower half of burial NW 73 displays torn and folded strips of linen used as binding tapes, and basket weave linen as the outermost layer

FIGURE 7.8   All of NW 73's outer layers were basket weaves, but the layer of linen closest to the body along the legs is plain weave (NW 73.21). Although not as refined as 68.19 (shown in Figure 7.6 above), it displays stylistic similarities to the body layer of NW 68 with its open warp near the fringe end, self-bands, and two shots of false purple wool

FIGURE 7.9   Many of the basket weave linen pieces appeared to be new and unused prior to burial, prompting the use of the term "shroud" in reference to them. This piece, NW 68.12, was cut to shape and laid over the foot area between the seventh and eighth overall shrouds

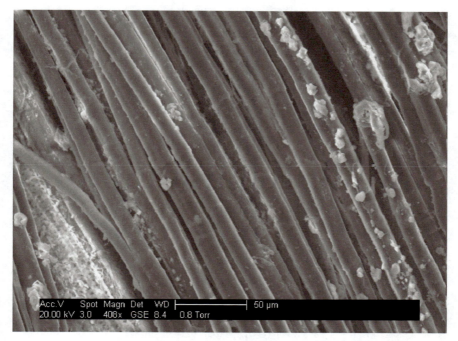

FIGURE 7.10 SEM photography of "new" linen from previously-excavated Fag el-Gamous burials (2000-SE-46.2). Note the utter absence of abrasion or breaking. These fibers appear strong and untouched by daily wear

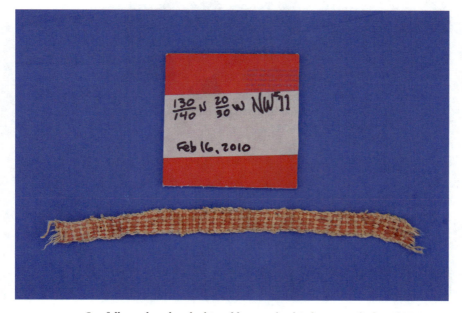

FIGURE 7.11 Carefully-made red-and-white ribbon used as binding tapes for burial NW 11

182   SOUTH

FIGURE 7.12   Burial NW 11 in situ, showing the presence of fine
red-and-white ribbon and a series of limestone blocks
covering the burial

FIGURE 7.13   Burial NW 88, if the hypothesis is correct, was one of the wealthiest
burials in this section. It included three-colored ribbon, palm sticks
supporting the body, and all of the layers of wrapping were
constructed in plain weave rather than basket weave

FIGURE 7.14   The three-colored ribbon from burial NW 88

FIGURE 7.15   Other objects associated with burial NW 65, perhaps indicative of higher
                          economic status

FIGURE 7.16   Burial NW 95 at the feet, showing a finer outer layer followed by basket weave
layers underneath

CHAPTER 8

Textiles and Jewelry at Fag el-Gamous

Joyce Y. Smith, Kerry Muhlestein and Brian D. Christensen

Elsewhere in this volume we discuss extensively the burial practices of the common man as represented in the Fag el-Gamous sand cemetery. While these burials must represent the common, or poorer, people of the area due to their large numbers, they are remarkable in regards to the amount of resources used for a common burial.[1] The two most frequently used types of goods associated with these burials, and probably the most expensive, are textiles and jewelry. In order to better understand these burials and the requisite resources marshaled by the deceased during their life and their loved ones after their death, this paper explores a few case studies of burial textiles and jewelry. By better understanding these two elements, we can more fully understand funerary culture of the area as a whole. For those who are interested, explanations of some terms specific to textiles are placed in footnotes.

1 The Weave of Burial Shrouds

"Textiles and clothing are perhaps the most significant markers of human existence," and say something about the identity of the person.[2] Of course the textiles we examine speak of their identity in death, or a hoped for identity in the afterlife, but they still say something about the self-identity of those who were buried at Fag el-Gamous. Linen is by far the most common material from which textiles for either the living or dead were made in Egypt,[3] and form the vast majority of textiles found in the cemetery. While we have found many burials at Fag el-Gamous that have intricate patterns and vibrant colors in their burial textiles, the majority have been much more plain. Most publications about textiles from Egypt have focused, understandably, on the most vibrant and intricate examples. These are the kinds of pieces that were brought

---

1 See the article on "Death of a Common Man" in this volume.
2 Jochen Sokoly, "Textiles and Identity," in Finbarr Barry Flood and Gülru Necipoğlu, eds. *A Companion to Islamic Art and Architecture* (New York: John Wiley & Sons Inc., 2017), 275; and Christina Riggs, *Unwrapping Ancient Egypt* (New York: Bloomsbury Academic: 2014), 120.
3 See Riggs, *Unwrapping Ancient Egypt*, 109–111.

back from Egypt and *made* their way to museums and university collections where they were later carefully studied and published.[4] In contrast, here we wish to focus on the more common burial. Thus we will first present information about more mundane and common fabric largely devoid of colorful patterns. Patterns are made by adding extra or colored lines to either the warp or weft threads[5] of a textile. The type of textile most frequently found in the burials at Fag el-Gamous is a rather coarse, basket weave[6] linen textile with a repeated pattern of ribs[7] designated by our analysts as the X-2-X-2-X pattern. ("X" represents the rib). The rib structures are formed by inserting additional weft threads per shot.[8] If there are a total of 5 threads forming the rib, it would be designated as "5X"; 3 threads in the rib would be "3X" etc. The number "2" represents the two shots of regular weave between the ribs. An X-2-X-2-X rib pattern is designated by the repetition of a rib, followed by two shots, then another rib, two shots, and a third rib. This rib pattern is generally repeated throughout the entire cloth at intervals ranging from 4 to 15 centimeters between the rib pattern structure. It may be a product that was manufactured specifically for use in burying the dead, possibly produced from local weaving workshops.

At Fag el-Gamous, fabrics used in life could become a shroud or covering for the dead, such as when well-worn tunics and or sheets of linen with evidence of patching and mending are found as burial coverings. At the same time, there are also numerous examples of newly woven pieces of linen, many of which are of the basket weave, 3-rib pattern. These textiles show no evidence of wear or use prior to padding and wrapping the deceased. Even under a microscope no fraying is visible. Since almost any use at all creates microscopic fraying, this indicates that these textiles were used only in death.

Often at Fag el-Gamous, fine white-bleached linen, plain (tabby)[9] weave shrouds are found held in place with red and white (or un-dyed) woven ribbon as the outer-most burial covering. It is also common to find several layers of

---

4   For example, see László Török, *Coptic Antiquities II, Textiles* (Rome: L'Erma di Brethschneider, 1993). This is an excellent publication of a number of very high quality and spectacular textiles.
5   Warps are the long threads held in place on a loom, wefts are the threads woven into and around the warp threads.
6   See the article on basket weave in this volume.
7   Ribs are raised lines across the width of the fabric.
8   A shot is a single pass of the weft thread woven through the lengthwise warp threads across the width of the fabric.
9   Gillian Vogelsang-Eastwood, "Textiles," in *Ancient Egyptian Materials and Technology*, Paul T. Nicholson and Ian Shaw, eds. (Cambridge: Cambridge University Press, 2000), 274.

coarse basket weave (or extended weave)[10] shrouds, made of un-dyed linen with the repeated pattern of weft ribs, beneath the outer white, plain weave shroud. These large pieces of cloth were newly constructed and seem to have been made specifically to be used at the time of burial. At Fag el-Gamous the earlier burials tend to employ more used and worn textiles for burial, but as time went on the trend turned more and more towards being buried in new textiles, presumably created for the purpose of covering the dead. While body fluids are responsible for textile deterioration on the torso of the body, the parts of shrouds wrapping the upper body and lower legs and feet are often still clean and supple. This same type of ribbed linen fabric is also found folded and used to provide additional padding and shaping around the body and is often found in the folded layers of face bundles. Torn strips of linen, 2–3 cm wide, are used in the same manner as the red and white ribbons, to bind or wrap around shrouds, particularly interior shroud layers. Often, there is no selvedge on the shroud itself, but the torn strips do have one selvedge edge. These strips often have an X-2-X-2-X pattern matching the pattern of the shroud, indicating that the torn, binding strips were taken from the same or similar piece of cloth.

FIGURE 8.1   An example of a plain weave, ribbed burial textile
PHOTOGRAPHY BY JOYCE Y. SMITH

---

10   Ibid.

FIGURE 8.2   A closeup of ribs with six threads (6X) within basket weave
PHOTOGRAPH BY JOYCE Y. SMITH

These textiles are best understood by looking at specific examples. The aforementioned patterns are evident in specific samples of textiles from burials
studied during the 2010 season. It should be noted that nothing was included
with any of these burials that allows us to determine a date.

From the area 190/200 N 30/40 E, excavated in 2009, Burial NE #22 was located at a depth of 110 cm. The third layer of textiles (from the outside) was
un-dyed linen, basket weave, measuring 35 cm in the warp direction, including
a 14 cm fringe, and 52 cm in the weft direction. Thread count was 22 warp and

10 weft, single ply threads, S twist, soft spun, and of medium thickness. There was a 4X-2-4X-2-4X weft rib pattern that was repeated every 6 cm. Torn linen strips were used as binding and had a rib pattern similar to the shroud.

Burial NE #56 was also from 2009 and analyzed during the 2010 season. It was linen basket weave cloth with ribs. It measured 58 cm in the warp direction, 81 cm in the weft. Threads were coarse, S twist, and medium spun with 12 warps per cm by 8 wefts per cm. The rib pattern was 7X-2-7X-2-7X with a 9 cm repeat, but only repeated 3 times on this portion of the shroud.

Also from 2009, Burial NE #66 layer 6 was of fine linen thread, basket weave with ribs in a 6X-2-6X-2-6X pattern. There was also a handkerchief as part of the face bundle measuring 24 cm in the warp direction by 30 cm weft.

Burial NE #67 from the 2009 season had several layers of un-dyed basket weave linen shrouds with a 6X-2-6X-2-6X pattern. Threads were fine, single ply, S twist, soft spun with counts of 18 warps and 12 wefts. The rib pattern began 4 cm from the fringe with pattern repeats 8 cm apart and then widening to 12 and 15 cm apart. These burials are only a few examples of the numerous appearances of this rib pattern in burial shrouds and wrappings. There are a variety of combinations of this X-2-X-2-X pattern making each shroud unique.

Continuing to use the 2009 season as an example, 66 complete burials were discovered in the northeast portion of the 190/200 N 30/40 E area at depths between 60 cm and 250 cm. Thirty-three burials have between 1 to 11 layers of basket weave linen with the X-2-X-2-X pattern. There were approximately 26 skeletalized burials with few, if any, fragments of textiles to study, and there are a few whose analysis is yet to be integrated into our database for use in studies.

It is possible this particular style of weaving was unique to a local workshop in the area of Fayoum.[11] More research is needed to come to any definite conclusion. Yet some of the burial cloths are of lesser quality with uneven weaves and aberrations in the pattern, which could indicate the existence of a small cottage-industry consisting of individuals who wove textiles outside of a larger, more regularized industry, but rather in their homes. A tradition of weaving could have been passed along multi-generationally in such a setting.

The search continues to find comparable textiles in other museum collections that clearly correspond to the ones with the X-2-X-2-X rib pattern found at Fag el-Gamous. Efforts to communicate with other textile analysts from different excavations, especially in the Fayoum, are ongoing, in an attempt to discover the extent of the use of this specific weave pattern. One small fragment

11   For more on workshops in this area see the article on the history of the Fayoum, Seila and Fag el-Gamous in this volume.

pictured in the Masada IV publication of the Yigael Yadin Excavations from 1963–1965 shows a similar three-rib pattern, but it is of plain weave and not a large enough fragment to suggest any repeat.[12] Another fragment with a rib pattern to consider is from the Katoen Natie collection in Antwerp, Belgium. It is a half-basket weave linen piece with colored wool pile-weave[13] decorations illustrating a lamp stand and two ankhs on either side of the lamp.[14] It is dated (with 95.4% probability) between 210–390 AD.[15] There are at least two X-2-X-2-X type of weft rib repeats in the linen ground and within the wool design. Still, at this point it seems that while the X-2-X-2-X pattern is common at Fag el-Gamous, it is not as common in other areas. As the study of weaving patterns in antiquity expands, we will be better able to make comparisons that will refine this picture.

2   Jewelry

While the majority of burials do not have jewelry associated with them, it is still one of the more common kinds of grave goods found in the cemetery. For example, in a sample of 336 burials, only 77 (23%) had any kind of grave goods. Of these, 12 (15.5% of burials with grave goods, 3.5% of all burials in the sample) had jewelry. Pottery (10% of the total burials in the sample) is the only more common kind of grave good interred with burials.

Jewelry could consist of beads (typically composed of glass, faience, clay, or shells), metal, leather, or combinations of these materials. Less commonly wooden, bone/ivory,[16] or stone objects were part of burial jewelry. We have found a number of bracelets that are simple rings of metal, often consisting of two or three bands. We have been able to test the chemical make-up of several metal pieces of jewelry using an XRF analysis. These objects are predominantly

---

12   Avigail Sheffer and Hero Granger-Taylor, "Masada IV," *The Yigael Yadin Excavations 1963–1965 Final Reports* (Jerusalem: The Hebrew University of Jerusalem, 1994), 174.

13   For an illustration of pile weave, see Elisabeth Grace Crowfoot, *Qasr Ibrim: The Textiles from the Cathedral Cemetery* (London: Egypt Exploration Society, 2011), 13.

14   Antoine De Moor, *3500 Years of Textile Art* (Tielt: Lannoo Publishers, 2009), 142–143.

15   Ibid.

16   In small, aged, worked pieces such as these, we cannot tell whether the objects are of ivory or bone. In such cases it is standard and most transparent to refer to the pieces as bone/ivory. See Olga Krzyszkowska and Robert Morkot, "Ivory and related materials," in *Ancient Egyptian Materials and Technology*, Paul T. Nicholson and Ian Shaw, eds. (Cambridge: Cambridge University Press, 2000), 321. If these objects are ivory, they would most likely be hippopotamus ivory. See Ibid., 326–327.

copper, with small amounts of zinc, iron, tin, arsenic and palladium also present. This is fairly similar to the composition of bronze.

In a sample of 33 pieces of jewelry from Fag el-Gamous stored at the Kom Aushim storage magazine, 13 (39%) had metal objects, with 7 of those consisting only of metal. 10 pieces of jewelry (30%) had glass[17] (most frequently in the form of beads), with 3 of those being pieces of jewelry that consisted only of glass besides whatever material had been used to string them together. 9 (27%) had faience as part of the piece, with one consisting of only faience.[18] 6 (18%) contained wooden objects, with 2 of those pieces of jewelry consisting solely of wood besides whatever kind of material had been used to string the wood. Additionally, 6 (18%) had leather delicately carved or woven into part of the jewelry, but most often as the material which held the jewelry together. Leather does not survive as well as the other kinds of jewelry mentioned thus far, so it is quite likely that it was used at a much higher rate than these statistics reflect. Most commonly, the leather was braided in some way. Leather was always found used in combination with other materials. There were also 6 (18%) that used clay, usually in the form of beads. Clay was also always used in combination with other materials. Bone/ivory was always used in combination with other materials, and was found in 3 (9%) jewelry pieces. Yarn was used to string or tie together 3 (9%) pieces of jewelry. Stone and shells were both used in 2 (6%) jewelry items and always in combination with other materials.

It should be noted that this survey of materials used in jewelry is only a small sample. A much larger sample would be more statistically significant. It is hoped that in the future a close study of field books and objects from this excavation and similar cemeteries will yield a more detailed study of jewelry in the Roman Fayoum. Still, this small collection provides a useful snapshot of the kinds of materials used to make jewelry in this area of the Fayoum. Even with this, a greater depth of understanding can be gained by examining in detail a few specific pieces of jewelry from the cemetery.[19]

---

17   Glass at this time period was most frequently what is known as natron glass, as opposed to earlier time periods that used plant ash more heavily in their construction. See Julian Henderson, *Ancient Glass, an Interdisciplinary Exploration* (Cambridge: Cambridge University Press, 2013), 92–98.

18   Faience is perhaps the earliest synthesized material, and is a very early forerunner to glass. See Ibid., 14. Faience was used in Egypt as early as 4000 BC and continued to be used throughout Egyptian history.

19   The jewelry of these two burials were discussed in an earlier article, which was coauthored by Joyce Y. Smith, one of the coauthors of this article. For the article see Joyce Y. Smith, Kristin South, C. Wilfred Griggs, and Giovanni Tata, "Jewelry and accessories from two Christian burials from Fag el Gamous Cemetery in Fayum Region, Egypt," in *Dress accessories of the 1st millennium AD from Egypt: Proceedings of the 6th conference of the*

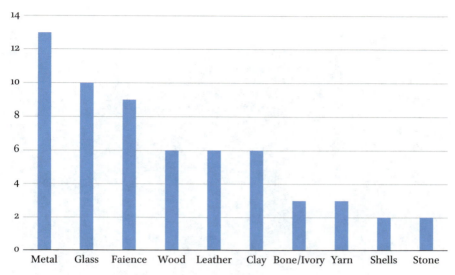

FIGURE 8.3   Material used in jewelry

While the two burials we now examine are from the sand cemetery and thus are, in large measure, from the "common man" by definition, the jewelry found with them is not common. This is partially because jewelry among these burials is uncommon overall and partially because among the small number that have jewelry, many have simple pieces (such as a band of metal forming a bracelet) that are informative, but not as flashy as other types of jewelry. Here we discuss two burials that seem to be common in most respects, yet are unusual in their jewelry. They also both had impressive textiles.

We first examine burial 190/200 N, 30/40 E, Southeast quadrant, #44, found at a depth of 152 cm (hereafter just referred to as burial 44). The burial was clustered with three other adult burials, lying directly beneath one of them. Burial 44 was a brown-haired female who passed away at about age 18. She was about 5 feet 2 inches tall (155 cm). While we cannot date this burial precisely, its depth suggests that it was interred somewhere around the material cultural height of the imperial Roman era, roughly between 200 and 400 AD. Its outer shroud was linen with a plain tabby weave with 7 cm bands of purple[20] wool

research group "Textiles from the Nile Valley," Antwerp, 2–3 October 2009, Antoine De Moor, Cäcilia Fluck, and Elisabeth Ehler, eds. (Tielt, Belgium: Lannoo, 2011), 204–219. Here we use some of the information from that earlier article, but we use it in a different way for a different purpose. We are grateful for the work done by our colleagues as represented in their article.

20   For more on the use of purple in the burials of Fag el-Gamous, see the paper on purple dye in this volume. While this particular textile was not among those we were able to test,

FIGURE 8.4   Purple "hue" weft bands from burial 44
                   PHOTOGRAPH BY JOYCE Y. SMITH

woven over every four warps. These bands were separated by three white linen threads. The purple bands extended from the face and head of the burial to its feet. A loop fringe was also part of the shroud. The shroud was then secured by the use of the kind of red and white ribbon that is common at the cemetery. They were wrapped in a diagonal, rhomboid pattern, which is also common.

A bead necklace was immediately apparent as the burial was uncovered. It was located under her chin and extending up to her right shoulder, which is where all of the beads were located. The beads were strung on braided leather strips. While the leather had largely disintegrated so that we cannot tell the exact original form of the necklace, the surviving arrangement makes it seem that it was a multi-strand necklace.

The necklace consisted of a striking number and variety of beads. The beads were strung on narrow (.2–.3 cm) braided leather strips. At intervals, a single strip looped over the outside of the bead to separate it from the next bead and hold it in place.

_____

based on the trend of purple dye at Fag el-Gamous, we assume the purple thread in burial 44 was not Tyrian purple.

FIGURE 8.5   Head of burial 44 with beads in situ on chest and right shoulder
PHOTOGRAPH BY JOYCE Y. SMITH

There were 78 bone/ivory beads, many of which had bands incised around the belly of the bead. Bone/ivory is carved into shape much as one would carve wood. The consistency and uniformity of the 78 barrel shaped ivory/bone beads indicates that they were probably turned on some kind of lathe after having had a hole drilled in them. Some of the beads have no incised lines around their belly, others have 2 or 3 incised belly lines. Lathe work is also evident in these precise, parallel, incised lines seen on the belly of 58 of the beads. Dyes and paints were sometimes used on bone/ivory pieces, however the decorative lines on these beads are blackened because they are dirt filled. When the dirt was removed there was no indication of dye or paint remaining in the incised lines.

There were also 21 glass beads, most with colored stringer designs in wave patterns, along with 25 small white shells and a small metal bell with a shell clapper. There was also a small metal ring (1.3 cm in diameter) and a larger metal ring (3.8 cm in diameter). These metal rings were similar to bronze in their chemical makeup. As the beads were strung on the leather strip, they were separated at intervals by a single strip looped over the outside of the bead. These beads are of the style known today as "stringer beads."

FIGURE 8.6   Beads from the necklace of burial 44 arranged by the excavation team
              PHOTOGRAPH BY JOYCE Y. SMITH

The shells on this necklace appear to be White Nassa or Dove shells with holes drilled artificially.[21] Several different gastropod (a kind of mollusk) shell beads were used, including discoidal, depressed, and elongate shapes. These are found both in the Red and Mediterranean Seas.

The faience beads are similar to those used in Egypt from its earliest history.[22] It is formed in a manner very similar to glass, except that heat is applied later in the process.[23] Silica, from ground quartz or sand crystals, was combined with sodium and lime and then was mixed with other minerals, such as calcium, magnesium oxide, potassium oxide, and copper oxide. The copper oxide, combined with varying amounts of other elements, is what causes the

---

21   A. Lucas, revised by J.R. Harris, *Ancient Egyptian Materials and Industries* (London: Histories and Mysteries of Man LTD, 1962), 41.

22   Paul T. Nicholson, "Faience Technology," in Willeke Wendrich, ed., *UCLA Encyclopedia of Egyptology* (Los Angeles: http://digital2.library.ucla.edu/viewItem.do?ark=21198/zz0017jtts), 2.

23   Ibid., 1–2.

turquoise or blue coloring.[24] Because of lower amounts of soda and lime than in glass, the silica does not melt completely, and thus it does not become glass, but rather small enough amounts of glass are formed to bind the rest of the material together in a hardened and glossy state.[25] As a result, Faience objects are molded in a clay-like state, and are then fired.[26] Faience could be molded by hand, molded in a form, created with a core that was burned away, or occasionally larger objects could be formed on a wheel, though this was much less successful than with ceramic clay.[27] As with the glass beads (see below), the faience beads in this necklace appear to have been core formed.

Some of the faience beads of Burial 44 are plain with no design, but most are in the popular, frequently found ribbed beads in melon form. Compared to other specimens of melon beads, these are not of the highest quality faience work, as indicated by the sometimes rough and un-evenness of the exterior glaze. They were predominantly hand formed of ceramic material employing the efflorescence method of glazing. Coloration is evenly distributed inside and outside the bead and appears to be integral with the body of the bead. Subtle color differences indicate that the beads were from at least two separate batches of paste mix and firing. The shine and texture of two of the beads indicate they were glazed by a different technique; either by cementation or the application method.

Three faience beads show signs of being formed with a mold. One exhibits unusually even, fine ribbing while the others appear to be hand formed with wide, somewhat random pressed ribs. Two of the plain beads are very smooth and unusually round indicating they may have been pressed into a mold. It is possible, however, for a highly skilled worker in hand formation to obtain such roundness without the use of a mold. As was noted above, core forming was probably the most common method for forming most of the faience beads.[28]

---

24   Ibid., 2; Paul T. Nicholson and Edgar Peltenberg, "Egyptian Faience," in *Ancient Egyptian Materials and Technology*, eds. Paul T. Nicholson and Ian Shaw (Cambridge: Cambridge University Press, 2000), 177–180. See also Carolyn Riccardelli, "Egyptian Faience: Technology and Production," *The MET Essays*, https://www.metmuseum.org/toah/hd/egfc/hd_egfc.htm; and Joshua J. Mark, "Faience," *Ancient History Encylopedia* online, https://www.ancient.eu/Faience/.

25   Nicholson, "Faience Technology," UEE, 2.

26   S. La Delfa, V. Formisano, and E. Ciliberto, "Laboratory Production of Egyptian Faiences and their Characterization," *Journal of Cultural Heritage* 9/1 (2008): 113–116.

27   Nicholson, "Faience Technology," UEE, 2–3; Riccardelli, "Egyptian Faience"; and Mark, "Faience."

28   William M.F. Petrie, *The Arts and Crafts of Ancient Egypt*, (Twickenham, UK, Senate, an imprint of Tiger Books International PLC, 1996), 119, was the first to propose this method.

FIGURE 8.7   Beads from burial 44
              PHOTOGRAPH BY JOYCE Y. SMITH

The glass beads of this burial appear to also be made by a core-forming method. Core forming glass-work was the forerunner of what is now called "lampworking." This method can also be referred to as the wound-bead flamework
technique, or torch working. This is now done with a single concentrated heat
source such as a blowtorch, but during the Roman era the glass was heated using a conical shaped furnace with vents. It is one of the earliest known glassmaking techniques.[29]

    The method of making these core-formed stringer beads has not changed
dramatically from the Roman era until now, though, as noted, more sophisticated tools are available today. In this method, glass "rope" rods or cane (cane
is pencil sized, while stringers are very thin cane) drawn and formed previously
are softened in the heat of the conical furnace to a molten state and are then
wound around a heat resistant metal core axis or mandrel (also called a pontil)
coated with a bead-release material (clay tempered with talc anciently.) The

---

29   "Glassmaking Technique: Core-Formed Glass," J. Paul Getty Museum, accessed December
      1, 2017, http://www.getty.edu/art/collection/video/142904/glassmaking-technique:-core-
      formed-glass/. Also see Henderson, *Ancient Glass*, 223–227 and 232–233; and Axel von
      Saldern, "Ancient Glass," *Boston Museum Bulletin* 64/335 (1966): 6.

glass bead is then heated several times as more layers of glass "rope" are wound around the mandrel to build it up to the desired size. Once the glass has cooled the core is removed, leaving a hollow spot inside the glass bead.

The successive applications of heat and layers of glass introduces the opportunity for decorating the piece. As the glass makers pull a point out from a hot gob of glass on a pontil rod with tweezers or a hook needle, the tip of the point is touched to another ball of glass on another pontil. Both rods are kept in the flame while working. The point sticks and a thread of glass "stringer" is pulled from point to point, leaving zig-zag lines around the sphere. The thread is broken or melted off and the pattern is melted flat to the more massive surface of the sphere.

In an attempt to fully understand the process, Professor Brian Christensen and his student, Noah Coleman, enacted a bead making process comparable to ancient methods. Employing kilns to melt the raw glass in ceramic crucibles, they drew out the molten glass, pulling it into colored glass rods (cane). Just as was described above, they then cut it into useable lengths before it was completely cooled and hardened. Instead of the clay and dung based (or possibly copper wire) mandrel (or core) that was probably used anciently,[30] they employed mandrels made of stainless steel, coated with a bead release of crystalline silica and alumina. Rather than using cone furnaces, they used a propaneoxygen blowtorch at 2500 degrees Fahrenheit to soften the cane and then applied one layer of glass "rope" at a time, adding more layers until the bead reached the desired size. Decorations were applied with thin glass stringers of various colors. Doing this, they were able to reproduce beads that were very similar to those found with burial 44.

The glass stringer beads of this burial seem to be in line with techniques and colors known to be used in Coptic Egypt. These beads were the result of practices that had originated in Egypt and then spread throughout the Mediterranean and Fertile Crescent much earlier, and were in use in both Greece and Rome,[31] and were particularly flourishing in Egypt at the time.[32] The Fayoum

---

30   While copper wire was used in some places, in Egypt the most common core was a mixture made primarily of clay and dung. See Paul T. Nicholson and Julian Henderson, "Glass," in *Ancient Egyptian Materials and Technology*, Paul T. Nicholson and Ian Shaw, eds. (Cambridge: Cambridge University Press, 2000), 202–203. See also Albert Neuburger, *The Technical Arts and Sciences of the Ancients,* Henry L. Brose, trans. (London: Kegan Paul Press, 2003), 155–156.

31   Frederic Neuburg, *Ancient Glass*, Michael Bullock and Alisa Jaffa, trans. (Toronto: University of Toronto Press, 1962), 18–20.

32   Ibid., 30–32. See also Albert Neuburger, *The Technical Arts and Sciences of the Ancients*; Frederic Neuburg, *Glass in Antiquity*, R.J. Charleston, trans. (London: Ranking Brothers Limited, 1949), 8–16; and A. Lucas, *Ancient Egyptian Materials* (New York: Green & Co., 1926), 44.

had Roman, Greek, Egyptian and Jewish populations. These were all cultures in which this kind of glass working had spread. Thus it is not surprising to find this type of glass work present at Fag el-Gamous.

The glass beads from burial 44 all had a black glass base bead form with white, green, blue, red and yellow lampworking. Some of the beads exhibit applied designs that were not heated to a point where the decoration fully integrated into the black base, resulting in the color design staying partially on the surface, creating a texture. Others were heated and melted into the black base completely creating a smooth, integrated design.

The glass beads are colorful and beautiful, but in some ways appear to not reach the craftsmanship one would expect from the high art achieved during the height of Roman glass production, especially in Egypt at the time.[33] The seeming defects in the beads suggest the possibility that the beads were made locally, not at a center of production that could achieve high artisanship.[34] The texture of the exterior of the glass exhibits symptoms of "sick glass," or a composition slightly deficient in calcium oxide (lime), that over a long period of time can cause visual defects in the glass, including opaqueness and an internal web of fine lines known as crizzling.

At the same time, core forming can be very sophisticated when feathering is applied to beads and vases. In many cases the opaqueness is intentional. It is possible that the apparent crizzling and opaqueness should not be viewed as a composition defect, instead they could be an intentionally created visual effect. The wavy patterns were also often part of the aesthetic of glassware. This kind of opaque and crizzling patterning created an organic look that was employed in Roman and later Venetian core formed glass.[35] For example, Venetian traditions use some of the same opaque feathering and stringer techniques on blown and solid glass. Thus it could be that the beads were of higher craftsmanship and their appearance is fully intentional.

---

33   During this era, Egypt became a serious producer of glass in both quantity and quality. This was so much the case that Roman emperors placed high taxes on Egyptian glass to offset the cheapness created by the quantity of their desirable glass. See Sandra Davison, *Conservation and Restoration of Glass* (Oxford: Elsevier Science, 2003), 23–24.

34   On the uniformity of glass making in production centers see E. Marianne Stern, "Glass Production," in *The Oxford Handbook of Engineering and Technology in the Classical World*, John Peter Oleson, ed. (Oxford: Oxford University Press, 2008), 520–521.

35   On Venetian glass, see Rosa Barovier Mentasti, "Glass and Glassmakers from the Renaissance to the Present Day," in *Glass Throughout Time, History and Technique of Glassmaking from the Ancient World to the Present*, Rosa Barovier Mentasti, Rosanna Mollo, Patrizia Framarin, Maurizio Sciaccaluga, and Anna Geotti, eds. (Torino: Skira Editore, 2003), 26–28.

Burial #13 of 180/190 North, 40/50 East, Southwest quadrant (hereafter referred to as burial 13) was uncovered in 2003 and analyzed during the 2007 dig season. The burial was an adult female, about five feet and three inches tall (162 cm). Again, we cannot provide a precise date, but the burial depth of 60 cm suggests she was interred somewhere around the Byzantine era.

The textiles and accessories of Burial 13 are extraordinary. While textiles are not the focus of this examination, it is worth noting that this woman had been wrapped in several layers of linen shrouds. Most of those were coarse linen[36] of simple weave, but one layer was a yellow weft faced woolen piece. This tunic had blue, yellow, green and red tapestry designs,[37] using slit, dovetail, and interlocking weaving methods.[38] A woolen sprang head covering consisting of red with yellow and green trimmings was held in place by hairpins, one made of gold and the other of ivory/bone. Brilliant red strands of wool bound her feet, and a wool loop of cordage was on her face, looping down to her chest and abdomen. The same red wool also encircled her pelvis.

On the upper left arm, fragments of ivory/bone bracelets remained. These fragments were pieced together to form four full bracelets with a portion of a fifth remaining. The bracelets were clasped with a small metal wire fastener. On this same arm a partial metal bracelet was also found.

There was more jewelry on this unusual burial. About her neck, lying on her chest, were the remains of three necklaces. Two necklaces were intact enough to present them as they were found. The beads and amulets were strung on thick two-ply red wool strands, with knots made in these strands between each bead in order to provide spacing, though the holes for many of the beads were large enough they could slip over the knots.

The most common piece on both of these necklaces was white beads, tubular in shape with ribbing stretching along their length. The ribbing is probably natural, for these beads are made from Scaphopoda dentalium, or tusk shells, which are typically ribbed in their native state.

The large, beautiful red pendants that were the focal point of these necklaces were both made of glass, which is only apparent when held up to the light. Such light exposure also reveals potential crizzling. Alternatively, the cracking could be due to a defect in what is known as "fit." Fit has to do with

---

36   Ancient Egyptian terms for linen include terms for different grades of linen. The fineness of the linen is determined by thread count, similar to sheets and other kinds of cloth in our day. From both texts and archaeological data it is clear that "smooth" or what is called today "coarse," linen was by far the most common. See Rosalind Hall, *Egyptian Textiles* (Buckinghamshire: Shire Publications Ltd., 2003), 9.

37   Tapestry designs in tunics were very common at the time. See Ibid., 33.

38   Vogelsang-Eastwood, "Textiles," 275.

FIGURE 8.8   Ivory/bone bracelets and fragment of a metal bracelet from burial 13
PHOTOGRAPH BY JOYCE Y. SMITH

FIGURE 8.9   A reconstruction of the pattern from the non-intact necklace of burial 13
PHOTOGRAPH BY JOYCE Y. SMITH

FIGURE 8.10   Shell beads and yarn from one of the intact necklaces of burial 13
PHOTOGRAPH BY JOYCE Y. SMITH

the coefficient of expansion in two kinds of glass. If one type expands or shrinks more than the other, cracks appear. Another possibility is thermal shock. Compressing glass between two surfaces could chill the exterior and crack it without breaking the whole piece if it were placed back in moderate heat to anneal quickly enough. Melting the surface would cure this, but it could have been put away to anneal without noticing.

The red glass amulets are probably pressed into their basic shapes on a marver (a heat resistant heavy metal sheet) rather than into a mold. Red glass is particularly difficult to produce. The colorant used most often was copper. Red glass has probably been under-recorded by Egyptologists due to its tendency to discolor to green.[39] These amulets have an appearance consistent with copper-red. Gold and selenium are also oxides that produce the color red. Though copper seems likely, gold cannot be ruled out since the use of gold can produce a similar look (because copper and gold have a very similar colloidal absorption rate), and is an oxide producing a red not likely to discolor

39   Paul T. Nicholson and Julian Henderson, "Glass" in *Ancient Egyptian Materials and Technology,* Paul T. Nicholson and Ian Shaw, eds. (Cambridge: Cambridge University Press, 2000), 199.

FIGURE 8.11   The two intact necklaces from burial 13
                       PHOTOGRAPH BY JOYCE Y. SMITH

into green.[40] Iron can vary from red to green,[41] but seems less likely in this case. Copper oxide causes this effect frequently, according to reduction or oxidation atmosphere.

Besides the beads, there are some other interesting pieces on these necklaces. Strung in the middle of one of these necklaces were two carved ivory/bone crosses.[42] Additionally, a brilliantly glazed faience amphora bead was present. This glazing was probably produced by cementation or application. The remains of what could be a kiln stilt mark that could be made during firing may suggest that the application method of glazing was employed. Another piece, which appears to be made of resin, seems to be either a fish or a bird. This same necklace contained two un-incised red glass beads that are quite large.

The third necklace contained the broken remnants of several red glass pieces. There was also an unbroken piece of red glass in a fan or tear drop

40   James E. Shelby, *Introduction to Glass Science and Technology* (Cambridge: The Royal Society of Chemistry, 1997), 205–206.

41   Ibid., 201–202, 204.

42   For a discussion of the possible meanings of these figures and others in the jewelry presented herein, see the excellent discussion on this topic in Smith, et al., "Jewelry and Accessories."

FIGURE 8.12   One of the glass medallions from a necklace of burial 13
PHOTOGRAPH COURTESY OF JOYCE Y. SMITH

FIGURE 8.13   The two intact necklaces of burial 13
PHOTOGRAPH BY JOYCE Y. SMITH

shape which had three horizontal lines scored across the top. Similar to the red glass used in the other necklaces, currently it is not immediately apparent that this piece is glass. It looks more like stone until it is held up to the light. Before being deposited in the sand for thousands of years, its glass nature would have been more apparent. This same necklace also contained several small, colored glass beads. Some of these beads were mock turquoise. Shell and faience beads were also included. These beads were decorated by opposing triangles. Pomegranate beads and a lotus seed vessel pendant made of high quality faience are present. The shell beads are Scaphopoda, a mollusk, also known as tusk shells. They naturally develop in the tubular form used in this necklace, complete with the "fluted" exterior. This necklace, as with the others, is a beautiful piece of jewelry. Together, the three necklaces formed a striking appearance.

We hope, in the future, to compile partial biographies of a number of individuals from this region, using textual, biological and other archaeological materials, so that we can more fully tell the stories of at least some of these individuals. While this will require a considerable investment of time and resources, we believe the stories of ancient lives revealed this way will be worth the investment. In this article we are not attempting to create archaeobiographies, but rather are attempting to use a few specific details to help paint the broad brush stroke background pictures that will help us understand the conglomeration of people from this place better. In our quest to understand the lives and deaths of the common man in the Fayoum of Roman Egypt, it is worth looking at that which is most common among them, as well as that which is unusual even among the common. It helps us glimpse the accessories of life and see how they viewed and valued existence for the dead. The plain textiles discussed above are among the most common element of the burials of the majority of people in the Fag el-Gamous area, though the particular style seems unusual outside of this area. Most of the textiles used in burial are not uncommon, yet they represent a significant amount of resource investment for the common class. At the same time, even these commoners had that which was unique about them, as is illustrated in the beautiful, singular, and unusual jewelry found on just a few of these common burials. While the possessors of the jewelry described herein did not receive an elite burial, they clearly had access to some degree of wealth. Furthermore, those who buried them must have felt that these objects were integral to the deceased, enough so that they were willing to bury with them objects of some monetary worth. All of this is evidence that even the common majority were each individually unique.

CHAPTER 9

They'll Never Be Royals: The "Purple" Textiles of Fag el-Gamous

Bethany Jensen, R. Paul Evans, Giovanni Tata and Kerry Muhlestein

1 Introduction

Excavations at the Fag el-Gamous necropolis have unearthed a unique collection of textile fragments, among which are some beautifully dyed pieces, including several featuring purple threads.[1] The purple threads used in the textiles come in a variety of hues, suggesting different dye sources for the threads. In the ancient world, the source for true, enduring purple dye came from the sea snail, Murex.[2] This dye was highly prized, very expensive, and was frequently used for royal garments.[3] Because of its desirable nature, purple dye was frequently imitated with mixtures of blue and red dyes, such as indigo (plant genus *Indigofera*) for blue and madder (plant genus *Rubia*) for red or cochineal (insect family *Margarodidae*).[4] Due to the variety of hues present in

---

1   C. Wilfred Griggs, "Excavating a Christian Cemetery Near Seila, in the Fayum region of Egypt," in *Excavations at Seila, Egypt*, C. Wilfred Griggs, Wm. Revell Phillips, J. Keith Rigby, Vincent A. Wood, Russell D. Hamblin, eds. (Provo, Utah: Religious Studies Center, Brigham Young University, 1988), 78.

2   Charlene Elliot, "Purple Pasts: Color Codification in the Ancient World," *Law & Social Inquiry* 33/1 (2008): 177; Zvi C. Koren, "Archaeo-chemical analysis of Royal Purple on a Darius I stone jar," *Microchimica Acta* 162 (2008): 381–382; David S. Reese, "Palaikastro Shells and Bronze Age Purple-Dye Production in the Mediterranean Basin," *The Annual of the British School at Athens* 82 (1987): 203.

3   Charlene Elliot, "Purple Pasts: Color Codification," 179–180, 183; Lloyd B. Jensen, "Royal Purple of Tyre," *Journal of Near Eastern Studies* 22/2 (1963): 104; Robert R. Stieglitz, "The Minoan Origin of Tyrian Purple," *The Biblical Archaeologist* 57/1 (1994): 46; W. Nowik, R. Marcinowska, K. Kusyk, D. Cardon, M. Trjanowicz, "High Performance liquid chromatography of slightly soluble brominated indigoids from Tyrian purple," *Journal of Chromatography A* 1218 (2011): 1244; Harald Bohmer and Recep Karadag, "New Dye Research on Palymra Textiles," *Dyes in History and Archaeology* 19 (2003): 90.

4   Zvi C. Koren, "A New HPLC-PDA Method for the Analysis of Tyrian Purple Components," *Dyes in History and Archaeology* 21 (2008): 26; Max Saltzman, "Identifying Dyes in Textiles," *American Scientist* 80/5 (1992): 479; Dominique Cardon, Witold Nowik, Hero Granger-Taylor, Renata Marcinowska, Katarzyna Kusuk, and Marek Trojanowicz, "Who Could Wear True Purple in Roman Egypt? Technical and Social Considerations on Some New Identifications of

this collection, it seems likely that the people using the cemetery at Fag el-Gamous were using imitation purple for their garments. This project determined what, if any, proportion of true purple was used in the textiles recovered from the necropolis and how the presence (or absence) of true purple informs our understanding of the ancient Egyptian population that used this cemetery.

2   Purple Dye

Purple in antiquity was seen as a luxury color. It was worn by the highest members of society and, in some periods, was only allowed to be worn by the emperor.[5] In contrast, indigo is chemically similar to shellfish purple, but never cost as must nor reached such a glorified status.[6]

According to Dominique Cardon, purple is defined as "a violet dye, ranging in shade from purplish-red to violet-blue, composed of colorants that are closely related chemically to the plant indigo, and obtained from various marine mollusks at present all classified in the *Muricidae* family."[7] Tyrian purple (6,6'-dibromoindigotin) is a violet-red color that is derived from the hypobranchial gland of mollusks. The color develops after the death of the animal from a colorless precursor.[8] These precursors (chromogens) are "water-soluble, colourless sulphate esters of indoxyl."[9]

      Purple from Marine Molluscs in Archaeological Textiles," *Purpureae Vestes III: Textiles y Tintes en la ciudad antigua* ed. C. Alfaro, J.-P. Brun, Ph. Borgard, R. Pierobon Benoit (Valencia, Spain: University of Valencia Press, 2011), 199–200; Naama Sukenik, David Iluz, Orit Shamir, Alexander Varvak, and Zohar Amar, "Purple-Dyed Textiles From Wadi Murabba'at: Historical, Archaeological, and Chemical Aspects," *Archaeological Textiles Review* 55 (2013): 50; Lloyd B. Jensen, "Royal Purple of Tyre," 111; Masanori Sato and Yoshiko Saski, "Blue and Purple Dyestuffs Used for Ancient Textiles," *Dyes in History and Archaeology* 19 (2003): 101; Jan Wouters, Ina Vanden Berghe, Ghislaine Richard, Rene Breniaux, and Dominique Cardon, "Dye Analysis of Selected Textiles from Three Roman Sites in the Eastern Desert of Egypt: A Hypothesis on the Dyeing Technology in Roman and Coptic Egypt," *Dyes in History and Archaeology* 21 (2008): 11.
5   Dominique Cardon, *Natural Dyes: Sources, Tradition, Technology and Science* (London: Archetype, 2007), 553.
6   Ibid., 551.
7   Ibid., 553.
8   Ibid., 554.
9   Ibid., 555.

2.1   *History*

Though largely associated with the Levant (especially Tyre), the first evidence of using mollusks to produce purple comes from Crete; large piles of mollusk shells have been discovered there that date between 1800 and 1600 BC.[10] Many Phoenician sites along the coast of the Levant have potsherds with molluskan purple residue with the earliest evidence of the dying process dating to the 13th or 12th century BC. Tyre, a major Phoenician city, is one of these sites and is the origin of the "Tyrian" moniker for the true purple dye.[11]

Beginning in the 1st millennium BC, purple was established under the Assyrians as a symbol of wealth. This subsequently carried over into other civilizations. Purple did not become associated with prestige in Egypt, however, until the time of the Ptolemies.[12]

For the Romans, purple did not become a status symbol until about the 3rd century BC. Rome started a thirst for purple that had never before been seen. Rulers dictated who could wear purple and in what qualities.[13] The most luxurious types of purple were reserved for the emperor. *Purpurae insania* (purple mania) reached its peak in the 2nd century AD. The variety of purples available ranged from expensive "true purple" derived from large quantities of mollusks to cheap imitations from plant dyes. Egyptian and Gaulish dyers were specialists at imitating purple.[14]

Under Diocletian and Constantine, official measures were put in place regarding the expensive purple. The higher quality dyes were even classified as "sacred purple." While the imperial court enjoyed the luxurious purple, customers from all social classes had access to imitation purple.[15]

2.2   *Dye Production*

A large number of mollusks was required to produce this purple dye. Research shows that on average one mollusk yields about 1.5 grams of dye. In order to dye three kilograms of wool more than 1000 mollusks would be required.[16]

To produce the purple dye, the shell of the mollusks must be broken and the hypobranchial gland must be ruptured. When this occurs, the cells in the gland die and release their contents. This results in the precursors coming into

---

10   Ibid., 571.

11   Zvi C. Koren, "Archaeo-chemical analysis of Royal Purple on a Darius I stone jar," *Microchimica Acta* 162 (2008): 382.

12   Cardon, *Natural Dyes*, 572.

13   Ibid., 573.

14   Ibid.

15   Ibid., 574.

16   Naama Sukenik et al., "Purple-Dyed Textiles from Wadi Murabba'at," 47.

contact with enzymes—aryl-sulphatases. The purple precursors then undergo one of two reactions depending on the type of mollusk. For one type, oxygen reacts with indoxyl derivatives to form tyriverdins which are converted to purple when exposed to light. In the other type of reaction, indoxyl derivatives form indigoid colorants quickly with exposure to oxygen.[17]

In antiquity the technique for extracting and processing the dye was written about by few authors. Three of the most helpful are Aristotle, Vitruvius, and Pliny the Elder, although Pliny's account is not sufficient to reconstruct the entire process. According to these writers, the first part of the process was to collect the secretions from the hypobranchial glands. Vitruvius wrote that the shells were broken open and the glands were pounded in mortars with honey. Salt was also added to the glands in proportion of about .570 kg of salt to 34.2 kg of purple mixture. The salt and gland mixture was left to macerate for no more than three days. Afterward the mixture was diluted with water. The amount of water varies between accounts. One account says that there should be one amphora (25.92 liters) of water for 50 pounds of the gland mixture.[18] Another source says that there should be 2,952 liters of water added to two kilograms of the gland mixture. After the water was added the mixture was heated and after about ten days the mixture was filtered and tested with ungreased sheep's wool. If the dye was ready, the rest of the wool would be added and left for five hours.[19]

Experimental archaeology has tried to replicate the process and has found that the record is incomplete. Purple dye has been successfully produced, but the vat technique of antiquity still remains a mystery.[20]

2.3   *Mollusks*

All mollusks used to produce purple dye belong to the *Muricidae* family of sea snails. *Muricidae* are carnivorous and feed on small worms and crustaceans. They are also know to feed on their own species. The size of *Muricidae* shells varies in size from about 6 mm in length to 20–30 cm.[21] There are about 1,300 species of *Muricidae* throughout the world, though mostly found in warm or temperate climates. It is unknown if all are capable of producing purple, and very few were actually used for that purpose.[22]

In the Mediterranean, three species became famous in the ancient world for producing purple dye: *Bolinus brandaris*, *Hexaplex trunculus* and *Stramonita*

---

17   Cardon, *Natural Dyes*, 555.
18   Ibid., 559.
19   Ibid., 560.
20   Ibid., 562.
21   Ibid., 565.
22   Ibid., 566.

haemastoma.[23] *Bolinus brandaris* yields Tyrian purple. *Hexaplex trunculus* yields a blue-purple.[24] *Stramonita haemastoma* yields a red-violet similar to Tyrian purple.[25]

2.4   *Purple in Egypt*

In Egypt, purple was created from a two-step process using indigo and madder (a red, plant based dye). This purple, while "false," was still of a high quality and became characteristic of purple dye in Egypt.[26] Few examples of Tyrian purple have been found in Egypt, indicating that this more economic method was wide spread, especially in the 1st millennium AD. When Tyrian purple has been found, it has been limited to small decorative elements because of the expensive nature of the dye.[27] Instead, the most common dyes used in Coptic textiles were madder, kermes (insect, *Kermes vermilio*), Armenian cochineal, and lac dye (insect, *Laccifer lacca*) for red and indigo for blue.[28]

2.5   *Indigo and Madder*

Indigo is a blue dye used in combination with other dyes to create purple. While created synthetically in modern times (it is used for denim jeans), the original source of the dye was plant-based.[29] Madder is a red dye that originates from several different plant species. It has also been manufactured synthetically and has since fallen out of use.[30]

3   The Textile Collection of Fag el-Gamous

The textile samples used in this study draw from several seasons of excavation at Fag el-Gamous. Excavation years include: 1987, 1992, 1994, 1998, and 2000.

---

23   Ibid.
24   Ibid., 579.
25   Ibid., 583.
26   De Moor et al., "Radiocarbon Dating and Dye Analysis of Roman Linen Tunics and Dalmatics with Purple Coloured Design," 44; Lloyd B. Jensen, "Royal Purple of Tyre," 111.
27   De Moor, et al., "Radiocarbon Dating and Dye Analysis of Roman Linen Tunics and Dalmatics with Purple Colored Design," 45.
28   Marek Trojanowicz, Jowita Orska-Gawrys, Izabella Surowiec, Bogdan Szostek, Katarzyna Urbaniak-Walczak, Jerzy Khel, and Marek Wrobel, "Chromatographic Investigation of Dyes Extracted from Coptic Textiles from the National Museum in Warsaw," *Studies in Conservation* 49/2 (2004): 116.
29   Encyclopædia Britannica, s.v. "Indigo," accessed April 13, 2015, http://www.britannica .com/EBchecked/topic/286171/indigo.
30   Encyclopædia Britannica, s.v. "Madder," accessed April 13, 2015, http://www.britannica .com/EBchecked/topic/355682/madder.

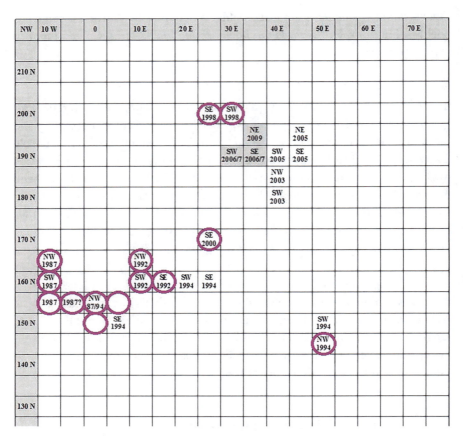

FIGURE 9.1   Location of textiles in this study; grid represents the cemetery; purple circles
             indicate squares that yielded textiles used in this study

Figure 9.1 shows a map of the locations for each season; squares with textiles
used in this study are circled in purple. Textiles were selected for study if it appeared that purple threads were used in the fragment. All samples were wool-
en threads. Although linen is the most common material used in burials at Fag
el-Gamous, the material does not hold dye well and is usually left undyed. This
study was as exhaustive as possible in trying to find all available[31] fragments
with purple threads. They span the life of the surface and 3-meter-deep shafts
in the cemetery ranging in use from 100 BC through 700 AD. Some fragments
were excluded if it appeared that in trying to extract a thread more harm would
be done to the fragment in the process than would be beneficial to the study.

---

31   All textiles were brought to Brigham Young University by formal and official agreement
      with the Supreme Council of Antiquities.

The samples were also limited to what was available in the collection at Brigham Young University.

Not all samples are immediately identified as purple. Some look black, blue, or even brown. These were included in the study with the hopes of providing data to aid future field and lab identification of color.

4   Methods of Dye Analysis

Dye analysis was conducted according to the process described in W. Nowik, R. Marcinowska, K. Kusyk, D. Cardon, and M. Trojanowicz, "High performance liquid chromatography of slightly soluble brominated indigoids from Tyrian purple," *Journal of Chromatography A* 1218 (2011): 1244–1252.

The first step was to collect the samples. The experiment requires 1–3 mg of textile sample for analysis; this is approximately 1–2 cm of a single thread. A few threads from each textile sample were collected and put in plastic screw-top vials. As it was not feasible to weigh the textile sample before removing a thread, a more visual standard was applied for collection. Sometimes, this was a single thread approximately 1–2 cm in length, other times it was several smaller pieces that resulted in a comparable measurement.

Once the threads were collected, 0.5 ml of dimethylsulfoxide (DMSO) was added to the vial. The vial with the textile sample and DMSO was incubated in a water bath at 80° C for 15 minutes.

The solution was then extracted out of the plastic vial using a pipette and filtered using a syringe and filter into glass vials to send to the high performance liquid chromatography (HPLC) lab to identify the dye components.

The BYU HPLC lab followed the experiment as outlined in the previously mentioned article. The results of HPLC analysis are given in minutes. HPLC analysis measures the flow rates of a solution after it has interacted with another material in the column. These flow rates make it possible to identify different compounds. We were able to compare HPLC profiles of pigments extracted from the Fag el-Gamous textiles with the profiles of a Tyrian purple standard (6,6' dibromoindigotin) and an indigo standard (Sigma-Aldrich, product 229296). Some samples were neither indigo nor Tyrian, and further testing must be done in order to determine the compound(s) used for the dye on these threads.

Analyses were conducted eight times. After four runs, a standard was included within each data set, resulting in four runs that were not attached to a standard and four runs that were attached. Thus, results from Runs 1–4 can be compared to one another, but they cannot be directly compared to Runs 5–8.

The standards used for Run 1 held for Runs 2, 3 and 4. Runs 5, 6, 7, and 8 were run in comparison with a standard contained in the sample set.[32]

Run 7 retested threads with inconclusive results from Run 1. While Run 7 is later chronologically than Runs 2–6, its results will be reported with Run 1 to provide the best comparison and understanding of the data.

Run 8 was conducted without a consistent comparison standard. It was not known until after this run of tests that the equipment in the HPLC lab can only analyze samples in batches of 20. While this did not affect results from earlier runs, it is clear that the results here are internally inconsistent. For this reason, the resulting data will be provided in Table 9.8, but there will be no additional analysis.

5   Results

5.1   *Data and Analysis – Standards*
5.1.1   Tyrian Standard

HPLC results of the Tyrian standard indicate that there is a peak at 13.742 (also 13.733) minutes for Run 5, 15.885 minutes for Run 6, 15.953 minutes for Run 7, and 15.877 minutes for Run 8. None of the textile samples show a peak at these times.

Indigo Standard:

HPLC results of the indigo standard show a peak at 12.913 minutes for Runs 1–4, 13.309 (also 13.315) minutes for Run 5, 14.974 minutes for Run 6, 15.489 minutes for Run 7 and 15.000 minutes for Run 8. Nearly every sample shows a peak at these times.

Tyrian and Indigo Standard Mixture:

HPLC results of a mixture of both indigo and Tyrian standards (Figure 9.2) from Run 6 show that Tyrian and indigo could be viewed separately. Earlier results were not clear in distinguishing two separate peaks (although Sample 53 from Run 5 came close). The first peak is from the indigo standard and the second is the Tyrian standard.

---

32   As each run was conducted, more about the process was understood, as a result the data does not look the same across the entirety of the project. For example, in the inaugural run, a Tyrian standard had yet to be obtained. Due to time constraints it was decided to move forward with the testing. Results not immediately identified as indigo were later retested.

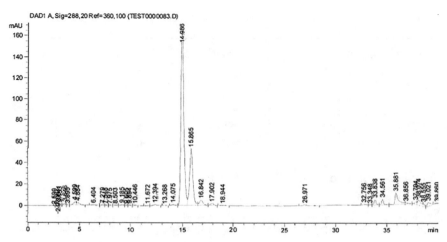

FIGURE 9.2 HPLC results of a mixture of Tyrian and Indigo Standards from Run 6 (Sample
        IT1)

5.2   Data and Analysis – Runs 1 and 7

The first run tested 8 different threads from 6 different textile fragments and
included an indigo standard. Results and descriptions are summarized in
Table 9.1. Images and some HPLC profiles of the samples can be seen in Figure
9.4 following the analysis.

5.2.1   Sample 1

200/210N 30/40E SW #50 is a textile fragment most likely from a tunic. The
clavus (vertical decorative stripe) is formed by two different shades of purple
wool and yellow wool.

A close up of 200/210N 30/40E SW #50 (Figure 9.3) shows the difference
between the two purple wools used in the tapestry design. One shade is very
dark, almost black, and is very similar to indigo. The other shade is lighter and
is very similar in color to other textiles that have been positively identified as
Tyrian purple.

Initial HPLC results from Sample 1, light purple wool from 200/210N 30/40E
SW #50, seemed to indicate that sample is Tyrian purple. The results were retested in Run 7, and all three samples were confirmed to be indigo (See Table
9.2 for Run 7 results). Samples 166, 167, and 168 (part of Run 7, but from the
same textile as Samples 1 and 2) are all nearly identical with peaks around 15.5
minutes. Sample 166 is from a broken portion of the tapestry design. Sample
167 is from a more intact portion of the tapestry design. Sample 168 is from the

TABLE 9.1   Dye analysis Run 1

Sample	Location	Description	Results (in minutes)	Conclusion
Sample 1 (S1)	200/210N 30/40E SW #50	Light Purple Wool	13.447 (and 19.539[a])	Inconclusive
Sample 2 (S2)	200/210N 30/40E SW #50	Dark Purple Wool	12.924	Indigo
Sample 3 (S3)	2000 Season (170/180N 20/30E) SE 12 Wool 1	Light Purple Wool (possibly discolored)	12.917	Indigo
Sample 4 (S4)	2000 Season (170/180N 20/30E) SE 12 Wool 1	Medium Purple Wool	12.923	Indigo
Sample 5 (S5)	160/170 N 10/20E SW #26A.2	Medium Purple Wool	12.908	Indigo
Sample 6 (S6)	Square 2 (150/160N 0/10E NW) #5	Medium Purple Wool	12.916	Indigo
Sample 7 (S7)	150/160N 0/10E SW Mud Brick Tomb	Dark Purple Wool	9.662	Undetermined
Sample 8 (S8)	2000 Season (170/180N 20/30E) SE #35	Dark Purple Wool	12.907	Indigo
Sample 9 (S9)	N/A	Indigo Standard	12.913	N/A

a   Some samples exhibited two peaks. When that is the case, both peaks are noted. If the peak is irrelevant to the current question (meaning it demonstrates a peak in an element that does not affect the color) then it is put in parentheses.

grape-like design at the bottom of the *clavus*. These results indicate that the light purple is indigo, but in a lesser concentration than Sample 2, which is the dark purple from 200/210N 30/40E SW #50. It is probable that the lighter purple is also mixed with another dye, though what that other component is remains to be discovered.

FIGURE 9.3 A close-up of 200/210N 30/40E SW #50

TABLE 9.2 Dye analysis Run 7

Sample	Location	Description	Results (in minutes)	Conclusion
Sample 166 (S166)	200/210N 30/40E SW #50	Light Purple from Broken Tapestry Design	15.512	Indigo
Sample 167 (S167)	200/210N 30/40E SW #50	Light Purple from more intact Design	15.608	Indigo
Sample 168 (S168)	200/210N 30/40E SW #50	Light Purple from Grape-like Design	15.619	Indigo
T2	N/A	Tyrian Standard	15.953	N/A
I2	N/A	Indigo Standard	15.489	N/A
IT2	N/A	50% Indigo 50% Tyrian (200/200μL)	15.560 and 16.438	N/A

5.2.2 Sample 2

The dark purple from 200/210N 30/40E SW #50 was also tested. Sample 2 was identified as indigo based on the initial run of the indigo standard. The indigo standard, Sample 9, was initially recorded at 12.9 minutes matching Sample 2 which was also recorded at 12.9 minutes.

5.2.3   Samples 3 and 4

Light purple wool that may have been discolored from 2000 Season SE 12 (wool) 1 was identified as indigo based on the initial run of the indigo standard. The indigo standard, Sample 9, was initially recorded at 12.9 minutes matching Sample 3 which was also recorded at 12.9 minutes.

Sample 4 from the same textile yielded the same result.

5.2.4   Sample 5

Medium purple wool from 160/170N 10/20E SW #26A.2 was identified as indigo based on the initial run of the indigo standard. The indigo standard, Sample 9, was initially recorded at 12.9 minutes matching Sample 5 which was also recorded at 12.9 minutes.

5.2.5   Sample 6

Medium purple wool from Square 2 #5 was identified as indigo based on the initial run of the indigo standard. The indigo standard, Sample 9, was initially recorded at 12.9 minutes matching Sample 6 which was also recorded at 12.9 minutes.

5.2.6   Sample 7

Dark purple wool from 150/160N 0/10E SW Mud Brick Tomb was identified as indigo based on the initial run of the indigo standard. The indigo standard, Sample 9, was initially recorded at 12.9 minutes matching Sample 7 which was also recorded at 12.9 minutes.

5.2.7   Sample 8

Dark purple wool from 2000 Season SE #35 was identified as indigo based on the initial run of the indigo standard. The indigo standard, Sample 9, was initially recorded at 12.9 minutes matching Sample 8 which was also recorded at 12.9 minutes.

5.2.8   Sample 9

Sample 9 is the indigo standard with a peak recorded at 12.9 minutes.

Based on these results, Samples 2, 3, 4, 5, 6, and 8 are indigo. Other threads from Sample 1 were retested in later runs and confirmed to be indigo. Sample 7 is undetermined, but is neither Tyrian nor indigo.

5.3   *Data and Analysis – Run 2*

The second run tested 11 threads from 10 different textiles. Results and descriptions are summarized in Table 9.3. Images of the samples can be seen in Figure 9.5.

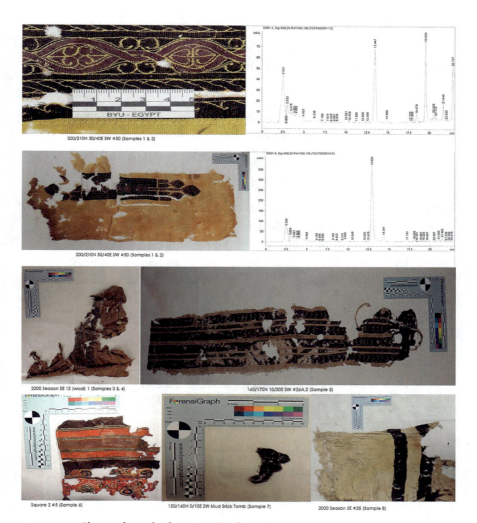

FIGURE 9.4 Photos of samples from Run 1 (and Run 7)

5.3.1   Sample 10
Medium purple wool from 200/210N 20/30E SE #8 was identified as indigo based on the initial run of the indigo standard. The indigo standard, Sample 9, was initially recorded at 12.9 minutes matching Sample 10 which was also recorded at 12.9 minutes.

5.3.2   Sample 11
Dark purple wool from 160/170N 10/20E SE #22A.1 was unidentified. Results were recorded at 11.4 minutes.

TABLE 9.3   Dye analysis Run 2

Sample	Location	Description	Results (in minutes)	Conclusion
Sample 10 (S10)	200/210N 20/30E SE #8	Light Purple Wool	12.904	Indigo
Sample 11 (S11)	160/170N 10/20E SE #22A.1	Dark Purple Wool	11.491	Undetermined
Sample 12 (S12)	150/160N 0/10W NE #14.2.2	Light Purple Wool	12.792	Indigo
Sample 13 (S13)	150/160N 0/10W NE #14.2.1	Medium Purple Wool	12.905 (and 19.237)	Indigo
Sample 14 (S14)	2000 Season (170/180N 20/30E) SE #12 (wool) 2	Dark Purple Wool (main)	12.901	Indigo
Sample 15 (S15)	2000 Season (170/180N 20/30E) SE #12 (wool) 2	Dark Purple Wool (small band)	12.898	Indigo
Sample 16 (S16)	150/160N 0/10E NW #13.2	Light Purple Wool (from tapestry)	12.896	Indigo
Sample 17 (S17)	150/160N 0/10E NW #13.1	Light Purple Wool (from tapestry)	12.893	Indigo
Sample 18 (S18)	160/170N 10/20E SW #26EFabric5.2	Medium Purple Wool	12.889	Indigo
Sample 19 (S19)	160/170N 0/10W SW #8AFolder1.1	Medium Purple Wool	12.891	Indigo
Sample 20 (S20)	160/170N 0/10W SW #8AFolder1.2	Medium Purple Wool	12.901	Indigo

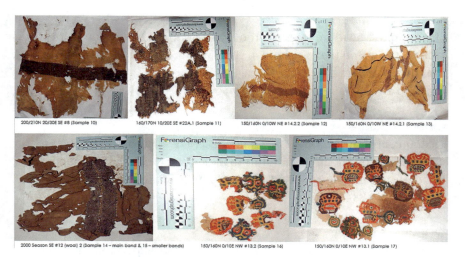

200/210N 20/30E SE #8 (Sample 10)   160/170N 10/20E SE #22A.1 (Sample 11)   150/160N 0/10W NE #14.2.2 (Sample 12)   150/160N 0/10W NE #14.2.1 (Sample 13)

2000 Season SE #12 (wool) 2 (Sample 14 – main band & 15 – smaller bands)   150/160N 0/10E NW #13.2 (Sample 16)   150/160N 0/10E NW #13.1 (Sample 17)

FIGURE 9.5 Photos of samples from Run 2

5.3.3 Sample 12

Light purple wool from 150/160N 0/10W NE #14.2.2 was identified as indigo based on the initial run of the indigo standard. The indigo standard, Sample 9, was initially recorded at 12.9 minutes nearly matching Sample 12 which was recorded at 12.79 minutes.

5.3.4 Sample 13

Medium purple wool from 150/160N 0/10W NE #14.2.1 was identified as indigo based on the initial run of the indigo standard. The indigo standard, Sample 9, was initially recorded at 12.9 minutes matching Sample 13 which was also recorded at 12.9 minutes. The other peaks are unidentified.

5.3.5 Samples 14 and 15

Both samples of dark purple wool from 2000 Season SE #12 (wool) 2 were identified as indigo based on the initial run of the indigo standard. The indigo standard, Sample 9, was initially recorded at 12.9 minutes matching Samples 14 and 15 which were recorded at 12.9 minutes and 12.89 minutes.

5.3.6 Sample 16

Light purple wool from tapestry from 150/160N 0/10E NW #13.2 was identified as indigo based on the initial run of the indigo standard. The indigo standard, Sample 9, was initially recorded at 12.9 minutes matching Sample 16 which was recorded at 12.89 minutes.

5.3.7   Sample 17
Light purple wool from tapestry from 150/160N 0/10E NW #13.1 was identified as indigo based on the initial run of the indigo standard. The indigo standard, Sample 9, was initially recorded at 12.9 minutes matching Sample 17 which was recorded at 12.89 minutes.

5.3.8   Sample 18
Medium purple wool from 160/170N 10/20E SW #26EFabric5.2 was identified as indigo based on the initial run of the indigo standard. The indigo standard, Sample 9, was initially recorded at 12.9 minutes matching Sample 18 which was recorded at 12.88 minutes.

5.3.9   Sample 19
Medium purple wool from 160/170N 0/10W SW #8AFolder1.1 was identified as indigo based on the initial run of the indigo standard. The indigo standard, Sample 9, was initially recorded at 12.9 minutes matching Sample 19 which was recorded at 12.89 minutes.

5.3.10   Sample 20
Medium purple wool from 160/170N 0/10W SW #8AFolder1.2 was identified as indigo based on the initial run of the indigo standard. The indigo standard, Sample 9, was initially recorded at 12.9 minutes matching Sample 20 which was also recorded at 12.9 minutes.

    Based on these results, Samples 10, 12, 13, 14, 15, 16, 17, 18, 19, and 20 are indigo. Sample 11 is undetermined, but is neither Tyrian nor indigo.

5.4   *Data and Analysis – Run 3*
The third run tested 11 threads from 11 different textiles. Results and descriptions are summarized in Table 9.4. Images of the samples can be seen in Figure 9.6.

5.4.1   Sample 21
Light/medium purple wool from 150/160N 0/10E NW #4 was identified as indigo based on the initial run of the indigo standard. The indigo standard, Sample 9, was initially recorded at 12.9 minutes nearly matching Sample 21 which was recorded at 12.58 minutes.

5.4.2   Sample 22
Light/medium purple wool from 160/170N 10/20E SW #22A.1 was identified as indigo based on the initial run of the indigo standard. The indigo standard,

TABLE 9.4   Dye analysis Run 3

Sample	Location	Description	Results (in minutes)	Conclusion
Sample 21 (S21)	150/160N 0/10E NW #4	Light/Medium Purple Wool	12.583	Indigo
Sample 22 (S22)	160/170N 10/20E SW #22A.1	Light/Medium Purple Wool	12.899	Indigo
Sample 23 (S23)	160/170N 10/20E SW #26CHead#1.2	Medium Purple Wool	12.900	Indigo
Sample 24 (S24)	200/210N 30/40E SW #25.2	Disintegrated Purple Wool	12.911	Indigo
Sample 25 (S25)	160/170N 10/20E SW #46C.1	Dark Purple Wool	12.908	Indigo
Sample 26 (S26)	160/170N 10/20E SW #16.2	Discolored Light Purple Wool	12.915	Indigo
Sample 27 (S27)	160/170N 10/20E SW #8.1	Purple/Blue Wool	12.910	Indigo
Sample 28 (S28)	160/170N 10/20E SW #8.5	Discolored Medium Purple Wool	12.916	Indigo
Sample 29 (S29)	160/170N 10/20E SW #14.2	Dark Purple Wool	12.912	Indigo
Sample 30 (S30)	160/170N 10/20E SW #39L.1	Dark Purple Wool	12.914	Indigo
Sample 31 (S31)	160/170N 10/20E SW #39L.3	Dark Purple Wool	12.907	Indigo

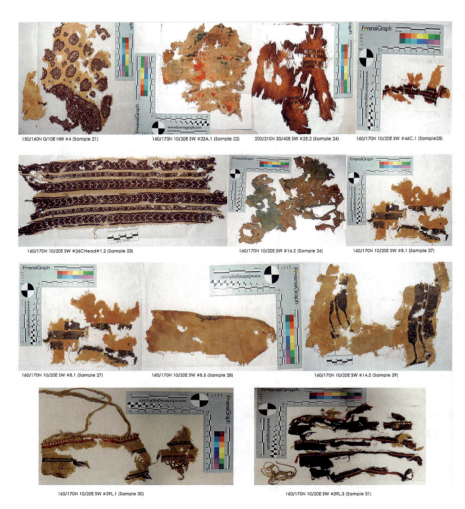

150/160N 0/10E NW #4 (Sample 21)   160/170N 10/20E SW #22A.1 (Sample 22)   200/210N 30/40E SW #25.2 (Sample 24)   160/170N 10/20E SW #46C.1 (Sample25)

160/170N 10/20E SW #26CHead#1.2 (Sample 23)   160/170N 10/20E SW #16.2 (Sample 26)   160/170N 10/20E SW #8.1 (Sample 27)

160/170N 10/20E SW #8.1 (Sample 27)   160/170N 10/20E SW #8.5 (Sample 28)   160/170N 10/20E SW #14.2 (Sample 29)

160/170N 10/20E SW #39L.1 (Sample 30)   160/170N 10/20E SW #39L.3 (Sample 31)

FIGURE 9.6   Photos of samples from Run 3

Sample 9, was initially recorded at 12.9 minutes matching Sample 22 which was recorded at 12.89 minutes.

5.4.3   Sample 23

Medium purple wool from 160/170N 10/20E SW #26CHead#1.2 was identified as indigo based on the initial run of the indigo standard. The indigo standard, Sample 9, was initially recorded at 12.9 minutes matching Sample 23 which was also recorded at 12.9 minutes.

5.4.4 Sample 24

Disintegrated purple wool from 200/210N 30/40E SW #25.2 was identified as indigo based on the initial run of the indigo standard. The indigo standard, Sample 9, was initially recorded at 12.9 minutes matching Sample 24 which was also recorded at 12.9 minutes.

5.4.5 Sample 25

Dark purple wool from 160/170N 10/20E SW #46C.1 was identified as indigo based on the initial run of the indigo standard. The indigo standard, Sample 9, was initially recorded at 12.9 minutes matching Sample 25 which was also recorded at 12.9 minutes.

5.4.6 Sample 26

Discolored light purple wool from 160/170N 10/20E SW #16.2 was identified as indigo based on the initial run of the indigo standard. The indigo standard, Sample 9, was initially recorded at 12.9 minutes matching Sample 26 which was also recorded at 12.9 minutes.

5.4.7 Sample 27

Blue/purple wool from 160/170N 10/20E SW #8.1 was identified as indigo based on the initial run of the indigo standard. The indigo standard, Sample 9, was initially recorded at 12.9 minutes matching Sample 27 which was also recorded at 12.9 minutes.

5.4.8 Sample 28

Discolored medium purple wool from 160/170N 10/20E SW #8.5 was identified as indigo based on the initial run of the indigo standard. The indigo standard, Sample 9, was initially recorded at 12.9 minutes matching Sample 28 which was also recorded at 12.9 minutes.

5.4.9 Sample 29

Dark purple wool from 160/170N 10/20E SW #14.2 was identified as indigo based on the initial run of the indigo standard. The indigo standard, Sample 9, was initially recorded at 12.9 minutes matching Sample 29 which was also recorded at 12.9 minutes.

5.4.10 Sample 30

Dark purple wool from 160/170N 10/20E SW #39L.1 was identified as indigo based on the initial run of the indigo standard. The indigo standard, Sample 9, was initially recorded at 12.9 minutes matching Sample 30 which was also recorded at 12.9 minutes.

5.4.11   Sample 31
Dark purple wool from 160/170N 10/20E SW #39L.3 was identified as indigo based on the initial run of the indigo standard. The indigo standard, Sample 9, was initially recorded at 12.9 minutes matching Sample 31 which was also recorded at 12.9 minutes.

Based on these results, Samples 21, 22, 23, 24, 25, 26, 27, 28, 29, 30, and 31 are indigo.

5.5   *Data and Analysis – Run 4*
The fourth run tested 8 threads from 8 different textiles. Results and descriptions are summarized in Table 9.5. Images of the samples can be seen in Figure 9.7.

5.5.1   Sample 32
Medium purple wool from 160/170N 10/20E NW #2.3 was identified as indigo based on the initial run of the indigo standard. The indigo standard, Sample 9, was initially recorded at 12.9 minutes matching Sample 32 which was also recorded at 12.9 minutes.

5.5.2   Sample 33
Dark purple wool from 160/170N 10/20E SE #2.2 was unidentified. Results were recorded at 9.6 minutes.

5.5.3   Sample 34
Mix of red and blue wool fibers from 160/170N 10/20E SE #10.3 was identified as indigo based on the initial run of the indigo standard. The indigo standard, Sample 9, was initially recorded at 12.9 minutes matching Sample 34 which was also recorded at 12.9 minutes.

5.5.4   Sample 35
Dark purple wool from 160/170N 10/20E SE #25B.2 was unidentified. Results were recorded at 9.6 minutes.

5.5.5   Sample 36
Medium purple wool from 160/170N 10/20E SW #21A Fabric6.2 was identified as indigo based on the initial run of the indigo standard. The indigo standard, Sample 9, was initially recorded at 12.9 minutes matching Sample 36 which was also recorded at 12.9 minutes.

TABLE 9.5   Dye analysis Run 4

Sample	Location	Description	Results (in minutes)	Conclusion
Sample 32 (S32)	160/170N 10/20E NW #2.3	Medium Purple Wool	12.908	Indigo
Sample 33 (S33)	160/170N 10/20E SE #2.2	Dark Purple Wool	9.646	Undetermined
Sample 34 (S34)	160/170N 10/20E SE #10.3	Wool – Mix of Blue and Red Fibers	12.918	Indigo
Sample 35 (S35)	160/170N 10/20E SE #25B.2	Dark Purple Wool	9.653	Undetermined
Sample 36 (S36)	160/170N 10/20E SW #21AFabric6.2	Medium Purple Wool	12.913	Indigo
Sample 37 (S37)	160/170N 10/20E SW #26Dhead#2.3	Medium Purple Wool	12.871	Indigo
Sample 38 (S38)	160/170N 10/20E SW #26B.2	Medium Purple Wool	12.911	Indigo
Sample 39 (S39)	160/170N 10/20E SW #39B.2	Dark Purple Wool	11.375	Undetermined

5.5.6   Sample 37

Medium purple wool from 160/170N 10/20E SW #26Dhead#2.3 was identified as indigo based on the initial run of the indigo standard. The indigo standard, Sample 9, was initially recorded at 12.9 minutes matching Sample 37 which was recorded at 12.87 minutes.

5.5.7   Sample 38

Medium purple wool from 160/170N 10/20E SW #26B.2 was identified as indigo based on the initial run of the indigo standard. The indigo standard, Sample 9,

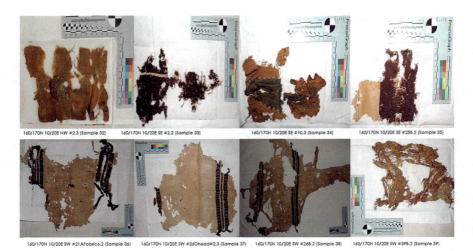

160/170N 10/20E NW #2.3 (Sample 32)   160/170N 10/20E SE #2.2 (Sample 33)   160/170N 10/20E SE #10.3 (Sample 34)   160/170N 10/20E SE #25B.2 (Sample 35)

160/170N 10/20E SW #21AFabric6.2 (Sample 36)   160/170N 10/20E SW #26Dhead#2.3 (Sample 37)   160/170N 10/20E SW #26B.2 (Sample 38)   160/170N 10/20E SW #39B.2 (Sample 39)

FIGURE 9.7   Photos of samples from Run 4

was initially recorded at 12.9 minutes matching Sample 38 which was also recorded at 12.9 minutes.

5.5.8   Sample 39
Dark purple wool from 160/170N 10/20E SW #39B.2 was unidentified. Results were recorded at 11.37 minutes.

Based on these results, Samples 32, 34, 36, 37, and 38 are indigo. Samples 33, 35, and 39 are undetermined, but are neither Tyrian nor indigo.

5.6   *Data and Analysis – Run 5*
The fifth run tested 11 threads from 9 different textiles and 7 standards. Results and descriptions are summarized in Table 9.6. Results from Samples 40–50 are compared with the results of the standards tested in Samples 51–57. Images of the samples can be seen in Figure 9.8.

5.6.1   Sample 40
Medium purple wool from band from 160/170N 10/20E SW #39G was identified as indigo based on the second run of the indigo standard. The indigo standard, Sample 51, was recorded at 13.3 minutes matching Sample 40 which was also recorded at 13.3 minutes.

5.6.2   Sample 41
Medium purple wool from roundel from 160/170N 10/20E SW #39G (Figure 9.8) was identified as indigo based on the second run of the indigo standard. The

TABLE 9.6   Dye analysis Run 5

Sample	Location	Description	Results (in minutes)	Conclusion
Sample 40 (S40)	160/170N 10/20E SW #39G	Medium Purple Wool from Band	13.362	Indigo
Sample 41 (S41)	160/170N 10/20E SW #39G	Medium Purple Wool from Roundel	12.738	Indigo
Sample 42 (S42)	160/170N 10/20E SW #39G	Dark Purple Wool from Band (bottom)	13.359	Indigo
Sample 43 (S43)	160/170N 0/10W NW #7D.3	Medium Reddish Purple Wool (vibrant)	13.363	Indigo
Sample 44 (S44)	160/170N 0/10W NW #7D.2.3	Medium Purple Wool	13.349	Indigo
Sample 45 (S45)	160/170N 10/20E SW # 38A	Medium Purple Wool from back of designs	13.336	Indigo
Sample 46 (S46)	160/170N 10/20E SW #46A.2	Medium Purple Wool	13.355	Indigo
Sample 47 (S47)	160/170N 0/10W NW #6F.2	Medium Purple Wool	13.335	Indigo
Sample 48 (S48)	160/170N 0/10W NW #6F.1	Medium Purple Wool	13.362	Indigo
Sample 49 (S49)	Not numbered; likely: 150/160N 0/10E NW #13 (From display – piece with yellow fork)	Dark Purple Wool	10.005	Undetermined
Sample 50 (S50)	160/170N 10/20E SW #39A	Red/Purple Wool	13.356	Indigo
Sample 51 (S51)	N/A	Indigo	13.309	N/A

TABLE 9.6   Dye analysis Run 5 (*cont.*)

Sample	Location	Description	Results (in minutes)	Conclusion
Sample 52 (S52)	N/A	Tyrian	13.742	N/A
Sample 53 (S53)	N/A	50% Indigo 50% Tyrian (200µL)	13.325 and 13.691	N/A
Sample 54 (S54)	N/A	25% Indigo 75% Tyrian (100/300µL)	13.331	N/A
Sample 55 (S55)	N/A	75% Indigo 25% (300/100µL)	13.327	N/A
Sample 56 (S56)	N/A	Indigo	13.315	N/A
Sample 57 (S57)	N/A	Tyrian	13.733	

indigo standard, Sample 51, was recorded at 13.3 minutes similar to Sample 41 which was recorded at 12.7 minutes.

5.6.3   Sample 42

Medium purple wool from band from 160/170N 10/20E SW #39G was identified as indigo based on the second run of the indigo standard. The indigo standard, Sample 51, was recorded at 13.3 minutes matching Sample 42 which was also recorded at 13.3 minutes.

5.6.4   Sample 43

Medium red/purple wool from 160/170N 0/10W NW #7D.3 was identified as indigo based on the second run of the indigo standard. The indigo standard, Sample 51, was recorded at 13.3 minutes matching Sample 43 which was also recorded at 13.3 minutes.

5.6.5   Sample 44

Medium purple wool from 160/170N 0/10W NW #7D.2.3 was identified as indigo based on the second run of the indigo standard. The indigo standard, Sample

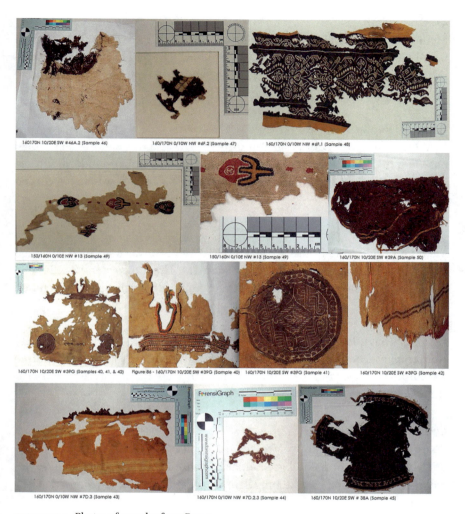

FIGURE 9.8 Photos of samples from Run 5

51, was recorded at 13.3 minutes matching Sample 44 which was also recorded at 13.3 minutes.

5.6.6   Sample 45

Medium purple wool from 160/170N 10/20E SW #38A was identified as indigo based on the second run of the indigo standard. The indigo standard, Sample 51, was recorded at 13.3 minutes matching Sample 45 which was also recorded at 13.3 minutes.

5.6.7   Sample 46
Medium purple wool from 160/170N 10/20E SW #46A.2 was identified as indigo based on the second run of the indigo standard. The indigo standard, Sample 51, was recorded at 13.3 minutes matching Sample 46 which was also recorded at 13.3 minutes.

5.6.8   Sample 47
Medium purple wool from 160/170N 0/10W NW #6F.2 was identified as indigo based on the second run of the indigo standard. The indigo standard, Sample 51, was recorded at 13.3 minutes matching Sample 47 which was also recorded at 13.3 minutes.

5.6.9   Sample 48
Medium purple wool from 160/170N 0/10W NW #6F.1 was identified as indigo based on the second run of the indigo standard. The indigo standard, Sample 51, was recorded at 13.3 minutes matching Sample 48 which was also recorded at 13.3 minutes.

5.6.10   Sample 49
Sample 49 was not numbered but is likely 150/160N 0/10E NW #13. Dark purple wool from the design in the center was unidentified. Results were recorded at 10.005 minutes.

5.6.11   Sample 50
Red/purple wool from 160/170N 10/20E SW #39A was identified as indigo based on the second run of the indigo standard. The indigo standard, Sample 51, was recorded at 13.3 minutes matching Sample 50 which was also recorded at 13.3 minutes.

5.6.12   Sample 51
Sample 51 is the indigo standard with a peak recorded at 13.3 minutes.

5.6.13   Sample 52
Sample 52 is a Tyrian Standard. Results were recorded at 13.7 minutes

5.6.14   Sample 53
Sample 53 was 50% Tyrian and 50% Indigo standard mix. This allowed for the identification of the two separate compounds (Figure 9.2).

5.6.15   Sample 54

Sample 54 was a mix of 25% Indigo standard and 75% Tyrian standard (100/300μL). This did not give the separate peaks that are given for Sample 53. There is an odd shaped peak at 13.331. (In this instance odd is meant that it peaks as normal, but when returning to the baseline on the right side there is a slight bump outward, though not enough to produce a separate result.)

5.6.16   Sample 55

Sample 55 was a mix of 75% Indigo standard and 25% Tyrian standard (300/100μL). This did not give the separate peaks that are given for Sample 53. There is a peak at 13.327 with a slight angle change near where the peak meets the baseline, though not enough to register a separate result.

5.6.17   Sample 56

A rerun of the Indigo Standard. Results are at 13.3 minutes.

5.6.18   Sample 57

A rerun of the Tyrian Standard. Results are at 13.7 minutes.

Based on these results, Samples 40, 41, 42, 43, 44, 45, 46, 47, 48, and 50 are indigo. Samples 49 is undetermined, but is neither Tyrian nor indigo. The mixture of the standards ensured that Tyrian and Indigo could be viewed separately in HPLC analysis. Sample 53 shows two peaks that are almost separated, consistent with peaks for pure indigo and pure Tyrian purple.

5.7   *Data and Analysis – Run 6*

The sixth run tested 24 threads from 21 different textiles and 3 standards. Results for samples 58–81 were based on the results of the standards T1, I1, and IT1. Results for the Tyrian standard were recorded at 15.8 minutes and 14.9 minutes for the indigo standard. Results and descriptions are summarized in Table 9.7. Images of the samples can be seen in Figure 9.9.

5.7.1   Sample 58–60

Samples 58–60 were a rerun of 200/210N 30/40E SW #50 (Samples 1 and 2). Light purple wool from Sample 58 was identified as indigo based on the third run of the indigo standard. The indigo standard, Sample I1, was recorded at 14.9 minutes matching Sample 58 which was also recorded at 14.9 minutes. The indigo standard also matched Sample 59, which was the dark purple wool in the

TABLE 9.7   Dye analysis Run 6

Sample	Location	Description	Results (in minutes)	Conclusion
Sample 58 (S58)	200/210N 30/40E SW #50	Light Purple Wool	14.979	Indigo
Sample 59 (S59)	200/210N 30/40E SW #50	Dark Purple Wool	14.991	Indigo
Sample 60 (S60)	200/210N 30/40E SW #50	Light/Dark Purple Mix (1 strand of each)	15.027	Indigo
Sample 61 (S61)	160/170N 10/20E SW #22B.3	Medium Purple Wool	15.041	Indigo
Sample 62 (S62)	160/170N 10/20E SE #17.1	Medium Purple Wool (from band)	15.040 (and 10.472)	Indigo
Sample 63 (S63)	160/170N 10/20E SW #17A.1	Dark Purple from border design	14.983	Indigo
Sample 64 (S64)	150/160N 0/10E NW #25.1	Dark Purple from Clavi	14.987 (and 10.442)	Indigo
Sample 65 (S65)	150/160N 0/10E NW #21	Medium Purple Wool	14.985	Indigo
Sample 66 (S66)	150/160N 0/10E NW #25.2	Medium Purple from Tapestry Square	15.007	Indigo
Sample 67 (S67)	150/160N 0/10E NW #25.2	Dark Purple from Clavi	15.033 (and 10.471)	Indigo
Sample 68 (S68)	160/170N 10/20E SW #17C.3	Dark Purple from design	15.031	Indigo
Sample 69 (S69)	150/160N 0/10E NW #13	Red/Purple Wool	15.037	Indigo
Sample 70 (S70)	160/170N 10/20E SW #21B.1	Red/Purple Wool from band	15.046	Indigo

Sample	Location	Description	Results (in minutes)	Conclusion
Sample 71 (S71)	160/170N 10/20E SW #21B.4	Dark Purple (discolored) from band	10.481	Undeter-mined
Sample 72 (S72)	160/170N 10/20E SW #39D.2	Medium Purple from band	15.013	Indigo
Sample 73 (S73)	2000 Season 170/180N 20/30E #13.3	Dark Purple from band	14.569	Indigo
Sample 74 (S74)	160/170N 0/10W NW #6J.2	Medium Purple Wool Embroidery	14.987	Indigo
Sample 75 (S75)	160/170N 0/10W NW #6J.1	Dark Purple Wool	14.993	Indigo
Sample 76 (S76)	160/170N 0/10W NW #6Sample2	Discolored Purple Wool (+ warps of unknown color)	14.991	Indigo
Sample 77 (S77)	160/170N 0/10W NW #6Sample5.1	Dark Purple from band	15.028	Indigo
Sample 78 (S78)	150/160N 0/10E NW #13B1	Medium Purple from embroidery	15.033	Indigo
Sample 79 (S79)	200/210N 30/40E SW #9.2	Dark Purple Wool	15.040	Indigo
Sample 80 (S80)	200/210N 30/40E SW #9.1	Dark Purple Wool	14.979	Indigo
Sample 81 (S81)	200/210N 20/40E SW #22.3	Dark Purple from band	14.986	Indigo
T1	N/A	Tyrian Standard	15.885	N/A
I1	N/A	Indigo Standard	14.974	N/A
IT1	N/A	25% Indigo 75% Tyrian (100/300µL)	14.986 and 15.865	N/A

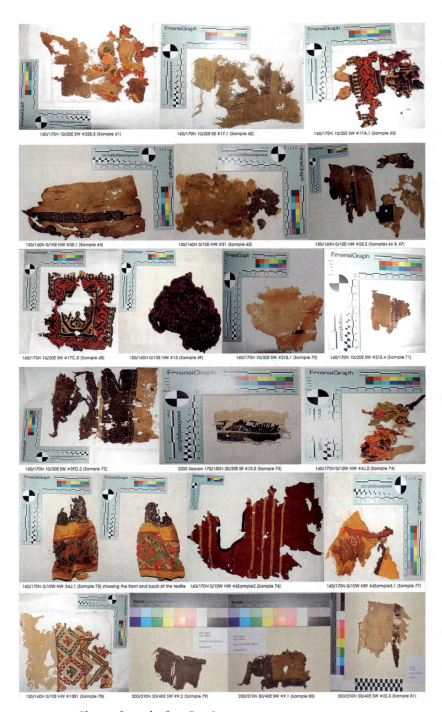

160/170N 10/20E SW #228.3 (Sample 61)   160/170N 10/20E SE #17.1 (Sample 62)   160/170N 10/20E SW #17A.1 (Sample 63)

150/160N 0/10E NW #25.1 (Sample 64)   150/160N 0/10E NW #21 (Sample 65)   150/160N 0/10E NW #25.2 (Samples 66 & 67)

160/170N 10/20E SW #17C.3 (Sample 68)   150/160N 0/10E NW #13 (Sample 69)   160/170N 10/20E SW #21B.1 (Sample 70)   160/170N 10/20E SW #21B.4 (Sample 71)

160/170N 10/20E SW #3FD.2 (Sample 72)   2000 Season 170/180N 20/30E SE #13.3 (Sample 73)   160/170N 0/10W NW #6J.2 (Sample 74)

160/170N 0/10W NW #6J.1 (Sample 75) showing the front and back of the textile   160/170N 0/10W NW #6Sample2 (Sample 76)   160/170N 0/10W NW #6Sample5.1 (Sample 77)

150/160N 0/10E NW #1381 (Sample 78)   200/210N 30/40E SW #9.2 (Sample 79)   200/210N 30/40E SW #9.1 (Sample 80)   200/210N 20/40E SW #22.3 (Sample 81)

FIGURE 9.9   Photos of samples from Run 6

textile, and Sample 60, which was a mix of the light purple wool and the dark purple wool from this textile. This clearly distinguished that both purples in this textile are indigo.

5.7.2 Sample 61

Medium purple wool from 160/170N 10/20E SW #22B.3 was identified as indigo based on the third run of the indigo standard. The indigo standard, Sample I1, was recorded at 14.9 minutes nearly matching Sample 61 which was recorded at 15.0 minutes.

5.7.3 Sample 62

Medium purple wool from band from 160/170N 10/20E SE #17.1 was identified as indigo based on the third run of the indigo standard. The indigo standard, Sample I1, was recorded at 14.9 minutes nearly matching Sample 62 which was recorded at 15.0 minutes.

5.7.4 Sample 63

Dark purple wool from border design from 160/170N 10/20E SW #17A.1 was identified as indigo based on the third run of the indigo standard. The indigo standard, Sample I1, was recorded at 14.9 minutes matching Sample 63 which was also recorded at 14.9 minutes.

5.7.5 Sample 64

Dark purple wool from *clavus* from 150/160N 0/10E NW #25.1 was identified as indigo based on the third run of the indigo standard. The indigo standard, Sample I1, was recorded at 14.9 minutes matching Sample 64 which was also recorded at 14.9 minutes.

5.7.6 Sample 65

Medium purple wool from 150/160N 0/10E NW #21 was identified as indigo based on the third run of the indigo standard. The indigo standard, Sample I1, was recorded at 14.9 minutes matching Sample 65 which was also recorded at 14.9 minutes.

5.7.7 Sample 66

Medium purple wool from tapestry square from 150/160N 0/10E NW #25.2 was identified as indigo based on the third run of the indigo standard. The indigo standard, Sample I1, was recorded at 14.9 minutes nearly matching Sample 66 which was recorded at 15.0 minutes.

5.7.8   Sample 67
Dark purple wool from *clavus* from 150/160N 0/10E NW #25.2 was identified as
indigo based on the third run of the indigo standard. The indigo standard,
Sample I1, was recorded at 14.9 minutes nearly matching Sample 67 which was
recorded at 15.0 minutes.

5.7.9   Sample 68
Dark purple wool from design from 160/170N 10/20E SW #17C.3 was identified
as indigo based on the third run of the indigo standard. The indigo standard,
Sample I1, was recorded at 14.9 minutes nearly matching Sample 68 which was
recorded at 15.0 minutes.

5.7.10   Sample 69
Red/purple unspun wool from 150/160N 0/10E NW #13 was identified as indigo
based on the third run of the indigo standard. The indigo standard, Sample I1,
was recorded at 14.9 minutes nearly matching Sample 69 which was recorded
at 15.0 minutes.

5.7.11   Sample 70
Red/purple wool from band from 160/170N 10/20E SW #21B.1 was identified as
indigo based on the third run of the indigo standard. The indigo standard,
Sample I1, was recorded at 14.9 minutes nearly matching Sample 69 which was
recorded at 15.0 minutes.

5.7.12   Sample 71
Dark purple wool (discolored) from band from 160/170N 10/20E SW #21B.4 was
unidentified. Results were recorded at 10.48 minutes.

5.7.13   Sample 72
Medium purple wool from band from 160/170N 10/20E SW #39D.2 was identified as indigo based on the third run of the indigo standard. The indigo standard, Sample I1, was recorded at 14.9 minutes nearly matching Sample 72 which
was recorded at 15.0 minutes.

5.7.14   Sample 73
Dark purple wool from band from 2000 Season 170/180N 20/30E SE #13.3 was
identified as indigo based on the third run of the indigo standard. The indigo
standard, Sample I1, was recorded at 14.9 minutes nearly matching Sample 73
which was recorded at 14.5 minutes.

5.7.15   Sample 74

Medium purple wool from embroidery from 160/170N 0/10W NW #6J.2 was identified as indigo based on the third run of the indigo standard. The indigo standard, Sample I1, was recorded at 14.9 minutes matching Sample 74 which was also recorded at 14.9 minutes.

5.7.16   Sample 75

Dark purple wool from 160/170N 0/10W NW #6J.1 was identified as indigo based on the third run of the indigo standard. The indigo standard, Sample I1, was recorded at 14.9 minutes matching Sample 75 which was also recorded at 14.9 minutes.

5.7.17   Sample 76

Discolored purple wool and warps of an unknown color from 160/170N 0/10W NW #6Sample2 was identified as indigo based on the third run of the indigo standard. The indigo standard, Sample I1, was recorded at 14.9 minutes matching Sample 76 which was also recorded at 14.9 minutes.

5.7.18   Sample 77

Dark purple wool from 160/170N 0/10W NW #6Sample5.1 was identified as indigo based on the third run of the indigo standard. The indigo standard, Sample I1, was recorded at 14.9 minutes nearly matching Sample 77 which was recorded at 15.0 minutes.

5.7.19   Sample 78

Medium purple wool from embroidery from 150/160N 0/10E NW #13B1 was identified as indigo based on the third run of the indigo standard. The indigo standard, Sample I1, was recorded at 14.9 minutes nearly matching Sample 78 which was recorded at 15.0 minutes.

5.7.20   Sample 79

Dark purple wool from 200/210N 30/40E SW #9.2 was identified as indigo based on the third run of the indigo standard. The indigo standard, Sample I1, was recorded at 14.9 minutes nearly matching Sample 79 which was recorded at 15.0 minutes.

5.7.21   Sample 80

Dark purple wool from 200/210N 30/40E SW #9.1 was identified as indigo based on the third run of the indigo standard. The indigo standard, Sample I1, was recorded at 14.9 minutes matching Sample 80 which was also recorded at 14.9 minutes.

5.7.22   Sample 81
Dark purple wool from band from 200/210N 30/40E SW #22.3 was identified as indigo based on the third run of the indigo standard. The indigo standard, Sample I1, was recorded at 14.9 minutes matching Sample 81 which was also recorded at 14.9 minutes.

Based on these results, Samples 58, 59, 60, 61, 62, 63, 64, 65, 66, 67, 68, 69, 70, 72, 73, 74, 75, 76, 77, 78, 79, 80, and 81 are indigo. Sample 71 is undetermined, but is neither Tyrian nor indigo.

5.8   *Data and Analysis – Run 8*
The eighth run tested 87 threads from 76 different textiles and 3 standards. Results and descriptions are given in Table 9.8.

Samples 82–90 and Samples 92–165 are likely indigo, though all results are undetermined due to the inconsistent application of the standard. All samples, excepting Sample 91, are thought likely to be indigo given their physical comparison with samples from Runs 1–7 as well as the relative consistency within the run (results common at 14.5, 15.0, and 15.5, with the indigo standard at 15.000 minutes, and no results as high as the Tyrian standard at 15.877).

TABLE 9.8   Dye analysis Run 8

Sample	Location	Description	Results	Conclusion
Sample 82 (S82)	200/210N 20/40E SW #22.5	Medium Purple Wool	15.495	Undetermined (likely Indigo)
Sample 83 (S83)	200/210N 20/30E SE #18.2	Dark Purple from band	15.476	Undetermined (likely Indigo)
Sample 84 (S84)	200/210N 30/40E SW #21.1	Dark Purple from band	15.492	Undetermined (likely Indigo)
Sample 85 (S85)	200/210N 30/40E SW #51.1	Dark Purple Wool	14.410	Undetermined (likely Indigo)

Sample	Location	Description	Results	Conclusion
Sample 86 (S86)	200/210N 30/40E SW #21.2	Dark Purple from band	15.494	Undetermined (likely Indigo)
Sample 87 (S87)	160/170N 0/10W NW #6.1	Medium Purple from Tapestry Design	15.477	Undetermined (likely Indigo)
Sample 88 (S88)	160/170N 0/10W NW #6.4	Medium Purple from Embroidery	15.472	Undetermined (likely Indigo)
Sample 89 (S89)	150/160N 0/10E NW #13A1	Medium Purple from Embroidery	15.507	Undetermined (likely Indigo)
Sample 90 (S90)	150/160N 0/10E NW #13A1	Dark Purple (probably black) Wool	14.451	Undetermined (likely Indigo)
Sample 91 (S91)	150/160N 0/10E NW #13B1.2	Dark Purple from Embroidery	10.772	Undetermined
Sample 92 (S92)	150/160N 0/10E NW #13B1.2	Dark Purple/ Red Mix (2 ply)	14.996	Undetermined (likely Indigo)
Sample 93 (S93)	150/160N 0/10E NW #13B1.2	Medium Purple from Embroidery	14.984	Undetermined (likely Indigo)
Sample 94 (S94)	150/160N 0/10E NW #13D1.2	Medium Purple Wool (loose)	14.996	Undetermined (likely Indigo)
Sample 95 (S95)	150/160N 0/10E NW #5G	Medium Purple from band	14.989	Undetermined (likely Indigo)
Sample 96 (S96)	150/160N 0/10E NW #5F.1	Medium Purple from band	14.555	Undetermined (likely Indigo)
Sample 97 (S97)	150/160N 0/10E NW #5F.2	Medium Purple from tapestry square	14.570	Undetermined (likely Indigo)
Sample 98 (S98)	150/160N 0/10E NW #5C.6	Medium Purple from tapestry design	14.996	Undetermined (likely Indigo)

TABLE 9.8   Dye analysis Run 8 (*cont.*)

Sample	Location	Description	Results	Conclusion
Sample 99 (S99)	150/160N 0/10E NW #5C.13	Medium Purple from tapestry design	14.999	Undetermined (likely Indigo)
Sample 100 (S100)	160/170N 0/10W NW #45C.1	Medium Purple wool	14.997	Undetermined (likely Indigo)
Sample 101 (S101)	160/170N 0/10W NW #29.1	Medium Purple	14.584	Undetermined (likely Indigo)
Sample 102 (S102)	160/170N 0/10W NW #29.1	Dark purple	14.989	Undetermined (likely Indigo)
Sample 103 (S103)	160/170N 0/10W NW #19B	Medium Purple from band	14.987	Undetermined (likely Indigo)
Sample 104 (S104)	150/160N 0/10W NE #15B	Medium Purple	14.991	Undetermined (likely Indigo)
Sample 105 (S105)	150/160N 0/10W #2A.1	Medium Purple from tapestry design	14.980	Undetermined (likely Indigo)
Sample 106 (S106)	150/160N 0/10W #2A.2	Medium Purple from tapestry design	14.581	Undetermined (likely Indigo)
Sample 107 (S107)	150/160N 0/10W NE #24B.4	Dark Purple	14.990	Undetermined (likely Indigo)
Sample 108 (S108)	150/160N 0/10E NW #7B.1	Red/Purple Tapestry Design	14.557	Undetermined (likely Indigo)
Sample 109 (S109)	150/160N 0/10E NW #5L.1	Medium Purple from band	14.553	Undetermined (likely Indigo)
Sample 110 (S110)	150/160N 0/10E NW #5K.1	Dark Purple from tapestry design	14.026	Undetermined (likely Indigo)

Sample	Location	Description	Results	Conclusion
Sample 111 (S111)	150/160N 0/10E NW #5K.1	Medium Purple Wool	14.573	Undetermined (likely Indigo)
Sample 112 (S112)	160/170N 0/10W NW #9B	Dark Purple from band (?)	14.711	Undetermined (likely Indigo)
Sample 113 (S113)	160/170N 0/10W NW #9B	Dark Purple from band (?)	14.696	Undetermined (likely Indigo)
Sample 114 (S114)	160/170N 0/10W NW #7G.1	Medium Purple from band	14.996	Undetermined (likely Indigo)
Sample 115 (S115)	160/170N 0/10W NW #7HFolder#1.1	Medium Purple	14.991	Undetermined (likely Indigo)
Sample 116 (S116)	160/170N 0/10W NW #7HFolder#1.2	Medium Purple from band	14.579	Undetermined (likely Indigo)
Sample 117 (S117)	160/170N 0/10W NW #7K.1	Medium Purple wool	15.002	Undetermined (likely Indigo)
Sample 118 (S118)	160/170N 0/10W NW #7K.2	Medium purple from neck opening	14.577	Undetermined (likely Indigo)
Sample 119 (S119)	160/170N 0/10W NW #7K.3	Medium Purple from band	14.991	Undetermined (likely Indigo)
Sample 120 (S120)	160/170N 0/10W NW #7L.1	Medium Purple from band	14.578	Undetermined (likely Indigo)
Sample 121 (S121)	160/170N 0/10W NW #8.1	Dark Purple from band	14.997	Undetermined (likely Indigo)
Sample 122 (S122)	160/170N 0/10W NW #8.2	Medium Purple from band	14.047	Undetermined (likely Indigo)

TABLE 9.8   Dye analysis Run 8 (*cont.*)

Sample	Location	Description	Results	Conclusion
Sample 123 (S123)	160/170N 0/10W NW #8.2	Medium Purple from band	14.992	Undetermined (likely Indigo)
Sample 124 (S124)	160/170N 0/10W NW #6K.1	Medium Purple Wool	14.014	Undetermined (likely Indigo)
Sample 125 (S125)	160/170N 0/10W NW #7A.1	Medium Purple from braided design	14.587	Undetermined (likely Indigo)
Sample 126 (S126)	160/170N 0/10W NW #7A.2	Medium Purple from tapestry band	14.591	Undetermined (likely Indigo)
Sample 127 (S127)	160/170N 0/10W NW #7A.3	Medium Purple from tapestry band	14.699	Undetermined (likely Indigo)
Sample 128 (S128)	160/170N 0/10W NW #7BFolder#1.1	Medium Purple from braid band	14.598	Undetermined (likely Indigo)
Sample 129 (S129)	160/170N 0/10W NW #7BFolder#1.1	Medium Purple from tapestry band	14.587	Undetermined (likely Indigo)
Sample 130 (S130)	160/170N 0/10W NW #7CFolder#2	Medium Purple band	14.602	Undetermined (likely Indigo)
Sample 131 (S131)	160/170N 0/10W NW #1.1	Medium Purple band	15.018	Undetermined (likely Indigo)
Sample 132 (S132)	160/170N 0/10W NW #1.2	Medium Purple from roundel	14.280	Undetermined (likely Indigo)
Sample 133 (S133)	160/170N 0/10W NW #5C	Medium Purple from band	15.752	Undetermined (likely Indigo)
Sample 134 (S134)	160/170N 0/10W NW #6AFolder1.1	Medium Purple tapestry band	15.722	Undetermined (likely Indigo)

Sample	Location	Description	Results	Conclusion
Sample 135 (S135)	160/170N 0/10W NW #6BFolder2.1	Medium Purple band	15.739	Undetermined (likely Indigo)
Sample 136 (S136)	160/170N 0/10W NW #6D.1	Medium Purple	15.312	Undetermined (likely Indigo)
Sample 137 (S137)	160/170N 0/10W NW #6E	Medium Purple Tunic	15.351	Undetermined (likely Indigo)
Sample 138 (S138)	160/170N 0/10W NW #6-31.2	Medium Purple Wool	15.708	Undetermined (likely Indigo)
Sample 139 (S139)	160/170N 10/20E NW #3–4	Medium Purple Wool	15.754	Undetermined (likely Indigo)
Sample 140 (S140)	160/170N 10/20E NW #38	Medium Purple Band	15.748	Undetermined (likely Indigo)
Sample 141 (S141)	160/170N 10/20E NW #5	Dark Purple Design	15.732	Undetermined (likely Indigo)
Sample 142 (S142)	200/210N 30/40E SW #44.4	Medium Purple from Roundel	15.724	Undetermined (likely Indigo)
Sample 143 (S143)	200/210N 30/40E SW #43.3	Medium Purple Wool	15.699	Undetermined (likely Indigo)
Sample 144 (S144)	2000 Season SE #7	Medium Purple Roundel	15.682	Undetermined (likely Indigo)
Sample 145 (S145)	Unknown (warm edge)	Medium Purple Band	15.680	Undetermined (likely Indigo)
Sample 146 (S146)	Unknown (no address 5)	Medium Purple Tapestry Design	15.692	Undetermined (likely Indigo)
Sample 147 (S147)	Unknown (no address 1)	Medium Purple Band	15.693	Undetermined (likely Indigo)
Sample 148 (S148)	Unknown (no address 1)	Medium Purple Tapestry Design	15.697	Undetermined (likely Indigo)

TABLE 9.8   Dye analysis Run 8 (*cont.*)

Sample	Location	Description	Results	Conclusion
Sample 149 (S149)	Unknown (no address 2)	Medium Purple Wool (unspun)	15.700	Undetermined (likely Indigo)
Sample 150 (S150)	200/210N 20/40E SW #22.4	Medium Purple Band	15.684	Undetermined (likely Indigo)
Sample 151 (S151)	200/210N 20/30E SE #36.1	Medium Purple Band	15.692	Undetermined (likely Indigo)
Sample 152 (S152)	200/210N 20/30E SE #38.2	Medium Purple Band	14.597	Undetermined (likely Indigo)
Sample 153 (S153)	200/210N 20/30E SE #40.5	Dark Purple Bands	15.666	Undetermined (likely Indigo)
Sample 154 (S154)	200/210N 30/40E SW #43.4	Medium Purple Wool	15.691	Undetermined (likely Indigo)
Sample 155 (S155)	200/210N 30/40E SW #43.6	Medium Purple Bands	15.658	Undetermined (likely Indigo)
Sample 156 (S156)	200/210N 30/40E SW #43.5	Medium Purple Roundel	15.652	Undetermined (likely Indigo)
Sample 157 (S157)	200/210N 30/40E SW #43.7	Medium Purple Band	15.659	Undetermined (likely Indigo)
Sample 158 (S158)	200/210N 30/40E SW #49.2	Medium Purple Band	15.018	Undetermined (likely Indigo)
Sample 159 (S159)	200/210N 20/30E SE #44.7	Dark Purple Band	15.009	Undetermined (likely Indigo)
Sample 160 (S160)	200/210N 20/30E SE #44.8	Dark Purple Tapestry Design	15.017	Undetermined (likely Indigo)

Sample	Location	Description	Results	Conclusion
Sample 161 (S161)	200/210N 20/30E SE #44.9	Dark Purple Roundel with Tapestry	15.022	Undetermined (likely Indigo)
Sample 162 (S162)	150/160N 0/10W NE #10A	Dark Purple Tapestry Roundel	15.154	Undetermined (likely Indigo)
Sample 163 (S163)	140/160N 50/60E NNW #7.1	Dark Purple Band	14.045	Undetermined (likely Indigo)
Sample 164 (S164)	140/160N 50/60E NNW #12.4	Dark Purple Wool	15.010	Undetermined (likely Indigo)
Sample 165 (S165)	150/160N 0/10E SE #3.4	Dark Purple Tapestry Design	14.992	Undetermined (likely Indigo)
T3	N/A	Tyrian Standard	15.877	N/A
I3	N/A	Indigo Standard	15.000	N/A
IT3	N/A	50% Indigo 50% Tyrian (200/200μL)	14.999 and 15.865	N/A

6   Conclusions

The Fag el-Gamous cemetery has yielded an extensive collection of textiles. The majority of the textile fragments are plain or basket weave linen, but there are a number of beautifully dyed wool pieces. Some of these textiles are visually very similar to textiles that were dyed with shellfish purple, but the wide variety of hues suggests that indigo (blue dye) and madder (red dye) were mixed to create purple in various proportions. Nearly all of the purple pieces analyzed in this study were determined to be made from indigo. Those not identified as indigo were determined to be neither indigo nor Tyrian. Tyrian purple is not present among any of the textile fragments analyzed in this study. This shows that the influence of "purple mania" did indeed reach as far as Fag el-Gamous, but "true purple" did not.

While it would be very interesting to find a textile dyed with Tyrian purple in this necropolis, it does not seem likely in this context. First, the Fayoum is removed from the main thoroughfares of trade. Geographically, the Fayoum is not close to the major ports and cities in Egypt. While trading certainly reached this far inland, it seems rather unlikely for this particular commodity to travel so far from its origin to a non-royal population. Second, those buried in the cemetery of Fag el-Gamous had rather poor burials, indicating that the inhabitants or those who buried them were of a lower socio-economic status in life,[33] and thus would not have had access to Tyrian purple-dyed textiles. The lack of Tyrian purple is consistent with what is currently thought about the people using this necropolis; they were not wealthy. Further excavation may improve upon this current understanding.

---

[33]   See the article on the burial of the common man in this volume.

CHAPTER 10

A Paleopathological Pilot Study of the Fag El-Gamous Cranial Collection

Casey L. Kirkpatrick

1 Introduction

Excavations at Fag el-Gamous have proceeded in most years since 1981, revealing over 1000 human burials.[1] The Fag el-Gamous cemetery also represents one of the earliest archaeological sites in Egypt to conduct a large scale on-site osteological study of human remains.[2] Despite the many years of bioarchaeological data collection, only a handful of bioarchaeological studies have been published.[3] This is in part due to the untimely death of the team member who first began doing bioarchaeological studies at the site.

This chapter presents a preliminary analysis of the osteological collection within the Fag el-Gamous storage magazine to determine the potential for further bioarchaeological analysis and academic contribution to knowledge. A small sample of the cranial collection was observed and documented using more comprehensive methods than those that were possible under the time constraints of previous seasons. Following a brief discussion of the site, cranial collection, and materials and methods used within this study, the resulting raw paleopathological data is revealed in this chapter, followed by a summary of the findings. Although in most cases the archived osteological records were not

---

1   R. Paul Evans, David M. Whitchurch, and Kerry Muhlestein, "Rethinking Burial Dates at a Graeco-Roman Cemetery: Fag el-Gamous, Fayoum, Egypt," *Journal of Archaeological Science: Reports* 2 (2015): 209–214.

2   Vincent A. Wood, "Paleopathological Observations and Applications at Seila," in *Excavations at Seila, Egypt*, C. Wilfred Griggs, ed. (Provo, Utah: Religious Studies Center, Brigham Young University, 1988), 31–44.

3   See: Vincent A. Wood, "Paleopathological Observations and Applications at Seila," 31–44; C. Wilfrid Griggs, Marvin C. Kuchar, Scott R. Woodward, Mark J. Rowe, R. Paul Evans, Naguib Kanawati, and Nasry Iskander, "Evidences of a Christian population in the Egyptian Fayum and genetic and textile studies of the Akhmim noble mummies," BYU *Studies Quarterly* 33 (1993): 214–247; Scott R. Woodward, Mary J. King, Nancy M. Chiu, Marvin J. Kuchar, and C. Wilfrid Griggs, "Amplification of ancient nuclear DNA from teeth and soft tissues," *Genome Research* 3 (1994): 244–247; T.B. Ball, C.W. Griggs, M. Kuchar, R. Phillips, and W.M. Hess, "Image analysis of Egyptian mummy hair," *Microscopy and Microanalysis* 8 (2002): 922–923.

---

available for comparison, with the knowledge of what characteristics had been documented in previous seasons, this study reveals the vast potential for further bioarchaeological studies at Fag el-Gamous and brings to light some previously unknown information about the individuals examined.

2 Fag el-Gamous Cemetery and the Cranial Collection

The Fag el-Gamous site is overlooked by the Seila Pyramid, perched atop a nearby hill, and is made up of some Middle Kingdom shaft tombs, some Ptolemaic and Roman era tombs carved into the mudstone escarpment, and a large cemetery composed of loose sand burials as well as simple shafts cut into the compacted sand.[4] These latter burials are from the Roman to early Byzantine periods.[5] The cemetery is very large (ca. 125 hectares) and densely packed[6] with generally well-preserved human remains as a result of the arid climate and ideal conditions for the natural desiccation and preservation of organic materials. As excavations have been largely focused on the Fag el-Gamous cemetery, the cranial collection is mostly made up of individuals excavated from the necropolis' sand cemetery. The cataloguing of skulls in the 2018 season (see below) will make it possible to check the skulls available against those for which we have more osteological and archaeological records. This will allow more complete studies in the future.

---

4 See the chapter on the history of the excavation in this volume for more details.
5 On the components of the Fag el-Gamous site: Leonard Lesko, "Seila 1981," *Journal of the American Research Center in Egypt* 25 (1988): 216–217; C. Wilfred Griggs, "Excavating a Christian Cemetery Near Seila, in the Fayum Region of Egypt," in *Excavations at Seila, Egypt*, C. Wilfred Griggs, ed. (Provo, Utah: Religious Studies Center, Brigham Young University, 1988), 74–84; C. Wilfrid Griggs, Marvin C. Kuchar, Scott R. Woodward, Mark J. Rowe, R. Paul Evans, Naguib Kanawati, and Nasry Iskander, "Evidences of a Christian population in the Egyptian Fayum and genetic and textile studies of the Akhmim noble mummies," *BYU Studies Quarterly* 33 (1993): 216. On the dating of the Fag el-Gamous cemetery: Kristin H. South, *Roman and Early Byzantine Burials at Fag El-Gamus: A Reassessment of the Case for Religious Affiliation* (Masters Thesis, Brigham Young University, 2012); R. Paul Evans, David M. Whitchurch, and Kerry Muhlestein, "Rethinking Burial Dates at a Graeco-Roman Cemetery: Fag el-Gamous, Fayoum, Egypt," *Journal of Archaeological Science: Reports* 2 (2015): 209.
6 Leonard Lesko, "Seila 1981," *Journal of the American Research Center in Egypt* 25 (1988): 223; C. Wilfrid Griggs, Marvin C. Kuchar, Scott R. Woodward, Mark J. Rowe, R. Paul Evans, Naguib Kanawati, and Nasry Iskander, "Evidences of a Christian population in the Egyptian Fayum and genetic and textile studies of the Akhmim noble mummies," *BYU Studies Quarterly* 33 (1993): 216, 228; Evans, et al., "Rethinking Burial Dates at a Graeco-Roman Cemetery," 209; Kristin H. South, *Roman and Early Byzantine Burials at Fag El-Gamus: A Reassessment of the Case for Religious Affiliation* (Masters Thesis, Brigham Young University, 2012), 36.

The relatively modest burial goods associated with sand cemetery burials suggests that there has been limited looting in the cemetery.[7] Most of the better-preserved skeletal remains were found wrapped in linen shrouds and/or clothing, sometimes bound by purpose-woven ribbons or rope, often with a bundle of linen placed over the face. Individuals were also sometimes placed atop wooden boards or a bundle of palm fronds, or wrapped in reed mats.[8] Although some burials show possible evidence of desiccation prior to wrapping,[9] it is possible that the local and surrounding populations were aware of this burial ground's fairly consistent ability to naturally mummify human remains. As such, it may be possible that the particularly large scale of this cemetery may have been partly a reflection of the continued preference for the preservation of the body after death, even after the classical dynastic methods of anthropogenic mummification had been abandoned. Of course, as there are other similarly arid areas in the desert surrounding the Fayoum, the location for this cemetery may have also gained importance due to other reasons-such as its proximity to the dynastic rock-cut tombs and the Seila Pyramid, a topic which is currently being researched.[10]

Past excavations of the cemetery burials at Fag el-Gamous were generally followed by the removal of textiles from the bodies, which were then examined by textile specialists. The human remains were then examined and documented in accordance with a short (1 double-sided page) osteological recording form. Due to time constraints and the sheer number of human remains excavated at Fag el-Gamous, prior studies of the human remains focused on the recording of preservation, burial treatments, burial contexts, basic demographic information (age, sex, and stature estimation), and any obvious anomalies or pathologies (including, but not limited to osteophytosis and dental disease). Initially the excavation did not emphasize osteological analysis, and not enough time was allotted for such analysis in a dig season.[11] This was exacerbated by the untimely death of Vincent Wood, the team member who was analyzing the skeletal remains. Given these time constraints and other obstacles, many skeletal variations and minor afflictions likely went undiagnosed.

7   Lesko, "Seila 1981," 223; South, *Roman and Early Byzantine Burials at Fag El-Gamus*, 1.
8   For more on these practices see the article on "Death of a Common Man," in this volume. Also see Lesko, "Seila 1981," 222; Wood, "Paleopathological Observations and Applications at Seila," 31–44; South, *Roman and Early Byzantine Burials at Fag El-Gamus*, 47–76.
9   South, *Roman and Early Byzantine Burials at Fag El-Gamus*, 52.
10   Kerry Muhlestein, 2014. Personal communication.
11   Vincent A. Wood, "Paleopathological Observations and Applications at Seila," in *Excavations at Seila, Egypt*, ed. C. Wilfred Griggs (Provo, Utah: Religious Studies Center, Brigham Young University, 1988), 31–44.

Advances in the field of osteology may also account for differences between the original preliminary reports and future analyses. The death of Vincent Wood and other changes in personnel have also made it so that many of these preliminary reports are lost, though we are still working on tracking them down. Still, a copy of the standardized recording sheet was available for review and provided important information about the types of data collected in past seasons. Under new directorship, the work of excavation has slowed as a new emphasis has been placed on analysis and conservation. As part of this emphasis, work is being done to organize and digitize the osteological archives for Fag el-Gamous. It is hoped that all data from future studies of individuals in the Fag el-Gamous magazine can be paired and compared with data from the previous studies and contextualized archaeologically through the use of these reports.

During the early excavations, the human remains were reburied after examination. Following the establishment of the storage magazine under the previous direction of Dr. C.W. Griggs, about one-third of the crania were stored in the storage magazine for further study and the infra-cranial remains were laid to rest in a tomb or reburied.[12] If criteria were used to decide which crania were kept and which were reburied, they were not recorded and are not currently apparent. Unfortunately, this separation of skeletal elements precludes any possibility for the re-examination of the infra-cranial remains in association with their respective crania. As such, future studies of the Fag el-Gamous cranial collection will be dependent on the archived osteological data for details regarding associated infra-cranial skeletons. The ongoing search for previous osteological reports and their integration into a useable database are part of why this is a preliminary report – an important but intermediate step. Nevertheless, this large well-preserved cranial collection has the potential to unveil a significant amount of new data, and could serve as a valuable study collection for the investigation of numerous bioarchaeological and Egyptological research questions. As older osteological reports are found, organized, and used, the potential for study will grow.

For a number of years, the osteological collection at the storage magazine was unorganized. During the 2014 season, the collection was examined both to assess its research potential, and to determine how to best organize and preserve the remains. The work of this season revealed that the collection remains in good condition and does not seem to have been affected by the usual storage

---

12   Vincent A. Wood, "Paleopathological Observations and Applications at Seila," in *Excavations at Seila, Egypt*, ed. C. Wilfred Griggs (Provo, Utah: Religious Studies Center, Brigham Young University, 1988), 31–44.

pests (e.g. rodents, insects, looters). Within the cranial collection, some of the skulls are still covered, or partially-covered, in mummified tissue and some individuals' hairstyles have even remained intact. Many other crania were discovered naturally skeletonized upon excavation, and some others have lost teeth post-mortem and/or have in some way been separated from their mandible. During the 2018 season, new storage facilities were created for the entire collection of skulls. Skulls were placed on 2 cm tall and 15 cm diameter micro-fiber rings, which we created to stabilize and protect the skulls. Skulls without attached hair were stored inverted (upside down) with the frontal and parietal bones resting on the rings to protect the teeth. Skulls with attached hair were stored with the base of the skull and the mandible, or the maxilla when the mandible was absent, resting on the microfiber ring. At the end of the study season, all shelves containing skeletal remains were also draped with clear plastic to prevent dust accumulation on the collection. This storage method will ensure that the recovered biological material will continue to remain in pristine condition for future studies and eventual re-interment. These skulls were also catalogued and their location within the storage magazine was mapped. This map will be included in the database that is now being created for the excavation. All of this has the excavation poised for more serious osteological studies in the future.

3   Materials and Methods

Twenty-one individuals were studied by the current author during the brief 2014 study season (6 working days were at the storage magazine, the rest of the season was spent at the Kom Aushim government facility where there are no crania); five of these crania were excavated during the previous season (2013) and retained their full infra-cranial remains as well as all of the information about their archaeological context. The remaining crania (n=16) were randomly selected for examination from the Fag el-Gamous magazine. In most cases, the archaeological context was recorded on the crania. For the purpose of this study, in cases where the archaeological contexts were missing or illegible due to fading, crania were assigned NN (no number) designations (i.e. NN1, NN2, NN3...etc.). The selected crania were examined and documented through photography and the use of a pre-determined combination of documentation methods from *Arizona State Museum's Skeletal Inventory Form*[13] and *Human*

---

13   Arizona State Museum, *Arizona State Museum's Skeletal Inventory Form,* (Tucson: Arizona State Museum, 2004).

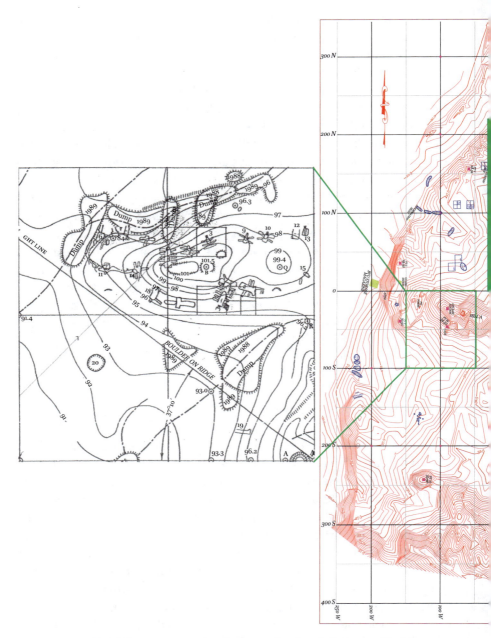

FIGURE 10.1   Fag el-Gamous: a map of areas excavated to date. *Left:* Map modified from an
original created by Dr. Brent Benson. Rock-cut tombs and selected dump sites
from previous seasons shown in association with Hill B at Fag el-Gamous.
Center: Map modified from Alexander Lovett Harold Mitchell, Todd Osborn
and Brent R. Benson, *Fag el-Gamous Cemetery* (Provo: Brigham Young

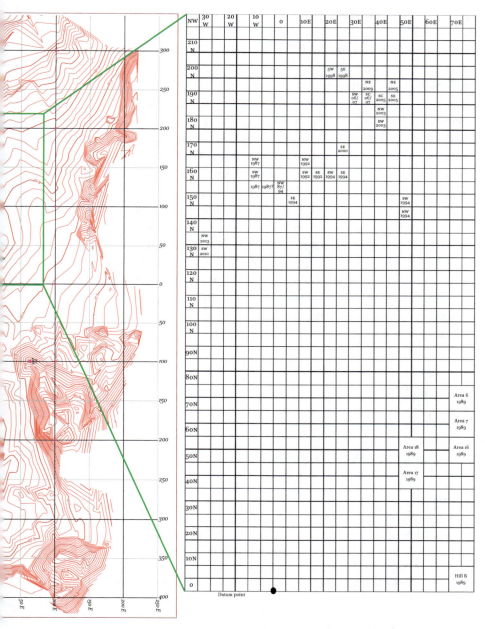

University, 2009). *Right:* Map modified from Kristin H. South, *Roman and Early Byzantine Burials at Fag El-Gamus: A Reassessment of the Case for Religious Affiliation* (Master's Thesis, Brigham Young University, 2012), 37, Figure 4. Area specifications and excavation years indicated for previously excavated squares on the Fag el-Gamous cemetery excavation grid

Remains Recording Sheet[14] with reference to *Standards for Data Collection from Human Skeletal Remains.*[15]

This chapter is focused on the inventory of the selected remains, their state of preservation, demographic information (i.e. age and sex estimations), and paleopathological data gleaned from this preliminary study. Crania were assigned age estimates based on the stages of dental development,[16] dental wear,[17] and cranial suture fusion.[18] Based on these indicators, individuals were assigned to the following categories: subadult (<21 years), young adult (21–34 years), middle adult (35–45 years), or older adult (45+ years). Sex determinations were based on observations of the nuchal crest, mastoid processes, supra-orbital ridge, glabella, mandibular eminence, gonial flaring, and mandibular rami.[19] Since current sex determination methods are unable to determine the sex of subadults with any accuracy, subadults were recorded as having undetermined sex. During the 2014 study season, metric data (quantitatively measurable) and non-metric (qualitatively observed) skeletal traits were also documented. However, given that the documentation of these traits is intended for large scale statistical analysis in the future, and they do not contribute meaningfully to the osteobiographies of individuals, their details are not included in this chapter.

4   Results

Grave: 130/140N, 20/30 W
Skeleton: NW 56
Excavation Date: March 14, 2013

---

14   Daniel Antoine, *Human Remains Recording Sheet,* (London: Institute for Bioarchaeology, 2011).

15   Jane E. Buikstra and Douglas H. Ubelaker, *Standards for data collection from human skeletal remains: proceedings of a seminar at the Field Museum of Natural History.* (Fayetteville: Arkansas Archaeological Survey, 1994).

16   Douglas H. Ubelaker, *Human Skeletal Remains: Excavation, Analysis, Interpretation,* 2nd Edition. (Washington, DC: Taraxacum, 1989), Figure 71.

17   Donald R. Brothwell, *Digging up bones: the excavation, treatment, and study of human skeletal remains.* (Ithaca: Cornell University Press, 1981), 72.

18   Jane E. Buikstra and Douglas H. Ubelaker, *Standards for data collection from human skeletal remains: proceedings of a seminar at the Field Museum of Natural History.* (Fayetteville: Arkansas Archaeological Survey, 1994), 32–38, 43.

19   Jane E. Buikstra and Douglas H. Ubelaker, *Standards for data collection from human skeletal remains: proceedings of a seminar at the Field Museum of Natural History.* (Fayetteville: Arkansas Archaeological Survey, 1994), 16–21; Daniel Antoine, *Human Remains Recording Sheet.* (London: Institute for Bioarchaeology, 2011).

Sex: Undetermined

Age: Subadult – Dental development: 6 years (+/- 24 months)

General Inventory: Mandible with missing right mandibular condyle.

Dental Inventory/Pathology: Mandible: exhibits post-mortem loss of six anterior teeth and two incompletely developed first molars. Two fully erupted deciduous premolars and two pre-eruption second molars remain inside their crypts.

General Pathology: No evidence of pathology.

• • •

Grave: 130/140N 20/30W

Skeleton: NW 63

Excavation Date: March 14, 2013

General Inventory: Skull is present and complete, with some damage to zygomatic bones. Left arm (humerus, radius, and ulna; carpals, metacarpals and phalanges) and sacrum are present.

Sex: Possibly female

Age: Subadult – Dental development: 15–20 years

Dental Pathology/Inventory:

Maxilla: All teeth are present with little wear. Third molars are present and erupting in their crypts on both sides. Gross caries lesions in the left first molar have destroyed the distolingual cusp and exposed the interior of the tooth. Linear enamel hypoplasias are present on anterior and cheek teeth.

General Pathology:

Pitting on left maxillary surface indicates a possible infection. Pitting is visible on the palatal surface, bones making up the base of the cranium, zygomatics, external auditory meatus, and mastoid processes. The individual has a deviated septum and an unfused first sacral vertebra, indicating spina bifida occulta.[20]

• • •

Grave: 130/140 N 20/30 W

Skeleton: NW 70

Excavation Date: March 18, 2013

---

20   Joseph E. Molto, Casey L. Kirkpatrick, and Jim Keron, "A Paleoepidemiological Analysis of Sacral Spina Bifida Occulta in Population Samples from the Dakhleh Oasis, Egypt," *International Journal of Paleopathology* 26 (2019): 93–103.

General Inventory: Cranium, mandible, right rib (bifurcated), right tibia (proximal 2/3 present, distal end missing, proximal growth plate missing; probably intrusive as it appears to be from a much younger individual), and metatarsals are preserved. Some hair and tissue associated with cranium remains.

Sex: Possibly female.

Age: Subadult – Dental development: 15–20 years

Dental Inventory/Pathology:

Maxilla: Full adult dentition present and erupted, except M3 (both left and right present, but not erupted, visible in crypts). Large carious lesion present on left M1 on the distolingual and occlusal surfaces.

Mandible: All teeth present with little to no wear and moderate calculus buildup on anterior teeth. Significant spaces between anterior teeth. Linear hypoplastic defects are on cheek teeth, and possibly on anterior teeth but these are obscured by the calculus. Third molars present in crypts and erupting. Alveolar bone fenestration present in association with anterior teeth.

General Pathology:

Cranial: There is extensive pitting around the external auditory meatus on left and right sides, and some pitting on the cranial base and sides. Zygomatic processes on left and right have vascular grooving but are broken off. Bifurcated right rib (15 cm maximum length, 3.3 cm at widest point of fork, 0.7 cm width of smaller tong, 1.0 cm width of larger tong): The smaller tong has part of an articulating surface visible, the larger tong is broken with no indication of articulation, and there is some pitting and a significant osteological ridge on the inferior surface of the rib near the costotransverse articulating surface.

Metatarsal has a bony growth extending ca. 2 cm from the inferior distal surface in a disc shape.

• • •

Grave: 130-140N, 20-30W

Skeleton: NW 73

Excavation Date: March 18, 2013

General Inventory: Skull and mandible, infra-cranial skeleton not inventoried due to time constraints.

Sex: Undetermined

Age: Young Adult – Dental Development: complete, dental wear: 17–25 years

Dental Pathology/Inventory:

Maxilla: Post-mortem loss of upper left first incisor, canine, second premolar and third molar.

Mandible: Post-mortem loss of lower left first incisor and unerupted lower left third molar. Post-mortem loss of right first and second incisors, canine and third molar. There is moderate dental wear on all remaining teeth.

General Pathology: Analysis incomplete due to time constraints. To be revisited in a future season.

• • •

Grave: 130/140N, 20/30W
Skeleton: NW 95
Excavation Date: March 21, 2013
General Inventory: Mandible is present with some mummified tissue attached; but it is missing the left mandibular condyle. Infra-cranial skeleton is still largely covered in mummified tissue, especially the lower legs and feet, and arms and hands, which still have nails attached.
Sex: Undetermined
Age: Older Adult – Dental wear: 45+ years
Dental Pathology/Inventory:
Mandible: There is generalized alveolar bone loss, significant calculus deposits on the lingual side of the anterior teeth. All remaining teeth are heavily worn with no remaining enamel on all but the canines and the right second lower incisor. All but four of the buccal teeth have been lost ante-mortem and the alveolar bone is found to be in different stages of resorption. This alveolar resorption likely contributes to the appearance of significant gonial flaring. A small cloaca can also be seen piercing the fully resorbed alveolar bone on the right side in the molar region. This suggests that there may have been an ongoing infection in the mandible that required drainage through this cloaca.
General Pathology: Analysis incomplete due to extensive presence of mummified tissue – radiographic study suggested. Osteoarthritis on distal left femur (eburnation present).

• • •

Grave: Area 14
Skeleton: 3
Excavation Date: 1989
General Inventory: Skull present and complete. Mandible absent.
Sex: Possibly male
Age: Older Adult – Dental wear: 45+ years, one tooth extremely worn, the other tooth slightly worn, ante-mortem tooth loss, suture fusion: 27–51 years

Dental Inventory/Pathology:

Maxilla: Two teeth are present, all others were lost ante- or post-mortem. Right first premolar is present with moderate wear, and the left second premolar is present with severe wear. The right first molar, the left first and second molars lost ante-mortem as evident through alveolar resorption, and the remaining sockets are remodelled with pitting indicating a possible infection. Periapical abscesses are present on left first and second premolar sockets. Pitting and slight resorption were observed in most sockets along with generalized periodontitis.

General Pathology:

This individual has a deviated septum and his zygomatic bones on both sides have an unusual scalloped shape on the inferior surface, possibly due to strong masseter muscles. Pitting was observed around the occipital condyles, on the sphenoid, on the palate, and around the external auditory meatus. Bony growths (layered new bone) were noted on the inferior surface of the petrous portion on the left and right temporals. There were also small bony growths/ridges on the palatal surface, and on the palatines. Large protruding pterygoid plates extend laterally on both sides and two small round bony outgrowths were observed at the anterior of the foramen magnum.

• • •

Grave: 150–160 N 0–10 E

Skeleton: SE 3

Excavation Date: 1994

General Inventory: Cranium is present with a broken right zygomatic bone, a broken left temporal bone separated from the skull with a missing superior margin, and a broken occipital bone with the inferior part missing. There is a small section of hair and textile present on the head, which is very well-preserved. The mandible is present and complete with slight post-mortem damage to the surface of the bone, and the infra-cranial skeleton is missing.

Sex: Undetermined

Age: Subadult – Dental development: 10 years (+/- 30 months)

Dental Inventory/Pathology:

Maxilla: Deciduous canine is present on the left side and deciduous first molars are present on left and right sides. Pitting is present in all visible sockets. Deciduous first molars on left and right sides have significant occlusal wear that is heavier on the palatal cusps. Third molars are present in crypts but not erupted. There is unusual lipping of the alveolar bone around the upper first incisor sockets and fenestration over the upper right canine root.

Mandible: Deciduous first molars are present on the left and right sides. The left and right third molars are present and unerupted in crypts, and all other teeth are missing post-mortem. Dental crowding is evident with the first premolar sockets located behind the incisor sockets. There is also pitting in all sockets and generalized periodontitis, with the sockets for the permanent first molars having more extensive pitting and resorption that looks typical of the end stages of alveolar eruption.

General Pathology:

There is uneven gonial flaring on the mandible with the right side much more flared. There is also pitting on the maxilla, palate, alveolar surface, cranial base, mastoid, external auditory meatus and temporo-mandibular joints (TMJ). Vascular grooving is also evident on nasals and beneath the nasal aperture. Pitting is also barely discernible in the eye orbits (possibly mild cribra orbitalia). A partial metopic suture is visible in the lower part of the frontal bone, and a multi-partite os inca is present. An osteolytic lesion on the left parietal bone is a probable pressure defect (approximately 1 cm x 1 cm) affecting the ectocranial table, possibly resulting from a soft tissue tumor or cyst.

• • •

Grave: 150-160N 0-10E
Skeleton: SE 5
Excavation Date: 1997
General Inventory: Cranium is present, although the sphenoid, temporal and occipital bones are broken with parts missing post-mortem. The majority of the left temporal bone is detached but present and the nasal bones are missing post-mortem. The mandible is present with post-mortem damage; the left mandibular condyle and right condyle and coronoid process are missing. Some small pieces of hair and tissue remain on the head as well as most of the tissue within the left eye orbit.
Sex: Undetermined
Age: Subadult – Dental development: 6 years (+/- 24 months)
Dental Inventory/Pathology:
Maxilla: The deciduous dentition has erupted, but most teeth have been lost post-mortem. Five erupted teeth remain present with little to no wear, and some adult dentition is visible. The incisive foramen is very large.

Mandible: Deciduous dentition is present with 4 erupted teeth remaining and the rest are missing from post-mortem loss, some adult dentition is visible in crypts.

General Pathology:

Porosity is visible around the external auditory meatus on both sides and on the palatal surface. The metopic suture appears to be partially obliterated with incompletely fused parts remaining on the lower and upper parts of frontal bone, including the wide-open sutures of the anterior fontanelle. The fusion of this open fontanelle appears to be significantly delayed in comparison with dental development. There are multiple wormian bones associated with the right lambdoidal suture.

• • •

Grave: 150-160N, 50-60E
Skeleton: NNW 19
Excavation Date: Unknown
General Inventory: Mandible present and complete
Sex: Undetermined
Age: Older Adult – Dental wear: 45+ years
Dental Pathology/Inventory:

Mandible: 7 complete teeth are present, all with extensive dental wear, plus a broken half of a molar root. There is possible agenesis of the third molars as well as agenesis of the right second incisor. There is ante-mortem loss of the left canine and first premolar with the alveolar bone almost completely resorbed at these sites. There is post-mortem loss of all molars with significant alveolar resorption in the posterior of the dental arch, and around the area of the second molars, indicating possible ante-mortem loss through infection. There is significant buildup of dental calculus on the lingual and labial surfaces of most remaining teeth. Enlarged mental foramina further support the probability of infection.

General Pathology:

Extensive pitting, new bone formation, and changes in the joint contours of both mandibular condyles indicate bilateral osteoarthritis of the temporomandibular joint.

• • •

Grave: 150/160N, 50/60E
Skeleton: SW 16

Excavation Date: Unknown

General Inventory: Mandible and cranium are present, but missing the basilar part of the occipital bone on the left side. The posterior of the left temporal bone and occipital bone appear to have been burnt with a heat-related crack extending from the lambdoidal suture through part of the occipital bone.

Sex: Undetermined

Age: Subadult – Dental development: 6 years (+/- 24 months)

Dental Pathology/Inventory:

Maxilla: All maxillary teeth are missing except the left second incisor, the first and second left deciduous premolars and left and right unerupted first permanent molars. The tooth crypts of the right first and second deciduous premolars show evidence of porosity and alveolar resorption.

Mandible: Mandibular first incisors are missing (post-mortem loss), and the deciduous second left premolar is missing, but may have been lost ante-mortem, given the porosity found in the remaining tooth crypt. First and second permanent molars are visible within open crypts but are unerupted. Lower deciduous second incisors are slightly rotated. There is no calculus buildup, no significant dental wear, and no visible dental caries. The mental foramina are enlarged.

General Pathology:

Small bilateral bone growths protrude from the palatal bone. There is also porosity bone on the palate, maxilla, nasal bones, frontal bone, mandible, zygomatic arch, sphenoid and temporal bones. Mild cribra orbitalia, or porosity in the eye orbits, was visible. There is significant porosity/bone growth in the external auditory meatus and petrous processes of the temporal bones. The individual also had enlarged infra-orbital foramina and an unfused maxillary bone.

• • •

Grave: 160/170N 10/20E

Skeleton: #13

Excavation Date: Unknown

General Inventory: Skull and mandible are present, both with remains of mummified tissue. Also the cranium is covered in hair.

Sex: Undetermined

Age: Subadult – Dental development: 15 years (+/- 36 months)

Dental Pathology/Inventory:

Mandible: Most of the adult dentition is erupted. All teeth are present except the right second premolar and first molar. Multiple linear enamel hypoplasias are on most mandibular teeth. There is a small buildup of dental calculus on lingual and labial surfaces of the anterior mandibular teeth. All crypts that are missing teeth show significant porosity in the alveolar bone within the crypt.

Maxilla: Most teeth were lost post-mortem, with 3 molars remaining; all have little to no dental wear. First upper right molar crypt shows signs of interproximal alveolar bone recession.

General Pathology:

The maxillary suture is minimally fused. Some porosity on maxillary bone is visible.

• • •

Grave: 160/170N, 10/20E
Skeleton: NW 22
Excavation Date: Unknown
General Inventory: Skull is present and complete, mandible is missing. Some mummified tissue and hair remain on the skull.
Sex: Possible male
Age: Adult – Dental development: complete, suture fusion: 20–42 years
Dental Pathology/Inventory:
Maxilla: All teeth are missing post-mortem, remaining sockets show that all teeth were present and erupted. Porous alveolar bone is present in the cheek teeth crypts.
General Pathology:
Porosity present on the palate, frontal bone, maxillary bone beneath the nose, parietal bones, lower occipital bone, temporal bones, sphenoid bones (particularly surrounding the external auditory meatus), and within the enlarged lacrimal fossae.

• • •

Grave: 160/170 N 10/20 E
Skeleton: SE 22
Excavation Date: Unknown
General Inventory: Cranium present and mostly complete. Some hair and tissue are present on the left side of the cranium.
Sex: Possible female
Age: Young to Middle Adult – Dental development: complete, suture fusion: 19–44 years.
Dental Pathology/Inventory:

Maxilla: All teeth are missing post-mortem, the remaining sockets show that all teeth were present and erupted at the time of death.

General Pathology:

A button osteoma is present on the right coronal suture (approximately 1 cm x 1 cm). The frontal bone is fused slightly lower than the parietals and there are small round indentations on the frontal bone that are worthy of further study. The right greater wing of the sphenoid has layered new bone growth near the pterion. There is pitting around the occipital condyles. There is also pitting near the right temporo-mandibular joints (TMJ) fossa and on the joint surface of the left TMJ fossa, that may indicate possible osteoarthritis. The vomer is warped and uneven, possibly resulting from post-mortem damage.

• • •

Grave: 160/170N 10/20E
Skeleton: SW 7
Excavation Date: Unknown
General Inventory: Skull is present, but is missing the occipital bone, the right temporal bone, and both zygomatic arches. The mandible is not present.
Sex: Male
Age: Young Adult – Dental development: complete, dental wear: 17–25, suture fusion: 27–44 years
Dental Pathology/Inventory:
Maxilla: Only the second and third right molars and the roots of the right first molar remain, along with the roots of the second left premolar and first and third left molar roots. All remaining roots were left when the crown broke away post-mortem. The crowns of the second and third right molars show slight dental wear and a slight buildup of dental calculus on the lingual and buccal surfaces. Missing teeth were likely lost post-mortem, however, there is porous alveolar bone between all tooth crypts.
General Pathology:
The parietal bones are asymmetrical, with rounded left parietal and slightly flatter left parietal. The Lambdoid suture is completely fused on the right side. There is probable synostic posterior plagiocephaly as indicated by this early fusion and the uneven shape of the skull outline. There are also defined temporal ridges on both sides of the skull and an abnormal bony growth (approximately 1.5 cm x 1.5 cm) posterior and superior to the left eye orbit in the calvarium.

• • •

Grave: 160/170 N 20/30 E
Skeleton: SW 12
Excavation Date: Unknown
General Inventory: Cranium and mandible present and complete.
Sex: Possible male
Age: Older Adult – Dental wear: 45+ years
Dental Inventory/Pathology:
Maxilla: Four adult teeth are present and broken. The left first molar is complete but demonstrates extensive wear and slight calculus build-up. There are periapical abscesses associated with the right second premolar and right first molar, and alveolar bone fenestration associated with the left second premolar. There is extensive alveolar resorption and remodelling at the left second molar, and right first and second molar sockets indicating ante-mortem tooth loss in these cases. Pitting is visible in all alveolar sockets.

Mandible: Two extremely worn teeth present; left second incisor and left first molar. Carious lesion observed on distal interproximal root of left first molar. All other teeth were lost post-mortem. Pitting is visible in all alveolar sockets and calculus is preserved on both remaining teeth.

General Pathology:
Pterygoid plates on the sphenoid are abnormally large and protruding. Extreme gonial flare on left and right sides of the mandible. There is temporo-mandibular joints (TMJ) osteoarthritis – extensive pitting, new bone formation, and resorption on the left and right TMJ surfaces on both mandibular fossae and mandibular condyles, with the left side having more severe changes anterior to the mandibular fossa. There is extensive pitting around the occipital condyles, the right external auditory meatus, and the palatal surface. A small bony growth was also observed on the interior surface of the superior part of the right orbit, on the medial side (approximately 5 mm x 5 mm, although there are no clear margins). Incisive foramen and both mental foramina are very large, indicating probable infection. There is a small bony growth on the left and right sides of the palatal surface, near the second molars making a slight groove.

• • •

Grave: 160/170 N 10/20 E
Skeleton: SW 18
Excavation Date: Unknown
General Inventory: Cranium present and mostly complete with hair.

Sex: Undetermined
Age: Older Adult – Dental wear: 45+ years
Dental Inventory/Pathology:
Maxilla: Right second molar is present with extensive wear and large caries lesion on the distal interproximal surface. All other teeth were lost ante- or post-mortem. Extensive pitting and some resorption in the alveolar bone indicate that several teeth were likely lost ante-mortem. The left and right third molars were probably lost ante-mortem, as indicated by the almost complete resorption of the alveolar sockets. A periapical abscess was observed in association with the right first incisor, right first molar, and left second premolar.
General Pathology:
Porosity was observed around the occipital condyles and on the palatal surface. The vomer is warped and curved to the right. There is very thin cortical bone on the posterior orbital surface and an indention on the medial interior orbital surface above the lacrimal groove.

• • •

Grave: 200/210N, 20/30E
Skeleton: SE 30
Excavation Date: Unknown
General Inventory: Cranium and mandible present and complete.
Sex: Possible Female
Age: Subadult or Young Adult – Dental development: abnormal, 15+ years, dental wear: no exposed dentine suture fusion: abnormal (craniosynostosis), 19–44 years
Dental Pathology/Inventory:
Maxilla: Most anterior teeth were lost post-mortem, however, all cheek teeth were retained. Adult dentition was erupted, except for the incomplete eruption of the left canine and third molars. The second left incisor has marked shoveling. Fenestration is visible on the labial side of many maxillary tooth roots. Linear enamel hypoplasia was present on several teeth.
Mandible: Most anterior teeth and premolars were lost post-mortem. The adult dentition is erupted, except for the incomplete eruption of the left canine and third molars. Both lower canines are rotated, and the right second incisor is slightly rotated. There is an abscess with signs of resorption at the left mandibular first molar crypt. There is a bony ridge on the alveolar bone adjacent to the right molars on the buccal side. The lower right first incisor has a significant deposit of calculus on the lingual surface. There is a

bony bridge over the right third molar crypt, and the third molar is not erupted.

Cheek teeth on the right side show extreme deposits of dental calculus, particularly on the buccal and lingual surfaces, covering both the maxillary and mandibular teeth, suggesting an inability to separate or move this side of the jaw.

General Pathology:

Abnormal bony growth reaches from the right mandibular body to the right zygomatic bone, where they join in an open suture. The temporomandibular joints (TMJ) show abnormal wear anterior to the mandibular fossae and on the mandibular condyles. The lateral pterygoid muscle insertion sites below both mandibular condyles are marked with disc-like indentations and porous bone. Asymmetrical parietal and occipital bones indicate probable craniosynostotic plagiocephaly. This individual also has a metopic suture and asymmetrical nasal bones. Additonally, the palate, occipital, temporal, sphenoid, maxillary and mandibular bones are porous.

• • •

Grave: Unknown
Skeleton: NN 1
Excavation Date: Unknown
General Inventory: Mandible present and complete
Sex: Undetermined
Age: Middle or Older Adult – Dental development: complete, ante-mortem tooth loss, osteoarthritis on mandibular condyles
Dental Pathology/Inventory:
Mandible: All teeth are missing (mostly post-mortem). There is an abcess at the right third molar crypt. There is an unerupted or completely resorbed crypt resulting from the loss of left third molar. Both first molars were lost ante-mortem with almost complete resorption of the left crypt and significant resorption of the right crypt. There is porous alveolar bone between teeth throughout the dental arch.
General Pathology: Evidence of osteoarthritis on both mandibular condyles.

• • •

Grave: Unknown
Skeleton: NN 2
Excavation Date: Unknown
General Inventory: Mandible present and complete
Sex: Undetermined
Age: Young Adult – Dental development: complete, dental wear: 17–25 years
Dental Inventory/Pathology:
Mandible: Anterior dental alveoli show extensive pitting, but little to no re-sorptions, indicating probable post-mortem tooth loss. Three molars are present with some enamel wear. The lower right first molar and lower left first molar were lost ante-mortem as evident through fully resorbed dental alveoli. The left second molar has a distal interproximal wear facet and car-ies lesion at the distal cemento-enamel junction (CEJ). The right second molar has a distal interproximal gross caries lesion at the CEJ, and the third molar has a mesial interproximal gross caries lesion at the CEJ. Both lesions penetrate into the dentine cavity and encompass the CEJ, interproximal enamel surface, and root surface.
General Pathology:
Pitting on right and left mandibular condyles.

• • •

Grave: Unknown
Skeleton: NN 3
Excavation Date: Unknown
General Inventory: Mandible present and complete
Sex: Undetermined
Age: Subadult – Dental development: 6 years (+/- 24 months)
Dental Inventory/Pathology:
Mandible: The deciduous dentition is represented by three anterior teeth and four premolars with little to no wear. A permanent first molar is erupt-ing on the right side, and an empty crypt for the adult first molar is visible on left side. Permanent second molars are visible in crypts on right and left sides. Permanent incisors are also visible in crypts. Pitting and slight resorp-tion are visible in the left deciduous second molar socket.
General Pathology:
Pitting on inferior interior surface of mandible.

• • •

Grave: Unknown
Skeleton: NN 4
Excavation Date: Unknown
General Inventory: Mandible present and complete
Sex: Undetermined
Age: Older Adult – Dental development: complete, significant ante-mortem tooth loss, osteoarthritis on the mandibular condyles.
Dental Inventory/Pathology:
Mandible: No teeth remain in this mandible. The left first incisor, second premolar, and molars (one, two, and three), and the right molars (one, two, and three) were lost ante-mortem as evidenced by the alveolar resorption in these sockets. As such, there is extensive alveolar remodelling in posterior portions of the dental arch. The right third molar socket is still somewhat visible with extensive pitting. Pitting is also visible in all other sockets.
General Pathology:
Some pitting was observed on the left and right mandibular condyles.

5   **Summary of the Results**

In this preliminary analysis of a small sample from the Fag el-Gamous storage magazine, I found that access to some skeletal information was impeded by the excellent preservation of some individuals who retained mummified tissue. Ideally, cases such as these would benefit from non-destructive examination methods such as radiography. It is hoped that permission will be granted to conduct radiographic studies in the future so that further paleopathological information may be obtained without compromising the integrity of the human remains. In the meantime, I present here a summary of the results of this preliminary study with the disclaimer that the results of this study are tentative, given the extremely small sample size and the resulting inability to conduct cohort-specific analyses. Nevertheless, this pilot project represents a new beginning in paleopathological study at the Fag el-Gamous cemetery and hopefully the first of many published studies to come.

During this study, it was discovered that although the human remains within the storage magazine remained excellently preserved, many teeth had been lost post-mortem, either at the place of burial, in transit, or during handling, study or storage. Despite this post-mortem dental loss, it was determined that this population had a significant amount of ante-mortem tooth loss and alveolar bone recession with relatively little evidence of dental caries (Figure 10.2). A number of dental abscesses were observed along with widespread periodontitis

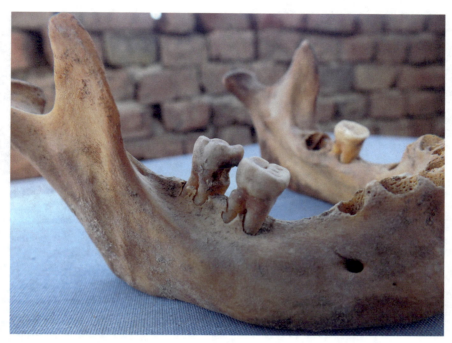

FIGURE 10.2   Individual NN2 – Large interproximal carious lesions on the adjacent surfaces of the first and second right molars, which also have severe alveolar recession. Ante-mortem tooth loss of the adjacent premolars.

and moderate to severe dental wear, perhaps indicating that issues of severe dental wear and/or periodontitis leading to abscess were responsible for more ante-mortem tooth loss than dental caries at this site[21] (Figure 10.3).

The relationship between dental wear and caries is complicated as ongoing dental wear can create an oral environment that is not conducive to the development of calculus deposits or the settlement of cariogenic bacteria, thus resulting in reduced caries rates.[22] This phenomenon is seen in many ancient Egyptian populations due to the apparently gritty or fibrous nature of their diets, which often results in significant to severe dental attrition and minimal dental calculus buildup.[23] However, in this population sample, several individuals were found to have significant dental calculus deposits in some teeth, even in the presence of severe dental wear (Figure 10.4) – perhaps indicating

21   Cf. Richard T. Koritzer, "An analysis of the cause of tooth loss in an ancient Egyptian population," *American Anthropologist* 70/3 (1968): 550–553.

22   George J.R. Maat and Edo A. Van der Velde, "The caries-attrition competition," *International Journal of Anthropology* 2/4 (1987): 281–292.

23   R.J. Forshaw, "Dental health and disease in ancient Egypt," *British Dental Journal* 206/8 (2009): 421–424.

FIGURE 10.3   160-170N 10-20E SW18 – Dental abscess and severe alveolar recession

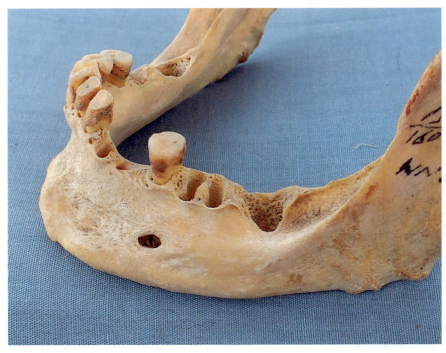

FIGURE 10.4   150-160N 50-60E NNW19 – Dental calculus and severe wear affecting the same
                 teeth

that in addition to gritty foods, a significant part of the diet consisted of soft, cooked foods which have a tendency to stick to the teeth in the absence of regular dental hygiene and/or normal occlusion. Having said this, as it was previously mentioned, it must be acknowledged that the very small sample size considered in this chapter cannot be considered to be representative of the greater trend at the site. Furthermore, if dental extraction of carious teeth was the norm in this population, we would expect to see similarly low rates of caries accompanied by high rates of ante-mortem tooth loss. Large dental caries can also lead to dental infection and result in dental abscess, potentially accounting for the abscesses seen in this population. Although these preliminary results generally support the trends noted by Wood,[24] further dental analysis is required to determine the true prevalence of dental disease in this cemetery population and the diets that contributed to the dental pathology. It is also crucial that future dental studies divide the population sample by sex and age cohorts as dental pathology may differ significantly according to these factors and may give further information regarding the diets, hygiene, and tooth use across different sectors of the population. Although the graves at Fag el-Gamous are relatively egalitarian with regard to the inclusion of grave goods and burial treatment,[25] it may also be interesting to compare oral and skeletal pathology according to socio-economic status where possible. Egyptological study of dental practices from this time period may also prove useful in the interpretation of dental anthropological results at Fag el-Gamous.

A very small number of the teeth examined in this study show evidence of linear enamel hypoplasia (Figure 10.5), which can be indicative of periods of significant physiological stress, such as starvation or febrile illness, during dental growth.[26] Although the source(s) of physiological stress cannot be determined in these cases, other indicators of possible illness were observed in the studied crania. Most of the crania exhibited non-specific indicators of inflammatory response, namely pitting, on the basilar bones of the skull, including the greater wings of the sphenoid and the inferior surfaces of the maxilla (Figure 10.6A). Although similar pitting on the basilar cranial bones has been

---

24   Vincent A. Wood, "Paleopathological Observations and Applications at Seila," in *Excavations at Seila, Egypt*, C. Wilfred Griggs, ed. (Provo, Utah: Religious Studies Center, Brigham Young University, 1988), 31–44.

25   South, *Roman and Early Byzantine Burials at Fag El-Gamus*, 22–23.

26   Alan H. Goodman and Jerome C. Rose, "Assessment of systemic physiological perturbations from dental enamel hypoplasias and associated histological structures," *American Journal of Physical Anthropology* 33/S11 (1990): 59–110.

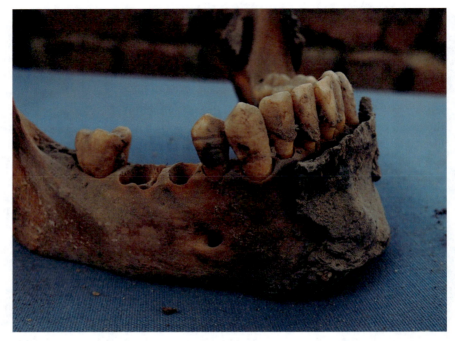

FIGURE 10.5   160-170N 10-20E #13 – Linear enamel hypoplasia on right canine and first
                premolar

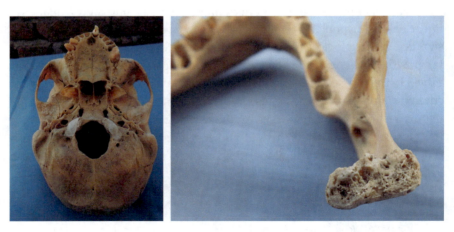

FIGURE 10.6   160-170N 20-30E SW12 – (A) Pitting on sphenoid, occipital, temporal and
                maxillary bones. Evidence of temporomandibular osteoarthritis on both sides.
                (B) Close-up of right mandibular condyle with evidence of osteoarthritis

attributed to a deficiency of vitamin C (scurvy) in some cases,[27] this diagnosis is questionable at Fag el-Gamous given the non-specific nature of this pitting, its apparent resilience through adulthood, a lack of associated cribra orbitalia, and the extension of this porosity to the temporal bones and external auditory meatus in particular, as well as the occipital bone and occipital condyles on occasion. This type of porosity is found under similar conditions at Dakhleh Oasis, where widespread scurvy has been deemed improbable.[28] As such, this condition warrants further investigation.

Some other forms of pitting in the crania may be attributed to more specific aetiologies. For example, cribra orbitalia and porotic hyperostosis are osseous responses to one of the genetic anaemias (sickle cell or thalassemia) or to an acquired anaemia, resulting from poor nutrition, infectious disease, parasitism, metabolic or blood disorders, weanling diarrhoea, or a combination thereof.[29] In many cases, these conditions can be attributed to a deficiency in vitamin B12, which is consumed almost exclusively from animal protein.[30] Children are more susceptible to this deficiency as adults contain stores of B12 in their systems, meaning that shorter periods of B12 deficiency are often evident in the bones of children while skeletal manifestations of B12 deficiency in adults are only apparent when their diet has been B12 deficient for years.[31] As such, a study of cribra orbitalia and porotic hyperostosis has the potential to reveal

---

27   Donald J. Ortner and Mary Frances Eriksen, "Bone changes in the human skull probably resulting from scurvy in infancy and childhood," *International Journal of Osteoarchaeology* 7 (1997): 212–220.

28   Joseph E. Molto, "Dakhleh Oasis Project: Human skeletal remains from the Dakhleh Oasis, Egypt," *Journal of the Society for the Study of Egyptian Antiquities* 16 (1986): 119–127; Scott I. Fairgrieve and Joseph E. Molto, "Cribra orbitalia in two temporally disjunct population samples from the Dakhleh Oasis, Egypt," *American Journal of Physical Anthropology* 111/3 (2000): 328.

29   Arthur C. Aufderheide, Conrado Rodríguez-Martín, and Odin Langsjoen, *The Cambridge encyclopedia of human paleopathology* (Cambridge: Cambridge University Press, 1998), 348–351; Michael Schultz, "Paleohistopathology of bone: a new approach to the study of ancient diseases," *American Journal of Physical Anthropology* 116/S33 (2001): 106–147; Donald J. Ortner, *Identification of pathological conditions in human skeletal remains* (New York: Academic Press, 2003): 102–105; Phillip L. Walker, Rhonda R. Bathurst, Rebecca Richman, Thor Gjerdrum, and Valerie A. Andrushko, "The causes of porotic hyperostosis and cribra orbitalia: A reappraisal of the iron-deficiency-anemia hypothesis," *American Journal of Physical Anthropology* 139/2 (2009): 109–125.

30   Phillip L. Walker, Rhonda R. Bathurst, Rebecca Richman, Thor Gjerdrum, and Valerie A. Andrushko, "The causes of porotic hyperostosis and cribra orbitalia: A reappraisal of the iron-deficiency-anemia hypothesis," *American Journal of Physical Anthropology* 139/2 (2009): 112, 114.

31   Phillip L. Walker, Rhonda R. Bathurst, Rebecca Richman, Thor Gjerdrum, and Valerie A. Andrushko, "The causes of porotic hyperostosis and cribra orbitalia: A reappraisal of the

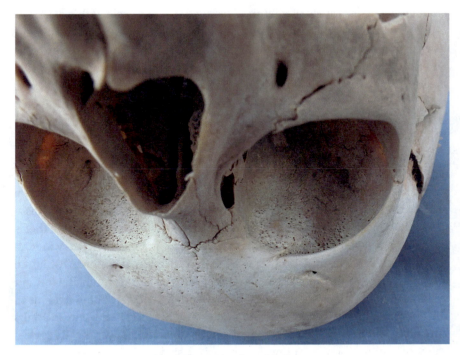

FIGURE 10.7   150-160N 50-60E SW16 – Mild cribra orbitalia

information about a paucity of animal protein in the diet and how long that
deficiency lasted. In this population sample, only one subadult individual
(6 years old +/- 24 months) was found with barely discernable porosity in the
eye orbits (150-160N 0-10E SE3) and one subadult individual (9-10 years old +/-
24 months) presented with more substantial porotic lesions in the eye orbits,
though both cases represent mild cribra orbitalia (Figure 10.7). Both of these
cases were found in association with widespread porosity in other cranial
bones as well as solitary lytic lesions in the skull, thus casting doubt on a dietary aetiology for these porosities. Given the lack of active cribra orbitalia in
adults within this small sample of individuals from Fag el-Gamous, there is no
evidence for a long-term population-wide deficiency of vitamin B12, and therefore dietary meat, during the lifetimes of the adults included in this preliminary study. As cribra orbitalia and porotic hyperostosis most commonly affect
young children, the relative paucity of these conditions in this sample may be
a result of the lack of infant and young children's remains included in this

iron-deficiency-anemia hypothesis," *American Journal of Physical Anthropology* 139/2
(2009): 111.

study, as the youngest individual in this sample was estimated to be aged 6 years +/- 24 months at the time of their death. As such, the analysis of a much larger sample with a more substantial representation of all age cohorts over time is required to rule out any population-wide or cohort-specific nutrient deficiencies throughout the history of the cemetery.

Osteoperiostitis, typically found on the extremities, is also often included in paleo-epidemiological studies of physiological stress along with cribra orbitalia and porotic hyperostosis. Osteoperiostitis results from a primary infectious condition or a secondary osteological response to bone trauma, infection or haemorrhage. It has also been positively correlated with nutritional deficiencies and metabolic disorders.[32] Given the paucity of skeletonized infra-cranial remains available for study in the selected sample, it should come as no surprise that osteoperiostitis was not observed in this sample.

Despite the paucity of infra-cranial remains, some notable pathologies and abnormal growths were observed. One older adult individual was affected by osteoarthritis in the left knee that resulted in light eburnation of the lateral condyle of the femur (130/140N, 20/30W NW 95), and a possibly male adult individual suffered from severe bilateral osteoarthritis of the temporomandibular joint (Figure 10.6A-B). Even in individuals where the infra-cranial skeleton was missing, some notable pathology was observed. For example, a benign button osteoma was found on the right coronal suture of the possibly female adult found at 160/170N 10/20E SE22, which resulted in abnormal cranial growth and suture fusion (Figure 10.8A). An adult male was also found to have an abnormally shaped cranium, likely resulting from the premature fusion of the right lambdoid suture (i.e. synostotic posterior plagiocephaly). This same individual, found at 160/170N 10/20E SW7, also had a small, abnormally shaped neoplastic bone growth in the calvarium behind his right eye orbit (Figure 10.8B).

A developmental abnormality was also found in a possibly female subadult (17-20-year-old) individual, 130/140N 20/30W NW70; namely, a bifurcated (or forked) rib (Figure 10.9). The smaller (and shorter) side of the forked end of the rib has the remains of an articulating surface on the sternal end, suggesting that both sternal ends articulated with the costal cartilage. This developmental abnormality occurs in around 1.2% of the world's population and can sometimes be associated with nevoid basal cell carcinoma syndrome (also known as Gorlin's syndrome) if found in association with a jaw cyst.[33] No jaw cysts were

---

32   Donald J. Ortner and W.G.J. Putschar, *Identification of Pathological Conditions in Human Skeletal Remains* (Smithsonian Institution Press: Washington, DC, 1985): 206–215.

33   Robert J. Gorlin and Robert W. Goltz, "Multiple nevoid basal-cell epithelioma, jaw cysts and bifid rib: a syndrome," *New England Journal of Medicine* 262/18 (1960): 908–912.

FIGURE 10.8   (A) 160/170N 10/20E SE22 – Button osteoma on right coronal suture, resulting
in abnormal suture fusion and cranial growth. (B) 160/170N 10/20E SW7 –
Small neoplastic growth behind eye orbit

FIGURE 10.9   130/140N 20/30W NW70 – Bifurcated (or forked) rib

visible in 130/140N 20/30W NW70, and although radiography would be needed
to exclude this possibility completely, supporting evidence for a diagnosis
of Gorlin's syndrome has yet to been found in this individual. As such, this bifurcated rib may be a simple congenital defect rather than an indicator of
pathology.

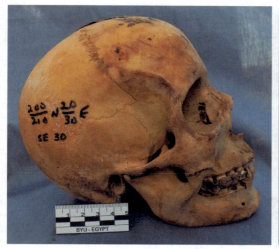

FIGURE 10.10   200/210N 20/30E SE30 – (A) Unfused connection of the abnormal growths
from the right mandible and zygomatic arch, and (B) the inferior surface of
the cranium, showing the articulating surface of the zygomatic growth and the
massive accumulation of dental calculus on the right side of the dentition (top
of photo) where the mandible was incompletely fused to the zygomatic arch

Another congenital abnormality was found in a possibly female adult individual, 200/210N 20/30E SE30. This individual had abnormal bone growths extending up from the right mandibular body and down from the inferior surface
of the right zygomatic arch. These two growths met at an unfused suture of
surfaces largely made up of trabecular bone. Although this abnormal suture
had not fused, the gross accumulation of dental calculus on the right side of
the dentition indicates that this condition did limit the mobility of the jaw,
especially on the right side (Figure 10.10 A-B). Both temporomandibular joints
show evidence of slight anterior displacement and eburnation resulting from
osteoarthritis. The pterygoid foveae and pterygoid muscle insertions on the
sphenoid show marked changes on both sides, indicating that the lateral pterygoid muscles responsible for opening the mouth and protruding the jaw were
unusually stressed. Similarly, the temporalis muscle insertion sites on the crania appear robust, and these muscles are responsible for closing the mouth and
retracting the jaw. Given that there is no evidence of stress in the masticatory
muscles that only help open and close the mouth, it is likely that the bony evidence of muscular stress in these two muscles represents evidence that this
individual may have been particularly reliant on horizontal movements of the
mandible for communication and/or consumption of foods.

It is notable that in this sample there are no clear indications of trauma,
though there are prior reports of high rates of evidence for violent trauma at
this site. Griggs and colleagues reported that "among the adults, 24 percent

died violently as indicated by trephinations in the skulls caused by sharp objects such as swords knives or axes... [with] nearly all of those violent deaths [found] in strata corresponding to the third and fourth centuries AD... [during which time period the adjusted rate of violence is] 58 percent".[34] While this small sample size did not contain evidence of trauma, a quick visual survey conducted while organizing the cranial remains during the 2018 season did reveal several instances of trauma. This will be the subject of a future analysis.

6   Paleopathological Research Potential and Future Studies at Fag el-Gamous

The skeletons that were analysed during this season have already produced significant information regarding the osteobiographies of selected individuals through this paleopathological study. However, a large-scale study of the population would further add to our collective understanding of the lives and deaths of those interred at Fag el-Gamous, as well as the environmental and cultural factors that affected the health and nutrition of those individuals. To this end, in the 2018 season, the Fag el-Gamous cranial collection was fully catalogued and rehoused in stable condition with a map noting each skull's location. For ease of data access and analysis, bioarchaeological data and photographs from this collection in the Bio-Archaeological Database Module (BADaBooM) osteological database.[35] This customizable database is currently primed to collect data regarding the inventory of the selected remains, their state of preservation, the demographic profiles of individuals (i.e. age and sex estimations), metric data, genetically linked non-metric traits, and the paleopathology of bones and teeth. This database is particularly suitable for this site as it allows for the inclusion of archaeological contextual information for each burial. This is important as bioarchaeological data can then be used to recognize data trends according to age, sex, burial type, archaeological context, estimated burial date, burial treatment, burial goods, and possible indicators of socioeconomic status.

34   Griggs, et al., "Evidences of a Christian Population in the Egyptian Fayum and Genetic and Textile Studies of the Akhmim Noble Mummies," 232.

35   Jessica Kaiser, "BADaBooM – a New Database Solution for Bioarchaeology," *84th Annual Meeting of the American Association of Physical Anthropologists* (2015); Jessica Kaiser, "The Giza Database," *Raising the Dead: The Bioarchaeology of the Saite and Roman Period Wall of the Crow Cemetery in Giza*, PhD Dissertation (Berkeley: University of California Berkeley, 2017): 132–146, Appendix XI.

With the use of BADaBooM, large scale studies of genetically-linked non-metric traits could give us a better understanding of the genetic relationships between individuals interred together, indicate whether there were familial preferences for different areas of the cemetery, and give a broad idea of the ancestral backgrounds of those interred at Fag el-Gamous.[36] A study of genetically inherited discreet traits would also be very useful in the context of a population study, as well as a comparative study with the non-metric analyses recently conducted at Kellis 2, Dakhleh Oasis on a cemetery population from the same time period.[37] Although analysis of dental morphology may be somewhat limited by the amount of ante-mortem and post-mortem tooth loss and high rates of dental attrition (dental wear), a dental and skeletal morphological analysis of the complete skeletal collection would be beneficial, as it has the potential to provide significant information about the genetic composition of the population interred at Fag el-Gamous and may contribute to our understanding of how the cemetery was established, through the possible identification of family groups and the ancestry of the people interred in this cemetery.

In addition to data on non-metric traits, metric data will be collected using an osteometric board, a sliding caliper, and a spreading caliper and will be recorded in BADaBooM to facilitate future analysis. This data can supplement studies of non-metric traits relating to ancestry and can be helpful in the assessment of malnutrition and pathology, as these physiological stressors can delay or suppress bone growth.[38] Significant differences in skeletal metrics will be identified through comparative studies with other Egyptian populations. When and if possible, radiographs will be taken of subadult and young adult long bones to identify any "Harris Lines," which would provide primary evidence of arrested bone growth (these lines are not present in older adults due

---

36   G. Richard Scott and Christy G. Turner, *The anthropology of modern human teeth: dental morphology and its variation in recent human populations*, Vol. 20 (Cambridge: Cambridge University Press, 2000); Joel D. Irish, "Who were the ancient Egyptians? Dental affinities among Neolithic through postdynastic peoples," *American Journal of Physical Anthropology* 129/4 (2006): 529–543; Heather J.H. Edgar, *Dental Morphology for Anthropology: An Illustrated Manual* (New York: Taylor & Francis, 2017); Lisa C. Brown, "Statistical analysis of nonmetric cranial trait interactions in a skeletal population sample from the Dakhleh Oasis, Egypt," *Electronic Thesis and Dissertation Repository*, 1516 (2013).

37   Brown, "Statistical analysis of nonmetric cranial trait interactions in a skeletal population sample from the Dakhleh Oasis, Egypt."

38   Alan H. Goodman and Debra L. Martin, "Reconstructing health profiles from skeletal remains," *The Backbone of history: Health and nutrition in the Western hemisphere* 2 (2002): 11–60; Sharon N. DeWitte, "Stress, sex, and plague: Patterns of developmental stress and survival in pre-and post-Black Death London," *American Journal of Human Biology* (2017) DOI: 10.1002/ajhb.23073.

to normal bone regeneration over time).[39] As seen in the above study, physiological stress can have a similar impact on dental enamel in the form of linear enamel hypoplasia (LEH).[40] These linear defects in enamel deposition can be viewed under oblique light and will continue to be noted in future analyses along with other non-specific indicators of physiological stress such as osteoperiostitis, porotic hyperostosis, and cribra orbitalia. These indicators will be used in cohort-specific comparative studies with other Egyptian populations to identify any significant differences in population frailty and susceptibility to infection and/or trauma.[41]

Although the aforementioned indicators of physiological stress are non-specific with regards to aetiology, additional paleopathological analyses will continue to be conducted at Fag el-Gamous in the future with reference to the standard paleopathological tomes[42] as well as more recent paleopathological and modern clinical literature. Mummified tissue will be observed for abnormalities and, if permitted, radiographic analysis will be used when possible to preserve the integrity of the human remains while revealing, or confirming, paleopathological conditions. Given that this cemetery spans periods of significant political, religious, and economic change, as well as a period of climatic change and the Cyprian Plague, there is great potential for paleopathological analyses to contribute to the historical narratives of these times of transition, particularly with regard to malnutrition, physiological stress, and chronic illness. Although the infra-cranial skeletons have been reinterred, this collection is an important resource for Egyptian paleo-epidemiological studies due to its large scale, the previous documentation of abnormalities in the infra-cranial skeleton, and the large time span represented within this cemetery population.

---

39   Amy B. Scott and Robert D. Hoppa, "A re-evaluation of the impact of radiographic orientation on the identification and interpretation of Harris lines," *American Journal of Physical Anthropology* 156/1 (2015): 141–147.

40   Simon Hillson, *Dental Anthropology* (Cambridge: Cambridge University Press, 1996); Alan H. Goodman and Debra L. Martin, "Reconstructing health profiles from skeletal remains," *The Backbone of history: Health and nutrition in the Western hemisphere* 2 (2002): 11–60; DeWitte, "Stress, sex, and plague: Patterns of developmental stress and survival in pre-and post-Black Death London."

41   Cf. Sandra M. Wheeler, "Nutritional and disease stress of juveniles from the Dakhleh Oasis, Egypt," *International Journal of Osteoarchaeology* 2/2 (2012): 219–234.

42   E.g. Tony Waldron, *Palaeopathology* (Cambridge: Cambridge University Press, 2008); Donald J. Ortner, *Identification of Pathological Conditions in Human Skeletal Remains* (New York: Academic Press, 2003); Arthur C. Aufderheide and Conrado Rodríguez-Martín, *The Cambridge Encyclopedia of Human Paleopathology*, Vol. 478 (Cambridge: Cambridge University Press, 1998).

In addition to skeletal paleopathology, further cohort-specific analysis of dental pathology (caries, periodontitis, dental wear, dental calculus, dental abscess, ante-mortem tooth loss, etc.), paired with mandibular and cranial morphology, will be used to provide information about diet, dental pathology, and dental hygiene in this population. Dental diseases are known to be highly correlated with diet and food processing methods and would give interesting and unique insight into the changes in the diets of those interred at the Fag el-Gamous cemetery throughout the history of its use.

7   Conclusion

Through this preliminary analysis of the Fag el-Gamous cranial collection, it was determined that this collection, and the further excavation of the Fag el-Gamous cemetery, have incredible potential for significant contribution to the fields of bioarchaeology, Egyptology and the history of occupation in the Fayoum. This conclusion is based on the excellent state of preservation of the remains, the large number of burials (excavated and unexcavated), and the large time span in which this cemetery was in use. If given the opportunity to expand the bioarchaeological study to include the use of advanced technologies (such as radiographic or biomolecular methods) in the analysis of the Fag el-Gamous cemetery population, this large site could give unprecedented access to information about changes in the health, diet and lifestyle of the Fayoum inhabitants spanning a long period of time, including significant periods of transition.

Regardless of the possibility for advanced scientific analysis, the Fag el-Gamous cranial collection has the potential to reveal a significant amount of information about the Fag el-Gamous cemetery and its occupants. As such, it is planned that the cranial collection will be studied in depth by paleopathologists and bioarchaeologists prior to the continued excavation at the Fag el-Gamous cemetery. With the information gleaned from this cranial collection and the archived osteological reports at hand, the excavations at Fag el-Gamous could proceed with more pointed research questions in the future and contribute significantly to Egyptian history.

Acknowledgements

First and foremost, I must thank the Egyptian Ministry of Antiquities and the Head of the Fayoum inspectorate, Ahmed Abdel Al and now Sayed Ali Elshora, for allowing us to continue the valuable work at Fag el-Gamous. I am also grateful for Manal Saied Ahmed's supervision over the 2014 season. Additionally, I feel the need to express my immense gratitude to Dr. Kerry Muhlestein for inviting me to work with his fantastic team, and to Dr. R. Paul Evans for enthusiastically welcoming me to join him in the examination of human remains at the site. My gratitude is also extended to Jennifer Willoughby, who assisted in the photographic analysis of some individuals included in this chapter. Finally, thank you to the reviewers of this chapter for their helpful feedback. This chapter is better as a result of your efforts and I accept any errors in this paper as my own.

CHAPTER 11

Fag el-Gamous Pottery with "Kill Holes"

Kerry Muhlestein, Brian D. Christensen and Cannon Fairbairn

1   Introduction

While a great deal of pottery sherds have been unearthed in the Fag el-Gamous cemetery, only a small percentage of burials have contained complete or semi-complete pieces of ceramic vessels. This may be due to the ancient practice of reopening burial shafts to inter a later burial, a process which can break and scatter pottery. The intact vessels have been routinely conserved and placed in storage magazines. During our recent conservation efforts we have revisited this pottery, both making sure it was properly stored and photographing and analyzing it for publication. During the 2014 conservation efforts, we noticed four ceramic vessels, and a fifth in 2018, all excavated by our predecessors, that exhibited an interesting feature. These five wheel thrown earthenware bowls, which all appear to be locally made and come from various time periods, had clean holes punched through the bottom. While pots can occasionally break in this area during the manufacturing process, these exhibit a pattern that is typical of being punched with a sharp blow. This intentional perforation allows us to fit these bowls into an important history. The purpose of this paper is not to extensively examine the practice, but rather to provide a brief background that allows the Fag el-Gamous pottery to be fit into its context, and to add the evidence of the Fag el-Gamous vessels to the larger discussion of this funerary practice.

All five bowls appear to be locally made since they do not fit well into standard vessel types. The semi-ragged holes presented in all five vessels are consistent with a sharp blow from a punch. If one were to press forcefully on the bottom of a ceramic vessel with a punch rather than striking it, the vessel would shatter completely. After creating similar vessels, we have tried punching pottery ourselves. Brian Christensen created ten ceramic hemispherical bowls similar to those in the Fag el-Gamous collection. Five were fired and five were dry but unfired. All bowls were struck using a hammer and a ½inch round steel rod. All unfired bowls completely shattered. Of the five fired bowls, three survived with a hole in the bottom. Each of these had been struck foot down on a piece of carpet. Two of them exhibited stress cracks around the rim. Clearly the process of punching bowls post production had to be done with fired bowls and was difficult enough that one would not do it this way if the bowl were intended for use.

As a follow-up to this experiment, we then made nine more replica vessels. For the vessel with the most complicated breakage pattern (FeG-Ka 112), Christensen made three copies. Two replicas were made of those vessels with fairly normal breakage patterns (FeG-KA 44 and FeG 3), and one each of the two vessels which displayed breaking that was easy to understand (FeG-KA 160 and FeG 2). All of these vessels were fired to 999 degrees Celsius (1,830 degrees Fahrenheit). This temperature was chosen because it approximately represents the low end of efficient maturity for most red earthenware clay worldwide. Red earthenware or redware is clay that contains high concentrations of naturally occurring iron. It is common clay, which will start to sinter, bloat, melt and distort above about 1,940°F. The iron itself is the flux which lowers the melting point of redware but also hardens it to maturity and makes it more efficient to fire with less fuel at lower temperatures than stoneware clays.

The punches in each of the ancient vessels, though spread out over time, are clean enough to indicate some kind of firm punching tool was used. In this, the second experiment, a ⅜ inch (9.5 mm) diameter metal punch was used. We found that the harder the hit to the punch the cleaner the break was. The vessels were placed on particle board. We presume a fairly firm surface was used in antiquity. Too hard a surface would result in chipping of the rim and vibration cracks or the destruction of the vessels, and too soft of a surface also results in more breakage from spreading of the walls. Again, these ancient vessels were created, used and interred in different time periods and thus were not all broken in necessarily the same way using the same tools and surfaces. Vessels with thicker walls required more power and were more likely to fracture. In our experiment, none of these fired vessels broke, though some exhibited stress fractures. The results of these experiments are discussed below with each individual vessel.

The kind of a punch holes found in these vessels could be made as part of the production process. Yet this does not explain why multiple potters would do this in various time periods with a variety of vessel types. If the pot were made on a wheel by a professional potter, as these pots certainly were, why would the potter punch a ragged hole? If the holed pots were used functionally for drainage it would be easier, quicker and less risky to the structure to press or cut a clean hole during a plastic clay stage. Functional potters would have consistently worked in the safest, most efficient manner, not wanting to waste their time or their materials. All of this suggests that these were not holes made for a utilitarian purpose as the vessels were created. The vessels seem to be made skillfully on the potter's wheel but also quickly and with very simple decorations, if any.

Taken together, these signs indicate that the vessels were punched post firing by the owners. This means that they were created for a variety of purposes, and at some point, their context changed in such a way that it was deemed necessary to intentionally perforate the vessel.

2 Vessel FeG-KA 44

The first vessel is object FeG-KA 44 (Figures 11.1 and 11.2). This is a small, coarse red-ware bowl or cup with white slip around the rim.[1] The bowls appear to be

FIGURE 11.1   FeG-KA 44
              PHOTOGRAPH BY BRIAN CHRISTENSEN

---

1   Slips are applied to part or all of the vessel pre-firing. See Anna Wodzińska, *A Manual of Egyptian Pottery, Volume 4: Ptolemaic Period-Modern* (Boston: AERA, 2010), 3. Due to the deterioration of the colored area, we are not completely certain it was applied pre-firing, but it appears to be.

FIGURE 11.2   FeG-KA 44
              PHOTOGRAPH BY BRIAN CHRISTENSEN

Nile silt/alluvium clay with many organic and varying inorganic inclusions
fired at a mid-high temperature.[2] Void marks are visible, and a section is broken from the rim to just below the white slip, or about half of the way down the
bowl. A hole has been punched through the base. It is about 8.5 cm wide and 6
cm tall. We lack details about the archaeological depth of this find, but know
the area in which it was discovered during the 1984 season (140/150 N, 0/10 E,
SE square). This vessel is best described as being from the Roman Era, though
not truly Roman for it has no real comparanda.[3] The Fag el-Gamous cemetery
seems to consist of largely Roman era burials,[4] and so we conclude that this is

---

2   Our gratitude to Krystal Pierce for help with the analysis of this bowl.
3   Our gratitude to Deborah Harris and Cynthia Finlayson for their aid in analyzing this
    pottery.
4   See R. Paul Evans, David Whitchurch and Kerry Muhlestein, "Re-thinking Burial Dates at a
    Graeco-Roman Cemetery: Fag el-Gamous, Fayoum, Egypt," *Journal of Archaeological Science:
    Reports* 2 (2015): 209–214.

most likely a local variation of a Roman era bowl. However, the kind of dripping slip present on the cup is often found in countryside Hellenistic areas, and somewhat similar vessels were created in Ptolemaic Egypt. Additionally, the style and the presence of some Hellenistic burials in the cemetery cause us to make the Roman dating of the vessel a tentative conclusion.

The concussion marks on the inside of the vessel were not large but were still present enough to indicate that the cup was punched while upside down. In order to validate this we broke one of our models right side up and one upside down. The look of the hole in the right side up vessel did not match that of FeG-KA 44, while the hole made when it was punched upside down matched very well. This confirmed our conclusion that the vessel had been punched upside down. It should be noted that this cup has a somewhat thick bottom, and when we punched our upside-down replica it took two strong blows to do so.

3   Vessel FeG-KA 112

The second vessel to be examined is object FeG-KA 112 (Figures 11.3 and 11.4). This vessel is a simple bowl with a rounded incurved rim and perforated pedestal base. The fabric appears to be a Nile silt clay with some organic and many inorganic inclusions, some of them large. The bowl is Early Roman 184, typically dated as Antonine (138–161 AD).[5] Manufacturing techniques appear to include external smoothing, internal wheel-marks, and a string-cut base.[6] Cracking is evident around much of the lip, which could be the result of the bowl being compressed on one side before firing, though another possibility will be noted below. Most of the cracks are surficial and do not extend all the way through the bowl. The center of the base is missing, and a hole has been punched in the bottom of the bowl. Traces of a white material on the surfaces appear to be environmental calcification rather than applied slip. Small burn voids and burn marks are visible on the exterior surface. It was deposited outside the entrance of a tomb in the midst of a complex of tombs carved into the mudstone shelving known as Hill B, Tomb 1. The burials in this part of Hill B seem to stem largely from the early Roman era, which is also when the closest parallels for this pottery occur. Some barley was placed under this bowl.[7]

---

5   Wodzińska, *Pottery Manual*, 4:136.
6   Our gratitude to Krystal Pierce for help with the analysis of this bowl.
7   See the botanical report in this volume for more on this grain and a picture of the tomb complex in which it was found.

FIGURE 11.3   FeG-KA 112
PHOTOGRAPH BY BRIAN CHRISTENSEN

The bowl seems to have been dropped or was compressed in some other way before firing so that it elongated very slightly. It should be noted that one possible reason for the hole is that since this bowl became somewhat misshapen it was then repurposed as a lid, somewhat similar to Early Roman 268, which was a lid that was pierced in order to release steam.[8] Yet FeG-KA 112 is dissimilar enough from these lids that it seems much more likely it was a slightly misshapen bowl that was later punched with a hole.

The concussion marks of FeG-KA 112 make it clear that it was broken upside down. We broke all three replicas upside down. One vessel took 3 blows to punch through, in contrast with the one blow needed for the other two replicas of FeG-KA 112. The repeated concussions of these blows caused small stress

---

8   Wodzińska, *Pottery Manual*, 4:162. John Gee suggested this possibility.

FIGURE 11.4   FeG-KA 112
                PHOTOGRAPH BY BRIAN CHRISTENSEN

fractures running horizontally just under the rim. While these were much smaller than those exhibited in the antique bowl, they are similar enough to suggest that the stress fractures apparent in FeG-KA 112 were caused by the force applied to the rim when punching the hole in the bowl while it was upside down resting on its rim.

4   Vessel FeG-KA 160

The third vessel in this study is object FeG-KA 160 (Figures 11.5 and 11.6). Found at 220 cm below the surface of the sand (in area 140/160 N, 50/60 E, NW square), a depth that typically indicates an early Roman era burial. This is a carinated jar with long wide neck, flaring rim, perforated ring base, and yellow painted surface treatment of dots and both horizontal and vertical lines. The fabric

FIGURE 11.5
FeG-KA 160
PHOTOGRAPH BY BRIAN
CHRISTENSEN

FIGURE 11.6
FeG-KA 160
PHOTOGRAPH BY BRIAN CHRISTENSEN

appears to be Nile silt with very few organic and some inorganic inclusions. The hole has been punched in the center of the base. We have found no true parallels for this jar, it seems to be a local variety of pottery.[9] The closest parallel, which has significant differences, such as the addition of a handle, is Early Roman 74, which is dated to the Hadrianic period (ca 117–138 AD).[10] The painting style is most typical of Late Roman vessels.[11]

The concussion marks indicate that this vessel was broken upside down. It is also unlikely that such a tall vessel would be punched right side up, for it would require a long tool and would be more awkward. Our experimental vessel was successfully punched and created a hole very similar to that in its ancient counterpart.

5   Vessel Feg 2

The fourth vessel, is object FeG 2 (Figures 11.7 and 11.8). It is a simple earthenware hemispherical bowl with depressed everted rim (which contains three large chips), perforated ring base, and red slipped interior. The fabric appears to be a marl clay with little to no organic and some inorganic inclusions. The majority of the temper appears to be very fine quartz. It appears to have been fired at a higher temperature than the other vessels, with wheel-marks present internally and externally. It has a dark red-purple fired clay slip. The interior is moderately burnished and smoothed with red slip. It has a partially smoothed salting/encrustation that is moderately present on the entire vessel. It was wheel thrown with a ring base measuring 8.1 cm in diameter. It has a wide but thin lip. The lip has a 2 mm wide groove running for 3 mm inside the lip. It is 2.3 cm wide and 7 mm thick. This thin lip is in contrast to the larger lip one would expect from a Roman bowl, again suggesting that this is a local variety. Still, there are many Early and Late Roman parallels for this vessel type, which is often referred to as a casserole vessel. The red slip seems to be more common in the Late Roman period.[12] About a third of the rim has been broken off. A large hole has been punched in the center bottom of the bowl, that is 4 mm across. Three radiating through cracks stem from this hole in approximately equidistant thirds. There is one additional through crack. There are also several

---

9   There are somewhat similar early Roman parallels, some of which have handles, none of which have this type of painting.

10   Wodzińska, *Pottery Manual*, 4:102.

11   Our gratitude to Krystal Pierce for helping to analyze this bowl.

12   Our gratitude to Krystal Pierce and Deborah Harris for help analyzing this bowl.

FIGURE 11.7   FeG 2
                PHOTOGRAPH BY KERRY MUHLESTEIN

exterior only cracks. Sadly, the bowl was left in the on-site storage magazine without anything that identifies where it was excavated beyond the Fag el-Gamous cemetery.

There is a compression crack that stems vertically up from the punched hole about half way up the bowl, and then spirals somewhat to either side. The concussion mark is on the bottom of the vessel, indicating that it was broken right side up. This could account for the compression cracks, since the bowl has to take more of the force of the blow when the punch quickly strikes the surface on which it rests, as opposed to the amount of force absorbed as the punch travels through open air before hitting a surface when the vessel is upside down. This was confirmed when we broke the replica of this bowl right side up and two very small compression fractures stemmed from either side of the hole, roughly 180 degrees apart from each other. It should be noted that similar cracks can appear from nesting close-fitting bowls in the kiln. Still we conclude that this bowl was punched right side up and that the visible compression fractures were likely created as part of this process.

FIGURE 11.8   FeG 2
PHOTOGRAPH BY KERRY MUHLESTEIN

6   Vessel FeG 3

The fifth object is FeG 3, a small coarseware bowl (Figures 11.9 and 11.10). It has a ring base and a thrown construction. It is roughly circular redware, slightly burnished on the exterior. Red slip was used, with some drips covering about half the object's exterior. Finger pull marks are visible on the inside, which is covered by fired dark grey slip.[13] The interior is smooth with a number of very small voids. The lip finish is missing. The wall thickness is 1 cm, as is the base. The remnant diameter is 12 cm at the top, and 6 cm at the base. It has no true comparanda, though it is somewhat similar to a few bowls, such as Early Roman 187[14] or Late Roman 152.[15] Again, it seems that this is a local variety of pottery.

---

13   The grey color is more likely a carbon stain from firing than that the slip was mixed to be grey.

14   Wodzińska, *Pottery Manual*, 4:137.

15   Wodzińska, *Pottery Manual*, 4:236.

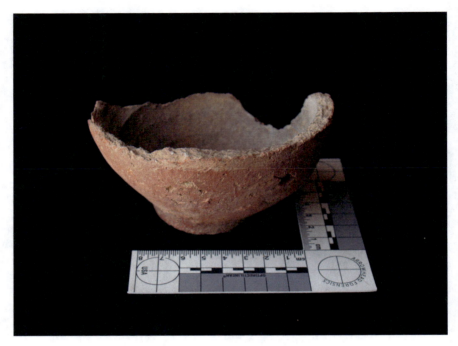

FIGURE 11.9   FeG 3
PHOTOGRAPH BY R. PAUL EVANS

The vessel has a hole punched in the bottom that is about 2.8 cm in diameter and is roughly circular.[16] It was struck from the bottom and the ball of percussion split off the inside of the bowl. Sadly, this bowl was also left with no identifying markers regarding where in the cemetery it was found.

Undoubtedly this vessel was punched upside down, for the concussion marks on the inside of the bowl are very clear. The replica that we punched upside down matched very well the breakage of the ancient original. Because it was so clear that this bowl was punched upside down, we took the liberty of punching the second bowl right side up to examine the difference. It developed very small stress fractures that were similar to those of FeG 2, again confirming that these fractures had been created because that vessel had been punched right side up.

All five vessels were of ordinary make and buried with common people.[17] The holes were created deliberately with a sharp blow or it would have shattered

16   Our gratitude to Deborah Harris for help analyzing this bowl.
17   See the article on burials in this volume for an explanation of what is meant by "common" burials in this cemetery.

FIGURE 11.10   FeG 3
PHOTOGRAPH BY R. PAUL EVANS

the bowl. It is not clear whether there was a uniform reason for perforating all
five vessels. It is clear that they were not all punched in exactly the same manner, as was discussed above. On the whole, besides the "kill" holes, a phrase to
be explained below, there does not seem to be anything unusual about these
vessels, and they do not share anything else specifically in common.

7   Global Context

The practice of creating holes in burial pottery is not unique to Egypt. Perforations could be created for a number of reasons, such as creating sieves, funnels,
lamps, incense burners, flower pots, etc. Yet these holes do not seem to fit a
functional purpose, and thus seem to fit more into the nebulous category of
"kill holes." One of the most recognized examples of pottery "kill holes" comes
from examples of Mimbres pottery in the North American South West (ca
1000–1250 AD). "The Classic Mimbres pottery tradition is characterized by
painted bowls decorated with geometric and figural designs in black on a white
ground. The bowls are usually found in human burials and appear to be used

to cover the face or head of the deceased. They often have a distinctive 'kill hole,' an intentional puncture at the base of the bowl which appears to be associated with this ceremonial function."[18]

"Kill holes" like this are also known from the Bari tribe, modern Sudanese tribes, Native American tribes of Florida, peoples of British Honduras, and ancient Nubia.[19] While it is informative to realize that this was a worldwide phenomenon, we must not assume that all of these cultures ascribed the same meaning to these holes. In order to understand the vessels of Fag el-Gamous it is most important to examine the Egyptian history of the practice. While there is not general agreement as to the reason for "kill holes" in Egypt, there is agreement that such practices stretch as far back as the Egyptian Old Kingdom.[20]

8   Egyptian Context

From early in Egyptian history, grave goods were broken in order to "kill" the object.[21] The tradition of breaking objects before burying them with the deceased began in the predynastic era, however this did not yet include pottery.[22] Stone vessels were "killed" most likely at the graveside.[23] During the Old Kingdom, objects, including pottery, were "killed," often by punching holes in the center, and buried with the deceased.[24] For example, the Petrie collection, housed in the University College, London, contains two stone bowls from the

---

18   Donna Yates, "Mimbres Pottery," in *Trafficking Culture,* last modified August 8, 2012, http://traffickingculture.org/encyclopedia/case-studies/mimbres-pottery/. See also Steven LeBlanc, "Mimbres Pottery," *Archaeology* 31/3 (May/June 1978): 8–11.

19   Leslie. V. Grinsell, "The Breaking of Objects as a Funerary Rite," *Folklore* 72/3 (1961): 477–479; Julia Budka, "Egyptian Impact on Pot-Breaking Ceremonies at El-Kurru? A Reexamination," in *The Fourth Cataract and Beyond: Proceedings of the 12th International Conference for Nubian Studies. British Museum Publications on Egypt and Sudan, 1* (Leuven: Peeters, 2014), 647; Leslie V. Grinsell, *Barrow, Pyramid and Tomb: Ancient Burial Customs in Egypt, the Mediterranean, and the British Isles* (London: Thames and Hudson, 1975), 62.

20   Nicola Harrington, *Living with the Dead: Ancestor Worship and Mortuary Ritual in Ancient Egypt* (Oxford: Oxbow Books, 2013), 38.

21   Robert K. Ritner, *The Mechanics of Ancient Egyptian Magical Practice. Studies in Ancient Oriental Civilization, no. 54* (Chicago: University of Chicago, 2008), 148.

22   Trude Kertesz, "The Breaking of Offerings in the Cult of Hathor," *Journal of the Institute of Archaeology of Tel Aviv University* 3/3 (1976): 134; Grinsell, *Barrow, Pyramid and Tomb,* 63.

23   R. Engelbach, ed., *Introduction to Egyptian Archaeology: With Special Reference to the Egyptian Museum, Cairo,* (Cairo: General Organization for Government Printing Offices, 1961), 236.

24   Grinsell, "The Breaking of Objects as a Funerary Rite," 481.

3rd–4th Dynasty with holes punched in the bottom.[25] Current thinking is that in this era such holes were made to "kill" grave goods,[26] though there is not agreement as to the reason for killing them (see below for other ideas as to the possible purpose of "kill holes").

Evidence for the practice of "killing" vessels has also been discovered in the Second Intermediate Period, where pots were found with small holes purposefully made in the bottom[27] or smashed against the ground[28] and then buried with the dead. In tombs of the 17th Dynasty at Dra Abu el-Naga, sherds of broken pottery that appear to have been shattered as part of the funerary meal were unearthed; however, some instead contained pots "killed" by holes knocked in the base.[29] The practice appears throughout the New Kingdom,[30] such as in the 18th Dynasty tomb of Djehuty (also at Dra Abu el-Naga, TT 11) where in a pit filled with broken pottery, bouquets, and funerary offerings, pots ritually "killed" by means of punched holes were also discovered.[31] Tombs at Dra Abu el-Naga also contained pottery that was possibly ritually killed, dating

25   William Matthew Flinders Petrie, *The Funerary Furniture of Egypt: With Stone and Metal Vases* (Warminster, England: Aris & Phillips, 1977), 4, nos. 38–39; L.V. Grinsell, "The Breaking of Objects as a Funerary Rite: Supplementary Notes," *Folklore* 84/2 (1973): 112; Grinsell, *Barrow, Pyramid and Tomb*, 63.

26   Ritner, *The Mechanics of Ancient Egyptian Magical Practice*, 148.

27   Engelback, *Introduction to Egyptian Archaeology*, 257; Grinsell, "The Breaking of Objects as a Funerary Rite," 481; Grinsell, *Barrow, Pyramid and Tomb*, 63; Julia Budka, "The Use of Pottery in Funerary Contexts During the Libyan and Late Period: A View from Thebes and Abydos," in *Egypt in Transition: Social and Religious Development of Egypt in the First Millennium BCE* (Prague: Czech Institute of Egyptology, Faculty of Arts, Charles University in Prague, 2010), 55.

28   M.J. López-Grande and E. Torrado de Gregorio, "Pottery Vases from a Votive Deposit Found at Dra Abu El-Naga (Djehuty Project Archaeological Excavation)," in *Proceedings of the Tenth International Congress of Egyptologists, University of the Aegean, Rhodes, 22–29 May 2008* (Leuven: Peeters, 2015), 417.

29   Harrington, *Living with the Dead*, 38–39; Anne Seiler, *Tradition und Wandel: Die Keramik als Spiegel der Kulturentwicklung Thebens in der Zweiten Zwischenzeit* (Mainz: Zabern, 2005), pl. 4b.

30   Grinsell, "The Breaking of Objects as a Funerary Rite," 481; Budka, "Egyptian Impact on Pot-Breaking Ceremonies at El-Kurru?," 646–647.

31   López-Grande and De Gregorio, "Pottery Vases from a Votive Deposit Found at Dra Abu El-Naga," 314; Harrington, *Living with the Dead*, 38–39. See also Susan J. Allen, "Tutankhamun's Embalming Cache Reconsidered," in *Egyptology at the Dawn of the Twenty-First Century: Proceedings of the Eighth International Congress of Egyptologists Cairo, 2000*, ed. Zahi Hawass (Cairo: The American University in Cairo Press, 2003), 27. Evidence of ritually broken pottery has been found as part of the burial of King Tutankhamun. These pots appear to have been smashed after the funerary meal and packed inside pots with other funeral-related items.

to end of the 20th Dynasty.[32] Pottery that appears to have been purposely broken was also discovered around the shared mortuary temple of Ramesses IV, Ramesses V, and Ramesses VI, near Deir el-Bahari.[33]

In a tomb-temple at Thebes, an Osiris bed was found accompanied by at least 45 jars that appear to have been ritually broken. One of these exhibited the features of a hole being punched in it.[34] While cultic in some sense, an Osiris bed also carries with it strong connotations of a funerary context. Still, the smashing of the pots rather than just perforating them makes this a difficult comparison.

In the same tomb-temple several 20th Dynasty storage vessels were found. The largest had a hole hammered into it between the shoulder and the rim.[35] A nearby amphora had two holes punched into it,[36] while two more amphorae had a single hole punched in each.[37] Interestingly, all of these non-smashed pots with perforations were in a funerary context, having been stored with the burial in a subterranean chamber.[38] While they are from a very different era, the holes and burial context make these a somewhat viable comparison with the Fag el-Gamous pottery.

Non-funerary contexts provide less of a parallel, but are also worth examining when they seem to serve a less common utilitarian function. This allows us to see the kinds of "kill holes" that the Fag el-Gamous vessels are not. For example, a large cache of New Kingdom (mid- to late-18th Dynasty) beer jars found at Tell el-Borg all exhibited holes.[39] Throughout the site the beer jars did not exhibit this feature, except in a large pit in which all jars were punctured. These holes were made before the vessels were fired, suggesting they were part of the functional use of the vessel, perhaps for intentional drainage as part of

---

32   Susanne Michels, "Cult and Funerary Pottery from the Tomb-Temple K93.12 at the End of the 20th Dynasty (Dra' Abu el-Naga/Western Thebes)," in *Vienna 2—Ancient Egyptian Ceramics in the 21st Century. Proceedings of the International Conference held at the University of Vienna, 14th–18th of May 2012*, Bettina Bader, Christian M. Knoblauch, and E. Christiana Köhler, eds. (Leuven: Peeters, 2016), 406.

33   M.J. López-Grande and F. Quesada, "Two Third Intermediate Period/Late Period Pottery Deposits at Herakleopolis Magna," in *Sesto Congresso internazionale di egittologia vol.* 1 (Turin: International Association of Egyptologists, 1992), 417.

34   Susanne Michels, "Cult and Funerary Pottery from the Tomb-Temple K93.12 at the End of the 20th Dynasty (Dra' Abu el-Naga/Western Thebes)," 406 and fig. 3.5.

35   Ibid., 407 and fig. 8.

36   Ibid., 407 and fig. 9.

37   Ibid., 407–408, figs. 10 and 11.

38   Ibid., 408 and fig. 15.

39   Personal communication with Rexine Hummel. See *Tell el-Borg II*, James K. Hoffmeier, ed. (Ann Arbor: Eisenbrauns, forthcoming in 2019), Plates VII and IX.

the cultic activity of the shrine. While they share the label of "kill holes," are interesting in their own right, and possess a partially shared history, they are essentially dissimilar from the Fag el-Gamous vessels.

An amphora with a hole punched in the shoulder was also uncovered at Tell el-Borg.[40] Holes punched in the shoulders of vessels are found at Amarna as well.[41] At Mendes, 19 of 88 beer jars (21.5%) found in connection with a shrine to the local fish goddess also exhibited punched holes, though in this case in the bottom of the vessel. Yet these early 19th Dynasty vessels seem to have also been punched before they were fired,[42] again suggesting that the holes served a utilitarian function, even if that function was part of a cultic act. Again, they may have some shared elements with the Fag el-Gamous killed vessels, but are not truly comparable.

Further intriguing evidence comes from el-Kurru, in Kush, from the era just before the 25th Dynasty. There, Egyptianized vessels were perforated in the bottom and then smashed.[43] Again, the distance in time and place, along with the smashing of the pot, does not provide a true parallel for what we see at Fag el-Gamous. Yet it is also clear that there are various ways of "killing" pots over a long period of time and over great distances of space, seemingly for different reasons.

Recently Julia Budka wrote of finding an 18th Dynasty pot in Nubia with a hole punched at the joint of the neck and body.[44] The practice is also attested during the Late Period, continuing into the Ptolemaic era.[45] For example, on another occasion Budka found a number of jars from the Libyan period that had been pierced during production and then were used in association with

---

40 Personal communication with Rexine Hummel, to whom we express gratitude.

41 Nicola Harrington, "The Eighteenth Dynasty Egyptian Banquet: Ideals and Realities," in *Dining and Death: Interdisciplinary Perspectives on the "Funerary Banquet" in Ancient Art, Burial, and Belief,* Catherine M. Draycott and Maria Stamatopoulou, eds. (Leuven: Peeters: 2016), 143.

42 Our gratitude to Rexine Hummel, who not only led us to the reference, but told us how she would re-date these vessels now. See Rexine Hummel, "Late New Kingdom Ceramics at Mendes," in *Delta Reports Volume I: Research in Lower Egypt,* Donald Redford, ed. (Oxford: Oxbow Books, 2009), 76 and figures 14–16 on Plate 15.

43 Budka, "Egyptian Impact on Pot-Breaking Ceremonies at El-Kurru?," 643. See also T. Kendall, *Kush, Lost Kingdom of the Nile: A Loan Exhibition from the Museum of Fine Arts, Boston, September 1981 – August 1984,* (Brockton, Mass: Brockton Art Museum, 1982), 23.

44 Julia Budka, "Exciting News—New Archaeological Project in Sudan Starts," AcrossBorders, accessed November 2017, http://acrossborders.oeaw.ac.at/a-killed-vessel-and-more-human-bodies-in-tomb-26/.

45 Budka, "The Use of Pottery in Funerary Contexts During the Libyan and Late Period: A View from Thebes and Abydos," 61.

the tomb of Osiris at Abydos.[46] As with the Mendes and Tell el-Borg vessels, these are not true parallels for the Fag el-Gamous pottery since the holes were created as part of their original use and since they are in a cultic rather than funerary context. Still, it is worth noting that some form of the practice was continuously in use in Egypt. Also at Abydos evidence exists of either the Ritual of Breaking the Red Pots, or a similar ritual from the Second Intermediate Period through the Ptolemaic era.[47] Evidence even suggests there was an increase in the ritual "killing" of pottery during the Ptolemaic era, at least in Thebes.[48] Budka believes that while they are associated with Osiris, these pots carry more of a funerary context.[49] Thus, in time and context they match more closely with the Fag el-Gamous pottery, but not in practice, since smashing was the method of "killing" them.[50]

While this is not an exhaustive discussion of all known examples of "kill holes," it is enough to illustrate both the possibilities and difficulties tied to examining the pottery found at Fag el-Gamous.

9   Meaning Behind the Practice

It is difficult to tell why such holes would have been created. An obvious association is with the ritual of Breaking of the Red Pots, wherein a certain type of pot was ritually smashed. Documented as early as the Old Kingdom, this ritual continued through the Ptolemaic era.[51] It was almost certainly a ritual that had to do with ending the potency of ritual objects once they no longer possessed the numinous and dangerous characteristic of being sacred. The ritual has connections with Pyramid Text 23 in addition to others and seemingly morphed into execration rituals, which ran parallel to, but did not replace, the ritual of Breaking the Red Pots.[52] However, this practice does not match precisely with

---

46   Ibid., 53–54.
47   Ibid., 54–55.
48   Ibid., 55 (see footnote 158).
49   Ibid., 55, 64.
50   Ibid.
51   Budka, "Egyptian Impact on Pot-Breaking Ceremonies at El-Kurru?," 645. See also Kerry Muhlestein, "Execration Ritual," in UCLA *Encyclopedia of Egyptology*, Jacco Dieleman and Willeke Wendrich, eds., Los Angeles, 2. http://digital2.library.ucla.edu/viewItem .do?ark=21198/zz000s3mqr.
52   Ritner, *The Mechanics of Ancient Egyptian Magical Practice*, 144–153; Samuel A.B. Mercer, *The Pyramid Texts in Translation and Commentary* (New York: Longmans, Green and Co., 1952), I:23, 74; II:114; Jan Assmann, "Spruch 23 der Pyramidentexte und die Ächtung der Feinde Pharaos," in *Hommages à Jean Leclant*, eds. Catherine Berger, Gisèle Clerc, and Nicolas-Christophe Grimal, 45–59 (Cairo: Institut français d'archéologie orientale, 1994).

the finds from Fag el-Gamous or many of the other "kill hole" vessels mentioned above. First, the finds from 17th to 18th Dynasty tombs attesting to the Breaking of the Red Pot consist of all the same red slipped ware. Second, many pots with "kill holes" also appear to have been smashed,[53] which is not the case at Fag el-Gamous. Yet the parallel is still strong, for the Breaking of the Red Pots was not only linked to the execration ritual, it also had ties to funerary meals,[54] and thus the funerary context of "decommissioned" pottery remains strong. We will return to this later.

Though the Breaking of the Red Pots is the only clearly documented ritual with a visibly long history in which pots were broken intentionally, there appears to have been many other pot-breaking or "killing" rituals, for not all finds of "killed" pottery match the pattern of this specific ritual.[55] The examples that serve as evidence for these other rituals include pottery that contains "kill holes" which were not smashed,[56] as was noted above. These pots range in time period, type, location, and context. They range from burial chambers to shafts to deposits in various cities or towns and appear in a variety of vessels, but all share deliberately made "kill holes."[57] Yet little is known about these rituals beyond the presence of the pottery and their archaeological context. We are coming to recognize that these perforated vessels seem to represent something different from the Breaking of the Red Pots ritual, though there may be some kind of connection between the ideas. It has become clear that there is a long history of perforating vessels in Egypt and the Sudan which needs to be further studied before we can come to a better interpretation.[58]

Thus, we lack a *communis opinio* as to why holes were punched in these pots. It is clear the holes were created to prevent further use of the object.[59] Perhaps the practice was to discourage tomb robbing, for after adding the

---

See also Kerry Muhlestein, *Violence in the Service of Order: the Religious Framework for Sanctioned Killing in Ancient Egypt*, BAR International Series 2299 (Oxford: Archaeopress, 2011), 19, 90.

53   Budka, "Egyptian Impact on Pot-Breaking Ceremonies at El-Kurru?," 645.

54   Ritner, *Mechanics of Ancient Egyptian Magical Practice*, 145; Budka, "Egyptian Impact on Pot-Breaking Ceremonies at El-Kurru?," 646; William Stevenson Smith, *A History of Egyptian Sculpture and Painting in the Old Kingdom*, (London: Oxford University Press, 1949), 206.

55   López-Grande and Quesada, "Two Third Intermediate Period/Late Period Pottery Deposits at Herakleopolis Magna," 417; Ritner, *Mechanics of Ancient Egyptian Magical Practice*, 149.

56   Budka, "Egyptian Impact on Pot-Breaking Ceremonies at El-Kurru?," 646.

57   Budka, "Egyptian Impact on Pot-Breaking Ceremonies at El-Kurru?," 646–647.

58   Budka, "Exciting News—New Archaeological Project in Sudan Starts."

59   Kertesz, "The Breaking of Offerings in the Cult of Hathor," 135.

holes, the vessels were useless to mortal man.[60] In a similar vein, could the holes be designed to keep other entities in the hereafter from appropriating the bowls?[61] Others propose that the practice stemmed from the belief that for the dead to use pottery (or other objects), it must be "dead" as well.[62] Thus "In the eyes of the people who practice in the breaking of the object is the equivalent of the death of the human being to whose service it is dedicated. It is thus killed in order that its ghost may follow the ghost of the dead into the spirit world, there to serve the purposes which it served in this world when made."[63] According to this line of thinking, upon "killing" the object, it then left this world for the world of the dead where it would be available to its now dead owner.[64]

Yet another idea is that the kill holes could symbolize the defeat and destruction of enemies, both in this world and the divine realm, as appears to be the case with the Breaking of the Red Pots.[65] Some even suggest that these enemies were the dead themselves, and breaking the pots drove the dead away and spared the living.[66] Edwin Oliver James suggested that breaking the objects prevented those living from being tempted to use the grave goods, thereby preventing anything bringing upon them the vengeance of the deceased.[67] Others suggest that some pots were broken to drive away the enemies of the deceased, such as the vulture.[68] In addition, it is possible that these pots, after having been used by mourners for a funerary meal, were considered unclean

---

60   John Garstang, *Burial Customs of Ancient Egypt as Illustrated by Tombs of the Middle Kingdom: Being a Report of Excavations Made in the Necropolis of Beni Hassan* (London: Kegan Paul, 2002), 159.

61   Our gratitude to Peter Robinson for this idea.

62   Garstang, *Burial Customs of Ancient Egypt as Illustrated by Tombs of the Middle Kingdom*, 159; Grinsell, "The Breaking of Objects as a Funerary Rite," 475.

63   E. Sidney Hartland, *Hasting's Encyclopedia of Religion and Ethics IV*, (Edinburgh: T & T Clark, 1991), 430, cited in Grinsell, *Barrow, Pyramid and Tomb*, 60.

64   Harrington, *Living with the Dead*, 37.

65   Grinsell, "The Breaking of Objects as a Funerary Rite," 477–478; Smith, *A History of Egyptian Sculpture and Painting in the Old Kingdom*, 206. On why this would be important, see Kerry Muhlestein, "Empty Threats? How Egyptians' Self-Ontology Should Affect the Way We Read Many Texts," in *The Journal of the Society for the Study of Egyptian Antiquities* 34 (2007): 115–130.

66   Harrington, *Living with the Dead*, 38; Geraldine Pinch, "Redefining Funerary Objects," in *Egyptology at the Dawn of the Twenty-First Century: Proceedings of the Eighth International Congress of Egyptologists Cairo, 2000*, Volume 2, Zahi Hawass, ed. (Cairo: The American University in Cairo Press, 2003), 446.

67   Edwin Oliver James, *Prehistoric Religion: A Study in Prehistoric Archaeology*, (London: Thames and Hudson, 1957), 141.

68   Ritner, *Mechanics of Ancient Egyptian Magical Practice*, 149.

and thus needed to be "killed."[69] Similarly, it is possible that if they were used in a funerary ritual they were thus rendered "holy," or "otherworldly," and the holes served to prevent them from being used in a mundane context.[70] Further, it has been proposed that the breaking of objects in funerary ceremonies was meant to call upon Hathor for help and direction. Hathor's offerings were often broken as they were given to the goddess.[71] Others suggest that in some cases the holes were used to offer a libation.[72] Associated with this is the idea that since the bowls serve as a kind of avatar for ceramics in the afterlife, bowls which had been used for other ritual purposes, ruining them for use in this life, were still suitable for burial. In this case, perhaps it was just a matter of economics for a poorer burial; those performing the burials used bowls that would no longer work for them but would be fine for the deceased.[73]

Another possibility should be mentioned. It has been suggested that some vessels owned by Jews were pierced when they had become ritually unclean in order to prevent their being confused as a clean vessel and being used, thus making those who used it ritually unclean.[74] While the presence of punched vessels throughout Egypt in clearly Egyptian contexts suggests that this is not what we are witnessing here, the known presence of Jews in the Fayoum[75] means that we should not ignore this possibility.

These vessels were not necessarily all punched for the same reason. Without further evidence or documentation, the ritual(s) or other purpose(s) associated with these holes is unknown. However, it seems likely that in some way these vessels had been used in a manner that required they be changed, or perhaps even decommissioned, before it was appropriate to use them in a funerary context. With only five of the many vessels discovered at Fag el-Gamous exhibiting kill holes, it seems that this was far from a common practice and may indicate that these five vessels were used for extra-ordinary purposes outside of the funerary realm. It is hoped that adding them to the known corpus of vessels with perforations will provide one more piece to a puzzle that hopefully will be solved in the future.

---

69   Harrington, *Living with the Dead,* 38–39.
70   This is hinted at in Harrington, "Eighteenth Dynasty Egyptian Banquet," 143.
71   Kertesz, "The Breaking of Offerings in the Cult of Hathor," 136.
72   Budka, "Egyptian Impact on Pot-Breaking Ceremonies at El-Kurru?," 649.
73   Again we thank Peter Robinson for articulating this idea.
74   See Jodi Magness, *Stone and Dung, Oil and Spit: Jewish Daily Life in the Time of Jesus* (Grand Rapids: Eerdmans, 2011), 59, for a summary of this idea.
75   Kerry Muhlestein and Courtney Innes, "Synagogues and Cemeteries: Evidence for a Jewish Presence in the Fayum," in *Journal of Ancient Egyptian Interconnections* 4/2 (2012): 53–59.

CHAPTER 12

Report on Botanical Macro Remains at the Fag el-Gamous Necropolis

Terry B. Ball and Kerry Muhlestein

The BYU Egypt Excavation Project has found only a few botanical remains over the many years of excavation. Two were grain offerings left outside of some of the largest tombs in the necropolis, and another, found near the Seila Pyramid, was a collection of inflorescences from some species of *Cyperus*. All three are presented here.

Grain offerings at tombs were common throughout Egyptian history. As early as the Predynastic Period, in cultures such as Badarian and Naqada, grain was among the items left in funerary offerings.[1] While the later Old Kingdom and Middle Kingdom saw grain offerings wane in favor of magical substitutes, there was a resurgence of actual grains offered at tombs during the New Kingdom.[2] Offering lists, especially those to Nepri, included grain.[3] Most of these practices carried over into the Ptolemaic period and on into the Roman era as well.[4] In fact, the Roman-era cemeteries of the Kharga Oasis contain a variety of offerings similar to those of the 2nd Dynasty.[5] Offerings were often left in or at the entry of tombs during this time,[6] similar to the grain offerings in one tomb or those at the entry to two others that are described below. Elsewhere in

---

1   A. Jeffrey Spencer, *Death in Ancient Egypt* (Harmondsworth: Penguin Books, 1982), 48–49; John H. Taylor, *Death and the Afterlife in Ancient Egypt* (Chicago: University of Chicago Press, 2001), 92; and Salima Ikram, *Death and Burial in Ancient Egypt* (London: Pearson Education, 2003), 132.

2   John H. Taylor, *Death and the Afterlife*, 92. Even King Tutankhamen's tomb had grain (and grinders) alongside its more fabulous artifacts. See Bridget McDermott, *Death in Ancient Egypt* (Stroud, UK: Sutton Publishing, 2006), 158–159.

3   Jan Assmann, *Death and Salvation in Ancient Egypt*, David Lorton, trans. (Ithaca: Cornell University Press, 2005), 343–345.

4   Françoise Dunand and Roger Lichtenberg, *Mummies and Death in Egypt*, David Lorton, trans. (Ithaca: Cornell University Press, 2006), 104–105.

5   Dunand and Lichtenberg, *Mummies and Death in Egypt*, 104–105.

6   Jennifer R. Drummond, "Burial and Funeral Practices in Roman Egypt: Ceramics from Three Sites in the Kharga Oasis" (MA diss., University of Southampton, 2013), 68, http://www.academia.edu/8102296.

Christian-Roman Egypt, grain offerings were a part of burials.[7] Barley and emmer were common for offerings throughout much of Egyptian history because they were traditionally the most common staple of food. Emmer was replaced by hard wheat during the Graeco-Roman era.[8]

In all respects, the grain offerings identified here fit in with the larger picture of funerary grain offerings in Egypt at this time. The offerings were barley, one of the major staples of consumption in the area.

1   KA FeG #107

These grains were found in a set of tombs carved into the mudstone escarpment of what has been designated as Hill B, Tomb 1. It is just to the east of the center of the cemetery. This particular set of tombs was dug deep into the hillside with a central aisle and several chambers carved on either side. Between two of these chambers, against the wall that divided them, a basket with a pile of grain had been left.

> **Provenance:** Area 3 (30/40 N 70/80 E, now renumbered as Hill B, Tomb 1), centered between chambers II and V
> **Collection date:** 23 February 1988
> **Description of material:** The grains are well-preserved, with lemmas and paleae typically still attached, along with some awn and rachis fragments. The grains are generally spindle shaped in dorsal, ventral, and lateral views, with lateral flattening. They are not keeled and are generally symmetrical in all planes of view. They have a clear and symmetrical ventral groove with no twisting. The maximum width of the grains is slightly off center. Grain length is typically 9.0–10.0 mm; breadth, 3.0–3.3 mm; and aspect ratio (length divided by breadth), around 3 mm.
> **Identification:** *Hordeum distichon* L. Two-rowed hulled barley

In the same set of tombs as described above, but this time inside one of the chambers, a pile of grain was left under an upside-down bowl on the floor of

---

7   Gillian E. Bowen, "Some Observations on Christian Burial Practices at Kellis," in *The Oasis Papers 3: Proceedings of the Third International Conference of the Dakhleh Oasis Project*, Gillian E. Bowen and Colin A. Hope, eds. (Oxford: Oxbow Books, 2003), 171.
8   Dorothy J. Crawford, "Food: Tradition and Change in Hellenistic Egypt," *World Archaeology* 11/2 (October 1979): 140.

FIGURE 12.1   The tombs where the baskets of grain were found. Originally the entire
                complex was covered, but over time the roof has caved in
                PHOTOGRAPH BY KERRY MUHLESTEIN

the burial chamber. We do not know if it was intentionally placed that way or
if the bowl fell at some point.

> **Provenance:** Area 3, Hill B Tomb 1, Chamber II found under a bowl
> **Collection date:** 23 February 1988
> **Description of material:** These grains and grain fragments are poorly
> preserved, some with lemmas and paleae still attached, along with some
> awn and rachis fragments. Whole grains are generally spindle shaped in
> dorsal, ventral, and lateral views, with lateral flattening. They are not
> keeled and are generally symmetrical in all planes of view. They have a
> clear and symmetrical ventral groove with no twisting. The maximum
> width of the grains is slightly off center. Grain length is typically 9.0–10.0
> mm; breadth, 3.0–3.3 mm; and aspect ratio (length divided by breadth),
> around 3 mm.
> **Identification:** *Hordeum distichon* L. Two-rowed hulled barley
> **Local history:** Barley and wheat have been cultivated from Neolithic
> times and constituted the primary cereal staples from Egypt, through the

FIGURE 12.2   KA FeG #107
PHOTOGRAPH COURTESY OF REVEL PHILLIPS

Levant, to Mesopotamia and Asia Minor.[9] Though barley makes an inferior flour and bread in comparison to wheat, being lower in gluten protein, it was still widely grown because it tolerates a much wider range of climates and soil types and ripens much earlier than does wheat. Barley was also widely used in brewing and as animal fodder.

This kind of barley is no longer as widely used because it does not flower as efficiently nor produce as much usable grain as six-rowed barley, which was developed over time and is more commonly used today.

While two-row barley is attested in the archaeological record from Egypt, and many examples can be found in archaeological collections, it is relatively rare in comparison with other kinds of barley or grains, at least partially because Egypt was moving towards using six-row barley.[10] Finding two-row

---

9   See Mary Anne Murray, "Cereal Production and Processing," in *Ancient Egyptian Materials and Technology*, Paul T. Nicholson and Ian Shaw, eds. (Cambridge: Cambridge University Press, 2000), 505–506.

10   Ibid., 512.

FIGURE 12.3   Close up of KA FeG #107
PHOTOGRAPH BY KERRY MUHLESTEIN

barley during this late era was unexpected. This makes these finds at Fag el-Gamous even more interesting, and makes it more imperative to report it to the larger academic community.

Provenance: Pyramid Area F
Collection date: 27 February 1988
Remains of another species of plant were found near the pyramid. Unfortunately, the notes made about the plant material's find are very sparse. The remains were found on the northern side, presumably in or near the cultic porch or chapel that also contained a libation altar, fragments of another altar or table, and fragments of a statue.[11] While it is not clear from the excavation notes that the remains were found in this structure, it seems the most likely place.
Description of material: The remains consisted of digitate to umbellate inflorescences that are well-preserved, typically with six to eight spikelets per spike. Spikelets are typically about 25 mm long. The rachillae are persistent, and the floral scales separate individually from the spikelets.
Identification: *Cyperus* sp. Because no achenes or styles are preserved in this sample, positive identification is difficult, but of the common Egyptian

---

11   See the two articles on the pyramid and its objects within this volume.

species, these inflorescences appear to most closely resemble those of *Cyperus rotundus* or *Cyperus esculentus.*

Local history: The genus *Cyperus* consists of hundreds of species of typically semiaquatic monocots. They generally grow in marshy areas or in still or slow-moving water. Tubers of various *Cyperus* species have historically been used for food, fiber, oil, and medicine. Though the most well-known *Cyperus* in Egypt is the papyrus (*Cyperus papyrus*), *Cyperus rotundus* (purple nutsedge[12]), which can grow to be about 75 cm tall,[13] also has a long history of use in the region, not only for food and medicine, but also as an aromatic and a water purifier.[14] Tubers of *C. rotundus* would be less often used as a food because they can have an unpleasant, bitter taste, and could be slightly toxic (less so if ground),[15] though it is clear they were used for food in some places at some times, perhaps even as a main source of carbohydrates in the Late Paleolithic period.[16] Its close relative, *C. esculentus* (yellow nutsedge,[17] or tigernut sedge), which our sample also resembles, is a more palatable, even sweet or nutty, flavored food source.[18] The tubers are starchy and still grow in the region today, flourishing in the same kind of environment in which barley grows.[19] The plants grow and reproduce easily (being considered a weed today, even "the world's worst weed"[20]), and are mature enough to eat in 3 to 6 weeks,[21] making them a ready food source available for offering. *C. esculentus* is more hearty and less affected by variations in temperature

12   See California Department of Food and Agriculture, "Weed Information – Yellow Nutsedge and Purple Nutsedge." (Available online at: http://www.cdfa.ca.gov/plant/ipc/weedinfo/cyperus.htm).

13   Mark Schonbeck, "Purple Nutsedge (Cyperus rotundus) in Greater Depth," https://articles.extension.org/pages/65213/purple-nutsedge-cyperus-rotundus-in-greater-depth.

14   Stephen Buckley et al., "Dental Calculus Reveals Unique Insights into Food Items, Cooking and Plant Processing in Prehistoric Central Sudan," *PLOS ONE* 9/7 (2014).

15   Mary Anne Murray, "Fruits, Vegetables, Pulses and Condiments," in *Ancient Egyptian Materials and Technology*, Paul T. Nicholson and Ian Shaw, eds. (Cambridge: Cambridge University Press, 2000), 613.

16   Ibid., 636–637.

17   See California Department of Food and Agriculture, "Weed Information – Yellow Nutsedge and Purple Nutsedge."

18   Ibid.

19   Theresa Friedman and Moshe Horowitz, "Biologically active substances in subterranean parts of purple nutsedge," *Weed Science* 19 (1971): 398–401.

20   J.E. Jordan-Molero, and Edward W. Stoller, "Seasonal development of yellow and purple nutsedges (*Cyperus esculentus* and *C. rotundus*) in Illinois," *Weed Science* (1978) 26: 614.

21   Ellis W. Hauser, "Development of purple nutsedge under field conditions," *Weeds* 10 (1962): 315–321.

and sunlight than *C. rotundus*,[22] and can grow in a wider temperature range,[23] making it an even more likely food source. Like all species of *Cyperus*, both *C. esculentus* and *C. rotundus* produce inflorescences consisting of umbel spikes with leaf-like bracts on a triangular shaped stem, similar to papyrus.[24] The sample found at the pyramid had deteriorated to the point that it was not possible to identify the exact species that produced it.

The presence of *Cyperus* stands in distinction to the grain offerings that were part of the nearby cemetery. Grain offerings are relatively common and understood. In contrast, the purpose of having this particular *Cyperus* species near the pyramid is unknown. If it were papyrus we would assume that it was used in conjunction with a lotus plant to represent Upper and Lower Egypt and would be in keeping with a ritual motif set by the red and black dirt that was ritually deposited at the foundation of the causeway, though it could fulfill that purpose as a representative of the sedge and bee.[25] However, as noted above, this particular *Cyperus* does not resemble papyrus, but appears to be some other species that likely was used for food, medicine, or as an aromatic. Though we cannot positively identify which species of *Cyperus* produced the inflorescences found at the site, nor be certain of precisely why it was there, it still appears safe to conclude that it had some ritual purpose.

---

22   Jordan-Molero and Stoller. "Seasonal development of yellow and purple nutsedges," 614–618.

23   Mark Schonbeck, "Yellow Nutsedge (Cyperus exculentus) in Greater Depth," https://arti cles.extension.org/pages/65211/yellow-nutsedge-cyperus-esculentus-in-greater-depth.

24   Mark Schonbeck, "Purple Nutsedge (Cyperus rotundus) in Greater Depth," https://arti cles.extension.org/pages/65213/purple-nutsedge-cyperus-rotundus-in-greater-depth.

25   See the article on excavating the pyramid in this volume.

CHAPTER 13

The Fag el-Gamous Papyrus Fragment

Lincoln H. Blumell

The BYU excavation of the Fag el-Gamous cemetery has yielded to date only one small papyrus fragment[1] with writing.[2] The fragment was excavated during the 1992 season in the northern part of the cemetery. In the field book, the papyrus bears the number KA, FeG09 and was reportedly found in the sandal of burial no. 39 who was buried at a depth of 127 cm. As papyrus (*papyrus/* πάπυρος) was used for a variety of purposes in antiquity, and did not just serve as the "paper" (*charta/*χάρτης) of the ancient world, it was not uncommon for inscribed papyrus to be repurposed after it was no longer needed and to be used for sandals,[3] or even for other items like ropes, cordage, baskets, and especially cartonnage and in the stuffing of mummified animals.[4] The present papyrus is made up of two small pieces that, when fitted together, measure 5.3x7.7 cm (HxW). The text consists of seven very partial lines of Greek text written with a dark brown ink along the fibers (recto) of the papyrus; the right margin is intact but the top, bottom, and left margins are missing. There is no way to determine how much text is missing before the start of each line and there is no writing on the back of the papyrus. The hand can be described as a cursive script where the writer tends to rapidly write letters without the lift of the pen. Most letters are written with a single stroke and overall there is a slight slant to the right. At the end of the line the last letter is often extended to the right margin with an exaggerated stroke extension. Some letters are ligatured

---

1 For editions of papyri, I have followed the abbreviations given in J.F. Oates et al. (eds.), *Checklist of Editions of Greek and Latin Papyri, Ostraca and Tablets* (5th ed.; BASP Suppl. 9, 2001). The online version is available at http://papyri.info/docs/checklist. I first autopsied this papyrus in February 2013 at the Kom Aushim storage magazine.

2 There is potentially a second papyrus, although its present whereabouts are unknown. The registry records that during the 1988 season another small papyrus fragment was discovered in the southern area of the cemetery, but it does not mention whether the papyrus preserved text.

3 W.M. van Haarlem, "A Pair of Papyrus Sandals," *Journal of Egyptian Archaeology* 78 (1991): 294–295. P.Ford.inv.00002 is a Ptolemaic letter that was later repurposed as a sandal as the papyrus has been cut to the outline of a sole of sandal and is entirely preserved.

4 When B.P. Grenfell and A.S. Hunt were excavating in Tebtunis on January 16, 1900 they discovered that a number of the mummified crocodiles had been stuffed with papyrus that had been previously inscribed.

to the next letter, most notably the alpha (ll. 4, 6), and the rho is written with a long vertical descender that can descend two lines (l. 4). There are no detectable phonetic or orthographic irregularities in the text and there is a sole abbreviation in line 7 marked by a supralinear stroke.

Given the small text sample, any paleographic analysis is tentative. But the text displays graphic trends that are indicative of documents written in the 4th century AD, with notable parallels to texts written at the beginning of the century: viz. P.Oxy. XLIII 3143 (May/Jun. AD 305; Oxyrhynchus); P.Oxy. LXV 4491 (May 9, AD 307; Oxyrhynchus); P.Oxy. XLVI 3270 (Sept. 14/15, AD 309). The fragment should therefore be tentatively dated to the first half of the 4th century. In terms of provenance, while the text was found in the Fag el-Gamous cemetery, there is no indication from the text itself where it originated. There is a reference to a "village" (κώμη) in line 7, but the toponym that follows is lost where the papyrus is broken off. In terms of the kind of document that the fragment preserves, it is difficult to determine as there is very little text and the extant portion contains only general vocabulary; there is no single phrase that appears in the extant portion of the text that definitively establishes its content or purpose. The phrase τὰ ἀπ' αὐτῶν that appears in line 3 does occur in documents dealing with sales and leases, but this phrase on its own is not conclusive regarding the type of text. All that can be said therefore about the piece is that it preserved a documentary, and not literary, text.

```
        _ _ _ _ _ _ _ _ _ _ _ _
  →            ].[
          ο]ὐκ ἀναπαύῃ
          ]ος τὰ ἀπ' αὐτῶν
          ]ον ἕκαστος γὰρ α-
  5       ].ετούμενον τῇ ν-
          ] γὰρ ἐν πάσῃ φυ-
        ]. ἐν κώ(μῃ)
        _ _ _ _ _ _ _ _ _ _ _ _
```

---

7. pap. κω̄.

1   **Translation**

... [if] he/she/it does not cease ... the [blank] from them ... for each ... [verb] to the ... for in every ... in the village of ...

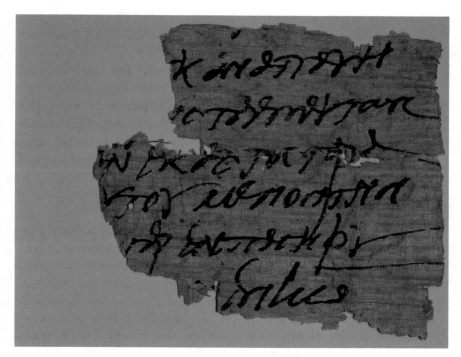

FIGURE 13.1   The papyrus fragment from Fag el-Gamous
PHOTOGRAPH BY LINCOLN BLUMMELL

Notes

2   ο]ὐκ ἀναπαύῃ. This phrase is not at present attested in the papyri, al-
      though the verb ἀναπαύω ("to cease") does appear. There are only a hand-
      ful of literary parallels: *Apoph. Pat.* 16.2, λέγει αὐτῷ ὁ γέρων· εἰ *οὐκ ἀναπαύῃ*,
      ἰδοὺ δέχομαι αὐτο (see also 7.9); *Vita Nicolai Sionitae* 44.3, Σὺ τί θλίβῃ ὧδε
      καὶ μοχθεῖς, καὶ *οὐκ ἀναπαύῃ* ἐν τῷ κελλαρίῳ ἔσω μετὰ τοῦ ἀδελφοῦ σου;.

3   ]ος τὰ ἀπ' αὐτῶν. Cf. P.Lond. III 1164.H.15 (p.164; AD 212; Antinoopolis) and
      P.Sijp. 46.7 (Sept. 4, AD 332; Hermopolis ?): τὰ ἀπ' αὐτῶν δίκαια; P.Mich. XV
      719.12 (III AD; Oxyrhynchus ?), P.Oxy. XIV 1698.16 (Sept. 10 AD 269; Oxy-
      rhynchus), and P.Oxy. XIV 1704.14 (AD 298; Oxyrhynchus): πάντα τὰ ἀπ'
      αὐτῶν περιεσόμενα; PSI XII 1310.40 (135/34 BC; Arsinoite): καὶ τὰ ἀπ' αὐτῶν
      πεσούμενα.

4   ]ον ἕκαστος γὰρ α-. The pronoun ἕκαστος (-η, -ον) is so common there is
      little that can be said of substance about this line of text. Since the phrase
      ἕκαστος γὰρ appears a few other times in the papyri and in every instance

it begins a new sentence, the same may be the case here: cf. BGU I 15.4
(AD 197; Arsinoite); BGU XVI 2644.9 (4 BC; Herakleopolite); P.Cair.Masp.
II 67151.209 (AD 570; Antinoopolis).

5   ]ετούμενον τῇ ν-. The termination of the verb establishes that it is either a
masculine accusative singular middle/passive present participle or a
neuter nominative/accusative singular middle/passive present participle. In the papyri the two verbs that most often end with this participial
termination are ὑπηρετέω ("to render service," sometimes in the context
of "military service") and ἐξυπηρετέω ("to assist to the utmost"). As both
verbs tend to take the dative case, what follows should probably be read
τῇ ν-: e.g. BGU XIII 2252.8–9 (AD 330; Arsinoite): ὑπηρετούμενον τῇ
δημο[σία]χρείᾳ; SB XVIII 13953.11 (AD 492; Herakleopolis): ἐξυπηρετούμενον
ταῖς δ[ημ]οσίαις χρείαις. While these two verbs appear as the most likely
candidates for the verb in this line, there are other possibilities.

6   γὰρ ἐν πάσῃ φυ-. The phrase ἐν πάσῃ appears about a dozen times in the
papyri but is never followed by a word beginning with φυ-. An interesting
chronological note about this phrase in the papyri is that outside of a
single reference (Stud. Pal. XX 1.30 [AD 83/84; Arsinoite]) it otherwise
only appears in texts dated to the 3rd century AD and later. See P.Ross.
Georg. V 6.5 (AD IV; Oxyrhynchus [?]).

7   ]. ἐν κώ(μη). The abbreviation κω̄ for κώμη is attested in the Ptolemaic,
Roman, and Byzantine periods, although it is especially well-attested in
the last period. On this and other abbreviations by suspension see N. Gonis,
"Abbreviations and Symbols," in R.S. Bagnall (ed.), Oxford Handbook of
Papyrology (Oxford: Oxford University Press, 2009), 171–174. When it is
governed by the preposition ἐν, the phrase typically has a definite article:
ἐν τῇ κώ(μη); however, it is also attested, as it is here, without the definite
article: ἐν κώ(μη). In the papyri this phrase is almost always followed by
the name of the village, which presumably appeared at the start of the
next line that is lost where the papyrus breaks off.

While ἐν κώ(μη) is almost certainly the correct reconstruction, it is also
possible that the phrase could be rendered ἐν κ(υρί)ῳ "in the Lord" and
then what we have here is a *nomen sacrum* – a "sacred name" abbreviated
in a Christian text. Though the supralinear stroke is written over the ome-
ga, suggesting that the abbreviation is based on the suspension κω( ), and
not the contraction κ( )ω, because it is not written over both letters, it is
not uncommon for the supralinear stroke in *nomina sacra* to be only
written over the second letter: e.g. P.Bas 16.21 (mid III AD; Egypt, provenance unknown) where it is written ἐν κω̄ but because it is part of a larger
valediction (ll. 19–21) it has to be a *nomen sacrum*, ἐρρῶσθαί σε εὔχομαι

ὁλοκλή[ρω]ς ἐν κ(υρί)ῳ ("I pray for your health in the Lord"). Beginning in the 3rd and 4th centuries, Christians began employing *nomina sacra* in papyrus letters as part of the initial greeting or valediction, although the practice is earlier in literary manuscripts of Christian origin. See L.H. Blumell, *Lettered Christians: Christians, Letters, and late Antique Oxyrhynchus* (Brill: Boston, 2012), 49–52.

CHAPTER 14

Philadelphia: A Preliminary Report

John Gee

The concession of the Brigham Young University Egypt Excavation Project has historically covered three areas: the Old Kingdom pyramid at Seila, the Greco-Roman cemetery at Fag el-Gamous, and the Greco-Roman town at Philadelphia. In the past, the efforts of the excavation have been focused on Seila and Fag el-Gamous. Others have recently done two seasons of work at Philadelphia, and so apparently the site has passed out of our concession. The work at Philadelphia needs to be done, because a local modern cemetery has been steadily encroaching on the site since 2011. Thus, this report will cover the town of Philadelphia. We hope it will further any work to be done there in the future, by ourselves or another team. However, what follows is based on my own research.[1]

1   The Standard Picture

The conventional picture of the site of Philadelphia is that "there is virtually nothing to see";[2] "nothing remains of the streets and houses."[3] "The Fayum was ... the site of a massive reclamation project under the early Ptolemies; many villages have no history earlier than the 3rd century BC,"[4] and Philadelphia was a "Ptolemaic foundation [that] probably took its name from the 'brother-loving' (*philadelphos*) title of Arsinoe, the sister-wife of Ptolemy II."[5] "It was laid out on a regular orthogonal plan, parallel to the new high-level canal which had opened up regular irrigation of this area. The grid seems to have

---

1   I would like to thank my colleague Kristin South who was present on the survey for correcting occasional details. Verena Lepper and Marius Gerhardt helped me locate material pertaining to the German excavations in the Zentralarchiv der Staatlichen Museen zu Berlin.

2   Roger S. Bagnall and Dominic W. Rathbone, *Egypt From Alexander to the Early Christians* (Los Angeles: The J. Paul Getty Museum, 2004), 135.

3   Euphrosyne Doxiadis, *The Mysterious Fayum Portraits: Faces from Ancient Egypt* (London: Thames and Hudson, 1995), 133.

4   Roger S. Bagnall, *Egypt in Late Antiquity* (Princeton: Princeton University Press, 1993), 111.

5   Bagnall and Rathbone, *Egypt From Alexander to the Early Christians*, 135–136; cf. Doxiadis, *Mysterious Fayum Portraits*, 133.

© KONINKLIJKE BRILL NV, LEIDEN, 2020 | DOI:10.1163/9789004416383_015

FIGURE 14.1   Philadelphia
               PHOTO BY JOHN GEE

been meticulously respected up to the end of occupation in the early 6th century AD."[6] The Arabic name of the site varies considerably in the literature,
being known as el-Rubayat, el-Riqqah, Darb Gerze, and Kom el-Kharaba el-
Kebir. The ancient Egyptian name for Philadelphia was *T3-nh.t* (Τάνεως).[7]

2   Excavation History

Philadelphia has a history of what we will term uncontrolled excavations, in
addition to some controlled excavations. One of the first known uncontrolled
excavations took place in the early 1880s and was the source of the archive of
the Thermouthas family, acquired in 1884.[8] This archive consists of four to six

---

6   Bagnall and Rathbone, *Egypt From Alexander to the Early Christians*, 136.
7   John Gee, "The Demotic Name for Philadelphia," *Enchoria* 35 (2016/2017): 195–197.
8   Katelijn Vandorpe, Willy Clarysse, and Herbert Verreth, *Graeco-Roman Archives from the
     Fayum*, Collectanea Hellenistica-KVAB 6 (Leuven: Peeters, 2015), 409–413.

papyri dating to the very end of the 1st century and beginning of the 2nd century AD (99-after 105).[9]

An extensive uncontrolled excavation in March of 1887[10] produced a number of mummy portraits sold through the Viennese antiquities dealer, Theodor Graf,[11] which Petrie noted in 1888, "have been found at er-Rubayat in the Fayum and have been greatly sought for and offered at fabulous prices in London and Paris. Wallis of South Kensington Museum has come out on purpose to get hold of them."[12] The portraits "excited much attention at the 1889 exhibitions in Munich and Berlin and many eminent painters showered praise on them."[13] Graf's exhibition went to other places, including "Paris, Brussels and London."[14]

One or more uncontrolled excavations occurred at the end of the 1880s or early 1890s. This produced four papyri archives, two of which were acquired in 1892. One was the archive of Tesenouphis son of Nikon; it consists of four or five papyri dating to about AD 211.[15] The other was the archive of Aurelius Ol, consisting of six papyri, dating to AD 370–390.[16] The archive of Flavius Abinnaeus, consisting of 80 documents dating between AD 342–351, was acquired in 1893.[17] Finally the archive of Hatres and Isas, comprising eight papyri dating between AD 276–314, was acquired sometime before 1895.[18] Loosely controlled excavations of Grenfell and Hunt in 1901 produced the archive of Hermolaos, or Apollonios, which contains four papyri, dating between 250-247 BC.[19]

Friedrich Zucker of the Staatliche Museen in Berlin excavated the site in 1908/1909,[20] assisted by Ludwig Borchardt.[21] More precisely, they started on

9   Vandorpe, Clarysse, and Verreth, *Graeco-Roman Archives from the Fayum*, 409–413.
10   Klaus Parlasca, "Mummy Portraits: Old and New Problems," in *Portraits and Masks: Burial Customs in Roman Egypt*, M.L. Bierbrier, ed. (London: British Museum, 1997), 127; Doxiadis, *The Mysterious Fayum Portraits*, 129–130.
11   Doxiadis, *The Mysterious Fayum Portraits*, 129.
12   W.M. Flinders Petrie, journal entry, 22–29 January 1888, quoted in Susan E.C. Walker, "Mummy Portraits in their Roman Context," in *Portraits and Masks: Burial Customs in Roman Egypt*, M.L. Bierbrier, ed. (London: British Museum, 1997), 3.
13   Parlasca, "Mummy Portraits: Old and New Problems," 127.
14   Doxiadis, *The Mysterious Fayum Portraits*, 131.
15   Vandorpe, Clarysse, and Verreth, *Graeco-Roman Archives from the Fayum*, 408.
16   Ibid., 97–98.
17   Ibid., 138–142.
18   Ibid., 162–163.
19   Ibid., 168–169.
20   H.I. Bell, "Review of Paul Viereck, *Philadelpheia*" in *Gnomon* 4/10 (1928): 584.
21   Paul Viereck, *Philadelpheia: Die Gründung einer hellenistischen Militärkolonie in Ägypten* (Leipzig: J.C. Hinrichs, 1928), 6.

30 December 1908,[22] and finished on 15 January 1909.[23] They were mainly looking for papyri, which they found, mainly in the cellars of the houses, and they
stopped looking once they stopped finding papyri.[24] They also found a cache
of sixty-eight ostraca from a cellar in Philadelphia; these date to either 210–204
or 193–187 BC.[25]

About two years later, an uncontrolled excavation found the eight papyri of
the archive of Kasios son of Taonnophris, which date between AD 155–175.[26]

The next year, 1911, was the first appearance of the 1,819 to 1,833 papyri of the
famous archive of Zenon son of Agreophon; these date between 263-229 BC.[27]

About 1920 there were more clandestine diggings and eight document cach-
es were discovered about this time. The archive of Nemesion son of Zoilos
contained between sixty-four and sixty-six papyri, dated to AD 30–61, and was
acquired about 1920.[28] The six papyri of the archive of Aurelia Tapais date to
AD 298–307 and were found during clandestine diggings in 1920.[29] The archive
of (Marcus) Lucretius Diogenes and Aurelius Sarapion, which comprises thirty-
four to sixty-nine papyri, dating between AD 132–248, were acquired 1920–23.[30]
About the same time (1920–1925), the eighty-one ostraca of the police of Philadelphia, dating between 299-00 BC, were acquired in 1920–1925.[31] The nine papyri of the archive of Ploutogeneia, wife of Paniskos, dating to about AD 297,
were acquired in 1923.[32] The eight papyri of the Isidoros versus Tryphon lawsuit, dating to AD 5–6, were acquired in 1923–24.[33] The six papyri of the archive
of Horos son of Patous Jr. dating to 199-184 BC, were acquired in 1925.[34] Finally,
the six papyri dating to 182–177 BC and belonging to Leontiskos and partners,
were also acquired in 1925.[35]

---

22   Bell, "Review of Paul Viereck, *Philadelpheia*," 584.
23   Friedrich Zucker, letter to the General-Verwaltung der Königliche Museen zu Berlin, 15
      January 1909, SMB-ZA I/ÄM 068 64–65.
24   Friedrich Zucker, letter to the General-Verwaltung der Königliche Museen zu Berlin, 15
      January 1909, SMB-ZA I/ÄM 068 64–65. My thanks to Marius Gerhardt for correcting my
      transcription of the letter.
25   Vandorpe, Clarysse, and Verreth, *Graeco-Roman Archives from the Fayum*, 259–260.
26   Ibid., 204–205.
27   Ibid., 447–455.
28   Vandorpe, Clarysse, and Verreth, *Graeco-Roman Archives from the Fayum*, 256–258.
29   Ibid., 80.
30   Ibid., 239–251.
31   Ibid., 322.
32   Ibid., 315–317.
33   Ibid., 184–185.
34   Ibid., 181–182.
35   Ibid., 238.

Two other archives come from Philadelphia. The archive of Leon, *toparches* of Philadelphia contains four or six papyri, dating to 190-187 BC, derived from mummy cartonnage acquired in 1935.[36] We have no acquisition information for the four self-dedications to the god Anubis dating to 209/208 or 192/191 BC.[37]

Nothing from clandestine excavations appears to have come on the market since the mid-1920s. There is every reason to believe that uncontrolled excavations have continued to the present but no other papyri archives from Philadelphia seem to have surfaced. We will examine some of the reasons for that later.

3   Occupation History

To date, no archaeological work at the site has established a history or timeline of occupation on the site. This leaves us with only textual sources from the site. These comprise archives of socioeconomic texts. From those we can see a basic outline of the history of the site.

Clarysse and Vandorpe count nineteen different archives from Philadelphia.[38] The papyri evidence for Philadelphia is mostly in Greek but some documents in Demotic are also known.[39] The papyri archives cover the following ranges of dates:

The archive of Hermolaos, or Apollonios, dates to the middle of the 3rd century BC (250–247 BC).[40] The Zenon archive covers a larger time period in the middle of the 3rd century (263–229 BC).[41]

The ostraca of the police of Philadelphia cover the 3rd and 2nd centuries BC (299–100 BC).[42]

The cache of ostraca from a cellar in Philadelphia date to the end of the 3rd century BC or beginning of the 2nd century BC (210–204 or 193–187 BC).[43] The

---

36   Ibid., 236–237.

37   Ibid., 364.

38   Ibid., 460–461.

39   Notably P. BM EA 10560, in Cary J. Martin, "A Demotic Land Lease from Philadelphia: P. BM 10560," *JEA* 72 (1986): 159–173; P. BM EA 10750, in H.S. Smith, "Another Witness-Copy Document from the Fayyūm," *JEA* 44 (1958): 86–96.

40   Vandorpe, Clarysse, and Verreth, *Graeco-Roman Archives from the Fayum*, 168–169.

41   Ibid., 447–455.

42   Vandorpe, Clarysse, and Verreth, *Graeco-Roman Archives from the Fayum*, 322.

43   Ibid., 259–260.

self-dedications to the god Anubis also date to the end of the 3rd century or beginning of the 2nd century BC (209/208 or 192/191 BC).[44] The archive of Horos son of Patous Jr. dates to the beginning of the 2nd century BC (199–184 BC).[45] The archive of Leon, *toparches* of Philadelphia dates to the first half of the 2nd century BC (190–187 BC).[46] The archive of Leontiskos and partners also dates to the first half of the 2nd century BC (182–177 BC).[47]

The lawsuit between Isidoros and Tryphon dates to the beginning of the 1st century (AD 5–6).[48] The archive of Nemesion son of Zoilos dates a bit later in the 1st century (AD 30–61).[49]

The Thermouthas archive covers the end of the 1st century to the beginning of the 2nd century (99-after 105).[50]

The archive of Kasios son of Taonnophris dates to the second half of the 2nd century (AD 155–175).[51]

The archive of (Marcus) Lucretius Diogenes and Aurelius Sarapion covers most of the 2nd and the first half of the 3rd (AD 132–248).[52]

The archive of Tesenouphis son of Nikon dates to the beginning of the 3rd century (about AD 211).[53]

The archive of Ploutogeneia, wife of Paniskos dates to the end of the 3rd century (AD 297).[54] The archive of Hatres and Isas dates to the end of the 3rd and beginning of the 4th century (AD 276–314).[55] The archive of Aurelia Tapais also dates to the same time (AD 298–307).[56]

The archive of Flavius Abinnaeus dates to the middle of the 4th century (AD 342–351).[57]

The archive of Aurelius Ol dates to the end of the 4th century (AD 370–390).[58]

All of this information is conveniently summarized in the following chart:

---

44   Ibid., 364.
45   Ibid., 181–182.
46   Ibid., 236–237.
47   Ibid., 238.
48   Ibid., 184–185.
49   Ibid., 256–258.
50   Ibid., 409–413.
51   Ibid., 204–205.
52   Ibid., 239–251.
53   Ibid., 408.
54   Ibid., 315–317.
55   Ibid., 162–163.
56   Ibid., 80.
57   Ibid., 138–142.
58   Ibid., 97–98.

TABLE 14.1   Papyri archives from Philadelphia by discovery date

Date of discovery	Archive	Number of papyri	Date of archive
Acquired 1884	Thermouthas	4–6	AD 99-after 105
Acquired 1892	Tesenouphis	4–5	AD 211
Acquired 1892	Aurelius Ol	6	AD 370–390
Acquired 1893	Flavius Abinnaeus	80	AD 342–351
Acquired before 1895	Hatres and Isas	8	AD 276–314
Excavated 1901	Hermolaos or Apollonios	4	250-247 BC
Excavated 1909	ostraca archive	68 ostraca	210-204 or 193-187 BC
About 1910	Kasios son of Taonnophris	8	AD 155–175
About 1911	Zenon	1819–1833	263-229 BC
Acquired about 1920	Nemesion son of Zoilos	64–66	AD 30–61
Acquired 1920	Aurelia Tapais	6	AD 298–307
Acquired 1920–23	Lucretius Diogenes and Aurelius Sarapion	34–69	AD 132–248
Acquired 1920–25	Police archive	81 ostraca	299-100 BC
Acquired 1923	Ploutogeneia, wife of Paniskos	9	AD 297
Acquired 1923–24	Isidoros versus Tryphon	8	AD 5–6
Acquired 1925	Horos son of Patous Jr.	6	199-184 BC
Acquired 1925	Leontiskos	6	182-177 BC
Acquired 1935	Leon *toparches*	4–6	190-87 BC
Unknown acquisition date	Self-dedications to Anubis	4	209/208 or 192/191 BC

So, the archives cover from the beginning of the 3rd century BC through the end of the 4th century AD, with a conspicuous gap during the second half of the 2nd century BC through the 1st century BC. I attribute this gap to accident

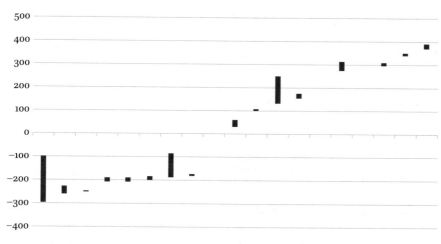

FIGURE 14.2

of preservation, but note that similar gaps in information about the same time occur in documentation at Thebes, and in demotic documentation in general.[59] There is also a lack of papyri archives after the end of the 4th century, although we do have some individual pieces that reference Philadelphia into the 8th century.

4   Archaeological Overview

On 23 February 2014, the BYU excavation team was able to conduct a preliminary survey of the site of Philadelphia. We did so because we feared for the site's integrity due to the encroaching local cemetery, and we wanted to assess the state of the site and the danger posed by the encroaching cemetery. We would like to thank the Egyptian Ministry of State for Antiquities and especially our inspector, Manal Saied Ahmed, who helped a great deal facilitating the preliminary survey. As we had not applied to do a surface survey, we photographed pottery and other finds on the south half of the site.

Most of the surface pottery consists of small broken sherds. Styles range from Ptolemaic to Byzantine period potsherds. The quality ranges from coarse to very fine. The pottery along the western slope of the city by the canal tended

---

59   Friedhelm Hoffmann, *Ägypten: Kultur und Lebenswelt in griechisch-römischer Zeit* (Berlin: Akademie Verlag, 2000), 26.

TABLE 14.2   Papyri archives from Philadelphia by date of archive

Date of archive	Archive	Number of papyri	Date of discovery
299–100 BC	Police archive	81 ostraca	acquired 1920–25
263–229 BC	Zenon	1819–1833	about 1911
250–247 BC	Hermolaos or Apollonios	4	excavated 1901
210-204 or 193–187 BC	ostraca archive	68 ostraca	excavated 1909
209/208 or 192/191 BC	Self-dedications to Anubis	4	unknown acquisition date
199–184 BC	Horos son of Patous Jr.	6	acquired 1925
190–87 BC	Leon *toparches*	4–6	acquired 1935
182–177 BC	Leontiskos	6	acquired 1925
AD 5–6	Isidoros versus Tryphon	8	
AD 30–61	Nemesion son of Zoilos	64–66	acquired about 1920
AD 99-after 105	Thermouthas	4–6	acquired 1887
AD 132–248	Lucretius Diogenes and Aurelius Sarapion	34–69	acquired 1923–24
AD 155–175	Kasios son of Taonnophris	8	about 1910
AD 211	Tesenouphis	4–5	acquired 1892
AD 276–314	Hatres and Isas	8	acquired before 1895
AD 297	Ploutogeneia, wife of Paniskos	9	acquired 1923
AD 298–307	Aurelia Tapais	6	acquired 1920
AD 342–351	Flavius Abinnaeus	80	acquired 1893
AD 370–390	Aurelius Ol	6	acquired 1892

to be of much finer make than the general pottery in the city. From that, we surmise that the rich of Philadelphia lived along the canal.

FIGURE 14.3   An example of a coarse ware surface sherd
PHOTOGRAPH BY JOHN GEE

Although streets are visible in area and satellite photographs, these were difficult to identify on the ground because of the wind-blown sand and the hap-
hazard preservation of walls.

The Zenon papyri reveal a number of details about structures in the city.
The city was comprised of temples to Greek gods, including a temple of Zeus,
a temple of Demeter, a temple of Dioscuri, and a temple dedicated to the gods
of Samothrace.[60] There are also a number of temples to Egyptian gods, including a temple of Souchos (Sobek), a temple of Poremanres (deified Amenemhet
III), and a temple of Thoeris (Taweret).[61] There was also a temple of Serapis, a
temple of Isis, and a temple to Ptolemy II and Arsinoe.[62]

---

60   Willy Clarysse and Katelijn Vandorpe, *Zenon, un homme d'affaires grec à l'ombre des pyramides* (Leuven: Presses Universitaires de Louvain, 1995), 50.

61   Clarysse and Vandorpe, *Zenon, un homme d'affaires grec à l'ombre des pyramides*, 50; Viereck, *Philadelpheia*, 14.

62   Clarysse and Vandorpe, *Zenon, un homme d'affaires grec à l'ombre des pyramides*, 51; Viereck, *Philadelpheia*, 14.

FIGURE 14.4   The remains of a better-preserved wall
                PHOTOGRAPH BY JOHN GEE

The Germans under Viereck and Zucker also found a small temple made of limestone rather than the mud brick of the houses.[63] The temple apparently showed signs of remodeling.[64] They took the limestone lintel from the gateway to Berlin (Inv. Nr. 19369).[65] The Demotic inscription reads:

> ḥsb.t 41 ꜣbd 3 prt sw 11 Pr-ꜥꜣ (Ptwlmys)|
> irm tꜣ Pr-ꜥꜣ.t (Qlwptrꜣ)| tꜣy=f ḥm.t nꜣ nṯr.w
> mnḫ ꜥnḫ ḏt Ḥr-mtn pꜣ nṯr ꜥꜣ nt
> di-ꜥnḫ Ḥr-pa-ꜣs.t sꜣ Ḏ-ḥ pꜣ mr-mšꜥ irm pꜣy=f ḫrṯ.w iir di ir=w wmṯy
> Year forty-one, month three of seedtime, day eleven of Pharaoh Ptolemy (VIII) and Cleopatra, his wife, the beneficent gods, living eternally. Harmotes, the great god, who saves Harpaese, son of Teos, the general, with his children, who have caused this threshold to be made.[66]

63   Viereck, *Philadelpheia*, 12–13.

64   Ibid., 14.

65   Ibid., 13.

66   Ibid., 13, Tafel IVb; S.P. Vleeming, *Some Coins of Artaxerxes and Other Short Texts in the Demotic Script found on Various Objects and Gathered from Many Publications* (Leuven: Peeters, 2001), 107.

This inscription identifies one temple, but not the temple mentioned in the papyri. Harmotes[67] is named after the twenty-second upper Egyptian nome, centered at Meidum, just 15 kilometers to the north of Philadelphia.[68] Thus the temple that the Germans found is not one of the ones mentioned in the Zenon papyri.

The term *wmty* in the inscription goes into Coptic as ογοντε which has two meanings, one being "tower" and the other meaning "threshold."[69] Spiegelberg,[70] Vleeming,[71] and the Chicago Demotic Dictionary have taken the former definition,[72] and understood it to refer to a pylon, but it would make more sense to take it in the latter definition. The inscription was found as part of a lintel, but based on the idea that a *wmty* was a tower, the excavator concluded that the inscription did not belong to the temple in which it was found: "Deswegen ist sie ja auch durch den Stucküberzug getilgt, und außerdem scheint sie ja von einem Pylon zu handeln, den aber der Tempel von Philadelpheia nie gehabt hat. Der Stein stammt also von einem andern, inzwischen verfallen Tempel, von wo man ihn herbeiholte, als man die Eingangstür zum Innern des Tempels neu baute."[73] Taking the term as a threshold eliminates the difficulty and identifies the owner of the temple.

The temple was undecorated except for a single scene,[74] and the Germans did not know to whom to ascribe the temple.[75] Where the temples to the other deities might be, the Germans said simply, "We don't know."[76]

Although we could see the location of the temple on the aerial photograph, we could not locate it on the ground. We did locate a stone structure north of the road that gives the appearance of small temple; the use of stone is unusual for the town as most of the town is mud brick. The use of stone for a temple in contrast to mud brick for habitations is a long-standing Egyptian tradition.

The Zenon papyri also mentions a royal palace, a stoa, a theater, and a gymnasium.[77] We have a possible location for the theater on the south-west edge of

---

67 Brief overview in Cary J. Martin, "A Demotic Land Lease from Philadelphia: P. BM 10560," *JEA* 72 (1986): 168 n. 8.

68 Rainer Hannig, *Großes Handwörterbuch Ägyptisch-Deutsch* (Mainz: Philipp von Zabern, 1995), 1351; Jean Winand and Alessandro Stella, *Lexique du Moyen Égyptien* (Liège: Presses Universitaires de Liège, 2013), 238.

69 W.E. Crum, *A Coptic Dictionary* (Oxford: Clarendon Press, 1939), 480.

70 Viereck, *Philadelpheia*, 13.

71 Vleeming, *Some Coins of Artaxerxes*, 107.

72 CDD W 79.

73 Viereck, *Philadelpheia*, 13.

74 Ibid., 13–14.

75 Ibid., 14: "Wem der Tempel gehörte, wissen wir nicht."

76 Ibid., 13–14.

77 Clarysse and Vandorpe, *Zenon, un homme d'affaires grec à l'ombre des pyramides*, 51.

the site, but this is not certain. Of all the structures mentioned in the papyri, we have been able to identify with certainty only one: the canal. In the papyri it is described as the great canal (τῆς μεγάλης διώρυγος)[78] which runs from north to south (<ἀπὸ> νό(του) εἰς βο(ρρᾶν)).[79] It is an unmistakable depression that runs in a line south to north along the western edge of the site, immediately before the modern cultivation.

Viereck noted that the streets were oriented to the cardinal directions and placed at right angles to each other.[80] Viereck identified three streets running north-south.[81] The Germans excavated nine blocks of houses.[82] These were built on limestone bedrock which had been leveled to create a flat foundation upon which to erect unbaked brick houses.[83] Baked bricks were usually used for floors and water basins.[84] A century ago, when the Germans excavated, the structures were between three and six meters high.[85] This height of preserved material helped the Germans explain, "the curious fact that there were neither doors nor windows in the house-walls which faced the street, and [Viereck] shows the reason to have been that they were placed not on the ground floor but on the first floor, which has now usually disappeared."[86] The doors on the upper floors were reached by stairs.[87] The Zenon papyri discuss mainly the doors of his villa which were painted, some had one leaf (μονόθυρος)[88] and others two (δίθυ(ρος));[89] a broken passage mentions a secret door (κρυπτὴν θύραν);[90] a door that led to the street is mentioned (παραδρομίδα δίθυρος) but the text does not specify which floor it was on.[91] Only two or three stories were preserved but, compared to house models, they may have been five or six stories high.[92] In most cases, upper stories were not preserved.[93] In only a few cases were the painted plaster of the walls preserved.[94]

---

78   P.Petr. III 145 19–20.

79   P.Petr. III 145 16.

80   Viereck, *Philadelpheia*, 7.

81   Ibid., 8.

82   Ibid., 8.

83   Ibid., 8.

84   Ibid., 8.

85   Ibid., 8.

86   Bell, review of Viereck, *Philadelpheia*, 585; Viereck, *Philadelpheia*, 9.

87   Viereck, *Philadelpheia*, 9–10.

88   P.Cair.Zen. 4.59764 31, 33, 35.

89   P.Cair.Zen. 4.59764 41.

90   P.Cair.Zen. 4.59764 25.

91   P.Cair.Zen. 4.59764 44.

92   Viereck, *Philadelpheia*, 10.

93   Ibid., 14.

94   Ibid., 14–15.

The Germans found evidence that portraits decorated the walls of buildings and they speculated that these portraits were then interred with mummies.[95] Earlier excavators had noted that "the portraits had been cut down to fit the format of the wrapped mummy."[96]

The Germans found "household wares of all sorts, papyri, wax tablets, and ostraca."[97] They published the papyri, wax tablets and ostraca in 1926,[98] but they published virtually none of the household wares. In another place, they mention that "unfortunately, there is not much preserved of furniture, household wares, cooking equipment, boxes and chests, jewelry and knickknacks, and all other sorts of things pertaining to the economy."[99]

In many ways Viereck and Zucker were ahead of their time. They sometimes published general findspots for some of the papyri and ostraca that they found.[100] This allows us to match papyri with findspots and determine something about the use of various parts of the town. Unfortunately, they published the findspots of only 68 out of 230 texts.[101] Most of these come from a single location and deal with the affairs of a single Ptolemaic period household. The museum numbers indicate that finds were entered into the museum according to the type of object, not according to where the object was found; so the museum acquisition number is not helpful in identifying where the object might have been found.

Zucker, however, provided a map of Philadelphia showing the location of the excavations that he carried out.[102] The road to the Fayoum in Zucker's day seems to follow the same course as the present road. He labeled the streets running north-south with letters and those running east-west with numbers. Sites of excavations were designated with Roman numerals and, since these show no particular pattern, we assume that they reflect a chronological pattern. The number of excavated sites, sixteen, also matches the number of days that Zucker excavated; as a working hypothesis, we might consider each the work of a separate day. He also provided an important clue in a letter that he

---

95   Ibid., 15–16.
96   Walker, "Mummy Portraits in their Roman Context," 4.
97   Viereck, *Philadelpheia*, 11–12.
98   Paul Viereck and Friedrich Zucker, *Papyri, Ostraka und Wachstafeln aus Philadelphia im Fayûm*, Aegyptische Urkunden aus den Königlichen Museen zu Berlin, Griechische Urkunden VII (Berlin, Weidmannsche Buchhandlung, 1926).
99   Viereck, *Philadelpheia*, 16.
100   E.g. Viereck and Zucker, *Papyri, Ostraka und Wachstafeln aus Philadelphia im Fayûm*, 203.
101   Viereck and Zucker, *Papyri Ostraka und Wachstafeln aus Philadelphia im Fayûm*, 14, 203.
102   Viereck and Zucker, *Papyri Ostraka und Wachstafeln aus Philadelphia im Fayûm*, Tafel I; Viereck, *Philadelpheia*, Tafel I.

wrote to the directors of the museum: "In der letzten Tagen haben wir einige Häuser an der Süd-nördl. laufenden Hauptstr. in Angriff genommen, aber bis jetzt keine Ergebnisse dabei gehabt."[103] A look at the excavation map shows that many of these locations are marked on the main street (Strasse C): Locations II, IV, V, VI, VIII, XIII, XIV all lie along the main street. The ostraca were found in location IX which is on the corner of Strasse D and Strasse 7, which is away from the main street. Zucker says that "Die Keller lieferten uns fast alles an Papyri u. an sonstigen Funden was uns die Grabung im Kôm bisher brachte."[104] Furthermore, these cellars belong to seven otherwise unprepossessing houses,[105] and the finds include the wax tablets, which were found in Locations I and V.[106] Our working hypothesis is that the papyrus finds also come from Locations I, V, and IX. Our own survey covered mainly the areas between Zucker's areas A2 and B7.

5   Looting

Looting at Philadelphia is nothing new. I have already traced something of the history of illicit excavation at the site. Bell noted in 1928 that "the ruins are, alas! steadily disappearing, the *sebakhîn* having now begun to use actual bricks of the houses for *sebakh*."[107] By 1929, Rostovtzeff reported that "all traces of ruins had disappeared."[108] This would explain why no papyrus archives or other artifacts from Philadelphia have appeared after the 1920s. This is not to say that depredations of the site have not continued. On our survey we found three looters' pits. The south-eastern quarter of the site is now occupied by a modern cemetery. Between the *sebakhin* and the looters the site is widely destroyed. The remaining walls are at most waist high, but usually ankle high. This has contributed to our difficulty in identifying streets when actually on site.

The looters' pits go down at least a meter below the level of the surface. Viereck's report claims that all the buildings were built on bedrock. The depth of the looters' pits indicates that the space between the walls are either filled with

---

103   Friedrich Zucker, letter to the General-Verwaltung der Königliche Museen zu Berlin, 15 January 1909, SMB-ZA I/ÄM 068 64–65.

104   Friedrich Zucker, letter to the General-Verwaltung der Königliche Museen zu Berlin, 15 January 1909, SMB-ZA I/ÄM 068 64–65.

105   Friedrich Zucker, letter to the General-Verwaltung der Königliche Museen zu Berlin, 15 January 1909, SMB-ZA I/ÄM 068 64–65.

106   Viereck and Zucker, *Papyri Ostraka und Wachstafeln aus Philadelphia im Fayûm*, 14, 203.

107   Bell, review of Viereck, *Philadelphia*, 584.

108   Doxiadis, *Mysterious Fayum Portraits*, 133.

FIGURE 14.5   Looter's pit 2014
PHOTOGRAPH BY JOHN GEE

sand so that they are actually higher than supposed, or that the German excavators did not actually hit bedrock. Other Greco-Roman sites, notably Antinoopolis, had paved stone streets.[109] Given the cursory nature of the German
excavation reports, it is difficult to reconcile their reports with what we
observed.

6   Prospects

This report sounds fairly discouraging. But there are a number of open questions that the excavation might still be in a position to answer.

The site looks denuded but there is still a chance to find out more about the
general layout of the city. Our survey indicates that the pottery is of better
quality in the south along the edge of the canal. This indicates that that neigh-
borhood was probably wealthier.

---

109   Judith McKenzie, *The Architecture of Alexandria and Egypt 300 BC-AD 700* (New Haven:
Yale University Press, 2007), 154.

FIGURE 14.6 Stone structure north of the road at Philadelphia
PHOTOGRAPH BY JOHN GEE

One of the major problems in the Fayum in the Roman period is the silting of the canals. Excavation of the canal could potentially discover much of the process and timing of silting.

One of the Demotic papyri from Philadelphia claims that Philadelphia "is on the northern side of the canal" (*nt ḥr pꜣ ꜥt mḥ.t ḥny*).[110] This is a bit difficult since the canal runs north-south at that point; this is recognized by a Demotic land lease that specifies that the canal is the eastern boundary of the land leased (*iꜣbṯ tꜣ ḥny*).[111] This situation needs to be clarified.

Philadelphia survived a few centuries into the Christian era, and we have papyrological records of Christians at the site. Individuals with Christian names appear within a decade or so of the Edict of Toleration.[112] We should expect there to be a church somewhere in the town. It might be a repurposed

110   P. BM EA 10750 line 4, in Smith, "Another Witness-Copy Document from the Fayyūm," 91, 93.
111   P. BM EA 10560 line 10, in Martin, "A Demotic Land Lease from Philadelphia," 161, 165.
112   E.g. Ἡλίᾳ in SB 14 11380 (AD 348).

temple or other structure; but we would expect that the Christians gathered to worship in a communal space.

There is a stone structure in the area around B1 that stands apart from the typical mud brick of the surrounding houses. Though it is not very large, it is possibly another temple.

Although the south-east portion of the site is now covered by a modern cemetery and most of the walls of the buildings disappeared a century ago, there is still more of the site left than one could ever hope to completely excavate.

CHAPTER 15

A Complete List of Publications about the Fag el-Gamous Necropolis and Seila Pyramid Excavations by Members of the BYU Egypt Excavation Team (Including Those from the Year that I.E.S. Edwards Was Part of the Team, and Those Resulting from Work at Kom Aushim)

Bethany Jensen and Masen Williamson

Ball, T.B., W. Griggs, M. Kuchar, R. Phillips, and W.M. Hess. "Image Analysis of Egyptian Mummy Hair." *Microscopy and Microanalysis* 8 (2002): 922–923. https://doi.org/10.1017/S143192760210729X.

Researchers have used image analysis to study Egyptian mummy hair to determine if significant morphological differences exist among races and sexes. These procedures were used with the intent of demonstrating differences between mummies from Fag el-Gamous and hair of living residents from the same region of Egypt, as well as Caucasoid and Oriental samples. It was determined that sex could be identified accurately 58%–69% of the time. Racial types were more difficult to discriminate between, but the overall conclusion was that there are still significant morphometric differences in hair types of various races and sexes.

Ball, T.B., C. Wilfred Griggs, M. Kuchar, R. Phillips, Nasry Iskander, and W.M. Hess. "Morphological Characteristics of Hair of Egyptian Mummies Compared with Hair from U.S. Caucasoids, Mediterranean Workers and Chinese." *Bulletin of the Australian Centre for Egyptology* 13 (2002): 7–15.

Previous studies have determined that it is possible for image analysis of hair particulates to track morphological comparisons for size and shape. The aim of this study was to use these morphological differences to differentiate the race and gender of mummies from Fag el-Gamous. Using 25 individual samples, the research team ran a discriminant analysis on the mummy hair. They determined that while Oriental hair samples were vastly different, the Mediterranean and Caucasoid samples were too similar for differentiation. Furthermore, gender was identified correctly 58% for males and 69% for females. The study concluded that significant morphometric differences exist in hair samples from different racial types and different sexes within racial types.

Ball, T.B., and W.M. Hess. "Determination of race and gender using image analysis of hair cross-sections." In *Proceedings of Fifty-first Annual Meeting of the Microscopy Society of America*, edited by G.W. Bailey and Conly L. Rieder, 216–217. San Francisco: San Francisco Press, 1993.

Previously published research demonstrated that image analysis can be utilized to study hair. This experiment aimed to capture statistical and image evidence to determine if scalp hair could differentiate individuals of different races or genders. Furthermore, the researchers hoped to find and evaluate reliable discriminant functions to make inferences about the race and gender of burials that lack identification. While they determined differences do exist between the sizes and shapes of hairs from subjects of different races and genders, there was not enough conclusive evidence to help identify mummies as either Caucasoid or Mediterranean. However, the hair analysis did establish a low confidence in the genders of the unidentified mummies.

Blumell, Lincoln H. "A Note on a Dedicatory Inscription to the God Soxis from Karanis." *Tyche, Beiträge zur Alten Geschichte, Papyrologie und Epigraphik* 29 (2014): 267–268.

This article is a result of the curators of the Kom Aushim storage magazine asking the BYU Egypt Excavation team to analyze texts kept there. It briefly details a translation of an inscription of a dedicatory note to the god Soxis. It was originally translated in 1975, but Dr. Blumell noticed an error in the initial translation when comparing it to the inscription. The first word was mistranslated, which changes the preceding titulature, though still references Ptolemy XII Auletes.

Blumell, Lincoln H., and Mostafa F. Hemieda. "The Curious Case of Kom Aushim Inv. no. 45: The Rediscovery of a Fragment from a Lost Inscription?" *Tyche, Beiträge zur Alten Geschichte, Papyrologie und Epigraphik* 28 (2013): 21–26.

The curators of the Kom Aushim storage magazine asked for the BYU team to translate and analyze some fragmentary inscriptions. The fragments of two Greek inscriptions illustrate unique parallels which possibly indicate that they were copies of a previously published inscription. Dr. Blumell continues to demonstrate these parallels by translating and evaluating the inscriptions, focusing on subtle abbreviations, numerology, and past scholarly research on these fragments by Seymour de Ricci.

Blumell, Lincoln H. "New Christian Epitaphs from the Fayum." In *Zeitschrift für Papyrologie und Epigraphik*, with contributions by Mohamed Hussen 193 (2015): 202–206.

During an excavation at Egypt, the curator at Kom Aushim asked the BYU excavation team to examine two unpublished inscriptions. These important discoveries were Greek epitaphs and clearly Christian because they contained distinct Christian markers such as crosses and *nomina sacra*. This article is a presentation of the two inscriptions, providing support to Fayumic provenance. The first stela has five lines of Greek on the top of the stone and is followed by small crosses. It is a funerary stela for a man named Thenes. The second stela is similar to the first in design and epitaph. This funerary stela, now for a woman named Kyra, also demonstrates a Christian influence with crosses carved along the bottom of the stone.

Blumell, Lincoln H., and Mohamed Hussen. "Two Coptic Epitaphs in the Kom Aushim Storage Magazine." *Chronique d'Égypte* 89, no. 178 (2014): 405–411.

In the storage magazine at Kom Aushim, at the behest of the curators, the BYU team analyzed two Coptic epitaphs which demonstrate features of the Fayoumic dialect. The first stela includes a funerary formula from this region. This inscription is similar to many Coptic Christian epitaphs and utilizes phrases, dating, and closing formulas of Christian inscriptions. The second stela also demonstrates Christian influences in its content and design. The authors highlight the religious influence by translating and commenting on the remains of these two epitaphs.

Clarke, Maribeth C., Rachel P. Haitt, Marvin C. Kuchar, and Mary H. Farahnakian. "Indexing and Cataloging Textiles From the Fag el Gamous Cemetery in Fayum, Egypt to Determine Their Relationship With Known Coptic Textiles." *Clothing and Textiles Research Journal* 21, no. 3 (2003): 120–129.

Analysis of ancient textiles excavated in 1998 from the Fag el-Gamous Cemetery in Egypt has led to questions about the cultural origin of the textile designs. The purposes of this study were to establish a means to index and catalog the textiles retrieved from Fag el-Gamous and determine a possible relationship between these textiles (dated 200 BC–800 AD) and textiles from known Coptic textile collections. Researchers acquired software for data collection, created a searchable image database, indexed and catalogued the Fag el-Gamous textiles, and drew comparisons to Coptic textiles. Although the Fag el-Gamous and Coptic textiles contained some similar structural elements, there were significant stylistic differences. This led to the conclusion that the Fag el-Gamous textiles were not Coptic in stylistic design. Thus, this unique collection of textiles may provide a significant bridge of textile artifacts between the Pharaonic and Coptic time periods.

Edwards, I.E.S. "The Pyramid of Seila and its Place in the Succession of Snofru's Pyramids." In *Chief of Seers: Egyptian Studies in Memory of Cyril Aldred*, edited by Elizabeth Goring, Nicholas Reeves, and John Ruffle, 88–96. New York: Kegan Paul International, 1997.

Dr. Griggs and a team of excavators from Brigham Young University uncovered two stelae, marking the owner of the previously unclaimed Seila Pyramid as Snefru. Though the precise date of the pyramid cannot be fixed within Snefru's reign, its position in the sequence of the king's pyramid can be established by studying several of its architectural features, such as the method of construction which appears to be roughly contemporaneous with the upper part of the Bent Pyramid.

Edwards, I.E.S. "Seila/Silah." In *Encyclopedia of the Archaeology of Ancient Egypt*, edited by Kathryn A. Bard, 721–722. New York: Routledge, 1999.

The site at Seila contains the largest pyramid of seven small step pyramids. Standing on the Gebel el-Rus, they overlook the Fayoum and Nile Valley. Excavations have been taking place at this site, with focus on the pyramid of Meidum, by Brigham Young University since 1981. Stelae found near the pyramid of Seila attributed it to Snefru, the first king of the 4th Dynasty. The other six pyramids have also been measured and evaluated to determine dates. Several suggestions have been made regarding the function of these pyramids, which lack the chambers and corridors found in the larger Pharaonic pyramids. One hypothesis is that they were cenotaphs for the birthplace of the queens, while another theory holds that they were used for ritual worship.

Evans, R. Paul and Kerry Muhlestein. "Death of a Child: The Demographic and Preparation Trends of Child Burials in the Greco-Roman Fayoum of Egypt." In *Handbook of Children of Antiquity*, edited by Lesly Beaumont, Matthew Dillon, and Nicola Harrington, Forthcoming.

While portions of the cemetery of Fag el-Gamous date earlier, especially in the mudstone escarpments, most of the burials in the cemetery are from the Roman/Byzantine period. Much of the research surrounding this excavation has centered on the burial textiles and possible markers of Christianity. Over time, members with osteological ability joined this team during a survey of burials from the cemetery and a substantial amount of data has now been collected. Concurrently, the abilities of the discipline to analyze juvenile skeletal remains has been greatly refined. Moreover, unlike the poor preservation and small sample sizes that have plagued many of the attempts to examine the children of antiquity, Fag el-Gamous has hundreds of well-preserved juveniles. All of this allows a significant contribution to be made to demographic studies of the ancient world, in particular with regards to children. At Fag el-Gamous there was about a 33% juvenile mortality rate. An analysis of cordage colors and linen wrapping techniques demonstrate that children do not seem to be in different types of graves overall, with only a few mass burials as exceptions.

Evans, R. Paul, David Whitchurch and Kerry Muhlestein. "Rethinking Burial Dates at a Graeco-Roman Cemetery: Fag el Gamous, Fayoum, Egypt." *Journal of Archaeological Science: Reports* 2 (2015): 109–114.

The research team at Fag el-Gamous studied the thousands of graves and exhumed bodies preserved at this cemetery, noting trends such as grave orientation and depth. The team studied a shift in the orientation of graves and this article covers the hypotheses postulated in answer to the question of this change. Using radiocarbon methods, they were able to determine that the shift began as early as the 2nd century AD and that the older graves were deeper, while the newer graves were more shallow. More analysis is necessary, but the shift in orientation may be attributable to the impact of the Roman empire and a Christian influence.

Greenfield, Judy. "Secrets of the Ancient World Revealed Through DNA: A lecture presented to the ESS by Dr. Scott Woodward, Professor of Microbiology, Brigham Young University, 20 April 2001." *The Ostracon: The Journal of the Egyptian Study Society* 12, no. 1 (Summer 2001): 21–23.

In this article, Greenfield summarizes a lecture presented by Dr. Woodward on DNA sequencing and analyzing DNA samples from ancient remains. While DNA often quickly decomposes, teeth have been found to be an excellent source for DNA extraction. The interior of a tooth can be drilled to access a clean sample that has not been contaminated by modern DNA. This research has been used while studying the remains from the cemetery of Fag el-Gamous. The DNA recovered from these sample remains has illuminated information such as epidemics of cholera and tuberculosis which would have impacted the population. Osteoporosis and abnormal growth also is evidenced in the DNA samples recovered. Finally, DNA has been used to track generations and understand family relations.

Griggs, C. Wilfred. "Burial Techniques and Body Preservation in the Fag el Gamous Cemetery." In *Actas del I Congreso Internacional de Estudios sobre Momias, 1992,* 659–662. Santa Cruz de Tenerife, Canary Islands, Spain: Museo Arqueologico de Tenerife, 1995.

Burial techniques and methods used in preserving bodies include some attempts at mummification in some pre-Christian burials, including an abdominal incision for removal of internal organs, removal of the brain through the nose, and application of preserving agents to slow decomposition. For all of the well-preserved burials, complex dressing and wrapping of the bodies is common and many females have elaborate coiffures. Burial direction also plays a role in the burial techniques and has provided one method for distinguishing potentially pre-Christian burials from Christian burials. Belief in the afterlife is attested by artifacts, burial procedures, and techniques throughout the history of the cemetery, regardless of the religion to which a burial is attributed.

Griggs, C. Wilfred. "Early Christian Burials in the Fayoum." In *Christianity and Monasticism in the Fayoum Oasis*, edited by Gawdat Gabra, 185–195. New York: American University in Cairo Press, 2005.

Dr. Griggs details the history of excavations at the cemetery at Fag el-Gamous, including the significant findings from these excavations. Beginning in the early 20th century, work began at the site by two British archaeologists: Grenfell and Hunt. Brigham Young University has now been studying the cemetery for decades, leading to many important discoveries. Most notably, a larger tomb containing a child's tomb complete with a heavy dark wood coffin, linens, and other ornamental accessories has given researchers insight into the culture and practices of ancient societies. The article also contains diagrams of the burial shafts and the interesting transition in burial directions, from head-west to head-east. This shift may be attributable to the influence of Christianity in the region.

Griggs, C. Wilfred. "Excavating a Christian Cemetery Near Seila, in the Fayum Region of Egypt." In *Coptic Studies: Acts of the Third International Congress of Coptic Studies: Warsaw, 20–25 August, 1984*, edited by Włodzimierz Godlewski, 145–150. Warszawa, Poland: Państwowe Wydawnictwo Naukowe, 1990.

This report, delivered by Dr. Griggs, covers the excavations at the archaeological site of Fag el-Gamous in the Fayoum depression. The researchers observed many aspects of the cemetery which highlight possible indicators of Egyptian culture and Christian influences. The jewelry, linens, burial positioning, and other factors were accounted for by the team to build a hypothesis for the lifestyle of people living in the region. Paleodontology also contributed to some of the findings because professionals were able to evaluate the teeth for periodontal diseases, gum deterioration, and decay in order to determine dietary habits. Overall, this cemetery has many burials for study. One of the main foci of study thus far has been exploring its possible ties to Christianity beginning in the early first centuries AD.

Griggs, Wilfred. "General Archaeological and Historical Report of 1987 and 1988 Seasons at Fag el Gamous." In *Actes du IVe Congrès Copte: Louvain-la-Neuve, 5–10 septembre 1988*, edited by Marguerite Rassart-Debergh and Julien Ries,

195–202. Louvain-la-Neuve: Université catholique de Louvain, Institut orientaliste, 1992.

This article recounts several studies completed at the Fag el-Gamous cemetery excavation site. These excavations yielded considerable information on the lifestyles of the people within the vicinity. A notable shift occurred in the direction of the burials, switching from head-west to head-east. The researchers hypothesized this change may be attributable to a Christian influence that lasted for the last seven hundred years that the cemetery was employed. Another key observation of the excavation team was the accessories included in the burials. The textile materials used also changed when the burial orientation shifted, indicating a new cultural influence. Finally, the symbol of the cross found on many head-east bodies is of great significance in determining possible Christian influence.

Griggs, C. Wilfred. "Rediscovering Ancient Christianity." BYU *Studies* 38, no. 4 (1999): 73–90.

In a Distinguished Faculty Lecture at Brigham Young University, Dr. Griggs outlines the definition of Ancient Christianity in the context of Latter-day Saint culture. He explains the notion that LDS Christianity is believed to be the restored version of an ancient Christianity, rather than a continuation of existing Christianity traditions, which is a more widely held view among the Christian community. He illustrates the influence of Christianity across the Mediterranean region by using historical figures as examples, including Valentinian, Origen, Eusebius, as well as groups of religious sects. Tying LDS beliefs to ancient Christianity's historical context, he leads into the BYU Egypt excavation and its ties to early Christianity.

Griggs, C. Wilfred, R. Paul Evans, Marvin C.J. Kuchar, Mark J. Rowe, and Scott R. Woodward. "The Genetic and Textile Analysis of the Hagarsa Mummies." In *The Tombs of el-Hagarsa*, by Naguib Kanawati, 51–66. Vol. 2. Sydney, Australia: Australian Center for Egyptology, 1993.

A Brigham Young University research team conducted an excavation of a cemetery at the Fayoum and gained important insights based in archaeological evidence. Analysis of genetic remains and textile samples are useful in determining many aspects of the lives of ancient peoples living in Egypt during the 1st through 3rd century. For example, several mummies tested were determined to be related to a single extended family. Furthermore, the genetic samples did not display characteristics of any epidemics or diseases found in similar populations. The genetic samples were obtained through endoscopic techniques and produced both mitochondrial and nuclear DNA for analysis. High-quality textiles indicated that the sample of mummies had access to a wealthier supply of materials which also demonstrate great spinning skill.

Griggs, C. Wilfred, R. Paul Evans, Kristin H. South, George Homsey, Anne Ellington, and Nasry Iskander. "Seila Pyramid / Fag el-Gamous Cemetery Project: Report of the 2000 Season." *Bulletin of the Australian Centre for Egyptology* 12 (2001): 7–23.

This study outlines the excavations and findings of a research team over several years in the cemetery of Fag el-Gamous, leading into a more detailed description of the excavation in 2000. It delineates the observations into three categories: archeology, biology, and textiles. Using artifacts, human remains, soil collection, and wrapping materials, the research team recorded observations they made about the cemetery. Key findings included an understanding of weaving techniques and burial practices of the people living on the edge of Fayoum. It further allows for a deeper study of textile technology and cultural practices regarding death in common villages.

Griggs, C. Wilfred, Marvin C.J. Kuchar, Mark J. Rowe, and Scott R. Woodward. "Identities Revealed: Archaeological and Biological Evidences for a Christian Population in the Egyptian Fayum." In *The Ancient Near East, Greece, and Rome*, edited by T.W. Hillard, R.A. Kearsley, C.E.V. Nixon, and A.M. Nobbs, 82–87. Ancient History in a Modern University. Grand Rapids, Michigan: Wm. B. Eerdmans Publishing Co., 1998.

The cemetery in the Egyptian Fayoum has provided vast amounts of information relating to the culture of the population which inhabited this area for approximately a millennium, beginning by at least the 3rd century BC. There is clear evidence of a major cultural revolution sometime during the latter half of the 1st century AD, resulting in a reversal of burial direction, new patterns of dressing the deceased, and the placing of particular artifacts in the graves. This cultural shift has been tentatively attributed to the arrival of Christianity, but more research must be done before a conclusion can be reached.

Griggs, C. Wilfred, Marvin C. Kuchar, Scott R. Woodward, Mark J. Rowe, R. Paul Evans, Naguib Kanawati, and Nasry Iskander. "Evidence of a Christian Population in the Egyptian Fayum and Genetic and Textile Studies of the Akhmim Noble Mummies." *BYU Studies* 33, no. 2 (1993): 214–243.

Beginning in 1981, teams from Brigham Young University have been excavating in Fayoum. They have uncovered hundreds of burials in this cemetery, including two extremely significant pre-Christian burials as well as evidence of early Christians in Egypt. This article details the major findings of the research to date covering the Seila Pyramid, pre-Christian burials in the hill tombs, shaft tombs, and genetic analyses of ancient burials. There is clear evidence of a major cultural revolution in the latter half of the 1st century AD, resulting in a reversal of burial direction, new patterns of clothing or dressing the deceased for burial, and the placing of particular kinds of artifacts in the graves. The researchers identified this cultural change with the arrival of Christianity and proposed that there is archaeological evidence here for some of the beliefs and practices of these early Christians. Many questions still are unanswered, but the team plans on using genetic and other analyses of ancient burials in Egypt to continue their research.

Hamblin, Russell D. "The Geology of the Gebel El-Rus Area and Archaeology Sites in the Eastern Fayum, Egypt." *Excavations at Seila, Egypt,* edited by C. Wilfred Griggs, 45–73. Provo, Utah: Religious Studies Center Brigham Young University, 1988.

The Gebel el-Rus area is an archaeological site in Fayoum in Egypt where Brigham Young University has been excavating with permission from the Egyptian Government. This chapter provides stratigraphic and lithologic information on this 40 square mile region. It covers major epochs in the history and geomorphology of the Fayoum to illustrate the natural excavation of the Fayoum depression over time.

Hamblin, Russell Dee. "Stratigraphy and Depositional Environments of the Gebel el-Rus Area, Eastern Faiyum, Egypt." *Brigham Young University Geology Studies* 34, no. 1 (1985): 61–83.

One of the best-exposed sequences of Tertiary strata in the western desert of Egypt occurs along the Nile-Fayoum divide, east of the Fayoum depression. Well preserved Eocene and Pliocene rocks are well preserved at the site and form many of the prominent ridges and peaks on Gebel el-Rus. Braided stream-alluvial fan deposits, largely composed of gravels and pebbly sands, mark the regression of the Pliocene gulf from the Gebel el-Rus area. Sedimentary structures in this upper member show that the clasts were from an ancient highland source area immediately to the west. During the Pleistocene the topography of the eastern Fayoum was reversed, creating the modern Fayoum depression.

Lee, Sophie. "Analysis of Ancient Egyptian Textiles: The Burial Ribbons of Fag al-Gamous." BYU *Journal of Undergraduate Research* (2010).

The textiles used at the Fag el-Gamous cemetery are potentially indicative of two different belief systems with a transition period, possibly as Christianity spread into Egypt. This article details the examination of body wrappings and bindings that were utilized at the cemetery. Based on the ribbon colors and widths, excavators created a typology of the ribbons to compare to other known Christian burials. While the ribbons alone cannot be used as a defense for Christian burials, they are strong evidence to support the case.

Muhlestein, Kerry. "From the Sands of Egypt: Results from the BYU Egypt Excavation Project." BYU *Religious Education Review* (Fall 2012): 6–7.

The ongoing BYU excavation project of a cemetery in the Fayoum has yielded a number of finds that cast a fascinating light on the lives of the area's ancient inhabitants. The clothing, accessories, and textiles found in the burials has illuminated interesting elements about the lifestyles, diseases, diet, and religious beliefs. Included in some of the graves are potential evidences of early Christian influence, specifically jewelry in the shape of the cross. Also part of this excavation is a pyramid built by Snefru, the first king of the 4th Dynasty and father of the builder of the pyramids at Giza. The pyramid being uncovered by the BYU team may be the first true pyramid constructed and has allowed researchers to analyze its dimension and construction techniques.

Muhlestein, Kerry. "Pyramids and Mummies: the BYU Egypt Fayoum Excavation Project." *Newsletter for the Society for the Study of Egyptian Antiquities* 1, no. 1 (Winter 2011–2012): 1–3.

The bulk of the excavation work undertaken by Brigham Young University, with initial support from UC Berkeley, has taken place at the cemetery near Philadelphia. The vertical burial shafts, first used during the Ptolemaic period, were reused for centuries by local residents. The cemetery was notably in use during the spread of Christianity in this area, and some graves reflect a definite Christian influence. These factors, including grave direction and textile customs, mark a significant change in burial practices that may be evidence of Christianity in this Roman society. The excavation also uncovered a pyramid approximately 2 kilometers from the cemetery, named the Seila Pyramid. Alongside the pyramid, two stelae were unearthed with inscriptions naming Snefru as the architect of the pyramid.

Muhlestein, Kerry. "Transitions in Pyramid Orientation: new evidence from the Seila Pyramid." *Studien zur Altägyptischen Kultur* 44, no. 1 (2015): 249–258, tables 37–38.

Snefru, first king of the 4th Dynasty, developed the true pyramid and set a new design for pyramid complexes that would be followed closely thenceforth. The architectural elements of his pyramids represent a transition period. One of those transitions is a change from a primarily north-south orientation to that of primarily east-west. While much of the evidence for this transition has long been known, excavations from his small pyramid at Seila add more information about this transition. Much of the information about the Seila Pyramid has not been previously published. This study outlines some of that evidence, demonstrating that the Seila Pyramid has elements of ritual activity on both the northern and eastern side of the pyramid, including a northern altar, statue and offering table, and an eastern ritual porch, stelae and causeway.

Phillips, Wm. Revell. "Ancient Civilizations and Geology of the Eastern Mediterranean." In *Excavations at Seila, Egypt*, edited by C. Wilfred Griggs, 1–18. Provo, Utah: Religious Studies Center Brigham Young University, 1988.

In this selected chapter, Phillips covers the geographical development of Egypt and the Mediterranean. He briefly discusses climate zones, fault lines, and tectonic plate movement. This background provides a foundation for why Egypt developed a thriving civilization with a geographically favorable position. The annual Nile river flooding supported the farms with a replenishing supply of soil and freshwater. Phillips also briefly introduces the Greek and Christian cultural influences that impacted Egypt in successive centuries.

Phillips, W. Revell and J. Keith Rigby. "Halite Tomb Fillings and a Distinctive Halite-Cemented Sandstone in the Middle Eocene Gehannam Formation, Egypt." *Journal of Sedimentary Petrology* 61, no. 3 (1991): 419–427.

Halite cement in a coarse sandstone channel-fill and long curving ribbons of fibrous halite have been observed during investigations of archaeology and geology in the Fag el-Gamous area in the eastern Fayoum depression, west of the Nile Valley. Curved ribbons of sodium chloride found in tombs are tens of centimeters long and are highly unusual halite crystal forms. The salt has several possible origins. First, it may have been leached from surrounding Eocene formations. Second, it may be related to shore-line evaporation of Holocene lakes in the Fayoum depression. Third, it may have been concentrated from wind-transported salt from the west and northwest. Fourth, it may be a result of deliberate human activities. None of these possibilities can be clearly disregarded or proven, but the salt is interpreted as probably a result of human activities. Salt may have been used to stabilize sand in the area of chamber tombs cut into deposits of the Eocene Gehannam Formation. It may also have been used to seal the tombs to all but aggressive plunderers and against moisture.

Rigby, J. Keith. "Potential for Geologic and Interdisciplinary Research in and Around the Fayum Depression in Egypt." In *Excavations at Seila, Egypt*, edited by C. Wilfred Griggs, 19–30. Provo, Utah: Religious Studies Center Brigham Young University, 1988.

The Nile Valley and Fayoum area in the Western Desert of Egypt demonstrate a range of potential research topics, due to its vast size, scope, history, and cultural diversity. This article is a survey of several studies that have been compiled regarding this area. By approaching this area through several disciplines, a team of researchers collected and analyzed data about ancient DNA, botany, archaeology, linguistics, zoology, and statistics. Interdisciplinary cooperation when studying the Fayoum area can lead to important discoveries and connections that have previously gone unnoticed.

Rowe, Mark J., Scott R. Woodward, R. Paul Evans, Marvin C.J. Kuchar, and C. Wilfred Griggs. "Ancient History and Modern Biological Tools: Endoscopic Sampling and Mitochondrial DNA Analysis of Ancient Tissue." In *The Ancient Near East, Greece, and Rome*, edited by T.W. Hillard, R.A. Kearsley, C.E.V. Nixon, and A.M. Nobbs, 77–81. Vol. 1 of *Ancient History in a Modern University*. Grand Rapids, Michigan: Wm. B. Eerdmans Publishing Co., 1998.

This article provides an overview of the positive effects of endoscopic sampling of ancient tissue. This type of evaluation preserves the integrity of ancient remains very well, but success of the procedure depends on which part of the body can be accessed. The preferred samples come from teeth, which can be ground into a pulp for evaluation, but access to the mouth can be blocked by the burial mask. Wraps and textiles also obstruct some ability to draw samples from the abdominal area. By employing endoscopic techniques, researchers are able to extract internal samples without compromising the source material integrity. The extracted DNA can then be analyzed for mitochondrial genes. Researchers employed these techniques on a group of Akhmim mummies and determined a close maternal relation among the group, which is a crucial beginning to establishing a putative three generation ancient burial.

Smith, Joyce Y., Kristin South, C. Wilfred Griggs, and Giovanni Tata. "Jewelry and accessories from two Christian burials from Fag el Gamous Cemetery in Fayum Region, Egypt." In *Dress accessories of the 1st millennium AD from Egypt: Proceedings of the 6th conference of the research group "Textiles from the Nile Valley" Antwerp, 2–3 October 2009*, edited by Antoine De Moor, Cäcilia Fluck, and Elisabeth Ehler, 204–219. Tielt, Belgium: Lannoo, 2011.

Using jewelry from the graves of two females at Fag el-Gamous, this study explores the possible techniques, process, and raw materials used to create these accessories. The jewelry is significant due to the symbols indicating a Christian belief in a glorious afterlife. The materials consisted of glass, ivory, shells, and bells highlighting the innovation and technological advancement of the ancient world. The Egyptian culture, which esteemed jewelry and fine accessories, adapted to include the Christian influence that began to spread into the area. The symbols on the jewelry in Fag el-Gamous are evidence of this new culture that began to disseminate through the Egyptian part of the Roman Empire.

South, Kristin H. "Minor Burial Textiles and Religious Affiliation: An Archaeological Case Study from Roman Egypt." In *Dressing the Dead in Classical Antiquity*, edited by Maureen Carroll and John Peter Wild, Stroud, Gloucestershire: Amberly Publishing, 2012.

This article surveys the findings of burials in Fag el-Gamous with observations
on the burial orientation, accessories, and textiles utilized in the burial cere-
mony. Importantly, many burials included "face bundles" which are cloth
structures used to cover the face rather than the more traditional Egyptian
mummy portraits. These face bundles are linked with early Christian burial
practices and may denote a Christian influence in Fag el-Gamous. While no
conclusive evidence may be taken from these "face bundles," it is clear that a
shift occurred, and more precise dating techniques and future research may
help illuminate this shift in practices of dressing the dead.

South, Kristin H. "Roman and Early Byzantine Burials at Fag el-Gamus, Egypt:
A Reassessment of the Case for Religious Affiliation." Master's thesis,
Brigham Young University, 2012.

The Late Roman necropolis of Fag el-Gamous on the eastern edge of Egypt's
Fayoum Oasis is a valuable archaeological site for exploring issues of personal and cultural identity in Roman Egypt. Former scholarship regarding
the people buried at Fag el-Gamous has claimed—based on narrow evidence—that they represent an exceptionally early Christian community in
Egypt. However, a more careful look at the evidence—using recent theoreti-
cal approaches, data-driven analyses, and comparisons with contemporary
sites throughout Egypt and neighboring areas—reveals a more complicated
portrait of their religious affiliation and other aspects of their identity. This
study examines several potential markers of religious affiliation at Fag el-
Gamous placed in the context of burials from throughout the Roman and
early Byzantine eras in Egypt. Aspects of burial that appear to be "Christian"
innovations, or first occur in the period during which Christianity first appears, are highlighted. Conclusions from this broader and more in-depth evidence suggests that the case for the early arrival of Christianity in Egypt is
highly ambiguous, and any arguments concerning it must be correspondingly
complex. The necropolis of Fag el-Gamous, due to its extensive size and excellent preservation, provides valuable evidence for the unfolding of this
slow and piecemeal change and for the discussion of multiple aspects of
identity, such as religious affiliation, ethnic or national affiliation, gender,

and wealth or status. These aspects are interwoven to become the complex idea captured by identity.

South, Kristin H., Marvin C. Kuchar, and C. Wilfred Griggs. "Preliminary Report of the Textile Finds, 1998 Season, at Fag el-Gamus." *Archaeological Textiles Newsletter* 27 (Fall 1998): 9–11.

This article outlines the findings of the excavation at Fag el-Gamous in 1998. The cemetery, dating back to the Roman and Byzantine empires, is designed with large burial shafts that could contain up to six bodies. The excavation team reported the textiles used in the burial ceremonies, noting the dye colors, cordage, and burial orientation (head-east or head-west) used. Significantly, only eastward facing burials exhibited exorbitant amounts of cordage and ribbons, which may reflect a shift in burial practices over time.

South, Kristin H., and Kerry M. Muhlestein. "Regarding ribbons: The spread and use of narrow purpose-woven bands in Late Roman Egyptian burials." In *Drawing the threads together: Textiles and footwear of the 1st millennium* AD *from Egypt*, edited by Antoine De Moor, Cäcilia Fluck, and Petra Linscheid, 56–73. Tielt, Belgium: Lannoo, 2013.

The necropolis at Fag el-Gamous is a fascinating cemetery that has engaged excavators from Brigham Young University for three decades. The teams noticed an interesting shift in burial patterns within the same few centuries. A study of ribbons and face bundles, used to adorn the bodies, led to closer examinations. These two adornments occur only among populations that included those who identified themselves as Christian. While this does appear to be a strong correlation, there are other external influences that must be considered, such as Middle Egyptian fashion trends. Excellent documentation of Christian burials from western oases allows for a safe estimation that thus far undyed or red ribbons have been used in likely Christian burials. Other evidences show that minor textiles played important roles in marking religious identity.

South, Kristin H., Joyce Y. Smith, Giovanni Tata, and C. Wilfred Griggs. "'Face bundles' in early Christian burials from the Fayum, Egypt." *Archaeological Textiles Newsletter* 48 (Spring 2009): 2–5.

In the cemetery Fag el-Gamous, burial shafts containing layered burials display an interesting shift. The more shallow graves gradually shift from a west-facing orientation to an east-facing orientation. The eastward facing burials also display a superstructure of textile wrappings which cover the faces of the mummies. These superstructures are referred to as "face bundles." The excavation team estimate the date of these burials exhibiting "face bundles" and an orientation shift to fall within the range of AD 200–600 and are attributed to a Christian population. Hundreds of bodies have been exhumed over the past three decades which demonstrate these Christian influences on the culture. The team discovered interesting variations on the pattern for future study, demonstrating that the study was not exhaustive, but it did yield unusual trends about the necropolis at this time period.

South, Kristin H., Joyce Y. Smith, Giovanni Tata, and C. Wilfred Griggs. "Textile Finds from a Typical Early Christian Burial at Fag el-Gamus (Fayum), Egypt." In *Purpureae Vestes III: Textiles y Tintes en la ciudad antigua* ed. C. Alfaro, J.-P. Brun, Ph. Borgard, R. Pierobon Benoit, 127–135. Valencia, Spain: University of Valencia Press, 2011.

This study covers the common burial practices of Roman Egypt, detailing important research on the essentials which were included in a common burial site. These practices would have been more universally utilized and representative of what most people received. Though lacking the accessories of many graves of wealthier people, the simplicity illuminates important practices and themes of the lifestyles of the common masses. The excavators described the lack of rich colors, the head wrapping styles, and linen binding tape as indicators for a common burial. By studying these aspects of this particular burial, the research team hopes to continue their study and document a more complete picture of the burial practices of the populations of Fag el-Gamous and the greater Roman world.

Whitchurch, David M., and C. Wilfred Griggs. "Artifacts, Icons, and Pomegranates: Brigham Young University Egypt Excavation Project." *Journal of the American Research Center in Egypt* 46 (2010): 215–231.

For nearly three decades, Professor Griggs and the BYU team of excavators have excavated at a necropolis located on the eastern edge of the Fayoum depression. The site includes two large Graeco-Roman cemeteries, some

Middle Kingdom tombs, and a small Old Kingdom pyramid that dates to the reign of Snefru in the 4th Dynasty. The project, as of 2010, has resulted in the discovery of a great number of burials. The information gleaned from these burials provides context of native Egyptian and Graeco-Roman populations and their exposure to the early influences of Christianity. This article provides an overview of the project and highlights a small intricately woven pomegranate textile discovered in 1987 as a means to demonstrate the significance of the project and potential body of knowledge that will be added to current scholarship. Although the pomegranate textile falls well within the interpretive possibilities of numerous cultures, evidence points to a burial date during the Byzantine Period and, therefore, establishes a greater likelihood of symbolic meaning associated with that time frame.

Wood, Vincent A. "Paleopathological Observations and Applications at Seila." In *Excavations at Seila, Egypt*, edited by C. Wilfred Griggs, 31–44. Provo, Utah: Religious Studies Center Brigham Young University, 1988.

Wood demonstrates the importance of paleopathological studies, dentistry, and x-ray scans of teeth found in human remains. Previously, human remains were often discarded by archaeologists. A more recent group of excavators began studying human remains to reconstruct possible ancient cultures. The information discovered by professionals in the medical and dental fields have illuminated many facets of the ancient world, such as diseases, health practices, trauma, occupations, and dietary habits. Application of new medical techniques in fields such as archaeology can provide numerous discoveries about the ancient world.

Woodward, Scott R., Marie J. King, Nancy M. Chiu, Marvin J. Kuchar, and C. Wilfred Griggs. "Amplification of Ancient Nuclear DNA From Teeth and Soft Tissues." *Genome Research* 3, no. 4 (February 1994): 244–247.

Teeth are useful sources of DNA material due to a naturally created barrier that blocks exogenous DNA from contaminating the ancient DNA. It also allows for a more in-depth study of bodies which were not naturally well preserved by the climate. The research team demonstrated the importance of this technique by extracting and evaluating DNA sequences from 18 Egyptian mummies. DNA was isolated from the teeth of mummies excavated in a cemetery at Fag el-Gamous. Many precautions were taken to reduce the risk of sample contamination; however, this was a major obstacle in the study that spanned the entire process. Overall, the study demonstrated the ability to extract non-contaminated and biologically active DNA from ancient teeth, allowing researchers to begin addressing many important questions regarding ancient population genetics.

Index

Printed in the United States
By Bookmasters